FANDOM

Fandom

*Identities and Communities
in a Mediated World*

SECOND EDITION

Edited by

Jonathan Gray,
Cornel Sandvoss, *and*
C. Lee Harrington

NEW YORK UNIVERSITY PRESS
New York

NEW YORK UNIVERSITY PRESS
New York
www.nyupress.org

References to Internet websites (URLs) were accurate at the time of writing. Neither the author nor New York University Press is responsible for URLs that may have expired or changed since the manuscript was prepared.

ISBN: 978-1-4798-8113-0 (hardback)
ISBN: 978-1-4798-1276-9 (paperback)

For Library of Congress Cataloging-in-Publication data, please contact the Library of Congress.

New York University Press books are printed on acid-free paper, and their binding materials are chosen for strength and durability. We strive to use environmentally responsible suppliers and materials to the greatest extent possible in publishing our books.

Manufactured in the United States of America

10 9 8 7 6 5 4 3 2 1

Also available as an ebook

CONTENTS

Introduction

Why Still Study Fans?

CORNEL SANDVOSS, JONATHAN GRAY, AND
C. LEE HARRINGTON

"Most people are fans of something"—with this assertion we began
the first edition of this anthology in 2007. Today, following continued
technological, social, and cultural changes, fandom is an even more commonplace experience. The proliferation and simultaneous transformation
of fandom are well illustrated, for instance, by the emergence of "fan" as
a common description of political supporters and activists. Shortly after
the first edition of this volume was published, Barack Obama's primary
campaign illustrated the capacity of grassroots enthusiasm through the
now-existent infrastructure of social media (combined with the effective
management of mainstream media) to transform his outsider's bid into
a two-term presidency. Much of what set Obama's 2008 campaign apart
from its predecessors were the enthusiasm, emotion, and affective hope
that his supporters, voters, *fans* invested in that campaign.

Much has happened since the celebrations of Obama's election
in November 2008. In the world of entertainment, streaming is now
a commonplace route to access music, television, and film for many
households across the world. The acceleration of the shift from physical media to digital distribution channels has created new incentives
for telecommunication providers and online retailers to gain controlling stakes in content rights and production, echoing similar efforts of
media hardware manufacturers in the 1980s with the arrival of home
VCRs. DVD rental turned streaming service Netflix and online retailer
Amazon are creating and/or co-funding serial fan objects from *House
of Cards* to *The Man in the High Castle* at increasing rates, and Netflix
regularly resurrects canceled or former fan-favorite programming. In

Britain, former state monopoly telecoms provider BT was so concerned by Rupert Murdoch–owned Sky's push into its domain of landline and Internet service provision that it acquired extensive soccer rights for the UK market as a response, pushing the value for domestic Premier League TV rights past seven billion dollars for 2016–19 (BBC 2015). These examples illustrate how the unparalleled availability of mediated content and entertainment via digital channels combined with the difficulties to monetize content in digital environments have put fans at the heart of industry responses to a changing marketplace.

As a consequence, representations of fans in mainstream media content have at times shifted away from pathologization to a positive embrace of fans' vital role for contemporary cultural industries, and are now commonly part of the narratives that constitute the textual fields of (trans)media events from the cinematic release of the latest *Star Wars* installment to global sporting events such as the Olympics. "We're all fans now" has become a familiar refrain in countless popular press think pieces, and was even the marketing slogan for the fifty-second Grammy Awards in 2010. And (a very particular form of) fan banter and identities have even been central to one of the most successful and lucrative television shows of the past decade, *The Big Bang Theory*, while *The Walking Dead*'s aftershow featuring fan debriefing of the night's episode, *Talking Dead*, often out-rates many otherwise hit shows. Yet with these changing and proliferating representations of fandom, a crucial point of reference to (early) fan studies has shifted, too.

Three Waves of Fan Studies Revisited

In the introduction to our first edition, we divided the development of the field of fan studies into three waves with diverging aims, conceptual reference points, and methodological orientations. The first wave was, in our reading, primarily concerned with questions of power and representation. To scholars of early fan studies, the consumption of popular mass media was a site of power struggles. Fandom in such work was portrayed as the tactic of the disempowered, an act of subversion and cultural appropriation against the power of media producers and industries. Fans were "associated with the cultural tastes of subordinated formations of the people, particularly those disempowered by any combination of gender, age, class, and race" (Fiske 1992: 30). Within this tradition that was foundational to the field of fan studies and that spanned from John Fiske's work to Henry Jenkins's (1992) canonical *Textual Poachers*, fandom was understood as more than the mere act of being a fan of something: it was seen as a collective strategy to form interpretive communities that in their subcultural cohesion evaded the meanings preferred by the "power bloc" (Fiske 1989). If critics had previously assumed fans to be uncritical, fawning, and reverential, first-wave scholarship argued and illustrated that fans were "active," and regularly responded, retorted, poached. Fan studies therefore constituted a purposeful political intervention that set out to defend fan communities against their ridicule in the media and by non-fans.

In its ethnographic orientation and often advanced by scholars enjoying insider status within given fan cultures, the first wave of fan studies can be read as a form of activist research. And thus we referred to this wave as "Fandom Is Beautiful" to draw parallels to the early (and often rhetorically and inspirationally vital) stages of identity politics common for other groups hitherto Othered by mainstream society. Similarly, early fan studies did not so much deconstruct the binary structure in which the fan had been placed as they tried to differently value the fan's place in said binary: consumers not producers called the shots. As such, and in this defensive mode of community construction and reinforcement, early fan studies regularly turned to the very activities and practices—convention attendance, fan fiction writing, fanzine editing and collecting, letter-writing campaigns—that had been coded as pathological by critics, and attempted to redeem them as creative, thoughtful, and productive.

The underlying advocacy of first-wave fan studies derived its legitimacy from fans' assumed disempowered social position and their problematic representation in both public and academic discourses. Mass media of the time had a near monopoly on the representation of fans (or any other group for that matter). Their often stereotypical portrayal of fans and fan practices has been widely documented and discussed since Joli Jensen (1992) highlighted the similarities in the portrayal of fans as part of an undifferentiated, easily manipulated mass in media representations and early mass communication scholarship (see, for example, Bennett & Booth 2016; Duffett 2013; Hills 2002; Sandvoss 2005). In 2007 we examined how such representations were still common, as in a *New York Post* spread on "Potterheads," which, like many other media representations before, constructed fans as the representational Other. Such negative representations can still be found—on occasion even at the hands of those engaged with the field of fan studies, such as academic and filmmaker Daisy Asquith's documentary for the British Channel 4 network *Crazy about One Direction*. Participant and One Direction fan Becky reported her dismay at what she perceived as the gross misrepresentation of her fan practices and attachments: "they made out like . . . I don't have no life, and that I just sit outside Harry's [Style, member of One Direction] house every weekend waiting for him to appear."

However, while caricatures of fans in mainstream media persist, their context has changed. As Asquith quickly learned in the aftermath of the broadcast of *Crazy about One Direction*, mediated discourses about fans have been transformed over the past decade through social media, which give fans themselves a voice and the opportunity to publicly respond. One Direction fans feeling misrepresented responded on Twitter and elsewhere with vehemence. A defensive Asquith sought to justify herself: "their response to the film is so much more extreme than anything I chose to include. It's really been quite shocking" (Izundu 2013: n.p.). Not only can and do fans now respond publicly to such representations, the caricatures now also sit alongside the many more humanizing and respectful depictions, reflecting the commercial imperatives of a digital marketplace noted above. Furthermore, there appears little evidence of the generic position of being a fan to inform such demeaning representations. Rather, belittling portrayals of fans reflect social and economic stratification that persists most notably along the lines of gender, ethnicity, class, and age, which in turn are reflected in *specific* fan cultures and the choice of fan objects. In other words, fan cultures commonly subject to ridicule and other negative forms of representation—from Potterheads to *Twilight* fans (Busse 2013; Click, Aubrey, & Behm-Morawitz 2010; Hills 2012), fans of *The Only Way Is Essex* in Britain (Sandvoss 2015), and funk fans in the favelas of Brazil (Monteiro 2015)—are those associated with the young, the female, the queer, the outsiders, the poor, the ethnically different. These fans are discriminated against, not as fans, but as members of groups that their fandom represents. Indeed, many dismissive representations of given fan cultures are interfandom discourses driven by fans seeking to enforce lines of demarcation and distinction between themselves and other fans (see Williams 2013), such as when, for example, rock fans lambast pop music fans in a move that is regularly aged and gendered, and based upon a desire to place rock above pop in a cosmic hierarchy of musical genres.

The second wave of fan studies moved beyond the "incorporation/resistance paradigm" (Abercrombie & Longhurst 1998), by finding a new conceptual leitmotif in the sociology of consumption by French sociologist Pierre Bourdieu (1984). This second wave of work on fans (see Dell 1998; Harris 1998; Jancovich 2002; Thomas 2002; Dixon 2013) highlighted the replication of social and cultural hierarchies within fan cultures and subcultures. In these studies, the answer to why fandom and its academic analysis matters is thus a very different one. Documenting how the choices of fan objects and practices are structured through fans' habitus as a reflection and further manifestation of our social, cultural, and economic capital, such studies were still concerned with questions of power, inequality, and discrimination, but rather than seeing fandom as an a priori tool of empowerment, they suggested that fans' interpretive communities (as well as individual acts of fan consumption) are embedded in existing social and cultural conditions. These studies were still concerned, for instance, with questions of gender, but they no longer portrayed fandom as an extraordinary space of emancipation and reformulation of gender relations. Instead, the taste hierarchies among fans themselves were described as the continuation of wider social inequalities (Thornton 1995). Finding its reference point in Bourdieu's conceptualization of the habitus and thus highlighting the importance of the specificity of fan objects and the individual and collective practices of fans—in other words, who is a fan of what and how—such work thus highlighted the task that subsequent scholarship in fan and audience studies increasingly embraced: the creation of a conceptual and typological apparatus that allowed scholars to position and compare specific studies and findings.

However, while the second wave of fan studies proved effective in demonstrating what fandom is not—an a priori space of cultural autonomy and resistance—it had little to say about the individual motivations, enjoyment, and pleasures of fans. If Fiske's (1989, 1992) explanation of fandom as subversive pleasure was overtly functionalist, so would be attempts to explain fans' interests and motivations through the notion of the habitus alone. As much as popular media representations of fans have failed to ask why audiences become fans and why "fans act as they do" (Harrington & Bielby 1995: 3), the academic analysis of fandom was now in danger of committing the same omissions.

In addition to engaging with the task of refining typologies of fandom following Nicholas Abercrombie and Brian Longhurst's (1998) foundational work in this respect (see also Crawford 2004; Hills 2002; Longhurst 2007), the subsequent body of work we described in the first edition as the third wave of fan studies sought to broaden the scope of inquiry to a wide range of different audiences reflecting fandom's growing cultural currency. (Indeed, one might regard the third wave as a dissipation of what was previously a loosely coherent subfield into multiple projects with multiple trajectories that *combined* still have the force of a new wave, but that individually have carried fan studies into many diverse neighboring realms.) As being a fan became an ever more common mode of cultural engagement, earlier approaches based on a model of fans as tightly organized participants in fan cultures and subcultures did not match the self-description and experience of many audience members who describe themselves as fans (see Sandvoss 2005). When Jenkins wrote *Textual Poachers* (1992), fan communities were often relegated to conventions and fanzines. Today, with many such communities' migration to the Internet, thousands of fan discussion groups, websites, and social media networks populate cyberspace, and plenty of lived, physical space too. Similarly, mobile media bring fan objects out with their users everywhere. In turn, these changing communication technologies and media texts contribute to and reflect the increasing entrenchment of fan consumption in the structure of our everyday lives. Fandom has emerged as an ever more integral aspect of lifeworlds, and an important interface between the dominant micro and macro forces of our time.

Third-wave work has thus sought to change the goalposts of inquiry. On the micro level of fan consumption, third-wave studies have explored the *intra*personal pleasures and motivations among fans, refocusing on the relationship between fans' selves and their fan objects (see Thompson 1995), and resulting in, for instance, a range of psychoanalytic or psychoanalytically inspired approaches (Elliott 1999; Harrington & Bielby 1995; Hills 2002, 2007; Sandvoss 2005; Stacey 1994). On the macro level, third-wave research on fans extends the conceptual focus beyond questions of hegemony and class, to the overarching social, cultural, and economic transformations of our time, thereby offering new answers to the question of why we should study fans. Here fandom is no longer only an object of study in and for itself. Instead, third-wave work aims to capture fundamental insight into modern life—it is precisely *because* fan consumption has grown into a taken-for-granted aspect of modern communication and consumption that it warrants critical analysis and investigation. Third-wave fan studies help us understand and meet challenges beyond the realm of popular culture because they tell us something about how we relate to ourselves, to each other, and to how we read the mediated texts around us.

Fans Studies between the Personal and the Collective

Such work exploring the intrapersonal dimensions of fandom has proven surprisingly contentious. To Henry Jenkins (2014: 286), for instance, within fan studies "there has always been a sharp divide between those who study individual fans and those who study fandom as an imagined and imaginative community," which Jenkins believes fails to reflect realities of contemporary fandom and which carries a regressive quality that appears to jeopardize the achievements of first-wave fan studies. Jenkins (2007: 361) points to his "concerns that a return to individual psychology runs the risk of reintroducing all those pathological explanations that we fought so hard to dismantle" in the afterword to the first edition of this volume. To Jenkins (2007: 361), a focus on the fan's self is especially problematic in an era in which networks of user productivity and connectivity have moved to the center of attention of media and communication scholars:

> It seems a little paradoxical that the rest of the people involved in this conversation are more and more focused on consumption as a social, networked, collaborative process ("harnessing collective intelligence," "the wisdom of crowds," and all of that) whereas so much of the recent work in fan studies has returned to a focus on the individual fan. [. . .] While

sometimes a useful corrective to the tendency of earlier generations of fan scholars to focus on the more public and visible aspects of fan culture, this focus on the individual may throw out the baby with the bathwater.

Jenkins is undoubtedly correct in the assertion that with the rise of digital technology the above themes have moved to the center of our discipline. However, we do not recognize the fault lines he sketches out. His intervention is a useful reminder that different traditions persist within fan studies. In using the label "waves" rather than "phases," we sought to reflect that different conceptual and methodological approaches reached their high watermarks at different points in the development of the field, yet that concerns and approaches of earlier waves have become far from irrelevant. As we have demonstrated above, while instances of demeaning representations of fans have become less common, certain fan cultures remain subject to representational othering. Conversely, some fan cultures were never confronted with the same type of pathologization, most notably fans of most highbrow arts. In the study of fans subject to persistent social stigmatization, the initial aims of the first wave of fan studies have lost little of their significance. Similarly, questions of hierarchization and structuration within fan cultures remain important for the persistence of precisely such inequalities.

Within such diversity, we recognize not a "sharp divide" but rather a reflection of an increasingly theoretically and empirically rich field of study. Moreover, the dichotomy between the study of the interpersonal and the intrapersonal seems to us misleading: as numerous prominent instances attest (see Harrington & Bielby 1995; Hills 2002; Sandvoss 2005; Bailey 2005), scholars who have sought to explore and theorize the intrapersonal bond between fan and fan object still acknowledge the collective and communal dimensions of fandom, too. Studying the intensely personal attachments of fans does not preclude understanding "fandom as an imagined and imaginative community" (Jenkins 2007: 361). Whether focusing on the role of place, pilgrimage, or *Heimat*, the interplay between fandom and academia, or the role of fandom within the life course, such work has examined the individual psychology of fandom within its wider social context.

To us, then, the intrapersonal and interpersonal dimensions appear to be complementary, intrinsically connected parts of the same ecosystem of analysis. Jenkins is undoubtedly correct to link the rise of convergence culture with the emergence of unparalleled forms of fan/user productivity and connectivity, of collective action and interest-centered networks, groups, and communities. However, a second trajectory of digital culture is equally obvious and, in fact, closely interlinked with the emergence of such communities: the rapid *personalization* of media content and media use brought by the unparalleled accessibility of digital content, the ubiquity of personal individual and mobile (screen) media, social media, customer relation management, and the general "algorithmization" of digital media encounters. While fields such as political communication have long turned to the analysis of the consequences of these processes of personalization (see, for example, Sunstein 2007), fan studies ought not to disregard questions of the interplay between a fan's self and processes of personalization in digital media as the relationship between fan and fan text is the most personal and affectively motivated relationship between text and reader we can find.

To be fair to Jenkins, his call is based in concern that earlier gains not be lost, though he does not object in and of itself to new work being conducted. Francesca Coppa is more orthodox in seeking to enforce a narrow definition of fandom and opposing broader sets of questions about a wider set of fans. In response to the introduction to the first edition of this book, Coppa (2014: 74) claimed:

> Arguably this broadening of subject represents a *change* of subject. It seems unfair to say that early fandom scholars *overlooked* the broad spectrum of regular fans to focus on "the smallest subset of fan groups" (Gray et al. 2007: 8)—the creators and participators for whom fandom was a way of life—when that was precisely their defined object of study.

Coppa's argument—though this remains unacknowledged in the text—is based on reinforcing a binary distinction between fans and "normal audiences" that much of the first wave of fan studies embraced, reaching as far back as Fiske's work (and most clearly articulated in Fiske 1992). The epistemological flaw here is apparent. The object of study is defined through its adherence to a preconceived conceptual position leading to a circular logic: fans are found to be highly networked and participatory, because to be considered fans they need to be highly networked and participatory. All definitions are, of course, normative constructions, but key criteria in this process are existing practices, uses, and experiences. Coppa points to the labels employed in Abercrombie and Longhurst's typology (1998) as not matching fans' self-descriptions, but seems less concerned that her proposed narrowing of the field disqualifies vast numbers of others, who either self-describe as fans or are commonly regarded as fans in everyday life discourse, as possible subjects of fan studies. As such, a resistance to exploring and understanding a wide range of fan types and practices risks entrenching a very specific form of fandom practiced predominantly by white Anglo-Americans for a starkly limited set of fan objects. Certainly, Mel Stanfill (2011) and Rebecca Wanzo (2015) note how white fan studies has been, while Lori Hitchcock Morimoto and Bertha Chin (in this volume) similarly note how Anglo-American it has been. Moving forward (and backward, in how it tells its history, notes Wanzo), a vibrant fan studies (third-wavers included) cannot examine only "fans like us," but must challenge itself to explore how fandom changes in mode and type across demographics and globally, so that the "us" expands.

Consequently, we are encouraged by the degree to which the third wave pushes ever outward, and we now see an exciting diversification of interests, questions, approaches, and subjects. Rather than a sharp dichotomy in either fan practices or the study of fan practices, fandom in its summative meaning (rather than being used synonymously to describe a given fan culture) constitutes a spectrum in which a multiplicity of practices, groups, and motivations span between the polarities of the personal and the communal—yet with either dimension informing aspects of fans' practices and attachments at least residually. Studies of fans need not all be discussing the same types of fans, practices, or engagements to have a symphonic quality when considered in total. What is important for our purposes here is a recognition that the key challenge remains to preserve the specificity of voices of diverse fan experiences, and where appropriate developing macro theoretical positions from them, while being able to place the specificity of studies of particular fan cultures or groups in a wider contextual understanding of typologies and maps of fandom across different genres, interpersonal and intrapersonal dimensions, rather than misreading particular fan groups as singularly representative of all fan practices and motivations. Such contextualization remains particularly important in a field in which the preferred methodological approach (ethnography) hitherto heavily leans toward capturing the voices of those who have a high degree of social connectivity and visibility to researchers.

It is, hence, in recognition of fan experience being both personal and communal to varying degrees that we chose the subtitle of this anthology: *Identities* and *Communities in a Mediated World*. Because fandom has become an increasingly important identity resource in a world that has undergone profound transformations over the past four decades—as a result not only of the rise of digital communication technologies but also of the related forces of globalization and post-Fordism giving rise to what Bauman (2005) usefully described as "liquid modernity"—being a fan may be as important to one's community memberships as one's sense of self. In an era in which traditional markers of identity in high modernity such as employment, class, marriage, and (national) belonging, but also age, religion, sexuality, and gender are increasingly instable, fluid, and on occasion ephemeral, the imagined but voluntary communities we join through fan attachments are as important as the self-identity that is constructed and narrated by fans individually (cf. Harrington, Bielby, & Bardo 2014; Sandvoss 2003, 2014).

The main trajectories of the third wave of fan studies are informed by this duality of community *and* identity. These include the continued methodological and epistemological reflections about the relationship between academic enquiry and fan cultures and reflection of the field itself; the study of anti-fans, fantagonisms, and conflict between fan groups; an examination of changing forms of (digital) textuality, including in particular the role of paratexts; reception and value in fandom; the interplay between space, place, belonging, and fandom; the role of fan identities, experiences, and practices in the life course; the intersection of fandom and formal and informal political processes and activism; and forms of fan-generated content, fan productivity, and the eroding boundaries between media production and consumption. Whereas we focused on the first two of these in the first edition of this volume—and while they have attracted extensive attention in edited collections elsewhere since (see Larsen & Zubernis 2012; Duits, Zwaan, & Reijnders 2014)—the remaining five themes constitute the sections through which this updated volume seeks to contribute to the key debates in contemporary fan studies and beyond.

Fandom, Technology, and Convergence Culture

Before we introduce each of these sections, we want to turn briefly to a wider theme that has come increasingly to inform and span across these third-wave trajectories, and the wider field of media and communication research more generally: the study of technological change and its impact on users' practices.

Digitization and convergence have had tremendous impact on how media are created and used in the past two decades. Thus, for instance, professional production processes and practices have been recalibrated (as documented by Caldwell 2008; Mayer, Banks, & Caldwell 2009; Banks, Conor, & Mayer 2013); new forms of mass entertainment such as gaming have grown in their wake (Banks 2013); the coproduction and the utilization of user-generated content has changed production regimes and business models; and the means and channels of distribution—and thus in turn the nature of texts as content reflects its digital form—have been "revolutionized" (Lotz 2014). Gray and Lotz (2012: 54–55) have pointed to the segmentation of televisual texts that has always been part of television's continuous, everyday life textuality, yet that dramatically excelled in the digital age so that "many shows are experienced all the more often in segmented forms, as Hulu, YouTube, Facebook, embedded clips in blogs and other platforms" that "allow viewers to circulate segments ripped from the remains of the text"—and thus, we may add, that allow enunciatively and textually active fans to post, repost, remix, and embed content in their commentary or other paratexts, thus constructing, amending, or reinforcing the boundaries of their fan object. In remaining true to advocacy as a key aim of his work in a predigital age, Jenkins's work in particular has shifted "from resistance to participation as the core frame of fandom studies" (Jenkins 2014: 294) as new communication technologies have necessitated cultural industries to work with and embrace fans, thus emphasizing the potential of forms of collaboration and cooperation within fan cultures, and between fan cultures and cultural industries.

It is this optimistic embrace of the potential to change regimes of cultural production—and its move away from the assumption of opposition between the cultural industries and political progress that has long been central to cultural studies—that has prompted a frequently critical and skeptical response, with some scholars warning that the new media era may be cause for more concern than excitement. Certainly, for all that seems different and new, the production of entertainment texts central to various fan cultures remains often within regimes established in the era of mass communication. Film, television, and music production regularly continues to follow a studio-, broadcaster-, or label-based production model, leading to notable continuities in the political economies of content production. It is easy to understand why those concerned with the consequences of such regimes have expressed considerable unease with the burgeoning body of work highlighting democratizing, participatory, and creativity-enhancing practices as an assumed consequence of the eroding boundaries between media users and producers, strongly associated with technological change and in many ways epitomized and summarized in the figure of the fan (see Turner 2011). Richard Maxwell and Toby Miller (2011: 594) declare, "The lesson of the newer media technologies is the same as print, radio and television: each one is quickly dominated by centralized and centralizing corporations, regardless of its multi-distributional potential." According to Maxwell and Miller, to see the real economic and ecological costs "through the fog of cybertarianism, we need to establish some 'autonomy from the industry and fan logics' (Beaty 2009, p. 24)" (2011: 594). Others within fan studies, no less, have voiced concern with the degree to which convergence culture tends to privilege the same straight white middle-class Anglo-American men that previous media regimes did, gifting fannish tools to them while excluding or containing the still-marginalized fans in ever more effective, insidious ways. They point, too, to media industries' savvy, if cynical, co-optation of fans as unpaid labor for content creation and promotion (Busse 2009, 2013, 2015; Coppa 2014; De Kosnik 2012; Scott 2011; Stanfill 2011, 2015; Stanfill & Condis 2014).

This "new screen ecology" that Stuart Cunningham (2015) sketches out in his research of digital video platforms and in particular YouTube is thus of course one that operates within the framework of a post-Fordist global capitalism, and in particular under Google's corporate control, raising a host of questions about the power of algorithm as a means of social control and possible exploitation of an outsourced freelance work force (see Morreale 2014). However, we agree with Cunningham (2016) that with its over one million content creators who receive some level of remuneration through YouTube, of which many have crossed from high-intensity fan enthusiasm to petty production, what he describes as the clash between the NorCal business models of tech giants and the SoCal framing of the traditional media entertainment industry has created more than just new packaging for traditional media entertainment content (such as Netflix). Instead, new forms of genres and textuality give voice to a different and often more diverse group of content producers. As Cunningham and Craig (2016: 5411) conclude, "platforms such as YouTube exhibit facilitation rather than content control and much greater content, creator, service firm, and language and cultural diversity than traditional media hegemons." This shift in representational power and by extension of the capacity not only to remix and rework existing fan objects but to create new fan objects and texts beyond their initial framing by traditional cultural industries does not in itself set us all on the path to textually productive fandom. Yet it also highlights the limitations of the opposing macro analysis that sees corporatist control alone, blind to significant changes underneath admittedly still at best oligopolistic ownership structures, and it invites contemporary fan scholars to make sense of these multiple dueling forces with greater nuance.

Positioning such diversity in its context is instructive with regard to the question of the interplay between technology and fandom but thus also offers a way forward for contemporary fan studies. The type of approach that Cunningham and Silver (2014: 150) describe as a "middle-range" approach that fills in the gaps between "raw empiricism and grand or all-inclusive theory" in our eyes offers an effective model for fan studies with its significant theoretical advances in recent decades alongside a rich ethnographic heritage, but still an underdeveloped contextualization of much of its qualitative research in particular. It is through such midrange approaches that we propose to explore the main trajectories of third-wave fan studies beyond the underlying theme of technology—textuality, space, temporalities, participation, and citizenship. In turn these themes reflect the spectrum of enquiry spanning from the intrapersonal to interpersonal dimensions of being a fan, from identity to community.

Five Directions between Identities and Communities

The first section is dedicated to the (changing) nature of the very point of reference against which fans' affective engagements and attachments are constructed: fan objects and their textual form. The first three chapters examine the categories through which we can evaluate and appreciate different fan texts aesthetically, culturally, and socially in a post-Bourdieusian era and thereby critique the neglect of aesthetics in contemporary cultural studies. Sandvoss, in juxtaposing traditions of textual criticism in literary theory and media studies, proposes a model of aesthetic judgment rooted in Reception Aesthetics that reemphasize the act of reading as a form of dialogue with a textual Other. Further exploring the boundaries of fan texts and fans' textuality alike, Kristina Busse explores strategies for the evaluation of fans' own textual productivity in the form of fan fiction, which according to Busse foregrounds intertextuality and communal performativity to a greater degree than most literary texts, though this remains a distinction of degree rather than kind. Matt Hills, in turn, rejects a notion of aesthetics that serves as functional political judgments, questions the role of fan scholars as both academics and part of media audiences, and suggests, based on a critical reading of Barthes's lectures on the neutral, a reflexive understanding of fan scholars' aesthetic judgments as hermeneutic constructions of self-identity. Fans' roles as cultural producers in their own right also raise legal issues concerning textual ownership and copyright explored by Rebecca Tushnet. In tracing legal judgments and controversies concerning fans' alleged infringement of copyright laws, Tushnet juxtaposes legal and moral dimensions of copyright, and suggests that fan practices shed light on the meaning and implications of copyright. Concluding this section, Katriina Heljakka's chapter broadens our analysis of fan texts to objects and examines the interplay of physical objects and performativity in fandom through the study of fan toys in adulthood. Rather than functioning as collectibles, these toys come to serve as means of "paedic" pleasure based on the practices long associated with fandom: appropriation, customization, textual productivity, and performance.

Shifting our focus from text to context, the second section examines the spaces of fandom and the framing of fan practices and identities through the places in which they are manifested, as much as the converse process of the shaping of fan spaces through fans' affective attachments, emotions, and actions. Continuing the analysis of material objects, Daniel Cavicchi examines artifacts from nineteenth-century American "music lovers" to explore how the commodification of music generated a new form of fandom engaged with music's own singular effects and the personal qualities of music performers, and investigates early models for cultural consumption predating the development of mass communication technologies, thereby highlighting the inherent symbiosis between fandom and modernity even preceding the formation of the term "fan" in late nineteenth-century sports coverage. The interplay between communication technologies and place is further examined in Lucy Bennett's study of the controversies among fans and artists surrounding the use, or nonuse, of smartphones or cameras to share and record concert attendances focusing on Kate Bush's recent London concert after a three-decade hiatus and her request to fans to abstain from recording any part of the show. In contrast to the general assumption of fans being on the forefront of embracing new, digital technologies, Bennett finds that Bush enthusiasts sought to construct a sense of authenticity through the rejection of the use of communication technologies in an in situ setting that allowed for the nostalgic performance of a space of belonging. Questions of the fan performance in space in the case of concertgoers are also the focus of Mark Duffett's study by exploring a type of performance so ingrained in many in situ attendances by fans, yet rarely studied: screaming. According to Duffett, screaming constitutes a secular form of what Durkheim has described as totemism through which the collective dimension of in situ fandom is exercised within the public realm and, hence, constitutes a meaningful form of performative citizenship. Moving from spaces of fan performance to spaces of fan pilgrimages, in reference to Robert Aden's (1999) work, Will Brooker juxtaposes the physical and virtual travels of *X-Files* fans by immersing themselves in their favorite texts. Brooker documents a dual process in which our experience of place is shaped through media consumption and vice versa. Finally, developing the theme of experiences and communities in mediated space and its interrelations to physical space, the type of midrange approach we have been advocating here is well illustrated in Lori Hitchcock Morimoto and Bertha Chin's analysis of fandom in its transnational contexts, which critically examines the use of generalized references to fandom and "fannish" practices in English-speaking fan studies that lack awareness of their geosocial specificity, thereby, albeit unwittingly, creating a normative identity position and experience expectation.

Alongside the by now well-established focus on the role of space and place in fan identities and communities, recent work has significantly advanced our understanding of the temporalities of fandom, both in respect to the longitudinal development of fan cultures and individual fan affiliations and with a particular focus on the role of fandom within the life course, marrying concerns of fan studies and gerontology. Melissa Click charts the interplay between the longitudinal developments of fan texts and fans' life course by examining fan reactions to Martha Stewart's rise, fall, and rebranding, offering a complex cultural resource through which fans negotiate changes in their personal lives as much as the wider world. The theme of loss in fandom, prominent in the experiences of Martha Stewart fans, is developed further in Denise Bielby and C. Lee Harrington's analysis of fan reactions and responses to the death of *Glee* actor Cory Monteith. Fans' reactions to Monteith's death and to the on-screen death of Monteith's character (Finn), the implications of these deaths for other elements of *Glee*'s storyworld, and fans' subsequent commemorative practices reveal how experiences of loss are linked at both individual (fan) and collective (fandom) levels. Further developing the theme of how fandom intersects with identity articulations throughout different life stages, Henry Jenkins examines one of the most common practices through which personal histories of being a fan are constructed and narrated: collecting. Arguing that examining the types of stories comics tell about collecting can offer new understanding of relationships between fandom, collecting, and consumer culture, Jenkins ultimately suggests these stories reveal collecting practices to be representations of the self, not of the Other. Alexis Lothian in turn proposes that at a time when LGBT representations at last seem to have become part of mainstream media entertainment, the temporalities of media space in which fans create transformative fan works such as "Friendly" and "Healing Station Argh" from seemingly outdated source texts maintain the capacity to create utopian readings freed of the narrow framing of queer mainstream texts that might facilitate substantive social progress in their dialogue between past, presence, and utopia.

Moving from the possibilities to the actualities of political engagement and action, the fourth section explores citizenship and political participation in and through fandom within and beyond popular culture. The intersection of popular and political communication is well illustrated in Jonathan Gray's analysis of news fans, demonstrating how fandom—a mode of media reception long derided as trivial, overly emotional, and peripheral to the political sphere—is in fact central to our engagement with information and entertainment alike. Gray sees these viewers' fannish proclivities as potentially contributing to, not detracting from, the serious functioning of politics and citizenship formation. Studying the converse process of traditional political narratives and concerns informing the textualities of popular culture, Abigail De Kosnik traces the development of such narratives in fan fiction, arguing that such works invite readers to form an affective investment in the political sphere. Next, Aswin Punathambekar explores questions of public culture and citizenship in contemporary Indian cinema and its associated fan cultures. Through an analysis of fans' engagement with Indian film music, Punathambekar challenges global media studies to treat seriously the implications of fan practices for the development of culture industries worldwide. Fan participations in the public sphere are also at the heart of Dayna Chatman's analysis of Black Americans' live Twitter commentary about the ABC prime-time drama *Scandal*. Chatman concludes that both Black fans and anti-fans of the program participate in a meaningful public discourse through everyday talk that carries the potential to support the emergence of collective politics and activism. Contrasting the experience of fans as potential activists, Lori Kido Lopez and Jason Kido Lopez chart the difficulties in activists' attempts to engage fans in a political cause, the thus-far-unsuccessful campaign to rename the Washington Redskins NFL team. Highlighting the centrality of sports fandom as an arena of political debate, Lopez and Lopez document some success of the campaign through activists' utilization of oppositional fandom within the NFL.

Activist campaigns by, with, or targeted at fans in turn all highlight the eroding boundaries between media production and use and the consequential empowerment of fans as commentators, disseminators, and content creators. Our final section documents and analyzes the different forms of fan labor and interactions between fans and producers informing these shifting boundaries. Mizuko Ito maps practices of fan-created subtitling as enabling access for global audiences to Japanese anime, arguing that they form part of the emergence of a hybrid public culture that combines commercial and noncommercial participation incentives. The role of the commercialization of fan practices is further examined in Anne Gilbert's study of the fan-producer relationship at San Diego Comic-Con. Mapping the asymmetrical power relations between professional producers and fans, we witness in situ manifestations of the clash between industry strategies and fan tactics echoing in its de Certauian distinction the canon of early work on popular audiences and serving as a reminder of the limits of change brought by digitization in the balance of power between media industries and fans hitherto. Highlighting the still potentially antagonistic relationship between producers and fans, Derek Johnson examines conflict and "fantagonisms" between rival fan factions, and between fans and the institutional producers of fan objects, each battling for control of the diegetic universe, focusing on *Buffy the Vampire Slayer*'s much-debated sixth season. In her analysis of fan interactions with actor Orlando Jones, Suzanne Scott argues for a move toward a more intersectional understanding of fan identities, and for a critical reflection on the form of fan identities that are privileged by industry as well as in academic enquiry. Beyond the qualitative dimension of fan identities, power relations between industries and fans are determined through the ways in which fan audiences are quantified and measured. Philip Napoli and Allie Kosterich examine the use of social media in audience measurements, arguing that the use of social media data—to the extent that they allow for an accurate reflection of fans' sentiments—strengthens the voice of fans in industry decision-making processes and in potentially facilitating greater diversity, though they remain acutely aware of the continuing prevalence of traditional audience ratings.

Fans 4.0: Will Studying Fans Still Matter?

With Napoli and Kosterich's concern for how to quantify fan audiences, and thus by extension how to draw the boundaries between fans and those who aren't, we return to a final but central question about the future of fan studies. In his afterword to the first edition of this volume, Jenkins

(2007: 364) speculated playfully whether the category of "fandom" will lose its analytic utility as being a fan becomes a virtually ubiquitous practice and as "maybe there is no typical media consumer against which the cultural otherness of the fan can be located." If anything, the concern over fans constituting a distinct category has become even more acute in the intervening years. As we have illustrated here—and as the chapters that follow document in greater detail—fan practices and affective attachments take many different forms across a wide spectrum of contemporary culture and far beyond what we have historically regarded as the "popular." At the beginning of this introduction, we pointed to forms of grassroots enthusiasm in American politics that rose to the fore in the 2008 presidential election as bearing parallels to, and possibly being a form of, fandom. Eight years later, what was once a sideways look at the political activism from the perspective of fan studies had become common currency in public discourse. In the 2016 presidential primaries, references to "fans" of given candidates not only abounded, but also were more accurate than ever: Vermont Senator Bernie Sanders's campaign, with its call for profound political and economic change, was driven by a level of youthful grassroots enthusiasm that outshined previous campaigns, including its forerunners in 2004 with Howard Dean and 2008 with Barack Obama. As news outlets now routinely resort to the label "fan" in describing those supporting given candidates, their wider rhetoric is strongly reminiscent of previous representations of dynamics between stars and their fans, as in ABC News' (2016) headline worthy of describing any papal encounter by the latest boy group- or actor-heartthrob: "Bernie Sanders Brings Excitement to Fans during Whirlwind Vatican City Trip." Many other news media including the BBC (2016) highlighted how affective investments of Sanders fans and Clinton supporters had led to intense manifestations of trolling and anti-fandom between the two rival camps. However, while the affectively invested support and collective grassroots action in support of a candidate appeared to be the domain of center-left politics in the early years of the digital era, recent years have witnessed the same forms of practices and motivations, from emotive attachments, digital interpretative communities, and fan-generated paratexts to public performances of fan identities and collective action, utilized in the emergence of reactionary movements such as the Tea Party in the United States or various anti-immigrant parties and movements in Europe such as the UK Independence Party and Pegida. As James Hay (2011) observes, Tea Party activists indeed carry many of the hallmarks of the participatory, textually active, and networked user. They are undoubtedly fans of a given cause and of given politicians representing this cause, such as former Alaska Governor Sarah Palin (see Ouellette 2012).

The supporters to whom the label "fan" was most naturally and possibly most frequently applied in the 2016 presidential campaign were equally found on the far right: those who in their millions lent voice to and proudly displayed their affiliation with property-developer-turned-reality-television-performer Donald Trump. The textuality of Trump-the-candidate was that typical of a fan object: intertextual, mediated, polysemic. His campaign persona in the Republican primaries was based on his performance as the host of *The Apprentice* (which in turn is based on Trump's previous media appearances and self-branding efforts). Like popular fan objects in sports, Trump sought tirelessly to brand himself under a banner of "success," inviting a self-reflective affective bond with his fans who were left to color in the then-still-substantive ideological blanks according to their own, often diverging, beliefs and convictions. And many had no hesitation in calling themselves a "fan" of their preferred candidate. Trump's rise during the 2016 campaign further illustrated Jenkins's (2014: 285) acknowledgment that "there is nothing about participatory culture that would inevitably lead to progressive outcomes" and further highlighted the extent to which being a fan permeates many spheres of mediated engagements—political, cultural, and economical—in our everyday lives. Does this then, as Jenkins (2007) pondered, not without mischief, erode the usefulness of the notions of fans and fandom in their academic analyses?

Our answer remains a resounding a "no." We believe that the ubiquity of fans and fan practices makes the case for studying fans and fan cultures more pressing than ever. Indeed, as many academic and popular think pieces have struggled to explain the rise of Trump—and related phenomena from Fox News, Breitbart, and Sean Hannity to the Tea Party and Sarah Palin—better answers will require an awareness of how being a fan and becoming part of a fandom work.

Similarly, such universality of fan objects does not allow for a conceptualization of fans and fandom that is dependent on binary distinctions, or for its universal and a priori embracement. If as ideologically and performatively diverse practices as, say, slash writing and right-wing campaigning draw upon identificatory investments and both articulate participatory fan practices, then there may indeed be no mainstream culture remaining against which to demarcate fans as generic sets of practice. Attempts to maintain such binaries through definitions that exclude those outside the sentiments expressed in "Anglo-American, typically imagined as white, middle-class, and heterosexual" (Morimoto & Chin, this volume) fan cultures of science fiction and television drama seem, as we suggested above, largely arbitrary attempts to fit the object of study to a preconceived conceptual or political position, which remain also unaware of the relative privilege of such fan cultures in a global context. To be clear, we do not, as Coppa (2014) suggests, argue that the fan cultures at the heart of first-wave approaches ought no longer be considered. They are clearly encapsulated in broader definitions of fans, as is reflected by their multiple inclusion in this volume. What we *do* argue for are approaches that enable us to meaningfully conceptualize the obvious differences but also the—possibly less apparent— similarities of such seemingly divergent practices, and that acknowledge the interplay between fan and fan object, between agency and structure, that inevitably shape the quality and texture of fans' emotions, practices, and performances. The rich and diverse trajectories of third-wave fan studies we have outlined here, combined with typological advances and the recognition of both the intrapersonal and interpersonal dimensions of fandom, seem best equipped to achieve this.

After a decade of studies have documented how fan practices and attachments have proliferated across cultures, territories, and genres, little doubt remains that the practices and affective motivations associated with being a fan have come to shape much of our reception of, and engagement with, mediated content. This process of "fanization" is, however, not an otherwise neutral process simply enhancing participation. It is precisely because being a fan is more than just participation, because it carries an affective and identificatory dimension, because it shapes and is shaped by the personal and interpersonal, that the concepts of "fan" and "fandom" continue to matter and differ vis-à-vis many other terms used in our discipline to describe prosumers, citizen journalists, activists, influencers, amateur content creators, etcetera. The implications of "fanization" span across many cultural spaces including entertainment, arts, commerce, citizenship, and politics. They are profound and significant in all these realms. However, it is possibly its manifestation in political processes and the public sphere that illustrates why studying and theorizing fandom matters most lucidly. Among may other things, fanization has contributed to young activists forming cornerstones in recent presidential campaigns; to the personalization of politics (cf. Corner & Pels 2003; Stanyer 2012) and to media celebrity converting into political capital ever more instantaneously; to a disjuncture between affectively invested form and fans' beliefs and convictions that lead to a loss of trust and disillusionment (Sandvoss 2012, 2013); to the rise of extreme political partisanship on the right as a form of anti-fandom as much as of fandom; and it has thereby contributed to—though far from being singularly responsible for—a remarkable and dramatic erosion of rationality, civility, and reason in contemporary political and public life in the United States and beyond.

The binary oppositions against which fandom could once be conceptualized as oppositional practice may be fast disappearing. Yet, as these examples illustrate, the more being a fan is commonplace and the more it is "just like being any other media user," the more it matters; the more it shapes the identities and communities in our mediated world and with it the culture, social relations, economic models, and politics of our age.

WORKS CITED

ABC News 2016, "Bernie Sanders brings excitement to fans during whirlwind Vatican City trip," abcnews.go.com.

Abercrombie, N & Longhurst, B 1998, *Audiences: a sociological theory of performance and imagination*, Sage, Thousand Oaks, CA.

Aden, RC 1999, *Popular stories and promised lands: fan cultures and symbolic pilgrimages*, University of Alabama Press, Tuscaloosa.

Bailey, S 2005, *Media audiences and identity: self-construction in the fan experience*, Palgrave Macmillan, New York.

Banks, M 2013, *Co-creating videogames*, Bloomsbury, London.

Banks, MJ, Conor, B, & Mayer, V (eds.) 2013, *Production studies, the sequel! Cultural studies of global media industries*, Routledge, New York.

Bauman, Z 2005, *Liquid life*, Polity, London.

BBC 2015, "Premier League in record £5.14bn TV rights deal," www.bbc.co.uk.

BBC 2016, "Bernie Sanders supporters get a bad reputation online," www.bbc.co.uk.

Beaty, B 2009, "My media studies: the failure of hype," *Television & New Media* 10(1): 23–24.

Bennett, L & Booth, P (eds.) 2016, *Seeing fans: representations of fandom in media and popular culture*, Bloomsbury, New York.

Bourdieu, P 1984, *Distinction: a social critique of the judgment of taste*, Harvard University Press, Cambridge, MA.

Busse, K (ed.) 2009, "In Focus: fandom and feminism," *Cinema Journal* 48(4): 104–36.

Busse, K 2013, "Geek hierarchies, boundary policing, and the gendering of the good fan," *Participations: Journal of Audience and Reception Studies* 10(1): 73–91.

Busse, K (ed.) 2015, "In Focus: feminism and fandom revisited: fan labor and feminism," *Cinema Journal* 54(3): 110–55.

Caldwell, JT 2008, *Production culture: industrial reflexivity and critical practice in film and television*, Duke University Press, Durham, NC.

Click, MA, Aubrey, JS, & Behm-Morawitz, E (eds.) 2010, *Bitten by Twilight: youth culture, media, and the vampire franchise*, Peter Lang, New York.

Coppa, F 2014, "Fuck yeah, fandom is beautiful," *Journal of Fandom Studies* 2(1): 73–82.

Corner, J & Pels, D (eds.) 2003, *Media and the restyling of politics: consumerism, celebrity and cynicism*, Sage, Thousand Oaks, CA.

Crawford, G 2004, *Consuming sport: sport, fans and culture*, Routledge, New York.

Cunningham, S 2015, "The new screen ecology: a new wave of media globalization?," *Communication Research and Practice* 1(3): 275–82.

Cunningham, S 2016, "Qualifying the quantified audience," CCI Digital Methods Summer School, Queensland University of Technology, February 19.

Cunningham, S & Craig, D 2016, "Online entertainment: A new wave of media globalization?" *International Journal of Communication* 10: 5409–25, www.ijoc.org.

Cunningham, S & Silver, J 2014, "Studying change in popular culture: a 'middle-range' approach," in T Miller (ed.), *The Routledge companion to global popular culture*, Routledge, New York.

De Kosnik, A 2012, "Fandom as free labor," in T Scholz (ed.), *Digital labor: the Internet as playground and factory*, Routledge, New York.

Dell, C 1998, "'Lookit that hunk of a man': subversive pleasures, female fandom and professional wrestling," in C Harris & A Alexander (eds.), *Theorizing fandom: fans, subculture and identity*, Hampton, Cresskill, NJ.

Dixon, K 2013, "Learning the game: football fandom culture and the origins of practice," *International Review for the Sociology of Sport* 48(3): 334–48.

Duffett, M 2013, *Understanding fandom: an introduction to the study of media fan culture*, Bloomsbury, New York.

Duits, L, Zwaan, K, & Reijnders, S (eds.) 2014, *Ashgate research companion to fan cultures*, Ashgate, Farnham.

Elliott, A 1999, *The mourning of John Lennon*, University of California Press, Berkeley.

Fiske, J 1989, *Understanding popular culture*, Unwin Hyman, Boston.

Fiske, J 1992, "The cultural economy of fandom," in LA Lewis (ed.), *The adoring audience: fan culture and popular media*, Routledge, New York.

Gray, J & Lotz, AD 2012, *Television studies*, Polity, Malden, MA.

Gray, J, Sandvoss, C, & Harrington, CL 2007, "Introduction: why study fans," in J Gray, C Sandvoss, & CL Harrington (eds.), *Fandom: identities and communities in a mediated world*, New York University Press, New York.

Harrington, CL & Bielby, DD 1995, *Soap fans: pursuing pleasure and making meaning in everyday life*, Temple University Press, Philadelphia.

Harrington, CL, Bielby, DD, & Bardo, AR (eds.) 2014, *Aging, media, and culture*, Lexington, Lanham, MD.

Harris, C 1998, "A sociology of television fandom," in C Harris & A Alexander (eds.), *Theorizing fandom: fans, subculture and identity*, Hampton, Cresskill, NJ.

Hay, J 2011, "'Popular culture' in a critique of the new political reason," *Cultural Studies* 25(4–5): 659–84.

Hills, M 2002, *Fan cultures*, Routledge, New York.

Hills, M 2007, "Essential tensions: Winnicottian object-relations in the media sociology of Roger Silverstone," *International Journal of Communication* 1: 37–48.

Hills, M 2012, "Twilight fans represented in commercial paratexts and inter-fandoms: resisting and repurposing negative fan stereotypes," in A Morey (ed.), *Genre, reception, and adaptation in the Twilight series*, Ashgate, Farnham.

Izundu, CC 2013, "Director defends Channel 4 One Direction documentary," *BBC Online*, www.bbc.co.uk.

Jancovich, M 2002, "Cult fictions: cult movies, subcultural capital and the production of cultural distinction," *Cultural Studies* 16(2): 306–22.

Jenkins, H 1992, *Textual poachers: television fans and participatory culture*, Routledge, New York.

Jenkins, H 2006, *Convergence culture: where old and new media collide*, New York University Press, New York.

Jenkins, H 2007, "Afterword: the future of fandom," in J Gray, C Sandvoss, & CL Harrington (eds.), *Fandom: identities and communities in a mediated world*, New York University Press, New York.

Jenkins, H 2014, "Rethinking 'rethinking convergence/culture,'" *Cultural Studies* 28(2): 267–97.

Jensen, J 1992, "Fandom as pathology: the consequences of characterization," in LA Lewis (ed.), *The adoring audience: fan culture and popular media*, Routledge, New York.

Larsen, K & Zubernis, L 2012, *Fan culture: theory/practice*, Cambridge Scholars, Newcastle.

Longhurst, BJ 2007, *Cultural change and ordinary life*, Open University Press, Maidenhead.

Lotz, AD 2014, *The television will be revolutionized*, 2nd ed., New York University Press, New York.

Maxwell, R & Miller, T 2011, "Old, new and middle-aged media convergence," *Cultural Studies* 25(4–5): 585–603.

Mayer, V, Banks, MJ, & Caldwell, JT (eds.) 2009, *Production studies: cultural studies of media industries*, Routledge, New York.

Monteiro, C. 2015, "'You shall not pass': How favela's new appropriation of funk brought social issues and the power of fans together to the mainstream," European Fan Cultures Symposium, Rotterdam, December 3–4, 2015.

Morreale, J 2014, "From homemade to store bought: *Annoying Orange* and the professionalization of YouTube," *Journal of Consumer Culture* 14(1): 113–28.

Ouellette, L 2012, "Branding the Right: the affective economy of Sarah Palin," *Cinema Journal* 51(4): 185–91.

Sandvoss, C 2003, *A game of two halves: football, television and globalization*, Routledge, New York.

Sandvoss, C 2005, *Fans: the mirror of consumption*, Polity, Malden, MA.

Sandvoss, C 2012, "Enthusiasm, trust, and its erosion in mediated politics: on fans of Obama and the Liberal Democrats," *European Journal of Communication* 27(1): 68–81.

Sandvoss, C 2013, "Toward an understanding of political enthusiasm as media fandom: blogging, fan productivity and affect in American politics," *Participations: Journal of Audience and Reception Studies* 10(1): 252–96.

Sandvoss, C 2014, "'I ♥ Ibiza': music, place and belonging," in M Duffett (ed.), *Popular music fandom: identities, roles and practices*, Routledge, New York.

Sandvoss, C 2015, "The politics of proximity in part-scripted reality drama: on fans of *The Only Way is Essex* and *Made in Chelsea*," in L Geraghty (ed.), *Popular media cultures: fans, audiences and narrative worlds*, Palgrave, Houndmills.

Scott, S 2011, *Revenge of the fanboys: convergence culture and the politics of incorporation*, PhD dissertation, University of Southern California.

Stacey, J 1994, *Stargazing: Hollywood cinema and female spectatorship*, Routledge, New York.

Stanfill, M 2011, "Doing fandom, (mis)doing whiteness: heteronormativity, racialization, and the discursive construction of fandom," *Transformative Works and Cultures* 8, doi:10.3983/twc.2011.0256.

Stanfill, M 2015, *Orienting fandom: the discursive production of sports and speculative media fandom in the Internet era*, PhD dissertation, University of Illinois.

Stanfill, M & Condis, M (eds.) 2014, "Fandom and/as labor," *Transformative Works and Cultures* 15, journal.transformativeworks.org.

Stanyer, J 2012, *Intimate politics: publicity, privacy and the personal lives of politicians in media saturated democracies*, Polity, Malden, MA.

Sunstein, CR 2007, *Republic.com 2.0*, Princeton University Press, Princeton, NJ.

Thomas, L 2002, *Fans, feminisms and "quality" media*, Routledge, New York.

Thompson, JB 1995, *The media and modernity: a social theory of the media*, Polity, Cambridge.

Thornton, S 1995, *Club cultures*, Polity, Cambridge.

Turner, G 2011, "Surrendering the space," *Cultural Studies* 25(4–5): 685–99.

Wanzo, R 2015, "African-American acafandom and other strangers: new genealogies of fan studies," *Transformative Works and Cultures* 20, dx.doi.org./10.3983/twc.2015.0699.

Williams, R 2013, "'Anyone who calls Muse a Twilight band will be shot on sight': music, distinction, and the 'interloping fan' in the Twilight franchise," *Popular Music and Society* 36(3): 327–42.

PART I

Fan Texts and Objects

1

The Death of the Reader?

Literary Theory and the Study of Texts in Popular Culture

CORNEL SANDVOSS

[handwritten note: Due to Tolkien's acclaim while LOTR has a fandom in the traditional sense it bridges a cultural gap + not seen as 'Mickey mouse']

Concerns over meaning and aesthetic value have continually haunted media and cultural studies. In many ways the field of fan studies epitomizes these concerns. The relative neglect of the question of aesthetic value (see also Hills, this volume) has made the field of media and cultural studies (hereafter cultural studies) a popular target as a "Mickey Mouse" subject. On the one hand, this is, quite literally, true: fan studies has focused on popular texts from horror films via sports events to, indeed, comics. Beyond this, however, the notion of a "Mickey Mouse" subject implies a lack of depth and theoretical rigor. It is on this level that it remains most hurtful, especially when such criticism is reiterated by those in neighboring disciplines such as literary theory. Echoing such themes and pointing to structuralism paving the way for the rise of cultural studies, Eagleton accuses the new discipline of taking advantage of the fact that

> methodologically speaking, nobody quite knew where Coriolanus ended and Coronation Street began and constructed an entirely fresh field of enquiry which would gratify the anti-elitist iconoclasm of the sixty-eighters. [. . .] It was, in its academicist way, the latest version of the traditional avant-garde project of leaping barriers between art and society, and was bound to make its appeal to those who found, rather like an apprentice chef cooking his evening meal, that it linked classroom and leisure time with wonderful economy. (1996: 192)

If Eagleton's words are addressed to the discipline as a whole, nowhere do they reverberate more loudly than in fan studies. Fan studies has indeed eroded the boundaries between audiences and scholars, between fan and academic more than any other field (see Hills 2002; Tulloch 2000). To Eagleton, the blurring of these formerly distinct categories has led to a decline in analytic depth and an ideological stagnation: "what happened in the event was not a defeat for this project, which has indeed been gaining institutional strength ever since, but a defeat for the political forces which originally underpinned the new evolutions in literary theory" (1996: 192). Eagleton's critique raises a number of important questions: Has fan studies unduly neglected aesthetic value and thus become complicit in the decline of literary quality and theory alike? Have sociological studies of fan audiences in their emphasis on the micro over the macro, on fans in their subcultural context over wider social relations, undermined progressive traditions and forms of radical enquiry, as Bryan Turner (2005) has recently suggested? Is fan studies unwittingly part of a revisionist wave that has suffocated the final sparks of 1960s radicalism? Or is Eagleton's critique just the bitter réplique of a scholar who in the shifting sands of history sees the scholarly foundations of his discipline running through his hands, witnessing the dunes of social, cultural, economic, and technological relations upon which all intellectual projects are built shifting from his field of inquiry to another?

In order to answer these questions by comparing the traditions and aims of literary theory with those of fan studies, we need to find a point of—if not compatibility—convertibility between these two fields. This point is found in the shared essence of both disciplines: the analysis and interpretation of meaning in the study of texts and their readings.

Texts and Textuality

While both disciplines share a focus on texts and the meanings that evolve around them, they already diverge in their definition of what actually constitutes a "text." Our common understanding of texts is rooted in the idealization and imagination of closed forms of textuality that have shaped the study of written texts from the rise of modern aesthetics in Enlightenment philosophy via the Romantics, who "denied any influence from previous writers and asserted the text's utter uniqueness" (Gray 2006: 20), to Edmund Husserl's phenomenological search for the author's pure intent in literary texts. "Textual studies" has thus, as Gray notes, "a long history of fetishizing the text as a solitary, pristinely autonomous object, and this notion of textuality has exerted consider-able pressure, particularly on literary and film studies" (2006: 19–20). In fan studies, however, the task of defining the text has been rather more complex. To understand the origin of this difficulty, we need to briefly draw the admittedly crude distinction between form and content. Take the following textual fragment or statement: "My name is Dr. Serenus Zeitblom, Ph.D." To those who share English as a common language, the content of this brief sentence appears clear, but it is quite impossible for anyone, myself included, to describe its content in any form other than its meaning or, even if I could, to communicate this content to others. When I summarize the content of this statement as "someone is called Serenus Zeitblom, and he has a doctorate in philosophy," I am already describing the meaning I have generated in the act of the reading. All encounters with textual structures thus require ideational activity that inherently ties the text to its reader. No text (and content) exists inde-pendently (see Fish 1981; Holub 1992; Iser 1978).

This is, of course, hardly news. Yet, while we cannot separate content from meaning, we can observe how meaning changes in different forms of communication. If we set the same utterance or textual fragment into different contexts, its meaning, or at least its possible meanings, change. In the case of face-to-face interaction—let's say we meet someone on the street who introduces himself with the above words—the someone who is or claims to be Serenus Zeitblom is effectively limited to the person who has been seen or heard to make this statement. Here, the reciproc-ity of the text limits its possible meanings. The reader of this chapter in contrast will have found it more difficult to identify who the name points to when reading the above statement. The utterer of these words does not correspond with the author, leaving you with countless possibilities as to who the possessive pronoun in "my name" refers to. It is this fundamen-tal difference in form between written and spoken texts that Paul Ricœur accredits with what he labels as "difficulties of interpretation": "in face-to-face interaction problems [of interpretation] are solved through a form of exchange we call conversation. In written texts discourse has to speak for itself" (1996: 56). Our observation that texts change meaning through their form, in conjunction with Ricœur's assessment of the changing role of authorial intent in written texts, points to two important differences between fan texts and literary texts. First, in studying media audiences, we are confronted with a variety of different textual forms around which fandom evolves: alongside written texts, these include audio and sound, visual texts, audiovisual texts, and hypertexts.

The second difference concerns the way fan texts are formed across these media. Here, I owe the reader three belated definitions of "fans," "texts," and "fan texts." In my earlier work, I defined "fandom as the regular, emotionally involved consumption of a given popular narrative or text" (Sandvoss 2005a: 8). In its inclusion of both texts and narratives, this definition mirrored a level of uncertainty. While we all have a sense of who fans are, conceptualizing the textual basis of their fandom seems far more difficult. Hills (1999) distinguishes between popular texts (fictional) and popular icons (factual) as possible fan objects. On the level of the author, this distinction is of course correct. In the cases of literary fandom (see Brooker 2005) or fandom based on television shows, texts are written or controlled by copyright and license holders; they are in one form or another authored. In contrast, we do not describe popular icons such as musicians, actors, or athletes, or other fan objects such as sport teams, as deliberately authored texts. Even where those in the center of the public gaze aim to maintain a public and hence staged persona, fans' interests often focus on what lies behind the public façade, as is exemplified in the title of celebrity biographies from *The Real David Beckham* (Morgan 2004) to Albert Goldman's (2001) notorious *The Lives of John Lennon*. However, the popularity of such biographies already signals that we cannot rely on authorship as a defining element of textuality; indeed, the success of these books is often based not on their actual author, who may be unknown to readers, but on the subject—the object of fandom. Whether a given fan object is found in a novel, on a television program, or as a popular icon, fan objects are read as texts on the level of the fan/reader. They all constitute a set of signs and symbols that fans encounter in their frames of representation and mediation, and from which they create meaning in the process of reading. Consequently, what is needed is a broad definition of texts that is based not on authorship, but on texts as frames of realizable meanings that span across single or multiple communicative acts, including visual, sound-based, and written communication. Yet, what the example of celebrity biographies shows is that we need to reflect on textual boundaries too. As we remove authorship as the essence of textuality, the notion of the single text that can be distinguished from other texts becomes impossible to maintain, as it is now not by the producer but by the reader that the boundaries of texts are set (Sandvoss 2005a, 2005b).

The capability of media audiences to define textual boundaries is inextricably linked with their media of delivery. The home-based and mobile media through which most fan texts are consumed—television, radio, magazines, Walkmen and iPods, the Internet—are firmly entrenched in the structure of everyday life in late industrialism, embedding the act of reading in a social and technological context not only that is nonreciprocal (Thompson 1995), but also in which textual boundaries at the point of production are evaded through the technological essence of such media as spaces of flow (see Williams 1974; see also Corner 1999). Television finds its true narrative form in seriality (Eco 1994), while the hypertextuality of the Internet forces the reader/user into the active construction of the text's boundaries. Moreover, through notions of genre and the capitalist imperative of market enlargements that drives them, textual motives from narratives to fictional characters and popular icons are constituted and reconstituted across different media. A sports fan will read and watch texts in reference to his or her favorite team on television, on the radio, in newspapers, in sport magazines, and, increasingly, on the Internet; soap fans (Baym 2000) turn to the World Wide Web and entertainment magazines as part of their fandom; the fan of a given actress will watch her in different films but also follow further coverage in newspapers or read the above-mentioned celebrity biographies. Fan objects thus form a field of gravity, which may or may not have an urtext in its epicenter, but which in any case corresponds with the fundamental meaning structure through which all these texts are read. The fan text is thus constituted through a multiplicity of textual elements; it is by definition intertextual and formed between and across texts as defined at the point of production.

The single "episodes" that fans patch together to form a fan text are usefully described by Gray, drawing on Genette, as "paratext" that "infringes upon the text, and invades its meaning-making process" (2006: 36). As the fan text takes different forms among different fan groups— namely, the audience sections "fans," "cultists," and "enthusiasts," with their different use of mass media, which Abercrombie and Longhurst (1998) describe—the balance between urtext and paratexts changes. In Gray's words, to the degree that "we actually consume some texts through paratexts and supportive intertexts, the text itself becoming expendable" (2006: 37). What follows is a radically different conceptualization of "texts" than in literary theory. Individual texts at the point of production are part of a wider web of textual occurrences and the meanings derived from them. These textual elements are read in the context of other texts. Intertextuality is thus the essence of all texts. While many contemporary fan texts such as *The Simpsons*, on which Gray focuses, or *South Park* are based on parody and thus more ostensibly intertextual than others, meaning construction through text and context does not by itself allow us to distinguish between literary and mediated texts. The field of comparative literature, for instance, draws on the long-standing tradition of motive and theme research. Yet in each and every case, the textual field in which the individual text is positioned will allow the reader to construct different meanings.

On a most obvious level, this relates to existing knowledge. Those readers with an interest in twentieth-century German literature will not have been quite as clueless about who the above-mentioned Serenus Zeitblom was. They will have recognized the sentence "My name is Dr. Serenus Zeitblom, Ph.D." as the opening sentence of the second chapter of Thomas Mann's *Doktor Faustus*, in which the narrator, Serenus Zeitblom, apologizes for his belated introduction. It is then a form of preexisting interest or what we might call an object of fandom (the work of Thomas Mann) that allows us to create meaning through contextualization that will have remained hidden to other readers—just as if the sentence in question had been "My name is Slim Shady," different paratexts would have come into play for different fan groups. Beyond this, Mann's *Doktor Faustus* serves as a lucid example of intertextuality in literary works in their literary and multimediated context: "the life of the German composer Adrian Leverkühn as told by a friend," as the subtitle of its English translations goes, is an adaptation of the Faust motive—the selling of one's soul to the devil for earthly talents, powers, or knowledge—that spans through all forms of textuality in European literature and storytelling, beginning with the late medieval German myth via Goethe's *Urfaust* to Bulgakov's *Мастер и Маргарита*, poetry (Heine's *Der Doktor Faust*), theater such as Paul Valéry's fragment *Mon Faust*, music by Berlioz, Wagner, Liszt, and the Einstürzenden Neubauten, filmic adaptations, including Murnau's *Faust: Eine Deutsche Volkssage*, and comic supervillains such as DC Comics' Felix Faust, to name only a few.[1] Beyond such direct adaptations, the Faust motive resurfaces in a plethora of popular texts including George Lucas's *Star Wars*. Yet, Mann's *Doktor Faustus* is not only part of an intertextual web; it also, like Mann's preceding work, is based on an ironic gesture of the narrator, the by now familiar Serenus Zeitblom, which takes back the narrative and the pretense of representing the real; a gesture in Mann's work that according to Adorno (1991) reflects the crisis of the narrator in the modern novel as a direct consequence of the proliferation of new modes and media of representation, namely, film (see also Benjamin 1983). The difference between intertextuality in mediated and literary texts is thus one of degree rather than kind. For both sets of textuality, the crisis of the text (in its boundaries at the point of production) is thus the crisis of the narrator as literary and actual figure: the author him- or herself.

The fan scholar, coincidentally, is thus no more or less an "apprentice chef" than the philologist. Both rely on intertextual knowledge to interpret text and context. To the degree that the fan text is constituted on the level of consumption, the reading position of the fan is actually the premise for identifying the text and its boundaries—rather than to an apprentice chef, the fan scholar compares to a restaurant critic, who to do his job also needs to know how to cook.

On a wider point, our reflections of what constitutes a text coincide with the critical reflections on authorship and textuality in structuralism and poststructuralism. The study of fans further underlines a process of growing intertextuality, multimediated narrative figures, and multiple authorship that has eroded the concept of the author that, as Barthes (1977) notes, reached its zenith in the formation of high modernity as the culmination of a rationalist, positivist capitalist system. It is indeed Barthes's analysis of Balzac's *Sarrasine* that accurately prefigures the condition of textuality as decentered and refocused on the level of the fan/reader I have sought to describe here:

A text is not a line of words releasing a single "theological" meaning [. . .] but a multi-dimensional space in which a variety of writings, none of them original, blend and clash. [. . .] A text is made of multiple writings, drawn from many cultures and entering into mutual relations of dialogue, parody, contestation, but there is one place where this multiplicity is focused and that place is the reader, not, as was hitherto said, the author. The reader is the space on which all the quotations that make up a writing are inscribed without any of them being lost; a text's unity lies not in its origin but in its destination. (Barthes 1977: 146–48)

If the poststructuralist turn in Barthes's work furnishes us with a conceptual basis for the study and analysis of fandom, it is his earlier work and structuralism in general that allowed cultural studies to extend the study of interpretation and meaning beyond literary texts. As Eagleton notes resentfully (1996: 192), "structuralism had apparently revealed that the same codes and conventions traversed both 'high' and 'low' cultures, with scant regard for the classical distinction of value." When Eagleton laments the disappearing boundaries between Coriolanus and Coronation Street, he has thus already identified the guilty party. Eagleton's critique of course fails to acknowledge that the formation of structuralism was itself a reaction to changing forms of textuality that much of literary theory had been unable to address, continuing the study of literary texts as if they existed in splendid isolation. This, however, is not to dismiss Eagleton's concern over value out of hand. Many studies illustrate how fans themselves—from Tulloch and Jenkins's (1995) and McKee's (2001) *Dr. Who* to Cavicchi's (1998) Springsteen and Thomas's (2002) *The Archers* fans—are concerned with value. Yet, if Eagleton's comparison between cultural studies and literary theory is ill judged for lacking recognition of the multiple methodological grounds for the rise of the former and the inability to address new forms of textuality of the latter, his warning that in its heightened emphasis on structuralist and poststructuralist approaches cultural studies has lost the vocabulary to evaluate texts is less easily dismissed.

The Death of the Author and Audience Activity

The notion of intertextuality has been pivotal to fan studies from its very beginning. Jenkins (1992: 67), in the context of new technological developments such as VCRs, explored the notion of "rereading." Jenkins differed from Barthes's description of the irregularity of rereadings, noting that they are commercially attractive to the television industry. This distinction between reading and rereading belongs to the less widely recognized aspects of Jenkins's work, not least because he admits that it is difficult to maintain, since in an intertextual-structuralist approach, reading and rereading are the same phenomenon. However, terminology aside, Jenkins finds himself in fundamental agreement with Barthes's model of reading. In his canonical work of the first wave of fan studies, a basic model of fan textuality thus emerges that has come to prevail until today. As fan studies found new conceptual grounds throughout the 1990s describing fandom as a form of spectacle and performance (Abercrombie & Longhurst 1998; see also Lancaster 2001), as a manifestation of subcultural hierarchies (Jancovich 2002; Thornton 1995), or as a transitional space (Harrington & Bielby 1995; Hills 2002), the implicit assumption remained a model of textuality that distinguished between "exceptional texts" and "exceptional readings" and that allocated the specificities of fandom on the side of the fan/reader rather than the text. With few exceptions, studies of fan audiences have challenged the idea of "correct" or even dominant readings. Hence, fan studies with its critical attention to the power of meaning construction not only underlines Barthes's pronouncement of the terminal state of the modern author but also inherits its inherent ideological stance:

> Once the author is removed, the claim to decipher a text becomes quite futile. To give a text an Author is to impose a limit on the text [. . .], literature by refusing to assign a "secret," an ultimate meaning to the text (and to the world as text), liberates what may be called an anti-theological activity that is truly revolutionary since to refuse to fix meaning is in the end, to refuse God and his hypostases—reason, science, law. [. . .] [T]he birth of the reader must be at the cost of the death of the author. (Barthes 1977: 147–48)

This self-proclaimed radicalism, which has marked poststructuralism and fan studies alike, fostering relativism in aesthetic judgment as radical rejection of positivism and science, is, according to Eagleton (1996), based on "straw targets." Eagleton sees poststructuralism as rooted in the specific historic moment of disillusionment, as 1960s oppositional movements were uncovered as complicit in the very structures they set out to overthrow, hence leading to a total rejection of all structures and thus the concept of truth: "an invulnerable position, and the fact it is also purely empty is simply the price one has to pay for this" (Eagleton 1996: 125).

Here, Eagleton has a point, not least because if all that fan studies can do is to highlight the relative value of all texts and the inherent supremacy of the reader over the text, the field has reached its conceptual and empirical frontiers. What, however, are the alternatives? Fan studies, drawing on the work of Pierre Bourdieu (1984), has too convincingly unmasked forms of judgment based on authenticity and originality—which persist among fans as well as scholars—as means of social and cultural distinction (and domination) for a return to textual critique on such grounds to be considered a possibility. If it is only in these terms that we can maintain a distinction between *Coriolanus* and *Coronation Street*, it is a distinction not worth making.

The Death of the Reader

If we cannot locate aesthetic value of texts in themselves—and Eagleton's (1996) discussion of hermeneutics admits as much—yet do not want to abolish questions of value altogether, it needs to be located elsewhere. The author, pronounced dead in poststructuralism, and in any case conspicuously absent in most mass-mediated forms of textuality, has proven an unsuitable basis for textual interpretation and evaluation. However, if we can distinguish texts and meaning creation as radically as Jenkins's (1992) distinction between exceptional texts and exceptional readings suggests, the reader appears to be a no-better indicator of the aesthetic value of texts, since exceptional readings would thus appear to be based upon forms of audience activity quite independent of texts themselves. If we cannot locate aesthetic value in the author, text, or reader alone, it is in the process of interaction between these that aesthetic value is manifested. Hence, we need to define the act of reading in a manner that may appear obvious but has profound normative consequences. By defining the act of reading as a form of dialogue between text and reader (see Sandvoss 2005b), in fandom and elsewhere, we enter into a wider social and cultural commitment as to what texts are for and what we believe the uses of reading to be.

In doing so, I want to turn to Wolfgang Iser (1971, 1978), who, like other reception theorists (see Jauss 1982; Vodička 1975), moves the focus of literary theory from the text to the processes of reading. The premise of Iser's argument is that texts acquire meaning only when they are being read. The process of reading, however, is no simple realization of prepacked meanings controlled by the author, but rather an interaction in which the structures and figures of the text collide with the reader's (subjective) knowledge, experiences, and expectations, all in turn formed, we may add, in an intertextual field. In this process of dialogue between text and reader, meaning is created as the reader "concretizes" the text. Hence Iser focuses on textual elements of indeterminacy that come to life only through the interaction with the reader: textual gaps and blanks. In contrast to hermeneutical approaches, including the work of Ingarden (1973), who similarly speaks of "spots of indeterminacy," textual gaps have no theological, metaphysical function but are constituted and filled in each individual act of reading. In their recognition of the absence of inherent meanings and universal aesthetic value, Iser and fellow reception theorists thus actually share fundamental assumptions with Barthes's work. Yet, in contrast to the poststructuralist approaches to textuality that have given birth to fan studies, Iser establishes a firm basis on which the aesthetic value of a given text can be assessed. According to Iser, the act of concretization is underscored by readers' inherent striving to "normalize" texts. The notion of normalization is in turn linked to textual gaps: in their attempt to concretize textual gaps, readers are required to draw on their own knowledge and experience—on what Jauss (1982) has described as "horizon of expectation." It is therefore an inherent aspect of all ideational activity to align the Otherness encountered in the text, its alien elements, as closely with our past experience as possible. If we are successful, the text is fully normalized and "appears to be nothing more than a mirror-reflection" of the reader and his or her schemes of perception (Iser 1971: 9).

We must not, as Eagleton does, confuse Iser's observations with normative claims. Eagleton denounces normalization as a "revealingly authoritarian term," suggesting that a text should be "tamed and subdued to some firm sense of structure" as readers struggle to pin down "its anarchic 'polysemantic' potential" (1996: 71). Eagleton's adventurous reading itself tests the boundaries of polysemy, as in fact, Iser argues the

opposite: normalization is an inherent aspect of cognition and all ideational activity, but one that the text can evade. It is precisely the ability
of a text to avoid normalization in which its aesthetic value lies. While
readers strive to normalize texts, the question is to what extent texts will
let them do so. If a text is readily normalized, it "seems trivial, because
it merely echoes our own" experience (Iser 1978: 109). Conversely, those
texts that profoundly contradict readers' experiences and thus challenge
our expectations require a reflexive engagement that reveals "aspects
(e.g. of social norms) which had remained hidden as long as the frame
of reference remained intact" (Iser 1978: 109).

In this formulation of aesthetic value as defamiliarization lies a profound challenge to mediated textuality and fan texts in particular. The
obstacles to normalization in literary texts, such as *Doktor Faustus*, are
rooted in a range of narrative and metaphorical techniques that depend
on defined boundaries at the point of production—and hence the persistence of, if not the author, then at least his or her chosen narrative
form. In mediated texts, as I have argued above, these boundaries are
eroded. As the object of fandom corresponds with a textual field of
gravity, rather than a text in its classical sense, readers gain new tools
to normalize texts and to reconcile their object of fandom with their
expectations, beliefs, and sense of self. As fans' semiotic power extends
beyond the bridging of textual gaps to the inclusion and exclusion of
textual episodes, fan readers exclude those textual elements that impede
the normalization of the text and fail to correspond with their horizon
of expectation (see Johnson, this volume). It is thus that Elvis can be
claimed as an object of fandom by white supremacists and black soul
singers alike (see Rodman 1996), that sport teams serve as spaces of
self-projection to fans with varying habitus, beliefs, and convictions
(Sandvoss 2003), and that Springsteen fans find themselves in his lyrics
(Cavicchi 1998). These fan texts are void of inherent meaning and thus
no longer polysemic, but what I have described elsewhere as "neutrosemic" (Sandvoss 2005a)—in other words, they are polysemic to the degree that the endless multiplicity of meaning has collapsed into complete
absence of intersubjective meaning.

In all conceptualizations of fandom spanning from the early work
of Fiske to the present day, fandom as a form of audienceship has been
defined by its use: as a tool of pleasurable subversion, as the rally-

ing point of communities, as focus of audiences' own textual activities or performances, serving a range of psychological functions or as
semiotic space of narcissistic self-reflection. Yet, in this emphasis on
audience activity, fan studies has neglected the act of reading as the
interface between micro (reader) and macro (the text and its systems
of production).

If aesthetic value is based on transgression and estrangement, the
reading of fan texts strives for the opposite: familiarity and the fulfill-
ment of expectations. Iser's work translates thus into a fundamental
question in the study of fan texts: can the reader survive the death of the
author? The fates of the author and reader are rather more intertwined
than Barthes suggests; the process of reading as an act of communication spans like a line between two poles—one depends on the other.
When the author is eradicated from the text, when all gaps disappear,
the meaning that fans create is based no longer on reading but on audience activity. However, the disappearance of the author and fundamental redrawing of textual boundaries at the point of consumption are
rarely complete, as is evident in fans' frequent sense of disappointment
with their fan texts. Most texts—mediated or literary—can be neither
fully normalized and thus emptied of all alien elements, nor truly fantastic, evading all forms of concretization. The extent to which (fan) texts
thus reflexively challenge our perception is a matter of degree and one
that requires a different answer in each and every case of text-reader
interaction.

Two conclusions follow. First, fandom as a mode of reading sits uneasily with the aesthetic principles of reception theory. It constitutes a
particular form of engagement with the text that presupposes familiarity and in which our expectations are more rigid, our determination to
construct meaning in reference to the function of fandom greater than
in other processes of reading. However, it does so in relation to no specific texts, but applies across the spectrum of textuality from Romantic
poetry to television cartoon programs. We can judge a text's aesthetic
value thus only in relation to its reader.

In turn, this means that manifested in the act or reading, aesthetic
value nevertheless persists and remains a category worthy of exploration in all forms of textuality from literary to fan texts. It is admittedly a
functionalist definition of value and one that Eagleton (1996) dismisses

with the same vigor as he attacks poststructuralism. While the latter is disregarded for its hollow political gesture, the functionalism of Iser faces the opposite charge: according to Eagleton (1996: 71), the value of estrangement is rooted in a "definite attitude to the social and cultural systems [. . .] which amounts to suspecting thought-systems as such" and is thus embedded in liberalism. This much is true—and it is equally true that those who do not share such a broad vision of emancipation through communication, those who do not share a belief in the necessity of reflexive engagement with our social, economic, and cultural norms and conditions may quickly dismiss such aesthetics, however curious a position this may be for anyone with the loosest affiliation to the Enlightenment project, not least those drawing their conceptual and ethical inspiration from Marxism—cultural studies and Eagleton included.

Yet this is precisely the lesson that emerges from the study of fan texts and my attempted synthesis between cultural studies and literary theory: the empirical study of fan audiences over the past two decades has indisputably documented the absence of universal and inherent aesthetic values of texts. However, to remain true to its own roots, our discipline needs to find new vocabulary and concepts to analyze aesthetic value in its function: the process of reading. Here, studies of fan audiences can learn as much from literary theory as vice versa: in a state of constant audienceship in which we consume mediated and fragmented texts and reconstitute textual boundaries in the act of reading in an intertextual field, we need to formulate aesthetic categories that avoid the absolutism of traditional textual interpretation as much as the relativism of poststructuralism and deconstructionism. Aesthetic value can thus not be an objective category with what have been unmasked to be subjective criteria, nor can we afford the aesthetic (and ultimately social and cultural) indifference of conveniently abolishing aesthetics by relegating them to a subjective category with subjective criteria. Instead, the synthesis of fan studies and Reception Aesthetics enables us to explore aesthetics as a subjective category with objective criteria. In doing so, fan studies will not avoid ridicule for analyzing texts and their audiences that to some appear trivial; but it will move further toward exploring why fan texts mean so much to so many people and the meaning of this affective bond between text and reader in a mediated world.

NOTE

1 For a critique of intertextuality, and Kristeva's work in particular, see Stierle (1996).

WORKS CITED

Abercrombie, N & Longhurst, B 1998, *Audiences: a sociological theory of performance and imagination*, Sage, Thousand Oaks, CA.

Adorno, TW 1991, "The position of the narrator in the contemporary novel," in R Tiedemann (ed.), *Notes on literature*, Columbia University Press, New York.

Barthes, R 1977, *Image, music, text*, Fontana Press, London.

Baym, NK 2000, *Tune in, log on: soaps, fandom, and online community*, Sage, Thousand Oaks, CA.

Benjamin, W 1983, *Das Passagen-Werk*, R. Tiedemann (ed.), Suhrkamp, Frankfurt aM.

Bourdieu, P 1984, *Distinction: a social critique of the judgment of taste*, Harvard University Press, Cambridge, MA.

Brooker, W (ed.) 2005, *The Blade Runner experience: the legacy of a science fiction classic*, Wallflower, New York.

Cavicchi, D 1998, *Tramps like us: music and meaning among Springsteen fans*, Oxford University Press, New York.

Corner, J 1999, *Critical ideas in television studies*, Oxford University Press, Oxford.

Eagleton, T 1996, *Literary theory: an introduction*, 2nd ed., Basil Blackwell, Oxford.

Eco, U 1994, *The limits of interpretation*, Indiana University Press, Bloomington.

Fish, S 1981, "Why no ones afraid of Wolfgang Iser," *Diacritics* 11(1): 2–13.

Goldman, A 2001, *The lives of John Lennon*, reprint, Review Press, Chicago.

Gray, J 2006, *Watching with The Simpsons: television, parody, and intertextuality*, Routledge, New York.

Harrington, CL & Bielby, DD 1995, *Soap fans: pursuing pleasure and making meaning in everyday life*, Temple University Press, Philadelphia.

Hills, M 1999, *The dialectic of value: the sociology and psychoanalysis of cult media*, PhD dissertation, University of Sussex, UK.

Hills, M 2002, *Fan cultures*, Routledge, New York.

Holub, RC 1992, *Crossing borders: reception theory, poststructuralism, deconstruction*, University of Wisconsin Press, Madison.

Ingarden, R 1973, *The cognition of the literary work of art*, Northwestern University Press, Evanston, IL.

Iser, W 1971, "Indeterminacy and the reader's response in prose fiction," in JH Miller (ed.), *Aspects of narrative*, Columbia University Press, New York.

Iser, W 1978, *The act of reading: a theory of aesthetic response*, Johns Hopkins University Press, Baltimore.

Jancovich, M 2002, "Cult fictions: cult movies, subcultural capital, and the production of cultural distinction," *Cultural Studies* 16(2): 306–22.

Jauss, HR 1982, *Toward an aesthetic of reception*, University of Minnesota Press, Minneapolis.

Jenkins, H 1992, *Textual poachers: television fans and participatory culture*, Routledge, New York.

Lancaster, K 2001, *Interacting with Babylon 5*, University of Texas Press, Austin.

McKee, A 2001, "Which is the best *Doctor Who* story? A case study in value judgments outside the academy," *Intensities* 1, www.cult-media.com.

Morgan, G 2004, *The real David Beckham: an intimate biography*, Metro Books, London.

Ricœur, P 1996, "Die metaper und das hauptproblem der hermeneutik," in D Kimmich et al. (eds.), *Texte zur literaturtheorie der Gegenwart*, Philipp Reclam, Stuttgart.

Rodman, GB 1996, *Elvis after Elvis: the posthumous career of a living legend*, Routledge, New York.

Sandvoss, C 2003, *A game of two halves: football, television, and globalization*, Routledge, New York.

Sandvoss, C 2005a, *Fans: the mirror of consumption*, Polity, Malden, MA.

Sandvoss, C 2005b, "One-dimensional fan: toward an aesthetic of fan texts," *American Behavioral Scientist* 48(7): 822–39.

Stierle, K 1996, "Werk und intertextualität," in D Kimmich et al. (eds.), *Texte zur literaturtheorie der Gegenwart*, Philipp Reclam, Stuttgart.

Thomas, L 2002, *Fans, feminisms, and "quality" media*, Routledge, New York.

Thompson, JB 1995, *The media and modernity: a social theory of the media*, Polity, Cambridge.

Thornton, S 1995, *Club cultures*, Polity, Cambridge.

Tulloch, J 2000, *Watching television audiences: cultural theories and methods*, Hodder Arnold, London.

Tulloch, J & Jenkins, H 1995, *Science fiction audiences: watching* Dr. Who *and* Star Trek, Routledge, London.

Turner, BS 2005, "Public intellectuals and British sociology since 1945," *British Journal of Sociology* Lecture, London School of Economics, October 11.

Vodička, FV 1975, *Struktur der Entwicklung*, Vogelkopf, Munich.

Williams, R 1974, *Television: technology and cultural form*, Fontana, London.

2

Intimate Intertextuality and Performative Fragments in Media Fanfiction

KRISTINA BUSSE

In the late nineties I started reading *X-Files* fanfiction. It was only my second fandom, and the first where I came upon a wealth of archived fanfiction, alphabetized, tagged, and searchable in *The Gossamer Project* and, for my slash desires, in *Down in the Basement*. In the latter, I found a strange Mulder/Krycek story in which an eggbeater featured centrally. And then another one. And then several more. At that point, I realized that I might be missing something. Even knowing the canon fairly well, I could not recall the centrality of eggbeaters. Eventually, I learned that there had been a challenge on the MKRA (Mulder/Krycek Romantics Association) mailing list in 1996 for stories of exactly five hundred words and an eggbeater.

Since then, I've learned to assume that there may indeed be intense meta-conversations, quirky challenges, or intra- and inter-fannish tropes behind seemingly surprising literary choices. And sometimes I see these ideas developing in real time, such as the Tumblr post where a fan bemoaned the fact that *Person of Interest* (then in season 2) wasn't a proper fandom yet, because it did not have an mpreg (male pregnancy) story. In response, one fan writer scripted such a story, which, in turn, spawned several sequels by others, all of which then got recorded and turned into podfic by multiple readers. The podfic collection was titled "violent amoral unicorn of justice gets knocked up," using one of the tags that connected all the stories. It played on very specific stereotypes of the main character played out in a series of Tumblr drawings in which this hypermasculine, hyperphysical crusader for justice was lovingly drawn as a unicorn—now, of course, pregnant.

Whereas the *X-Files* story took me by surprise and I had to painstakingly retrace the contextual origins, more than a decade later I understood the fannish conventions and tropes and could appreciate many of the layers of inside jokes and intertextual references that made the *Person of Interest* story meaningful above and beyond its actual intertextuality with the show itself. More specifically, both examples exhibit the ludic interplay of viewers turned readers turned writers, all of which are fans connected through their love for the show and for fandom. Requests shape stories and create tropes, which in turn shape our perceptions and create more stories. Accordingly, in this essay I challenge the discourses that merge all forms of transformative works, without taking into account the creative relationships within and between fan communities and the often ephemeral contexts in which fanfic is written.[1]

Mainstream media and self-reflexive fan discourses often connect fan writing with professional transformative works, which range from mythological adaptations like the *Iliad* and *Aeneid* to postmodern rewrites like *Wide Sargasso Sea* or *Wicked*. Even as media convergence erodes the dichotomy between fan and professional, fanfiction's raison d'être should be understood on its own terms, as a series of personal—if not intimate—textual engagements. That centrality of affect, compounded by fanfiction's near ephemeral intertextuality (with source text, cultural and literary context, and, most importantly, other derivative interpretive texts), suggests that we lose an important layer of interpretation and meaning if we divorce fanfiction from its contexts and equate it with other forms of transformative creativity. There exist four interrelated aspects that are not restricted to fanfiction but that tend to be more pronounced in amateur transformative works written within a specific community: (1) fragmentation, the way fanfiction often tends to be part of an ongoing conversation; (2) intertextuality, a given story's dependence on community and fantext; (3) performativity, the conversational, community interaction component of many stories; and (4) intimacy, the emotional and often sexual openness and vulnerability readers and writers exhibit in the stories and surrounding interaction.

It is against these particular community aspects that the recent increase of professionally released fanfiction and its fannish and academic responses should be understood. While it is certainly worthwhile to study popular former fanfic franchises in terms of their aesthetic characteristics and narrative tropes, I want to focus on the aspects that get lost in translation, the parts of fanfiction that are specific to its dialogic amateur community status. Fanfiction in general relies more heavily on intertextuality and ephemerality. In fact, part of the goal of this essay is to show how fanfiction can throw into relief aspects of reading and writing often overlooked or minimized in literary texts: it foregrounds certain collective and intertextual aspects that traditional theories of reading and writing often like to ignore and brings them front and center. Nevertheless, when I suggest that fanfiction exemplifies certain characteristics that deeply embed it in a particular time and place and restrict its easy legibility, I describe dominant tendencies, not absolutes. All writing is intertextual, communal, and performative to a degree; fanfiction just tends to be more so, on individual and collective levels.

"Arcana" as Case Study

E. L. James's *Twilight* fanfiction "Masters of the Universe" turned *New York Times* number-one best-seller *Fifty Shades of Grey* clearly constitutes a watershed for fanfiction studies concerned with defining a particular fannish aesthetic. Perhaps the most astounding aspect of comparing the two versions is how little they differ. In her side-by-side comparisons, Jane Litte (2012) finds an 89 percent match, which is quite high when taking into account that all proper names were changed. Yet even though the two texts are virtually identical, Anne Jamison points to a fundamental difference that is contextual rather than text intrinsic: "I'm not arguing that Fifty Shades somehow *can't* stand on its own (more than twenty million readers say otherwise), but rather that the same work was more literary (read: more complex, discursive, critical, stylistically motivated) when it didn't" (2012: 316). Effectively, "Masters of the Universe" offers more interpretative possibilities when read in its fanfictional context. There are many reasons why *Fifty Shades* remained comprehensible and enjoyable even when stripped of all its initial contexts and intertexts: as an Alternate Universe, its direct relationship to the source text was already a step removed, using the archetypal ideas that Bella and Edward represent rather than the actual specific characters. And while Jamison describes a text that is clearly in dialogue with some of the fannish tropes in *Twilight* fandom, the fandom contains a large number of first-time fans, which made it somewhat insular, and the author has repeatedly stated her disinterest in the collective nature of fandom.[2]

Thus to show the complexity of fannish interrelations, I use a much lesser known text that moved into the non-fannish eye for a short while and whose negative reception exemplifies the complexities of comprehensively reading, analyzing, and evaluating fanfiction and the dangers when a fan text loses its specific context. In May 2005, Em Brunson's "Arcana," a work-in-progress (which has remained unfinished) *Harry Potter/CSI* mpreg crossover slash crack challenge response, was longlisted for the James Tiptree, Jr. Award, an "annual literary prize for science fiction or fantasy that expands or explores our understanding of gender" (tiptree.org). In the wake of the announcement, the feminist SF community surrounding WisCon (www.wiscon.info), a feminist science fiction convention at which the award is given, began questioning the story's appropriateness for the award and its literary merits. The debate soon moved into criticism of fanfiction in general, and issues of intended audiences, close(d) communities, interpretive contexts, and shame became central. I go back to this older story not only because it exemplifies all four aspects (i.e., fragmentation, intertextuality, performativity, and intimacy) of fanfiction, but also because it was rejected by mainstream readers because of it. And while the increased professional publication of fanfiction has evacuated some of the rebuttals fans immediately raised in response to "Arcana," I would suggest that many of the voiced concerns still apply.[3] Moreover, the discussions following the initial release and publicity illustrate how fans themselves are highly aware of what they do and how their writing may indeed foreground different concerns and goals.

Fanfiction as Fragment

All fiction has implicit and explicit restrictions, in terms of both accessibility (i.e., length, language, typeface, illustrations, etc.) and marketing (i.e., audience appeal, modes of distribution, etc.). Fanfiction has by necessity and choice often sidestepped commercial publishing: sometimes, this represents a purposeful anti-commercial stance; other times, it is the result of certain types of stories that do not appeal to a wider audience. Unlike professional fiction, which endeavors to make a profit and attempts to reach the widest reach of readers, fanfiction by its very nature has specific freedoms regarding content, form, and length. Ironically, as Louisa Stein and Kristina Busse have shown, fans often relish and creatively thrive from internal, external, and technological limits. As fans add creative constraints of their own, such "multiple restrictions of text, intertext, and interface help generate the immense spectrum of fan fiction, art, and analyses" (2009: 192).

Content may be the most obviously prescribed feature of commercial fiction, which requires genre categories and potentially assured readerships. One reason fanfiction is often known in popular media for pornographic content only is that writers are free to include explicit material in ways they cannot in professional publications. Moreover, writers can spend as much or as little time as they want on background, world building, characterization, or action: a writer may create an action scenario in one story and an emotional reflection in another. In fact, one huge difference between fanfiction and its close relative the tie-in novel is the fact that the latter cannot easily uproot the basic characters or worlds: mostly, writers are asked to leave the media property the way they found it (TWC Editor 2010). In contrast, fanfiction can freely kill off characters, make one evil and redeem another, or blow up the world entirely and imagine a postapocalyptic future. Finally, while writing only for art's sake might be the ideal, most professional authors need to appeal reliably to broad readerships in order to secure publishing opportunities. Fanfiction, on the other hand, may write stories for only a small handful of readers—who may be the only others interested in this particular plot and characterization but may also directly encourage and/or offer feedback to the writer.

While some fan writers play with form and create visual artifacts, multilayered story lines, text games, or hybrids thereof, fanfiction has remained surprisingly text based. Whether it is a nod to its print publication precedents or to its ASCII limited early Usenet days, fanfiction is on the whole more adventurous with content and length variations than it is with form. Notable exceptions exist that merge fan art, photo manips, vids, and entire web pages and social network accounts, but the predominance of central archives often invites a more traditional text-based narrative. Finally, length is entirely variable for fan writers, which means that a story gets to be exactly as long (or short) as the plot and characterizations require. Rather than modeling a story to fit a 60,000 to 80,000 word count, fic writers can end their narrative at 15,000 or expand to 130,000 without any concern for print cost and publication house requirements.

More specifically, the communicative nature of online fanfiction publishing, which offers immediate feedback to partial drafts, has created the work in progress (WIP). WIPs are exemplary fanfiction for a variety of reasons: they advertise their open status and writerly quality, to use Barthes's term (1990: 5–6). Rather than a closed text with fixed meaning, the very form of the WIP asks readers to collaborate in the meaning production, either imaginatively by envisioning various narrative threads as they wait for an update or literally by inviting feedback and discussions about the story line. Often, WIP fanfiction is episodic and thus, like televisual texts, easily enjoyed in parts. Nevertheless, the serial publication of many fan stories indicates one of the characteristics of what Cat Tosenberger (2014) has called fanfiction's "unpublishability." Unfinished stories are mostly unpublishable by definition, and WIPs often showcase all the virtues and vices of extemporaneous writing that is raw not only stylistically and grammatically but also in terms of plot and character development or even world building. The unfinished ending may exist in the mind of the fan writer and just hasn't (yet) been written down, but it may never be envisioned, which leaves the WIP as fragmentary ephemera at its best.

"Arcana" as a story was abandoned and has remained a WIP for over a decade now. It was nominated for the Tiptree as a WIP, and while its word count suggests a more conventional novel length, the story ends all but mid-scene, leaving the reader with a complex dilemma, unsolved relationship issues, and two worlds that have collided with no resolution in sight. As such, it is impossible to evaluate it as a complete and closed text even without the various other aspects (challenge response, crackfic, crossover) that make it such an apt example of fanfiction's unreadability. Moreover, its WIP status further foregrounds fan critics' need not just to analyze stories aesthetically but to understand them at the same time as deeply embedded cultural artifacts. Busse and Hellekson expand the meaning of WIP accordingly to include the entirety of fan productions. Calling "the entirety of stories and critical commentary written in a fandom" *fantext*, they describe it as an ever-expanding, ever-changing, self-contradictory collaboration (2006: 7). As such, every story, fragment or not, is always also an added part to the never-ending WIP that constitutes the fantext itself.

In fact, this fantext is not a purely text-based phenomenon: the online environment in which most fanfiction is shared relies heavily on multimedia and hypertextual interaction. Blogging tools such as Live-Journal (LJ), Twitter, or Tumblr not only offer easy sharing of image and video with text, but also invite interaction, response, and transformation (Stein & Busse 2009; Wood & Baughman 2012; Petersen 2014). So, even when individual stories do not feature multimedia, experimental, or hypertextual elements, the fantext, the entirety of fan responses can be understood as a highly experimental text whose interactive and transitory components span many sites, often interlinked with and more often creatively indebted to one another (Derecho 2006).

Fanfiction in Context

As a result, fanfiction is in conversation not only with the source text but usually also with other stories in the fandom and the discussions that permeate the community. Thus, it seems useful not to look at a story as if it were a distinct and isolated piece of art but instead to acknowledge its social and communicative aspects. Fan stories always are a response to the source text, often are produced in communication with several other fans, and likely are part of a conversation with other stories and discussions. In fact, while some stories are envisioned as autonomous artifacts and thus can be read by anyone unfamiliar with the source text, a large (if not larger) number of stories rely on an audience that is familiar with the source text and likely also the fantext, that is, the ever-growing collection of other fan stories.

In the case of "Arcana," there are multiple contexts necessary for understanding the story: (1) the two source texts of children's book *Harry Potter* and forensic procedural *CSI*; (2) the fan communities surrounding these shows; (3) general fannish tropes such as slash itself and mpreg and the rules of crossovers; and, more specifically, (4) the particular circumstances of the story, including the community in which it was posted and the challenge to which it responded. *Oh_No_Nicky* is an LJ community that was created in response to the season 5 finale of *CSI*, in which crime scene investigator Nick Stokes was abducted and buried alive. The community defined its central purpose as "organized flailing" in a "place where folks can come to be googly and crazy and cry and go wild about Nicky and all things CSI and no one will judge." Tone and diction indicate clearly a specific reading of the characters and the show as well as a focus on particular types of stories.

"Arcana" was one of several responses to a community mpreg challenge, that is, the story was expected to include male pregnancy and a particular fannish version of Nick as protagonist. Losing this particular intertextual context makes it difficult for readers to comprehend or enjoy the story—after all, they weren't its audience. In her involved post that spawned expansive discussion, Matociquala describes the specificity and often quite limited audience of fanfiction as follows:

> Fanfiction is written in the expectation of being enjoyed in an open membership but tight-knit community, and the writer has an expectation of being included in the enjoyment and discussion. It is the difference, in other words, between throwing a fair on the high road, and a party in a back yard. Sure, you might be able to see what's going on from the street, but you're expected not to stare. (LJ, May 18, 2006)[4]

There are several aspects that Matociquala points out here that are important. The author in fanfiction tends to be in a conversation with other fans just like her; that is, there is a conversation going on that often includes the writer, thus rejecting literary models that tend to privilege authors. Moreover, there tend to be specific and limited audiences for every story—sometimes the recipient in a gift exchange, other times all fans of a particular pairing—and these particular audiences often share a sizable number of assumptions with the writer that won't be spelled out and are thus often invisible to outsiders.[5]

Fanfiction as Ephemeral Traces

Most importantly, however, Matociquala's metaphor of the "party in the back yard" suggests a level of immediacy and performativity that we associate with theater, ballet, and opera rather than novels and short stories. Francesca Coppa points out this similarity when she argues that "fanfiction develops in response to dramatic rather than literary modes of storytelling and can therefore be seen to fulfill performative rather than literary criteria" (2006: 225). Moreover, the party metaphor showcases fanfiction's ephemerality: the process of its production is often as important as are the textual remnants. In fact, researchers should be careful not to take the resulting artifacts for the thing itself. Like any anthropological recovery, artistic products may need to be studied as artistic artifact *and* as ephemeral trace.

José Esteban Muñoz defines "ephemeral traces" as that which is left behind a performative event, both hinting at and hiding the originating social engagements. Ephemera thus is "a kind of evidence of what has transpired but certainly not the thing itself. It [. . .] includes traces of lived experience and performances of lived experience, maintaining experiential politics and urgencies long after those experiences have been lived" (1996: 10). Applying this notion to fannish artifacts helps us remain aware that much of the text's meaning can be tied in with a specific place, time, and community in ways that make it difficult to read (let alone judge) these artifacts. In fact, most of the social media platforms that fandom uses provide varying degrees of structural built-in ephemerality: older posts and comments disappear off the clearly visible top page and can be recovered only with some difficulty, and the rhizomatic structure of the Internet supports the concurrence of multiple conversations in separate spaces. As such, going back to a given post later on can make it difficult to understand all contributing aspects, since only parts are available.

But it is this layering of conversations, analyses, and fiction that not only constitutes the necessary context to explain and understand a given narrative but also offers a paratextual frame complementing fanfiction. And it is often in such frame debates that competing understandings of literary and cultural definitions and values become visible. Fanfiction challenges many attempts at traditional aesthetic valuation, because critics who ignore the guiding frameworks of how, when, and where a fan text was created can easily misread and misjudge. This is exacerbated because while much of the ephemeral performative aspects of fan writings occur on social networks, the stories are often archived on personal web pages, fandom-specific archives, or general fan archives. And whether by design or necessity, archives tend to "valu[e] the document over event" (Schneider 2012: 140) or, in our case, the story over the creative process, communal betaing, critical responses, and all other paratextual detritus.[6]

In the case of "Arcana," the contextual ephemerality is the particular community and challenge response as well as the partaking in a communal activity, the posting of parts that people responded to, the shared enjoyment over a particular version of Nick Stokes, and the back-and-forth within the feedback comments. It thus showcases how much of fannish writing is part of a dialog. Indeed, fanfiction can easily serve other purposes, ranging from personal interaction like a gift to intervening in fannish debates. And while the results may indeed be excellent, the event itself, the fan engagement is often more important than the actual product, that is, the few sentences of fictional prose. Likewise, role-playing games follow a similar logic where the actual play is the event itself with the textual traces leaving a remnant, a hint toward the event but not encompassing the event in its entirety (Stein 2006; McClellan 2013).

Fanfiction and the Id

The network of interconnected conversations, not only about the shows and fanfiction but also about personal and public events, remains the current model of fan interaction. The medium not only clearly exhibits the layers of multiple intersecting contexts, but also illustrates how the personal and the fictional sit side by side: a personal triumph or defeat, commentary on national and international politics, TV reviews, and fanfic snippet—shared in a single post or aggregated and displayed together on one's feed. The intimate details of one's life and fannish fantasies comment on one another in many ways, whether as escape, working through, or acting out. And while these are features common to much fiction, fanfiction's rawness and immediacy often make these aspects more visible. Moreover, fanfiction often tailors to our very desires, our innermost fantasies, sexual or not.

Ellen Fremedon introduces the term "Id Vortex" into fannish discourse to describe the tailored and customized writing that caters to the writers' and/or readers' kinks, that creates stories that move us emotionally not only because we already care about the characters but also because they use tropes, characterizations, scenes that appeal viscerally:

[I]n fandom, we've all got this agreement to just suspend shame. I mean, a lot of what we write is masturbation material, and we all know it, and so we can't really pretend that we're only trying to write for our readers' most rarefied sensibilities, you know? We all know right where the Id Vortex is, and we have this agreement to approach it with caution, but without any shame at all. (LJ, December 2, 2004)

It is this celebration of the id that seemed to spawn the criticism driving much of the discussions around "Arcana" *within* fandom. Even though many critics foreground their concern about quality issues, the story's crackfic premise is mentioned often enough in the debates to suggest that its id aspects are at least partly to blame for large parts of the criticism. In general, a lot of the responses seem to be exemplified by this comment: "If fanfic is going to get press/award nominations, why can't it please be fanfic that makes the genre look *good*?" (comment in Matociquala, LJ, May 15, 2006). So while Ellen Fremedon describes fandom as collectively embracing the Id Vortex without shame, clearly some hesitation to share these feelings with the world at large remains. In fact, in their book-length study on celebration and shame in fandom, Lynn Zubernis and Katherine Larsen describe how "a pervasive sense of shame permeates both fan spaces and academic approaches to the subject" (2012: 1).

So whether fans fault the story for not following traditional literary aesthetics or for not fulfilling their own specific desires, at issue is the choice of a story whose appeal is narrow and predicated on specific established genre expectations. This is not to suggest that this intense emotional writerly investment is either necessary for fanfiction or absent from pro writing. Nevertheless, the context of production, dissemination, and reception differs substantially: whereas much of the editorial process in pro writing distances the writer from her story, fanfiction purposefully encourages and thrives on intimacy and pleasing the Id Vortex. In fact, fan writing often is purposefully tailored toward narrow audiences, and fanfiction headers and tags tend to signal these specific genre elements, characterizations, and tropes.

Where fandom, pairings, and warnings provide the broadest selection, fans fine-tune their searches much further (Johnson 2014). Certain terms may signal specific characterizations shared by a small subset of fans and carrying with it a whole host of associated assumptions: in "Arcana," the mpreg tag invokes not just the fact of male pregnancy but a host of specific genre implications, while the reference to Nicky suggests a very specific interpretation of character Nick Stokes that feminizes if not infantilizes him. At its most extreme, a story may try to perfectly please one person rather than offering a mere moderate appeal to many. It is ultimately irrelevant whether fans like a given story and its tropes for sexual or other affective reasons. The fact that fans share these kinks and that fanfiction is an easy way to write and read specific desired story lines, characterizations, and tropes is a feature rather than a bug. Fandom should celebrate its ability to appeal to narrow audiences, and yet the events surrounding "Arcana" clearly suggest that wide appeal remains a quality for many even within fandom.

Conclusion

Many fan reactions to "Arcana" (just like those to *Fifty Shades of Grey* several years later) were predicated on the question as to how well it represented fanfiction as a whole. One fan writer analyzes her ambivalent reaction to the nomination of "Arcana": "So, you know, a crackfic CSI/HP mpreg angst-heavy h/c [hurt-comfort] crossover is not the poster child I would have picked, but as a representative of the way we are getting down in the muck of the id with dirt under our fingernails over here, I'm not sure that it's *wrong*" (Shalott, LJ, May 18, 2006). Looking at the discussions surrounding the story's nomination both within and without fandom suggests that far from being a bad representative for fandom, "Arcana" is actually exemplary in that it testifies to the focused narrowness of much of fan writing. It may not be a story that easily translates or that can be effortlessly or even enjoyably read by people outside of the community for which it was written, but then they aren't its audience. So, while fandom does produce artistic artifacts that can easily be judged valuable by traditional literary aesthetic values (often modernist and emphasizing complexity), we would miss large sections of fannish creation and its effects if those were the only criteria we employed. By understanding fanfiction in its fannish context and as a performative act that may have been written for a specific purpose or person, we can value fanfiction as both text and artifact, as a literary work and a cultural engagement.

We thus cannot simply divorce fanfiction from its context and equate it with other forms of derivative creativity. Fannish artifacts that are removed from their initial setting require us to be aware of the fact that we may see only traces rather than the entire textual and community engagement. And yet, even with fanfiction's peculiar status as always already social and intertextual, it still begs the question as to why it may require a distinct discussion. Or, said differently, my entire line of reasoning doesn't address whether fanfiction is indeed so fundamentally different that traditional models of literary theory cannot contain it. Rather than attempting to find a clear boundary that might distinguish fanfiction, however, I'd like to suggest a differentiated focus based less on absolute difference and more on degree. In other words, fanfiction is not necessarily wholly unlike other fiction in its creation, dissemination, and reception, but it markedly foregrounds communal and intertextual performativity that often caters to highly individualized reading desires. As a result, studying fanfiction may allow us to observe all of writing's social and contextual aspects in an exemplary environment, where intimate community engagement and contextual performative encounters accompany, affect, and shape all textual artifacts.

NOTES

1 The main argument I am juxtaposing here is one that looks at fanfiction as literature and thus focuses in particular on the way fan texts engage with an earlier source text. As a result, most highly intertextual and citational literature can be seen as fanfiction. See Pugh (2005), Derecho (2006), Jamison (2013), and Romano (2010).

2 For a comparison of published novels with the fanfiction they are based on, see Woledge (2005). For a close analysis of the relation between slash and romance fiction, see Kaplan (2012).

3 Often when fanfiction is removed from its environment and placed in different contexts, fans collectively react quite negatively. Recent events include the public reading of fanfiction at the *Sherlock* season 3 premiere event (Romano 2013), the inclusion of fanfiction on the book review site Goodreads (fanlore.org), and a fanfiction class that assigned reading and commenting on various stories (fanlore. org).

4 I do not link fan commentary on social networking sites such as LiveJournal (LJ) directly, but instead reference parenthetically with name, site, and date.

5 Over the past two decades, online fandom has moved from protected spaces into public view, which has increased debates over what constitutes private and public spaces. Fans often assume a form of "layered public," where interactions occur in public places, yet outsiders are expected "not to stare." See Busse and Hellekson (2012) and note 3.

6 For the relationship between fan archives, memory, and ephemera, also see Lothian (2013). For a discussion of *Fifty Shades* and fan archives, see De Kosnik (2015).

WORKS CITED

Barthes, R 1990, *S/Z*, Blackwell, London.

Busse, K & Hellekson, K 2006, "Works-in-progress," in K Hellekson & K Busse (eds.), *Fan fiction and fan communities in the age of the Internet: new essays*, McFarland, Jefferson, NC.

Busse, K & Hellekson, K 2012, "Identity, ethics, and fan privacy," in K Larsen & L Zubernis (eds.), *Fan culture: theory/practice*, Cambridge Scholars, Newcastle.

Coppa, F 2006, "Writing bodies in space: media fan fiction as theatrical performance," in K Hellekson & K Busse (eds.), *Fan fiction and fan communities in the age of the Internet: new essays*, McFarland, Jefferson, NC.

De Kosnik, A 2015, "*Fifty Shades* and the archive of women's culture," *Cinema Journal* 54(3): 116–25.

Derecho, A 2006, "Archontic literature: a definition, a history, and several theories of fan fiction," in K Hellekson & K Busse (eds.), *Fan fiction and fan communities in the age of the Internet: new essays*, McFarland, Jefferson, NC.

Jamison, A 2012, "When *Fifty* was fic," in L Perkins (ed.), *Fifty writers on* Fifty Shades, BenBella, Dallas.

Jamison, A 2013, *Fic: how fanfiction changed the world*, BenBella, Dallas.

Johnson, SF 2014, "Fan fiction metadata creation and utilization within fan fiction archives: three primary models," *Transformative Works and Cultures* 17, dx.doi.org/10.3983/twc.2014.0578.

Kaplan, D 2012, "'Why would any woman want to read such stories?' The distinction between genre romances and slash fiction," in SSG Frantz & EM Selinger (eds.), *New approaches to popular romance fiction: critical essays*, McFarland, Jefferson, NC.

Litte, J 2012, "*Master of the Universe* versus *Fifty Shades* by E.L. James comparison," *Dear Author*, March 13, dearauthor.com.

Lothian, A 2013, "Archival anarchies: online fandom, subcultural conservation, and the transformative work of digital ephemera," *International Journal of Cultural Studies* 16(6): 541–56.

McClellan, A 2013, "A case of identity: role playing, social media and BBC *Sherlock*," *Journal of Fandom Studies* 1(2): 139–57.

Muñoz, JE 1996, "Ephemera as evidence: introductory notes to queer acts," *Women & Performance* 8(2): 5–16.

Petersen, LN 2014, "*Sherlock* fans talk: mediatized talk on Tumblr," *Northern Lights: Film & Media Studies Yearbook* 12(1): 87–104.

Pugh, S 2005, *The democratic genre: fan fiction in a literary context*, Seren, Brigend, Wales.

Romano, A 2010, "I'm done explaining why fanfic is okay," *LiveJournal*, May 3, 2010, bookshop.livejournal.com.

Romano, A 2013, "Why fans are outraged at Sherlock and Watson reading sexy fanfic," *Daily Dot*, December 16, 2013, www.dailydot.com.

Schneider, R 2012, "Performance remains," in A Jones & A Heathfield (eds.), *Perform, repeat, record: live art in history*, Intellect, Bristol, UK.

Stein, L 2006, "'This dratted thing': fannish storytelling through new media," in K Hellekson & K Busse (eds.), *Fan fiction and fan communities in the age of the Internet: new essays*, McFarland, Jefferson, NC.

Stein, LE & Busse, K 2009, "Limit play: fan authorship between source text, intertext, and context," *Popular Communication* 7(4): 192–207.

Tosenberger, C 2014, "Mature poets steal: children's literature and the unpublishability of fanfiction," *Children's Literature Association* 39(1): 4–27.

TWC Editor 2010, "Interview with Jo Graham, Melissa Scott, and Martha Wells," *Transformative Works and Cultures* 5, doi:10.3983.

Woledge, E 2005, "From slash to the mainstream: female writers and gender blending men," *Extrapolation* 46(1): 40–65.

Wood, M & Baughman, L 2012, "*Glee* fandom and Twitter: something new, or more of the same old thing?" *Communication Studies* 63(3): 328–44.

Zubernis L & Larsen, K 2012, *Fandom at the crossroads: celebration, shame and fan/producer relationships*, Cambridge Scholars, Newcastle.

3

Media Academics *as* Media Audiences

Aesthetic Judgments in Media and Cultural Studies

MATT HILLS

In this chapter I want to argue that the dismissal of aesthetic considerations from much work in media/cultural studies—a foundational gesture aimed at distinguishing academics from both "naïve" consumers and "imposed" ideologies—does not, in fact, work to install critical rationality or desired neutrality (Barthes 2005). I will suggest that via its anti-aesthetics (see also Sandvoss, this volume) much cultural studies work has constructed cultural distinction for itself by implying that its scholars are exempt from the domains of fan culture and/or popular culture (Hills 2002, 2005a). However, such a fantasized exemption has not at all produced an escape from "popular aesthetics" (Bird 2003) but has instead recoded aesthetic judgments within the supposedly pristine spaces of academia.

If attempts to displace aesthetics produce only distorted shadows of the very problematic they seek to short-circuit, then might aesthetics not be returned more positively to circulation in cultural studies? As Hunter and Kaye have pointed out, scholars are usually "urged [. . .] not to take aesthetic judgements for granted. We should understand them instead as [. . .] exertions of social power" (1997: 3). But what would aesthetics look like if it were not treated merely as an ideological imposition?

By way of exploring this possibility, I will suggest that a rehabilitated aesthetics might emerge from the fact that media academics are themselves members of media audiences (Osborne 2000; Wright Wexman 1999), quite apart from the issue of whether or not they are also media fans. Curiously, debates in media/cultural studies have frequently returned to the question of whether the media academic who is also a media fan represents some kind of problematic or scandalous figure

(Hills 2002; Michael 2000; White 2005). My concern is that this apparent destabilizing of scholar versus fan identity may have worked as a kind of academic-ideological feint. That is, for some it may operate to restore the illusion that academics who can announce their non-fandom are in the clear, as it were, their modernist, rational, scholarly selves safely set apart from their simultaneous identities as "ordinary" media consumers. However, going beyond fan audiences—but still learning from work in fan studies—we should perhaps really be asking not "what it means if an academic studying fans is also a fan" but rather "what it means when an academic studying the media audience is also part of a media audience." This latter question also includes those who may not directly or obviously be part of a media audience, since contemporary media are dispersed into everyday life and culture rather than being isolated to specific screens at specific times (Abercrombie & Longhurst 1998; Bird 2003).

Oddly, only scholar-fans have been interpreted as carrying some hybridized or logically regressive identity in relation to their academic status—that is, they have been viewed in some quarters as "not proper academics"—whereas I want to argue here that this is in fact a special case of a more general problem. Academics, far more generally, are "not proper academics" either, if by this we mean that their scholarly selves cannot be cleanly separated out from their media-audience-based identities. Criticisms of specific scholar-fans, or even specific scholar-fan conferences, may arguably carry more weight (see Burr 2005), but all too often attacks on scholar-fandom have sought to attack this hybrid category per se for its supposed transgression of scholarly detachment, while exempting academia in general from any related critique or censure.

I will set out my argument here in three sections: (1) how the exclusion of aesthetics produces academic distinction; (2) how academic distinction recodes aesthetic judgment; and finally (3) how a general theory of hybridized academia—going beyond fandom—can restore the aesthetic.

How the Exclusion of Aesthetics Produces Academic Distinction

There can be little doubt that aesthetics has been powerfully detached from the academic study of popular culture. Analyzing this, Geraghty suggests "a number of reasons why making judgments about aesthetics has proved to be a difficult task in [...] the broader areas of media and cultural studies" (2003: 27). These include

> the impact of semiotics [...] with its pseudo-scientific claims about objectivity; the impact of postmodernism with its emphasis on diversity, decentring and play; the need to establish popular culture [...] as worthy of study that involved refusing the traditional modes of judgement; the impact of feminist work, with its demand that certain kinds of denigrated fictions should be taken seriously; the notion, coming rather differently from Foucault and Bourdieu, that to make aesthetic judgements was to impose the cultural norms of the powerful. (2003: 27–28)

Geraghty's list takes in the role of different academic schools of thought such as feminism, structuralism (figured as "semiotics"), and post-structuralism (represented as postmodern "play"). And yet, some of Geraghty's stated reasons have not been restricted to the operation of specific intellectual movements, or wider philosophies, and have instead formed parts of the general legitimation of academic study of the popular. Among these accounts of why aesthetics has found no place in media/cultural studies we might number "claims to objectivity," the refusal of "traditional modes of judgment," and the argument that making aesthetic judgments means imposing "cultural norms of the powerful." These rationales for abandoning aesthetics can all be said to work in one way. They each discursively construct media/cultural studies academics as "set apart" from popular culture, and as "set above" its consumers and fans (Hills 2005a, chaps. 6–7).

By laying claim to the nonaestheticized study of popular culture, scholars have sought to discursively distance themselves from what are viewed as normative practices of media consumerism. Consumers routinely assess what they like and dislike, fans passionately favor certain texts (Sandvoss 2005), and anti-fans equally passionately detest others (Gray 2003), but almost magically set outside these domains of taste, academia is positioned as carrying its own distinctive "imagined subjectivity" (Hills 2002: 3). That is, the academic's self-legitimating and claimed identity—split off from his or her identity as a media consumer—has typically been imaged and imagined as one of critical rationality, objectivity, and neutrality. As Barthes has written,

> I define the Neutral as that which outplays [. . .] the paradigm, or rather . . . everything that baffles the paradigm. [. . .] The paradigm, what is that? It's the opposition of two virtual terms from which [. . .] I actualize one to produce meaning. [. . .] Whence the idea of a structural creation that would defeat, annul, or contradict the implacable binarism of the paradigm by means of a third term. (2005: 6–7)

And media/cultural studies scholarship has, I am suggesting, adopted this kind of desired and desiring role as "tertium" (Barthes 2005: 7). Here, scholarly identity has formed a kind of third term that assumes an ability to "outplay the paradigm" of media consumer/producer, with the theorist adopting a performed role supposedly outside the identity of the "naïve" media consumer who proclaims his or her pop-cultural tastes, while also going beyond the identity of the ideology-imposing or ideology-circulating media producer. Neither imposing ideological strictures nor being subjected to them, there stands the properly disciplined media/cultural studies exegete.

Aesthetic judgments are treated as something belonging outside media/cultural studies. They are enacted and carried out by others, often fans of pop-cultural texts. Though writers such as Bird (2003) and Miller (2003) have reached very different conclusions over the value and elitism, or lack thereof, of fans' aesthetic judgments, they have nevertheless both advanced the notion that aesthetic criteria exist properly and firmly only outside media scholarship (Hills 2005b). Miller is especially scathing about fan practices of aesthetic judgment, which he depicts as an anathema to the anticanonical and anti-elitist ethics of cultural studies:

> These forms of fandom are straight-forwardly dedicated to replicating a college of aficionadi, who by their knowledge of elevating texts are somehow superior to the rest of us. This [. . .] replicates the very forms of quality discourse that were supposedly toppled by anti-canonical cultural studies. Instead, the best readers of the best texts are back, armed with

their best interpretations. No thank you. [. . .] Leave spotting trainspotters to trainspotters. (Miller 2003: 22)

However, such a rejection of aesthetics does not constitute the only possible academic strategy of distinction. For example, in "film studies,
the decisions about which texts deserve a place in the canon have often
been achieved through aesthetic judgements" (McKee 2001: 4). In this
context, the legitimation of academic study proceeds by appropriating
rather than opposing aesthetic discourses, with film being positioned as
worthy of study precisely because it can be viewed as "a particular sort
of aesthetic experience" (Kuhn 2005: 401).

Outside of film studies, however, aesthetics has remained something
of a dark art in media/cultural studies. Aesthetics can be studied, but
aesthetic judgments must not corrupt the media/cultural scholar's disciplinary reason and situated neutrality. Thomas J. Roberts carefully ne-
gotiates this terrain in *An Aesthetics of Junk Fiction*:

What shall we say is the difference [. . .] between a discipline and a
fan club, however learned? This difference, at least, is worth noticing: a
fan club says, "What we love, you should love too," but a discipline says,
"What we are discovering about what we love will be useful to you in your
investigations of what you love." (1990: 5–6)

At the very moment when Roberts entertains the possibility that studying culture may involve "loving" some cultural texts, he nevertheless
converts this into a curious kind of impassioned neutrality. For Roberts,
work in an academic discipline should never seek to convert or critique
the tastes of others but should seek only to generalize from its understanding of how (beloved) cultural texts operate on their readers. Again,
the "imagined subjectivity" of the scholar is rendered distinct from that
of the fan club member, who supposedly believes his or her aesthetic
judgments are the only right ones. By marked contrast, even where aesthetic judgments seem to move dangerously close to academic work,
Roberts suggests that they can be sublimated and transformed into a
more generalizable or objectively useful knowledge.

Although it is fandom that has repeatedly borne the brunt of cultural
studies scholars' need to bracket themselves off from the aesthetic judg-

ments of media audiences, I want to go beyond the issue of fandom here, arguing that the anti-aesthetics of media/cultural studies simply cannot achieve its aim of securing academic distinction from media consumers and industries. This is so, because regardless of whether or not any given academic is a "fan" of what he or she is studying, the "cultural analyst is at once 1) a reader/interpreter and member of a community of recipients [of media messages . . .]; and 2) an analyst of the messages at another level, via a different theoretical problematic" (Osborne 2000: 116).

Purging aesthetics as a marker of what Osborne terms this "level 2" difference does not, unfortunately, do away with the fact that media/cultural studies academics remain "level 1" media and cultural consumers, with all that this might imply about their tastes, distastes, identities, and affective engagements with media culture. "Making a reading" at level 2—for example, a disciplined structuralist/poststructuralist reading—is not ever fully coterminous with the analyst's embodied "reading experience" of that same text (Pearce 1997: 215 & 220).

However, a focus on the intersections of fandom and academia in the wake of Jenkins's (1992) seminal work has, I would say, succeeded in rendering relatively invisible the issue of academia's far more wide-reaching complicities with popular and media culture. The general question of whether or not academic identities can be distanced from consumer identities has not been convincingly tackled, since this logical regression—the academic studying media consumers and industries who is placed within the object of study as a media consumer of such industries—has been neglected in favor of picking over the special rather than the general case, that of the scholar who is also a fan of the type she or he is analyzing. If this special case is marked as a category violation demanding attention, the general case whereby "scholars, like others, have [. . .] interests at stake: we are not only critics but also consumers" (Wright Wexman 1999: 89) is left unmarked. As Wright Wexman has argued, "Critics customarily consider themselves disinterested observers [. . . although their activities lead . . .] to practical valuations of [. . .] texts, [and] one can view current scholarly practices in the light of these valuations. Why are certain [. . .] texts chosen for special attention?" (Wright Wexman 1999: 77).

This is the question I will now consider, arguing that the supposed removal of aesthetics from media/cultural studies has not, in fact, fully secured academics' cultural distinctions from "ordinary" media consumers, but has instead worked to recode aesthetic judgments in a variety of ways. Focusing only on the situation of academics who are also fans has been a highly effective way of sustaining the academic-ideological illusion that, for everybody else studying media culture, it's just "disinterested" and symbolically "set apart" business as usual.

How Academic Distinction Recodes Aesthetic Judgment

S. Elizabeth Bird has pointed out that the suspension of explicitly aesthetic judgments in media/cultural studies has been strongly linked to "the replacement of aesthetic standards by political and social ones" (2003: 118). The evaluation of texts has not, by any means, been taken off the scholarly agenda: far from it. Instead, alternative evaluative criteria have been set out, operating largely within what I've termed a "decisionist" approach to the cultural politics of media texts (Hills 2002: 182). Here, texts are routinely judged for their reactionary/progressive representations and meanings.

As if Derridean thought had never existed, this exercising of scholarly judgment assumes that clear lines can be drawn between the politically good and the politically bad text. Such an approach also assumes, of course, that Osborne's "level 1" aesthetic responses to media texts can be wholly divorced from distinctively "level 2" theoretical problematics— that is, that the political evaluation of texts can proceed without any reference to academics' "ordinary" consumer tastes or distastes for certain media texts. "Decisionist" analyses of popular media may also attempt to invert Osborne's "level 1" and "level 2" responses to texts, implying that a rigorous and rational political evaluation can actually underlie, at all times, scholars' more personal "level 1" tastes and distastes.

In film studies, which I've already noted has been historically less fearful of aesthetic judgment, some screen theory scholars went as far as explicitly collapsing together aesthetic and political evaluations. However, this generalizing compression of politics and aesthetics was soon subjected to critique for its reductiveness (see MacCabe 1981a, 1981b; McArthur 1981). Adornian and Frankfurt School approaches to aesthetics, which again construe the aesthetic primarily as a category of the political, would appear to be similarly problematic, since they too assume that aesthetics can be reduced to stable, fixed, and functional political codifications or judgments.

Seeking either to ground the aesthetic in the political or wholly to divorce the two modes of evaluation, "decisionist" approaches have hence sought to identify texts, and audiences, that "resist" dominant ideologies. Despite the fact that many media/cultural studies writers have long recognized the problems inherent in isolating out resistance (Abercrombie & Longhurst 1998; Jenkins 1992), the lure of being able to decisively sift out resistant or politically good texts has not passed away. In a review of my book *Fan Cultures* (2002) that claims that my own attack on decisionist narratives is decisionist itself, Christine Scodari argues that "resistance (or not) with respect to particular operations of power (including commodification) . . . might well [still] be determinable" (2003b: 182). In other words, scholarly machineries of political evaluation can continue onward, even if specific assumptions of active resistance and passive incorporation are inverted (Scodari 2003a: 125).

What I want to suggest here is that the foundational gesture of decisionist media/cultural studies—that aesthetic judgments can supposedly be grounded in, or displaced by, political evaluation—does not, in fact, evade the properly aesthetic: that which intersubjectively exceeds a priori pure reduction to, or pure separation from, the plane of political effectivity. Rather, aesthetic judgments are frequently recoded by media/cultural studies as strictly political ones. The aesthetic and the political are never as cleanly separable, nor as clearly interrelated, as decisionist strategies prefer to assert. Aesthetic judgments therefore remain surreptitiously and excessively in place, being masked behind or carried within supposedly purely political evaluations.

The recoding of aesthetic judgments results in a number of problems for media/cultural studies. The primary one can be described succinctly as the canon problem. By this, I mean that a severely limited range of media texts (and audiences) has been subjected to detailed academic study. Both scholar-fans and scholar-anti-fans or scholar-non-fans have contributed to this state of affairs.

Scholar-fans are those scholars who are also self-identified fans of what they study (Hills 2002: 11–15). By contrast, what we could call scholar-non-fans or scholar-anti-fans (following Gray 2003) are those who parade their disinterest in, or distaste for, specific media texts.

Each faction of media/cultural studies academics has played a part in the "canon problem." Scholar-fans have tended to study texts that they profess to love, and this has resulted in specific taste cultures being over-represented academically, with certain texts being far more likely to be canonized in academic study: "there is a tendency to favour programs and genres that may be considered edgy, avant-garde, or attracting a 'cult' audience. [. . .] I have rarely heard a [conference] presentation about successful 'middle-of-the-road' offerings—and never from scholars who identified as fans" (Bird 2003: 121).

Texts aimed at upscale audiences, favoring reflexive sophistication or postmodern playfulness with genre, or enacting a "cult" anticommercial and antimainstream ideology, are all thus more likely to meet with academic fervor and canonization. However, this limiting of academic attention is far from being only a result of celebratory scholar-fandom. It is also attributable to the critical work of scholar-anti-fans, who enact their distaste for certain forms of popular culture by dismissing, ignoring, or stereotyping them. As Jonathan Gray has said of anti-fans: "[they] construct an image of the text [. . .] sufficiently enough that they can react [. . .] against it. [. . . They routinely] engage in distant reading, responding to texts that have not been viewed" (2003: 71).

This would appear to be an accurate description of a range of critical theorists in media studies, who don't actually seem to closely read the texts they are so quick to condemn. Alan McKee has written of this type of scholar,

> I have noticed that many [. . .] teaching Media Studies, strongly organize their viewing schedules around public service broadcasting at the expense of commercial programming. Of course, this is not in itself problematic—unless the academics in question then begin to speak as experts about all television. At this point, a refusal to actually watch the medium being discussed seems [. . .] to be a little odd. (2003: 181)

There is indeed a kind of scholarly "distant reading" going on here, as academics write in a cursory, nondetailed, and dismissive manner about highly commercial or middle-brow TV shows (and other media) they feel an aesthetic distaste for. Bird argues that, as a result, academics' aesthetic judgments are replayed not only through scholar-fan celebrations of favored texts but also through neo-Marxist, anti-fan, or non-fan critiques of disfavored texts:

> [Critical] scholars do not care to define what is "wrong" with the middle-brow [and the commercial] in terms of taste or aesthetic judgement; they just ignore it. Yet inherent in that ignoring is a clear aesthetic judgement; these cultural forms indeed [are assumed to] constitute a vast wasteland, and people who consume them are probably not that capable of refined aesthetic judgement. (2003: 121–22)

The "canon problem" thus emerges out of two seemingly opposed currents of thought that, in actuality, work in concert to restrict which texts are studied in detail and canonized. Celebratory scholar-fans and critical scholar-anti-fans both demonstrate tendencies to marginalize the middle-brow and the commercial, favoring "cult" forms that symbolically enact a certain distance from "the mainstream," as well as favoring public service TV, which enacts a not-unrelated anticommercial ideology. Though the binary of "cult" versus "mainstream" can clearly be deconstructed—and an increasing number of texts are both cultish and very much mainstreamed (Brooker 2002; Gray 2006; Hills 2003, 2004)—I would argue that these cultural categories continue to be used within the sense-making practices of scholar-fans and scholar-anti-fans. In each case, "level 1" aesthetic judgments are recoded as "level 2" theoretical problematics, in a way that thus goes firmly beyond the issue of whether academics are also fans, to encompass the more general issue of how media academics are always-already media audiences. Moreover, they are audiences with specifiable aesthetic tastes that cannot simply be read off from their scholarly cultural politics.

The problem of restricted canonization (Hills 2004, 2005c) therefore devolves into two related forms of aesthetic judgment underpinning academic work: celebratory scholar-fandom and critical scholar-anti-fandom. In extreme instances of the latter, any attention to media fictions is wholly devalued in favor of "real" engagements with political issues (Philo and Miller 2001). Replaying a powerful cultural system of value that favors the factual over the fictional, and the supposedly real object over the aesthetic creation (Harrington & Bielby 1995: 135–36), such approaches install fatal blind spots within their analyses by neglecting to address how media fictions, as well as media reportage, can work to construct and circulate a variety of (de)politicized meanings about the world. Again, a type of aesthetic judgment is recoded in the somewhat infantilized and autoheroic writing of Philo and Miller (2001), albeit a judgment that refutes the aesthetic as being worthy of study tout court.

Meanwhile, the celebratory tones of certain scholar-fans have been picked apart in relation to a very much canonical object of study, the TV series *Buffy the Vampire Slayer*. Levine and Schneider have argued that many *Buffy* "scholars are [. . .] projecting, and 'acting out' their fantasies in relation to the program. They love BtVS" (2003: 299). These writers go on to imply that scholar-fans have prioritized their fandom—their "level 1" aesthetic responses—over their scholarly identities:

> BtVS is often entertaining, amusing, gripping—even exciting and titil-
> lating. But it is little more. Primarily, BtVS scholars are the ones who
> attempt to make the show out to be [. . .] something more than this.
> [. . .] If Joss Whedon is in fact a "genius," this is not because he manages
> to do any of those things that BtVS scholars bizarrely claim he does by
> erecting their own fictions and fantasies about what is going on in various
> episodes. (2003: 297–98, 299)

Scholar-fans such as David Lavery and Rhonda Wilcox stand accused of "emotivism" (Friedman & Squire 1998: 14), where moral judgments over the goodness or not of an object proceed on the basis of one's feelings in relation to that thing. In other words, these scholars allegedly let their enthusiasm for *Buffy* run away with them.

Buffy scholarship has provided rich pickings for those wanting to assess the impact of taste cultures on academia. In a study of the Slayage academic conference on *Buffy the Vampire the Slayer*—held in Nashville, May 2004, and affiliated with the online journal *Slayage* (McKee 2002: 69)—Vivien Burr gathered written responses from thirteen attendees, and supplemented these with her own participant observations. Burr's findings resonate with the concerns of Levine and Schneider, suggesting that "level 1" fannish aesthetics may have potentially usurped academic "level 2" theoretical problematics:

> Many delegates felt that fandom interfered with academic rigour on oc-
> casion. For example, Holly said, "I believe there was significant resistance

in the audience to a reading of Buffy that was not laudatory." [. . .] Alan remarked that [. . .] "the tone of [some questions . . .] and the ensuing discussion was more on a level of people's personal opinions and tastes about this character or another." (Burr 2005: 377–78)

To reiterate, these are not problems restricted to the intrusion of fannish aesthetics into academic work. They are more wide-ranging than this, moving far outside the matter of scholar-fan hybridity to take in the "anti-fandom" (Gray 2003) of critical media theorists who prefer to attack or ignore "commercial" forms of television/film, or even ignore media fictions altogether. Neither impassioned scholar-fans nor "disinterested" political-economy critics disclaiming their objectivity automatically have any monopoly on virtue. Aligning the academic self with one side of the reason/passion binary (Burr 2005: 380–81) does not ward off the problem of aesthetics in media/cultural studies. Instead, some (not all) scholar-fans and some (not all) scholar-anti-fans or scholar-non-fans have been structurally implicated in the recoding of aesthetic judgments, and hence in the "canon problem."

But how can media academics' status as media audiences be properly tackled, acknowledged, even utilized, without audience-based identities and tastes being seen as a "threat to academic identity" (Burr 2005: 378)? To consider this question means going beyond fandom, and conceding that the distinctive expulsion of aesthetics—resulting in its various scholar-fan and anti-fan recodings—is a general rather than a special problem in media/cultural studies.

How a General Theory of Hybridized Academia—Going beyond Fandom—Can Restore the Aesthetic

As Geraghty has argued, media/cultural studies may benefit "from academics being more explicit about the evaluative judgements we inevitably make" (2003: 40). However, it is hardly the case that aesthetic judgments have been properly expelled from these areas of study. It is, perhaps, fairer to say that they have continued, either in the name of political evaluation or via the impassioned critical/celebratory analyses of scholar-anti-fans and scholar-fans. Despite this recoded continuation, aesthetic judgments have also partly been nominally ruled out of media/

cultural studies as a result of the work of Pierre Bourdieu (1984, 1993).
Bourdieu argues that aesthetic judgments are inseparable from the
exercising of "cultural capital" and are thus linked to the cultural reproduction of systematic power inequalities (see Hills 2002; Williamson
2005). Debates concerned with more fully restoring aesthetic judgments
to media and cultural studies have tended to revolve around whether it
is necessary or desirable for scholars to uphold specific notions of quality media (Jacobs 2001; Thomas 2002), and in this ongoing discussion,
the work of Bourdieu—and his argument that aesthetics are linked to
macro-level cultural reproduction—has been somewhat suspended in
favor of more micro-level textual analysis. Aesthetic judgments, it seems,
steadfastly refuse to go away (see Bérubé 2005; Hills 2005a: 142–44).

One way to move forward would be to argue that film studies can
provide a model for media/cultural studies. Opposition to aesthetics
could be replaced by an appropriation of art discourses, with "television art" finally taking its place alongside long-established disciplinary
discussions of film art. This is Turnbull's (2005: 368–69) argument, as
she ponders whether media studies might make a place for "ekphra-
sis," the linguistic re-expression of a text's aesthetic impact on the self.
Though this seems promising, the question that remains is how ekph-
rasis would connect up with media/cultural studies' theorizing. Is it the
place of such theory to re-express subjective and aesthetic experiences,
or should these experiences be remediated, worked over, or even modified through the reflexivity of theory? Turnbull seems to take media/
cultural studies back to the collapsing together of politics and aesthetics
that marred the screen theory of MacCabe (1981a, 1981b), or to the pri-
oritizing of subjective aesthetics over politics.

Another way forward would be not to ape film theory, but rather to
pay attention to a path not taken in Barthes's lectures on the neutral.
Challenged as to whether his desire for the neutral is in some sense itself
merely an ideological restatement of the "petit-bourgeois [. . .] ideology
of the balanced account" (2005: 79), Barthes responds,

> I could, and it is, by the way, what I am doing, recognize that in me there
> are "petit-bourgeois" elements in my tastes, in my discourse are petit-
> bourgeois features (without going into the discussion of this cursed
> denomination here). [. . .] These features are not clandestine. [. . .]

However, that's not the direction I will take to answer. I will say: the Neutral is connected with [petit-bourgeois-ideological] neither-norism and nevertheless is absolutely different from it. (2005: 79–80)

Barthes's argument is that petit-bourgeois ideology is "social" and grants a "subject-position," whereas his discourse is "existential" and suspends any subject-position (2005: 80). We could hardly wish for a more condensed statement of the ideology of the nonplaced, free-floating academic who is assumed to stand outside social affiliations and contexts, thereby representing a near mystical tertium.

And yet Barthes's preceding and refuted acknowledgment is, I would say, actually a more promising answer to the question posed, even though it undermines the autoheroics of the allegedly acontextual academic always symbolically distanced from ideology. Barthes comes close to conceding that his discourse, even while it seeks to demystify and politically evaluate, is also permeated by the very ideology it opposes and unveils. This, I think, offers a better way forward for media/cultural studies: not a rise in aesthetic subjectivism, but instead a reflexive approach to scholars' aesthetic judgments as hermeneutic constructions of self-identity (Bailey 2005; Sandvoss 2005), and a recognition of how these may be both ideological and opposed to specific ideologies. The problem addressed by Barthes also captures a far wider difficulty, since all those working in the humanities and social sciences are, in a range of ways, caught up in versions of this binary: disciplinary knowledge versus cultural identity and experience. The literary scholar is an "ordinary" reader as well as a scholar; the political scientist is both a citizen and an academic; the sociologist is always part of a society; and so on. Disciplined scholarship may always require a series of Others from which it can disentangle its own supposed purity and specificity. However, such processes of Othering and their cultural exclusions can also be highlighted and challenged (Hills 2005a), and thus should not be assumed to be monolithically fixed, inevitable, or essential in their specifiable forms and contents.

Work in media/cultural studies may, then, benefit from shifting its legitimating discourses away from the anti-aesthetic, moving toward an acknowledgment that present-day scholarship can no longer be "set apart" from the culture and ideology it studies, but is rather "set in relation" with these contexts (Hills 2005a: 172–73). Though critical scholars have been happy to redescribe the worlds of media audiences, for example, shifting audience "leisure" into the register of "labor" (Meehan 2000; Shimpach 2005), the possibility of redescribing scholarship's own foundational self-descriptions has rarely been pursued. Recognizing that media academics are always-already media audiences, whether or not they are fans, would mean giving up the notion that media and cultural studies are enterprises outside the paradigm of consumer/producer, and outside the realms of aesthetic taste as well as ideology.

Will the entire edifice of media/cultural studies crumble away if we surrender the legitimating prop that academic work is essentially and purely different to the tastes/ideologies of everyday consumer and media-industry culture? I would say not: indeed, it may be easier for both critical scholar-anti-fans and celebratory scholar-fans to articulate exactly which cultural texts and media systems they are "for," without the need to cloak and recode aesthetic judgments. It may also allow the "canon problem" to be openly addressed and creatively opened out, with a wider range of cultural tastes and identities—a wider range of "projects of self"—then being archived and canonized by scholarship.

For some, the cost will undoubtedly be too high. Ideology will only ever be elsewhere in their worldview. But this splitting of the cultural world into highly legible heroes and victims is really a very simple story, however many lengthy words it loves to use. Recognizing the generalized hybridity of contemporary media academics—academics who are also audiences and consumers of the type they write about—surely means letting go of an infantile fantasy of omnipotence in which scholars are imagined as the bearers of pure, anti-ideological thought. At the same time, it means going beyond viewing fan audiences as the problematic site of aesthetic judgments—hence concomitantly depicting scholar-fandom as a threatening hybridity—in order to safely reconjure notions of academic authenticity.

WORKS CITED

Abercrombie, N & Longhurst, B 1998, *Audiences: a sociological theory of performance and imagination*, Sage, Thousand Oaks, CA.

Bailey, S 2005, *Media audiences and identity: self-construction in the fan experience*, Palgrave Macmillan, New York.

Barthes, R 2005, *The neutral*, Columbia University Press, New York.

Bérubé, M (ed.) 2005, *The aesthetics of cultural studies*, Blackwell, Oxford.

Bird, SE 2003, *The audience in everyday life: living in a media world*, Routledge, New York.

Bourdieu, P 1984, *Distinction: a social critique of the judgment of taste*, Harvard University Press, Cambridge, MA.

Bourdieu, P 1993, *The field of cultural production*, Polity, Cambridge.

Brooker, W 2002, *Using the force: creativity, community, and Star Wars fans*, Continuum, New York.

Burr, V 2005, "Scholar/'shippers and Spikeaholics: academic and fan identities at the Slayage Conference on *Buffy the Vampire Slayer*," *European Journal of Cultural Studies* 8(3): 375–83.

Friedman, EG & Squire, C 1998, *Morality USA*, University of Minnesota Press, Minneapolis.

Geraghty, C 2003, "Aesthetics and quality in popular television drama," *International Journal of Cultural Studies* 6(1): 25–45.

Gray, J 2003, "New audiences, new textualities: anti-fans and non-fans," *International Journal of Cultural Studies* 6(1): 64–81.

Gray, J 2006, *Watching with* The Simpsons: *television, parody, and intertextuality*, Routledge, New York.

Harrington, CL & Bielby, DD 1995, *Soap fans: pursuing pleasure and making meaning in everyday life*, Temple University Press, Philadelphia.

Hills, M 2002, *Fan cultures*, Routledge, New York.

Hills, M 2003, "*Star Wars* in fandom, film theory, and the museum: the cultural status of the cult blockbuster," in J Stringer (ed.), *Movie blockbusters*, Routledge, New York.

Hills, M 2004, "*Dawson's Creek*: 'quality teen TV' and 'mainstream cult'?," in G Davis & K Dickinson (eds.), *Teen TV: genre, consumption, and identity*, BFI, London.

Hills, M 2005a, *How to do things with cultural theory*, Hodder Arnold, London.

Hills, M 2005b, *The pleasures of horror*, Continuum, New York.

Hills, M 2005c, "Who wants to be a fan of *Who Wants to Be a Millionaire*? Scholarly television criticism, 'popular aesthetics,' and academic tastes," in C Johnson & R Turnock (eds.), *ITV cultures: independent television over fifty years*, Open University Press, Maidenhead, UK.

Hunter, IQ & Kaye, H 1997, "Introduction," in D Cartmell et al. (eds.), *Trash aesthetics: popular culture and its audience*, Pluto, Chicago.

Jacobs, J 2001, "Issues of judgment and value in television studies," *International Journal of Cultural Studies* 4(4): 427–47.

Jenkins, H 1992, *Textual poachers: television fans and participatory culture*, Routledge, New York.

Kuhn, A 2005, "Thresholds: film as film and the aesthetic experience," *Screen* 46(4): 401–14.

Levine, MP & Schneider, SJ 2003, "Feeling for Buffy: the girl next door," in JB South (ed.), Buffy the Vampire Slayer *and Philosophy*, Open Court, Chicago.

MacCabe, C 1981a, "Days of Hope, a response to Colin McArthur," in T Bennett et al. (eds.), *Popular television and film*, BFI/Open University Press, London.

MacCabe, C 1981b, "Realism and the cinema: notes on some Brechtian theses," in T Bennett et al. (eds.), *Popular television and film*, BFI/Open University Press, London.

McArthur, C 1981, "Days of Hope," in T Bennett et al. (eds.), *Popular television and film*, BFI/Open University Press, London.

McKee, A 2001, *Australian television: a genealogy of great moments*, Oxford University Press, Melbourne.

McKee, A 2002, "Fandom," in T Miller (ed.), *Television studies*, BFI, London.

McKee, A 2003, "What is television for?," in M Jancovich & J Lyons (eds.), *Quality popular television*, BFI, London.

Meehan, ER 2000, "Leisure or labor? Fan ethnography and political economy," in I Hagen & J Wasko (eds.), *Consuming audiences? Production and reception in media research*, Hampton Press, Cresskill, NJ.

Michael, J 2000, *Anxious intellects: academic professionals, public intellectuals, and enlightenment values*, Duke University Press, Durham, NC.

Miller, T 2003, *Spyscreen: espionage on film and TV from the 1930s to the 1960s*, Oxford University Press, Oxford.

Osborne, P 2000, *Philosophy in cultural theory*, Routledge, New York.

Pearce, L 1997, *Feminism and the politics of reading*, Arnold, London.

Philo, G & Miller, D 2001, "Cultural compliance," in G Philo & D Miller (eds.), *Market killing*, Pearson Education, Essex, UK.

Roberts, TJ 1990, *An aesthetics of junk fiction*, University of Georgia Press, Athens.

Sandvoss, C 2005, *Fans: the mirror of consumption*, Polity, Malden, MA.

Scodari, C 2003a, "Resistance reexamined: gender, fan practices, and science fiction television," *Popular Communication* 1(2): 111–30.

Scodari, C 2003b, "Review of fan cultures," *Popular Communication* 1(3): 181–83.

Shimpach, S 2005, "Working watching: the creative and cultural labor of the media audience," *Social Semiotics* 15(3): 343–60.

Thomas, L 2002, *Fans, feminisms, and "quality" media*, Routledge, New York.

Turnbull, S 2005, "Moments of inspiration: performing Spike," *European Journal of Cultural Studies* 8(3): 367–73.

White, C 2005, *The middle mind: why consumer culture is turning us into the living dead*, Penguin, London.

Williamson, M 2005, *The lure of the vampire: gender, fiction, and fandom from Bram Stoker to Buffy*, Wallflower, New York.

Wright Wexman, V 1999, "The critic as consumer: film study in the university, 'Vertigo,' and the film canon," in B Henderson & A Martin (eds.), *Film Quarterly: forty years—a selection*, University of California Press, Berkeley.

4

Copyright Law, Fan Practices, and the Rights of the Author (2017)

REBECCA TUSHNET

Fans of popular media who write stories about their favorite characters, draw pictures of them, and edit music videos reworking the original sources occasionally stop to think about whether what they are doing is legal under copyright law. In the past, many fans assumed that these creations were technically illegal—in copyright-specific terms, infringing—but not harmful to copyright owners and therefore not truly wrong, at least as long as fans kept relatively quiet about their creative practices (e.g., Brook n.d.). More commonly these days, fans think that fan creations count as "fair use," and thus as noninfringing, at least as long as no one is making any money from selling them (e.g., Gran 1999). Regardless, fans often see their legal status as similar to their social status: marginal and, at best, tolerated rather than celebrated as part of the universe of creators. Recent attempts to monetize or license fanworks, such as Amazon's Kindle Worlds or Paramount's guidelines for tolerating fan films that do some crowdfunding, remain a relatively small part of fans' creative worlds; though they offer some opportunities for fans looking for a path to commercialization, they cannot and will not substitute for fair use (Tushnet 2014).

Shortly after I found online fandom, I wrote an article on the subject (Tushnet 1997). I concluded that most fan fiction, particularly that disseminated on the Internet, would be classified as fair use under US copyright law.[1] Since then, much has changed. Fan fiction has regularly entered the legal discussion, usually as an example of fair use (Fanlore n.d.); I co-founded the Organization for Transformative Works (OTW), whose mission is to protect and defend noncommercial fan activities; and the Copyright Office has recognized that enough fan videos are fair use to justify a legal exemption to the general prohibition on "ripping" DVDs and streaming video to get clips.

The formal legal landscape is generally more favorable to fans than it was twenty years ago, as courts have been increasingly willing to protect "transformative" unauthorized uses against copyright owners' allegations of infringement. Transformative uses are those that add new insights or meaning to the original work, often in ways that copyright owners don't like. Like a book review that quotes a work in order to criticize it, a retelling of a story that offers the villain's point of view sympathetically or adds explicit sexual content can be a transformative fair use. Recent cases emphasize that copyright owners can't suppress unwanted interpretations of their works by asserting copyright. The most notable litigation involved a book by Alice Randall, *The Wind Done Gone*, which retold the story of Margaret Mitchell's *Gone with the Wind* from the perspective of a new character, the mixed-race daughter of a slave and a master. A federal court of appeals held that Randall's book was likely to be a fair use, largely because of the ways in which it criticized the racism of the original (*SunTrust Bank v. Houghton Mifflin Co.* 2001).

Legal doctrine is not all that matters, however. When copyright owners aggressively alleged infringement, threatening fans with massive civil penalties, fans in the past usually chose to shut down or hide their activities rather than standing their ground. The noncommercial fan community has still not given rise to litigated cases, but the presence of the OTW and increasing awareness of fair use among fans have enabled them to resist copyright owner threats, and in all the instances of which I am aware, copyright owners have decided not to follow up on informal threats when fans making noncommercial uses resisted.

Despite the absence of cases, fan practices do offer lessons for copyright law. Among other things, fan practices provide insights into moral rights, a category of authors' rights that is well recognized in Europe but has been far less successful in the United States. Various types of moral rights allow an author (or an author's heirs) to control the attribution of a work, to withdraw it from circulation, or to protect it from mutilation or distortion by unwanted adaptations or alterations. Moral rights theory posits a deep and unique connection between author and text such that an insult to the text is an assault on the author. Moral rights thus seem inherently in conflict with fans' willingness to take liberties with source texts. The few licensing attempts directed at fanworks have been consistent with fears about distortion, and contain both vague prohibitions on "offensive" content and specific directives to avoid matters of special importance to the copyright owner—from Paramount's ban on using anyone involved in an official *Star Trek* production in a fan film to G.I. Joe's ban on making Snake Eyes into a Yankees fan (*Star Trek Fan Films* n.d.; Tushnet 2014).

Yet not all moral rights claims are inconsistent with fan interpretive practices. Although protection against *distortion* conflicts with much fan creative activity, moral claims to *attribution* are widely recognized in fandom, and attribution rights are far less disruptive to ordinary interpretive practices than other kinds of moral rights. In addition, fan practices demonstrate that attribution can come from context, while the law has tended to assume that only explicit credit suffices to give authors proper acknowledgment.

Search engines have made it simple for anyone, including copyright owners and non-fans, to find fanworks. The now-archived Television Without Pity website, for instance, had many user forums that included discussions of fan creations, and TV producers regularly read the fan forums (though they may not have read the fan fiction threads in those forums) (Sella 2002). Someone who enjoys watching a show may now slide easily into the world of fan-generated content, without any prior screening and without much effort. This accessibility means that a reader's view of Harry Potter may be altered by an unexpected encounter with a sexually explicit or graphically violent story about him, which initially increased copyright owners' anxieties about losing control of their characters' images.

When I first wrote about fan fiction in 1997, it was possible for a diligent person to attempt a comprehensive listing of fan fiction sites, from *The A-Team* to *Zorro* (KSNicholas n.d.). I was amazed by the scope of online fandom—there were hundreds of sites listed! In 2015, Google listed over 13.5 million results for a search of the phrase "fan fiction" (an order of magnitude more than the results in 2008). If you're one in a million, you can find 250 blogs on Tumblr for people just like you. Even if your fandom is smaller, there's the yearly Rare Fandoms Challenge to connect the one person who wants to read a story with the one person who wants to write it (*The Yuletide FAQ* 2005). The quality of what is available varies wildly, and so do the people who participate and their reasons for doing so. There are twelve-year-olds just having fun sharing stories with their friends and there are published writers practicing their craft for a guaranteed audience. Likewise, the publicly visible *types* of fan productions are more varied than when I first engaged with the legal aspects of fandom. Fan fiction is the phenomenon to which legal scholars have paid most attention, but cosplay, fan drawings, photo manipulations, and music videos are also widely available.

This visibility is important. Fans who find fan fiction, art, and videos often feel a sense of validation, and they may feel that their own interests are more normal. For the many people still in transformative fandom who joined it when it flew below the radar, the visibility initially created a sense of exposure, and a certain fear that the powers that be might crack down if the fans weren't careful. Visibility invites study, and sometimes legal threats, as shown by the section of chillingeffects.org that hosts copies of cease-and-desist letters received by various fan sites. However, visibility has also produced a greater sense of normalcy, even for initially wary older fans. Though young people know that they aren't truly anonymous, the use of pseudonyms and fan-oriented sites allows a sense of protection. And fans often have a greater sense of what fair use allows; the OTW has tried to promote such legal literacy.

In addition, copyright owners have generally realized that threatening their fans makes much less sense than co-opting them. It's not accidental that the cult TV show *Supernatural* called its two-hundredth episode "Fan Fiction," and featured an unauthorized play very loosely based on the in-show *Supernatural* novels that was explicitly described as "transformative" by the playwright. *Supernatural*, like many other franchises, preferred to hail and engage its creative fans rather than to suppress them. The cease-and-desist letters have trickled to a near halt, and the new challenges for noncommercial fandom largely involve how to avoid being sucked into the vast wealth-extraction machine that is creative production in late capitalism.

Who Gets the Credit?

When I first wrote about fan fiction, disclaimer statements by fan authors were common and prominent: the author would state that she did not own the copyright to the characters and situations, name the entity that did (or the original creator, who is usually not the copyright owner), and sometimes add a request that the copyright owner not sue her. While I have not conducted a scientific survey, my strong impression is that disclaimers are far less common today. When they are present, they may not seem all that much like pleas for forbearance. For example, the tone of a disclaimer discussed in Esther Saxey's essay on *Buffy the Vampire Slayer* fan fiction (2002: 208) is casual enough that it is difficult to tell what is being disclaimed: "Joss moves in mysterious ways. But, damn his eyes, he owns the two lovlies and their auras. He created them, made them what they are, and I bow to you [*sic*]." Or, at the extreme, consider this (slightly fanciful) timeline from verygaygirlfriendspookymulder:

> author's notes in 1998: these characters, of course, do not belong to me !!! :) all rights reserved!!! just borrowing them for some fun!!!! heehee. i lov 2 obey the law

> author's notes in 2014: literally ignore all of canon. the author is dead. i own these assholes now.

As another OTW cofounder observed, "My work here is done!" (Cesperanza n.d.).

I think this informality is tied to a sense of greater normalcy. Fewer fan creators are worried that they are somehow doing something wrong, and they are more likely to expect that their readers will understand their basic premises. After four hundred disclaimers, the four hundred first is likely to seem a lot less important. Another likely related factor is that with the increasing variety and visibility of fan creativity, new fans are not always initiated by more experienced ones. They may not learn the norms of the preexisting community when they start sharing their own stories and art, including earlier online norms of explicitly disclaiming ownership.

Are fanworks part of a breakdown of respect for intellectual property and authors' interests? Generally, no. Fans who create derivative works tend to be sensitive to the interests of copyright owners in getting attribution for the original, canonical versions of their characters, offering "subversive respect" (Saxey 2002: 208). Fans also acknowledge copyright owners' legitimate economic interests, but maintain that their activities do not hurt and even help revenues from authorized works, by increasing loyalty to and interest in the official versions (Tushnet 1997: 669). A Lockean theory of adding value through labor plays a role in fan concepts of artists' rights. Few pure downloaders would claim to have invested labor in any relevant sense when they search for and select music or TV shows to copy. Fan authors and artists, by contrast, seek recognition from their peers for adding new aesthetics and twists to the official texts. Creation breeds respect for creation, along with respect for the appropriate limits of creators' control: as Henry Jenkins et al. write, "young people who create and circulate their own media [including remixes] are more likely to respect the intellectual property rights of others because they feel a greater stake in the cultural economy" (Jenkins et al. 2006: 12).

An absence of disclaimers might be thought to show unconcern for proper attribution. But that interpretation would ignore the importance of context: if I say that life is "A tale/Told by an idiot, full of sound and fury/Signifying nothing" without attribution, I don't expect you to think I made up those words myself. No more do fans expect other fans—their intended audience—to think that they created Superman or Captain Kirk. Fan creators are usually highly concerned with proper attribution. Plagiarism, that is, verbatim copying without attribution where the copier apparently expects to receive credit for the words or images as if they were her own, remains one of the most serious offenses against the fan community, and when discovered the plagiarist is generally publicly excoriated (e.g., Lady Macbeth 2004; *The Lois & Clark Fanfic Archive FAQ* n.d.).

Disclaimers were never intended to inform other fans. It was always fairly easy to tell an authorized *Star Trek* novel from an unauthorized fan creation. Rather, disclaimers were directed at an imagined audience, the copyright owners/original creators—disclaimers often included the request "Please don't sue." At the same time, most fans never thought that the copyright owner would actually read fan fiction in the first place. The ebbing of the disclaimer therefore signals not a sea change in fans' attitudes toward attribution, but a change in the need to cater to this imagined non-audience.

Fan practices surrounding attribution may have several lessons for the law. Trademark law is centrally concerned with attribution: its goal is to help consumers easily find the products they want, ensuring that a can of Coke is really made in a Coca-Cola bottling plant. Trademark can also protect against false claims of credit, for example if a new soda company put Coke in its bottles in order to deceive people into thinking that the new soda was just as good. In the past, authors have used trademark law to assert their rights to get proper credit and to keep their names off of unwanted projects, as when Stephen King stopped a movie studio from calling its film *Stephen King's The Lawnmower Man* (*King v. Innovation Books* 1992).

Early this century, the Supreme Court decided *Dastar Corp. v. Twentieth Century Fox Film Corp.* (2003), which involved a videotape series about World War II that was mostly composed of footage from an earlier series; the earlier series was no longer protected by copyright. A lower court had ruled that Dastar, the series producer, had violated federal trademark law by failing to attribute the footage to the (former) copyright owner, Fox, which had purchased the rights from Time-Life. The Supreme Court disagreed with the lower court, holding that using trademark law as a means to enforce attribution rights would threaten infinite battles over the true source of a work's ideas or expressions—some of the footage in the Time-Life series, for example, came from films made by servicemen for the US government. Justice Antonin Scalia, engaging in unattributed borrowing from Dastar's briefs (Band & Schruers 2005: 15), refused to require later creators to engage in a "search for the source of the Nile and all its tributaries" (*Dastar* 2003: 36).

As fan practices reveal, however, there can be a social consensus within a relevant community about how far to trace and when, providing a limiting principle enforceable by norms if not by law.[2] Often, missing credits aren't deceptive. Justice Scalia's uncredited borrowing from a party's legal brief escapes condemnation because the social context of his copying makes him a jurist, not a plagiarist. Similarly, fan creations, even without disclaimers, announce their unauthorized status so clearly through context that no deception is likely.

Nonetheless, traditional trademark law presumes that the presence or absence of a name is important. False advertising law is a better model for issues about attribution of texts, because that body of law takes into account whether a particular claim or omission makes a difference to consumers' decisions. An advertisement that does not mention an item's price is not therefore misleading: consumers know that goods have prices.

Analogously, in the fan context, lack of explicit attribution is regularly an immaterial omission because the audience already knows that the fan is not the original creator of the overall "universe." Moreover, fans are unlikely to know or care about the complex web of contracts and law that regulates relations between individual creators and the large corporations that usually own the rights to popular works. Though fans sometimes offer explicit disclaimers that refer to a specific creator or copyright owner, the relevant information is that the fan makes no ownership or authorship claims to the characters and situations.

Fan practices are not unique in their contextualization of the idea of proper credit. Jonathan Band and Matt Schruers point out that historical scholarship has similar norms that distinguish between the attribution owed when dealing with the in-group and that acceptable when dealing with the out-group (2005: 16–17). That is, historians expect that scholarly monographs will credit the work of other historians much more often and more specifically than popular historical works such as textbooks and encyclopedia entries (American Historical Association 2005). Historians, who generally rely on reputation more than money as compensation for their contributions to the sum of knowledge, care more about proper attribution within the profession than outside it.

More generally, audiences value attribution in a different way than they value trademarks for ordinary goods like soda. Authorization, which is what trademark law protects, is different from authorship. Consider a copy of Tom Clancy's *The Hunt for Red October* published by a pirate publisher in India versus an authorized "Tom Clancy's Op Center" novel written by a ghostwriter. Even if the pirate introduced a number of typographical errors into *The Hunt for Red October*, many of us would feel that the pirated book had a stronger claim to being a real Tom Clancy novel than the authorized book.

Fan texts are a third type of creation, neither pure copies of another author's work nor authorized additions to the original. Because they are not canonical, fan stories can offer a thousand different ways that Mulder and Scully first slept together, none of which contradict the others, or one author can write "Five Things That Never Happened"—five alternate histories for a favorite character, all of which are, as the title states, repudiated by the author (*Because AUs Make Us Happy* n.d.). Lack of authority, which stems from lack of authorization, allows a freedom unavailable to an official canon striving for internal consistency. Off on a frolic of their own, fans' very diversity operates as a signal that each fan is offering her own interpretations or revisions, not those of a commercial owner.

Who Gets the Blame?

Related to attribution and to moral rights against distortion is the question of who is *responsible* for the interpretations of the original text provided by fan creators. Texts invite interpretation, and making a text available to the public necessarily cedes some control over it, though copyright law has struggled to deal with this truism. When defendants have altered the content of what they have copied, courts often—though not always—have looked for some commentary on the original; more generally, they have sought new meanings or new messages. According to the Supreme Court, a parody, by distorting elements of the original, causes readers to rethink the messages of the original, while a satire merely uses the original to "avoid the drudgery in working up something fresh" and has less of a claim to fair use, although it is not automatically condemned (*Campbell v. Acuff-Rose Music, Inc.* 1994). Under the definitions used by fair use doctrine, a parody mocks the original specifically, like Weird Al Yankovic's "(This Song's Just) Six Words Long," which is set to the tune of "Got My Mind Set on You." A satire borrows a familiar work to get its audience's attention and to make fun of something other than the original, like a satirical song using a popular tune to lambaste a politician.

Using the parody/satire division as a guide, courts have found that a legitimate transformation exists when the new work makes overt that which was present in the original text covertly (at least as some readers saw it): transformative fair uses make subtext text. In two important parody cases involving the Barbie doll, for example, Mattel's attempts to protect its doll's image by using copyright law were thwarted by courts that found that overtly sexualizing Barbie constituted commentary on Barbie *because Barbie already had sexual connotations* (*Mattel, Inc. v. Walking Mountain Productions* 2003; *Mattel, Inc. v. Pitt* 2002). Another court used similar reasoning to reject Mattel's trademark claims against Aqua's popular novelty song "Barbie Girl" (*Mattel, Inc. v. MCA Records, Inc.* 2002).

Even more fascinating is the discussion in the *Wind Done Gone* case about the relevance of homosexuality and miscegenation to fair use. The Mitchell estate didn't want *Gone with the Wind* to be associated with such controversial topics. The Eleventh Circuit Court of Appeals held that Alice Randall's insertion of homosexuality, in the form of a gay Ashley Wilkes, into the world of *Gone with the Wind* was an important part of what made her book transformative. The court quoted *Gone with the Wind*'s description of the Wilkes family as artistic and "queer" (*Suntrust* 2001: 1270n26), a term already widely used to describe homosexuals when Mitchell wrote the novel (*Dictionary of American Slang* 1967: 415). (The similarities to slash fan fiction, which picks up on homoerotic elements in the original texts, are evident.)

In other words, the court held that *The Wind Done Gone*'s transformation consisted of making clear or exaggerated what was opaque or limited in the original text.[3] As a result, the legal defense of parodies and other literary transformations protects critics as creators in their own right more strongly when they draw deeply from a preexisting well. A court's determination that a work is parodic rather than satirical is therefore also a ruling that the original author is partly responsible for the content of the critical work, often content the author finds extremely objectionable. As a result, the concept of transformation requires the law to embrace the ambiguity of meaning.

Common fan understandings of good characterization are consistent with the idea of drawing deeply from canon to make something new: a story succeeds when it convinces readers that yes, Superman could have reacted that way if he woke up in a female body, or yes, the treatment of a female character by the original narrative was extremely unfair. Most fan creators are concerned to some extent with making the characters they use recognizable as related to the official versions. If they show Captain Kirk and Mister Spock having a sexual relationship, they want readers to see them as extensions of the canonical characters, not as two random men who happen to have the names "Kirk" and "Spock." Different readers may disagree about whether proper characterization has been achieved, but the goal itself is common, though not universal.

Fans, like courts analyzing transformative fair uses, thus see their work as related to the source texts, bringing meaning out as much as they are putting meaning in. Even without containing explicit criticism, a fanwork exists in dialogue with the original as well as with the fannish community, situating itself as a distinct entity that couldn't substitute for its commercial inspiration.

Significantly, transformation by engagement with what's already present also means that the original author did not have full control over the original text—that the text was not received in just the way she wanted it to be received. The more successfully a work is transformed in the technical legal sense, the more we are likely to be able to see that the evidence supporting the transformation was present all along in the original: Ashley Wilkes was always a little gay, wasn't he? While this is a perfectly standard result from the perspective of literary theory, the law rarely makes explicit what fans have always known: meaning cannot be imposed by authors or owners but rather is negotiated among texts, authors, and audiences.

But not all fanworks involve commentary, or at least commentary that would be legible to non-fans. Many theorists who believe that copyright has gone too far believe that the presence of authorship alone should favor fair use. Criticism shouldn't be the only kind of transformativeness; while the original author should have economic rights to control straightforward adaptations, like the movie version of a book, fair use should have a broad scope beyond that. Recently, the Second Circuit took a major step in this direction, refusing to require Richard Prince, a well-known appropriation artist, to have an articulable criticism of the original where his work plainly had a new *meaning* in the art world, distinct from that of the original photographs he copied and altered (*Cariou v. Prince* 2013). The distinct purposes and functions of the new works made them (mostly) transformative fair uses.

This reasoning has an analogy in fandom, where fanworks regularly provide fans with ways to work out their own interests in gender roles, romance, and other subjects, using existing characters as an important medium of communication. While fans often feel that only certain texts engage them enough to prompt a creative response, outsiders may not see the tie to a particular text as easily as the court did in the *Wind Done Gone* case. Fans may instead appear more like appropriation artists, settling on particular examples of popular culture because of their more general characteristics (engagement with the hero's journey, tendency to put women in refrigerators to further the story of a man, availability of a possible romantic threesome that is unlikely to become canonical, or something else) rather than because of a unique feature in need of criticism. Nonetheless, by retaining some basic connection to the original media source, fans identify their works as being in a particular fandom—a *Star Trek* Alternate Universe where the characters are all twenty-first-century bartenders is still a *Star Trek* fanwork—and thus connect themselves to the larger *Star Trek* fan corpus.

Attribution and Moral Rights

Concepts of attribution and credit play a major role in fan creators' theories of intellectual property (Tushnet 1997: 678–80). The practices of a community may provide attribution where it is not apparent on the face of the text, and the connections between original and fan creations are complex, with credit properly going in part to the original author and in part to the fan.

The legal concept of transformative use denies the author the authority to control all interpretations of a text, not just practically but conceptually. This rule is in obvious tension with moral rights against distortion, and many legal scholars conclude that moral rights don't fit into the American copyright system. But, as fan practices demonstrate, not all moral rights are the same: attribution, though it may not be explicit, can and should regularly be given to creators even if total control is denied them.

By contrast, moral rights against distortion appear even more ill-suited to the realities of creativity once we accept that criticism, mockery, and other uncomfortable transformations draw on material present in the original works. What an author intends to produce and what others understand her to have produced often diverge. Fan practices that emphasize the indelible yet unpredictable connections between originals and unauthorized creative responses can thus help illuminate the meaning and implications of copyright, just as copyright's fair use doctrine gives fans reasons why their unauthorized creations are neither unlawful nor immoral.

NOTES

1 My focus has been on US law even though media fandom is a global phenomenon because US law is unusually open-ended, whereas many other countries have limited exceptions to copyright for which fan creations are less likely to qualify, and also because US copyright owners, like many other US entities, are relatively swift to threaten lawsuits when they perceive an interference with their rights.

2 As Francesca Coppa pointed out to me, the social consensus about credit might be morally questionable, as when white performers take credit for popularizing African American forms of music, and a consensus might also change over time as political and social trends lead to different origin stories. This is another reason that using law to enforce credit-tracing norms might not be a good idea.

3 Miscegenation, the other taboo topic, is even more deeply buried in *Gone with the Wind*. One might say that, in a slave society, miscegenation is inevitably part of the context.

WORKS CITED

American Historical Association 2005, *Statement on standards of professional conduct*, www.historians.org.

Band, J & Schruers, M 2005, "*Dastar*, attribution, and plagiarism," *AIPLA Quarterly Journal* 33: 1–23.

Because AUs Make Us Happy n.d., strangeplaces.net.

Brook, M n.d., *The fan fiction FAQ*, www.meljeanbrook.com.

Campbell v. Acuff-Rose Music, Inc., 510 US 569, 580 (1994).

Cariou v. Prince, 714 F.3d 694, 706 (2d Cir. 2013).

Cesperanza n.d., cesperanza.tumblr.com.

Dastar Corp. v. Twentieth Century Fox Film Corp., 539 US 23 (2003).

Dictionary of American Slang 1967, Thomas Y. Crowell, New York.

Fanlore n.d., *Legal analysis*, fanlore.org.

Gran, J 1999, *Fan fiction and copyright*, www.alternateuniverses.com.

Jenkins, H, Purushotma, R, Weigel, M, Clinton, K, & Robison, AJ 2006, *Confronting the challenges of participatory culture: media education for the 21st century*, MIT Press, Cambridge, MA.

King v. Innovation Books, 976 F.2d 824 (2d Cir. 1992).

KSNicholas n.d., *Site map*, web.archive.org.

Lady Macbeth 2004, *Plagiarism—please help stop its spread*, forum.mediaminer.org.

The Lois & Clark Fanfic Archive FAQ n.d., www.lcfanfic.com.

Mattel, Inc. v. MCA Records, Inc., 296 F.3d 894 (9th Cir. 2002).

Mattel, Inc. v. Pitt, 229 F. Supp. 2d 315 (S.D.N.Y. 2002).

Mattel, Inc. v. Walking Mountain Productions, 353 F.3d 792 (9th Cir. 2003).

Saxey E 2002, "Staking a claim: the series and its slash fan fiction," in R Kaveney (ed.), *Reading the vampire slayer: the unofficial critical companion to Buffy and Angel*, IB Tauris, London.

Sella, M 2002, "The remote controllers," *NY Times Magazine*, October 20, 68.

Star Trek Fan Films n.d., www.startrek.com.

SunTrust Bank v. Houghton Mifflin Co., 268 F.3d 1257 (11th Cir. 2001).

Tushnet, R 1997, "Legal fictions: copyright, fan fiction, and a new common law," *Loyola L.A. Entertainment Law Journal* 17: 651–86.

Tushnet, R 2014, "All of this has happened before and all of this will happen again," *Berkeley Technology Law Journal* 29: 1447–88.

The Yuletide FAQ 2005, www.yuletidetreasure.org.

5

Toy Fandom, Adulthood, and the Ludic Age

Creative Material Culture as Play

KATRIINA HELJAKKA

Introduction: Adults and Toys in the Ludic Age

While the ludic activity of (digital) gaming has opened up a more allowing arena for explorations in adult play, toy play at adult age is still a largely underdeveloped area of academic inquiry even in fan studies. Adult toy fandom and activities related to toys most often seem to be referred to as hobbies related to collecting. The persistent rhetoric on collecting that encompasses adult relations and pastimes with toys of all kinds does not fully address the nature of the sometimes parasocial relationships adults have with their toys, nor does it do justice to contemporary creative practices that link their solitary object play with socially shared play experiences.

Although the concept of adulthood is culturally bound, ambiguous, and therefore often hard to define, it entails the idea of psychological maturity associated with a capability to act self-sufficiently and responsibly. In my appropriation of the term, an adult, in the context of contemporary toy fandom, is a person in his or her twenties or above with a keen interest in various forms of toy-related activities in association with creative cultivation of toys, such as storytelling or building of toy characters or constructions. Still, a dialogue between father and son in *The Lego Movie* (Lord & Miller 2014) illustrates the ongoing tension between the different object relations, toy fandom, and related practices of children and adults:

> DAD: You know the rules. This isn't a toy.
> FINN: Um, well, it kind of is.

> DAD: No. Actually it's a highly sophisticated interlocking brick system.
> FINN: We bought it at the toy store.
> DAD: We did. But the way I'm using it makes it an adult thing.

In this movie, the father is interested, with the help of Kragle (Krazy Glue), to preserve his own LEGO creations exactly as they are in their staged scenarios: immovable and in his son's opinion "unplayable." Yet, I question why the gluing of the bricks would eliminate the element of play from this activity or the status of a toy from the brick system by referring to it as an "adult thing."

Star Wars has the biggest collector base of any (toy and entertainment) brand (Geraghty 2006: 217). The most collected Star Wars merchandise is the action figures (*The Force of Three Generations* 2011). In 2011, I had the opportunity to ask Howard Roffman of Lucas Licensing how he sees the adult as a potential Star Wars player: "The adults would certainly not admit to playing with the toys. When the products are right for kids, the products are also right for adult collectors" (*The Force of Three Generations* 2011).

In Rogan's terms, "Collecting is a process where the ludic aspect is clearly present" (Rogan 1998: 47), but the possibility of play is often hidden under the guise of collecting. The challenges in approaching adult toy fandom through the lens of ludic activities, or rather *play*, include the stigmatizing labeling in association with adult consumption of any commodity or entertainment product considered classic children's media, including toys, and the fear of being categorized as an infantile and regressed adult. Even in times of the ludic turn, this fear still seems to cast a shadow over discourses around adults and toys in reference to both the toy industry and adult toy fans themselves.

Nevertheless, in the ludic age (e.g., Combs 2000), adult engagement with physical toys, such as LEGO or various character toys (dolls, action figures, or soft toys), can be more easily perceived because of what is made possible by the communicational means of digital media. The once ephemeral practices of adult toy fandom have become perceivable in coordinance with the emergence and popularity of social media, content creation platforms, and online cultures. It is no longer justifiable to categorize adult toy fandom single-handedly as a type of collecting dictated by a nostalgic attitude or "rejuvenalization." Rather, it should be viewed as an activity that is justifiably seen as a form of play that uses new technologies, media services, and so on with the same ease as it employs material objects—the toys themselves—to bond and co-create with like-minded audiences.

Cultures of Toy Collecting

To have a collection means to possess a group of objects under a connective theme. The collection comes to exist by means of its principle of organization. According to Sutton-Smith, collections are mixtures of imagination and mastery (Sutton-Smith 1986: 192). "A collection is not a collection, until someone thinks of it in those terms," says Pearce (1994: 158). According to Phoenix, multiples reinforce each other: "One action figure is just a toy, but ten figures are a collection" (Phoenix 2006: 7). The quest for a perfect collection may never be fulfilled, but the state of an unfinished collection is not satisfactory either (Kalliala 1999: 261). Completion, in fact, is central to all forms of collection, narration, and achievement, Arrasvuori, Boberg, and Korhonen assert (2010: 6).

Emerging technologies and developments of social media have enriched the cultures of collecting by making it possible to care for the collection as well as share documentation of it simultaneously. Despite increasingly digitalized environments, the traditional activities of accumulating, arranging, and displaying physical objects have survived as popular pastimes to our day. Contemporary popular culture recognizes the figure of the adult collector, as with Al McWhiggin, the rapacious toy collector of *Toy Story 2*. The plot of this toy trope unfolds around the idea that the toy cowboy character Woody is being bought by a shameless collector who does not want to play with the toy, but instead display it on a shelf. This represents to Woody's friends what death represents to us humans. After all, toys are meant to be manipulated in *play*, not only adored from a distance.

Collecting itself is a creative act (Hills 2009), but how does this act of creating manifest itself in material practices related to toys consumed by adult toy fans? What are fans who identify themselves as toy *collectors* (but who find it difficult to see their activities as play) actually doing with these objects?

Earlier research on the principles of adult play in contemporary toy cultures suggests that mature fans of toys can be organized into four groups; (1) toy collectors, (2) "toying" artists, (3) toy designers, and (4) "everyday players" (Heljakka 2013). It is in these terms possible to distinguish between collectors (who see their toy collections both as investments and as objects of research, and are interested in organizing their toys according to certain rules) and other types of players, less systematic in their collecting. The toying artists as well as toy designers often have their own toy collections but also a motivation to play with their toys by manipulating them for both professional and leisurely reasons. Finally, there are the "everyday players," whose enthusiasm toward toys may be driven by reasons beyond goal-oriented collecting or professional play. For the everyday *social object players* (Heljakka 2013), collections afford several possibilities of "toying." The once-hidden toy treasures are now proudly assembled and displayed to the world through unboxing videos, collection run-throughs, play tutorials, and published "photoplay"— imaginative, creative, and socially shared storytelling.

Adults as Toy Collectors

The history of toys is also a history of adult collecting (Lehto 1996: 6). Gröber writes that the habit of collecting toys began toward the end of the Middle Ages when craftsmen, who had formerly earned their living making objects for the use of churches, had to turn their hands to making smaller things for private patrons (in Daiken 1963: 195). As early as the sixteenth century it was in fashion for wealthy Europeans to have closets with toy collections (Nelson & Svensson 2005, 13). Hertz asserts that the mainstream of toy collecting derived from model railroading, a hobby that began to attract substantial attention as a serious adult hobby in the 1930s (Hertz 1969: 18, 27, 29).

The motivations to collect toys are manifold: In 1948, Eleanor St. George wrote that "women collect dolls for beauty, for associations, and for the memories they invoke of dolls they had in their own childhood" (St. George 1948: 1). Nostalgia that relates to childhood may also have an effect on a contemporary collector's motivations to search for toy experiences. Selim Varol, a collector of some fifteen thousand toys, says, "I think everyone is born with the hunter gatherer instinct, which essentially means you hunt for things and collect them. Maybe the experience of losing all my toys when I was twelve made this instinct stronger in me than my peers" (Deitch, de Oliveira, & Oxley 2012: 189).

The aesthetic experience of collecting is situated in the encounter of the person and the object (Rogan 1998: 42). The motivation to collect may also arise from the impulse to seek contact and to have close relationships with others (Formanek 1994: 329). In this way, it is viable to see how toys form a material resource for adult fans that is both personally significant and communally important (Hills 2009). The social aspect of toy collecting manifests in interactions in both physical and mediated playgrounds. Pushead, a graphic illustrator, says, "It's always interesting to see what people have in their collections, as true collectors rarely go out and talk about what they have" (*Super7 The Book* 2005). On the other hand, social media provide a platform for showcasing one's collection. Even though toy play of adult toy fans is often a solitary practice, it also has social dimensions just like any other activity in which knowledge about objects of fandom is accumulated. Collectors tend to form communities (Hills 2009). These are the adult toy fans who put the playthings into creative play and appropriate the objects in material, digital, and narrative practices that manifest on one hand both physically and solitarily, and on the other hand digitally and socially.

"What you have in your collection identifies your level of fandom," argues Geraghty (2014: 181). I could extrapolate by claiming that what you do with your collection defines your qualities as a player. For some, collecting is a serious form of play where time and dedication go into research of toys, intense immersion in their hyperdiegetic worlds, and perhaps also game-like precision in arranging the objects. Engaging playfully with toys with less goal-oriented motivations in mind represents another type of play.

For some, collecting means to play a game. Contest—an idea closely linked with the playing of games—is a feature of play that is frequently discussed in literature by scholars such as Huizinga (1955) and Caillois (1961). Some even go on to argue that collecting is a sport (Rogan 1998: 45). However, collecting is much more than *ludic*, a competitive game where rigid rules are followed. To instead consider adult fan practices in reference to toys as *paedic*, involving playful or less structured play instead of only a game, opens up possibilities beyond perceiving the ac-

tivity bluntly as consumption, or mere hunting and gathering. Collecting can also be seen as a productive activity that generates joy, as the
collecting and classifying of objects and experiences is a source of joy
to both adults and children (Danet & Katriel 1994): "collecting is much
more than a matter of distinction and social emulation. It is also fun and
play" (Rogan 1998: 44).

The "Wow" of Object Play in Toy Fandom

According to Hertz (1969), who writes about toy collecting in the late
sixties, the vast majority of toy collectors desire only commercially
manufactured toys. The situation has changed to a degree since, as DIY
cultures have become more prominent. However, the mass-produced
toy object is recognized as a collectible for which the "entertainment
supersystem" (Kinder 1991) creates a raison d'être and for which the toy
industry develops strategies of marketable persuasion. Limited editions
of toys either tied with transmedia-inspired content familiar from TV,
films, comics, and games or, alternatively, based on fashion or famous
brands originating in the toydom themselves are created and launched
in a fast-forward fashion.

Toys become objects of desire because of their capacity to *wow*. The
traditional toy industry continues to wow the toy audience with a constant flow of new toys, of which only a handful carry on their lives as
classics. The wowability of contemporary toys is defined by the designers
working either independently or within the toy industry, or even outside
of it. Today, the toy industry faces competition both from independent
toy makers funded by crowdsourcing campaigns and, furthermore, from
global manufacturers and marketers of lifestyle products, such as IKEA
and H&M. Still, the largest toy companies in the world thrive because
of their well-established toy brands and wide distribution networks that
operate across media. As such, the market of physical toys and games is
a fashion industry largely dependent on the success of other entertainment products and trends, and—today even more so—on the development of communicational technologies, related appliances, and digital
culture.

Hills notes that mass-market merchandising both "constrains and
enables the individual collector" (Hills 2009: n.p.). Selling collectibles,

or "things worth collecting," is of high interest to any toy company, but in order for a toy to become potentially alluring for the collecting players, clever marketing tactics need to be employed. Blom (2004) notes, for example, that Bandai (the Japanese company behind the Pokémon craze) showed great insight by choosing and employing their slogan "Gotta catch 'em all!" in marketing. Again, Ty, the company that made the Beanie Babies plush toys extremely popular among adult collectors in the 1990s, used a similar strategy by reminding the consumers: "Get them before they're gone" (Walsh 2005: 271).

Blom writes of collector's editions as items produced explicitly for collectors and *not for use* (Blom 2004). Barbie dolls are an example of toys that are frequently launched as pricey collector's editions intended for adult buyers. Coveted, limited edition series of LEGO, Masters of the Universe figures, Kenner's vintage Blythe dolls, and Star Wars toys— the biggest toy phenomenon collected by adult fans—are recognized to wow adults with toy interests and sold for hundreds, even thousands of dollars online, at sites such as eBay. Another category of collectibles paralleling mass-marketed "special editions" is artist-created toys and originally mass-produced, then artistically customized toys, which are often sold in specialized outlets such as Etsy and fan forums dedicated to designer toys. The value of these toys (also *art toys*) often depends on the limited numbers of their releases. Kidrobot, a designer toy outlet, characterizes their products as exclusive toys, which are extremely rare and collectible. When one of their toys is sold out, "it's sold out forever."

Selim Varol, a collector with a keen interest in both designer toys and other character toys such as action figures, collects original work almost exclusively from artists whom he has met personally (in Deitch, de Oliveira, & Oxley 2012: 190). Designer toys are figures with purely artistic backgrounds, either "fantasy" characters or variations on well-known, usually commercial figures. "Today they've developed into a form of subculture, the names of their creators are well-known and their collectors are in principle barely distinguishable from art collectors" (Blume 2008: n.p.).

In Blom's thinking, collector's editions represent an apotheosis of consumption, since in their case the utilitarian object is intended not to have a use, but to be placed on a shelf, skipping utilization altogether. However, collecting objects does not mean that they would be deprived of their utilitarian function. On the contrary, the collecting of artifacts equals the use of them in play.

Adult toy fans are interested in finding all kinds of toys that make them go wow, may they be antique, limited collector's editions, any mass-marketed and globally known toy brands, design-oriented art toys, or even handmade one-offs as seen on, for instance, Etsy. However, adult fans of famous toy brands or toy-types tend to be more organized and perceivably present in online spaces, for example, and the "everywhere-ness" of mass-marketed toys attracts wide fan bases.

In my research, I have been able to acquaint myself with the collections of toy designers, artists, and "everyday players." In their cabinets of wonder(ful) toys, examples of popular mass-produced toys collected in contemporary toy cultures include dolls such as newer toy-types of Blythe, Pullip, Monster High and Uglydolls, and Star Wars and Masters of the Universe action figures, and other classic character toys such as My Little Pony. The interest in toys that originated in the 1980s suggests that these characters still have their place on the lists for most collected toy-types in the 2010s. Furthermore, the culture of vinyl (designer) toys of the past decennium has proved the ongoing allure of plastic toys.

Brands and backstories communicated on toy packaging add elements to the toy's possible wowability. However, contrary to Matt Hills's argument about the lessening importance of toys' physical properties and an increasing interest in the narrative worlds framing them (2009), there is again a possibility to see more acknowledgment and appreciation addressed to the raw materials of contemporary toys: with new toy design—especially designer-created toys—more value is accrued to the raw materials and the innovative approaches in terms of using materials other than plastic, such as textiles, metal, or wood. At the same time new narratives not necessarily familiar from transmedia contexts emerge. The contemporary toy itself may become, because of this, the starting point for brand-new storyworlds in the hands or imaginations of either the toy designer or the adult fan.

The collecting activity extends to the packaging (and "unboxing") of toys as well, and toy collectors use a similar terminology to what is used for collected items in general: MIB means that the artifact is in good condition, in other words "mint" in its original box, NRFB means "never removed from box," and MWMT means "mint with mint tags."

Visual artist Geo Fuchs explains: "As soon as the figures are unpacked their value drops. There are collectors who never open the boxes, never allow them to see the light of day" (Heusermann 2008: n.p.). The term "MWMT" illustrates how even a toy's tag (or booklet) including the character's name and hints to a backstory, or personality description, may become valuable. MWMT has been important for toys such as Ty's Beanie Babies, as their tags include the name and birthday of the toy character—significant details for collectors interested in the hierarchy and release time of the toy among other characters, but also for the collector interested in the possibilities to anthropomorphize the toy character by, for example, developing its personality further.

Geraghty suggests that both the production and collecting of toys in the late twentieth and early twenty-first centuries would be seen as a new form of cultural capital (2006: 210). What remains unexamined in many studies on adult use of toys so far is the ways in which adult fans are being creative in their play with this cultural capital in more ways than just collecting. Besides the emotional and cognitive investment, such as "the passion for acquisition and preservation" and "the learning of prices, rarities, variants, histories," which Hills (2009: n.p.) acknowledges as relevant for a collector (of toys), I would like to add the acts of creation to the main principles needed to be recognized as important for contemporary adult toy fandom.

The Flow of Creative Play

Having duplicates of a collected toy allows the collector to employ one of the artifacts *in play* and one in pristine NRFB condition. According to Robbins, who writes about collecting Star Wars merchandise, this idea of buying one for play or display and the other one for "collecting" purposes sealed in its original package (Robbins 2006: 198) opens up the possibility of differentiating between a playful and casual form and a more serious and goal-oriented attitude toward toy collecting. For some collectors, it is of interest if the toy has been manipulated by human hands after the original sales transaction, or if the object has been outside of the box, but still considered to be in good condition.

Following Csikszentmihalyi's (1975) ideas, collectors frequently experience a holistic, autotelic sensation, "flow." Flow is derived during play acts with toys, in the manipulation of physical objects besides collecting—play patterns such as customization of toys, creating stories of toys, and cosplaying with them. The sensuous aspects of collecting—the handling, touching, playing with, and caring for the collection, as noted by Danet and Katriel (1994: 228–29)—are important for the adult toy fan. The tactile qualities of toys thus contribute to their capacity to invite their fans to playful engagement, and to successfully dissolve the toy's wow into the experience of flow.

As explained by Belk and Wallendorf (1994: 245), the collection invites one to play with imagination as it allows the collector to play with multiple images of the self and multiple images of others. Today, even toy brands may serve as a tool for consumers' performances of identity (Hills 2009). Belk and Wallendorf (1994: 322) claim that collections are used not only to express aspects of one's own direct experiences, but also to express fantasies about the self. When employed, for instance, in "avatarial" play, character toys also serve not only as extensions of our bodily selves, but as the physical extensions of our fantasies and thus as our toyified mini-mes (Heljakka 2012).

According to Sihvonen (2009: 225), the combination of realistic and fantastical elements is typical of children's play but also of the collecting hobbies of adults. A lot of adult engagement with physical toys also has to do with the imagination: fantasies about toy characters' personalities and their adventures in both physical and imagined spaces have to do with the mature fans' capacity to continue or completely replay what has been informed in a toy's backstory in reference to its marketing or transmedially communicated meanings.

In many ways, especially character toys such as dolls, action figures, and plush toys (i.e., *toys with a face*) will acquire personalities and may even be anthropomorphized as companions in play. More extremely, an individual toy will be given an even more significant role and presence in the intimacy of the home, or when taken out on excursions as "travelling toys" or in the name of toy tourism (Heljakka 2013). To some collectors, dolls may even function as child substitutes, notes Holz (1982: 3).

Adults most often like to keep their toys away from the "messy paws of children" and, if part of families, dedicate space for and distinguish their toys from the other playthings in the home. The notion of the *Wunderkammer* lives on in today's toy collections with the exception that spaces beyond closets and glass cabinets are dedicated to both singularly and collectively displayed playthings. Toys of adult fans reside as eye candy in homes and work spaces and as parts of either temporary or permanent scenes as displayed in dioramas or dollhouses. Toys' role as eye candy still describes only one of their possible functions: as my studies with adult toy fans have shown, toys are rarely left on the shelf. Instead, after acquiring the toy (or multiples thereof), the adult may engage in many types of playful interactions.

Articulation, poseability, and possible "huggability" of character toys (dolls, action figures, and soft toys) are considered key affordances as adult toy fans "re-create the toy store" in their homes by aesthetic arrangement. A collection does not need to be complete in order to be displayed. Instead, toy fans actively arrange and rearrange their toys in displays or specially built and decorated dioramas. A toy may also gain value from this act of manipulation. For precious dolls, for example, the manipulation of them may (in the mind of the collector) give these artifacts added value, which contributes to a certain *glow* around the toy.

Fans' DIY crafting, such as customization practices with character toys and the creation of dioramas, dollhouses, dresses, and props for play scenarios, including the reappropriation of everyday materials, has become evident with the rise of popularity in fan practices on social media and represents notable directions of creative play practices of recent times. Moreover, it is interesting to see what role technology has played for contemporary toy fandom employing physical toys. Mobile devices and digital cameras enable and inspire *photoplay* (photographing toys; see, for example, Heljakka 2012) and make the sharing of toy experiences, creativity, and fandom more perceivable in social media. Toy portraiture (both professional and amateur making of toyish portraits of popular icons) and the "replaying" of popular narratives with toys has become increasingly notable and present on blogs, Instagram, and Etsy, among other sites. Furthermore, digitally and socially shared play calls out for others to join in, as when the ritual of *unboxing* a toy is first documented and then shared on YouTube, inviting both children and adults to toy fandom through information, entertainment, and interaction. At the same time, the importance of encounters with other toy fans is undeniable: coming together at cons, cosplaying with and "as" toys with others, and meeting toy designers are essential facets of adult toy fandom even in the digitally mediated ludic age.

Conclusion: Aspects of Play in Adult Toy Fandom

In conclusion, what has been formerly addressed as the activity of *collecting* toys can be seen as a form of play. The adult toy fan in his or her playing activity comes to value meanings that the toy has (1) toward the player, (2) in relation to other fans, (3) in terms of preserving and continuing the lifecycle of a toy, toy-type, or series, (4) as a monetarily valued artifact, and (5) as an artifact that affords play patterns in relation to creative practices: aesthetic appreciation, accumulation, studying, manipulating, organizing, displaying, and sharing of the toy collection.

Although adults still represent a minority among toy consumers in the world, interest toward toys at mature age has risen. It is important to note that collecting is play activity that explains to a certain extent the phenomenon of adult toy fandom, but does not provide an exhaustive explanation of it. Nevertheless, it is in the hands of the collectors, how toy culture is preserved, and considered in terms of wider cultural interest and appreciation.

As Geraghty points out, "super collectors" contribute to the transforming status of collectibles by making them "objects of cultural history, transforming the notion of the museum and what should be preserved there" (Geraghty 2014: 8). One example is European collector Selim Varol, whose collaboration with artists Daniel and Geo Fuchs has contributed to some of the toys in his collection now attracting visitors to art museums as features of both photographic play and installations (Heusermann 2008).

"A work of art draws it's [*sic*] aura from its uniqueness, but a metamorphosed, everyday object may borrow its aura from age and authenticity" (Rogan 1998: 43). In adult toy fandom, the objects of play come to gain an auratic glow exactly in this way: from the physical manipulation and continued stories that circulate the playthings in conversations and communications between fans.

What researchers should consider in the future is the possibility of long-term object relations of adult toy fans: based on my assumptions, the life cycles of relations with toys may be longer in adult toy fandom because of the dedication given and investments made for either singular toys or even larger collections. The strategies for exiting toy fandom are largely underresearched. According to my findings, many adult fans have the destinies of their toys well planned for the future: consideration is given to where the toy(s) will go when it is time for the fan to move into other playgrounds.

Adults as a recognized target group for toys may have more importance in the near future as generations who have had access to a multitude of toys in their childhood mature. To continue dismissing the adult toy enthusiast's willingness to invest more and more devotion on play experiences as delivered by all kinds of physical toys—whether purposefully targeted as rare collector's items, art toys, or simply exactly the same toys children are now playing with—would not be wise for the toy industry, nor for any researcher interested in toy cultures.

Toys invite us to play and suggest play performances. Acquiring toys or creating a toy collection is an individual project with multifaceted motivations linked with either ludic goals of completion or paedic pleasures gained in reference to creative play—customizing, costuming, creating displays, or staging scenes with toys and then photoplaying with them. Fandom for toys is a matter of not only celebrating collecting enslaved by the entertainment supersystem, but also socially engaging with the creative players of today—the toy designers, artists, and everyday players. A toy fan, in the truest sense, is not only a collector of objects either, but a creative player of materials and storyworlds, and a fan of anyone who dreams them up.

WORKS CITED

Arrasvuori, J, Boberg, M, & Korhonen, H 2010, "Understanding playfulness: an overview of the revised play experience (PLEX) framework," in *Proceedings of the 7th Design & Emotion Conference*, Chicago.

Belk, RW & Wallendorf, M 1994, "Of mice and men: gender identity in collecting," in SM Pearce (ed.), *Interpreting objects and collections*, Routledge, New York.

Blom, P 2004, *To have and to hold: an intimate history of collectors and collecting*, Woodstock, New York.

Blume, E 2008, "Daniel & Geo Fuchs in Toyland," in D & G Fuchs, *Toygiants* (exhibition catalogue), Silver edition, Gingko Press, Berkeley.

Caillois, R 1961, *Man, play and games*, University of Illinois Press, Urbana.

Combs, JE 2000, *Play world: the emergence of the new ludenic age*, Praeger, Westport, CT.

Csikszentmihalyi, M 1975, *Beyond boredom and anxiety: the experience of play in work and games*, Jossey-Bass, San Francisco.

Daiken, L 1963, *Children's toys throughout the ages*, Spring Books, London.

Danet, B & Katriel, T 1994, "No two alike: play and aesthetics in collecting," in SM Pearce (ed.), *Interpreting objects and collections*, Routledge, New York.

Deitch, J, de Oliveira, N, & Oxley, N 2012, "Interview with Selim Varol," in *Art & Toys Collection Selim Varol*, Me Collector Room (exhibition catalogue), Stiftung Olbricht.

The Force of Three Generations 2011, interview with Howard Roffman, Licensing Academy at Brand Licensing Europe, October 20, London.

Formanek, R 1994, "Why they collect: collectors reveal their motivations," in SM Pearce (ed.), *Interpreting objects and collections*, Routledge, New York.

Geraghty, L 2006, "Aging toys and players: fan identity and cultural capital," in MW Kapell & JS Lawrence, *Finding the force of the Star Wars franchise: fans, merchandise, and critics*, Peter Lang, New York.

Geraghty, L 2014, *Cult collectors: nostalgia, fandom and collecting popular culture*, Routledge, New York.

Heljakka, K 2012, "Aren't you a doll! Toying with avatars in digital playgrounds," *Journal of Gaming and Virtual Worlds*, 4(2): 153–70.

Heljakka, K 2013, *Principles of adult play(fulness) in contemporary toy cultures: from wow to flow to glow*, PhD dissertation, Aalto University.

Hertz, LH 1969, *The toy collector*, Funk & Wagnalls, New York.

Heusermann, A 2008, "Nice to meet you," in D & G Fuchs, *Toygiants* (exhibition catalogue), Silver edition, Gingko Press, Berkeley.

Hills, M 2009, "Interview with Dr. Matt Hills," pt. 2, doctorwhotoys.net.

Holz, L 1982, *Developing your doll collection, for enjoyment and investment*, Crown, New York.

Huizinga, J 1955, *Homo Ludens: a study of the play element in culture*, Beacon, Boston.

Kalliala, M 1999, *Enkeliprinsessa ja itsari liukumäessä: Leikkikulttuuri ja yhteiskunnan muutos* [The angel princess and suicide in a slide: play culture and change in society], Gaudeamus Yliopistokustannus University Press, Finland.

Kidrobot, www.kidrobot.com.

Kinder, M 1991, *Playing with power in movies, television and video games: from Muppet Babies to Teenage Mutant Ninja Turtles*, University of California Press, Berkeley.

Lehto, M-L 1996, *Huwikaluja lapsille: Vanhat suomalaiset lelut* [Amusing things for children: old Finnish toys], Tammi, Hämeenlinna.

Lord, P & Miller, C 2014, *The Lego Movie*, Warner Bros, Village Roadshow Pictures, RatPac-Dune Entertainment, The Lego Group, Vertigo Entertainment, Lin Pictures, Warner Animation Group, Warner Bros. Animation.

Nelson, A & Svensson, K 2005, *Barn och leksaker i lek och lärande* [Children and toys in play and learning], Liber, Stockholm.

Pearce, SM 1994, "The urge to collect," in SM Pearce (ed.), *Interpreting objects and collections*, Routledge, New York.

Phoenix, W 2006, *Plastic culture: how Japanese toys conquered the world*, Kodansha International, Tokyo.

Robbins, A 2006, "Controlled scarcity: the making of a mass produced collectible," in I Vartanian (ed.), *Full vinyl: the subversive art of designer toys*, HarperCollins, New York.

Rogan, B 1998, "On collecting as play, creativity and aesthetic practice," *Etnofoor* 11(1): 40–55.

Sihvonen, T 2009, *Players unleashed! Modding the Sims and the culture of gaming*, PhD dissertation, University of Turku.

St. George, E 1948, *The dolls of yesterday: dolls and doll collecting in Europe and America during the past 200 years*, Charles Scribner's Sons, New York.

Super7 The Book 2005, 5.1, Super7Media Inc., Gingko Press, Berkeley.

Sutton-Smith, B 1986, *Toys as culture*, Gardner Press, New York.

Walsh, T 2005, *Timeless toys: classic toys and the playmakers who created them*, Andrews McMeel, Kansas City.

PART II

Spaces of Fandom

6

Loving Music

Listeners, Entertainments, and the Origins of Music Fandom in
Nineteenth-Century America

DANIEL CAVICCHI

After having attended the opera four nights in a row in 1884, twenty-
four-year-old Lucy Lowell chastised herself by writing in her diary,
"I suppose it can't be good for a person to go to things that excite her
so that she can't fix her mind on anything for days afterwards" (Lowell 1884: April 19).[1] Lowell was the daughter of Judge John Lowell and
a member of one of the first families of Boston. While many young
women of her social standing spent their time attracting appropriate
male suitors by acquiring rudimentary skills in singing and piano playing or self-consciously showing themselves off in the boxes of the city's
growing number of concert halls and theaters, Lucy eschewed such
social intrigue and instead became truly obsessed with onstage sound
and spectacle. She attended performances by almost every touring
opera and symphonic star that passed through Boston, every rehearsal
and concert of the new Boston Symphony Orchestra, and many local
festivals, band concerts, and musical theater productions. In the seven
volumes of her diary, which she wrote between 1880 and 1888, she wrote
page after page of description about her experiences of hearing music.
She only mechanically mentioned attending singing lessons on Mondays
and Thursdays; she sometimes referred to expectations about her own
socially mandated performances with disdain. "Had a dinner party for
Miss Tweedy. Mabel + Hattie were the other girls, John Howard Messers,
G. D. Chapin, L. Pierce + R. Loug, gentlemen," she wrote in 1880. "I had
to sing in eve'g. Bah!" (Lowell 1880: January 28).

Lowell was not alone; since the mid-nineteenth century, increasing numbers of young people in America's rapidly growing cities had

formed a unique and sustained attachment to the world of public concerts. People had listened to music before the 1850s, of course; indeed, concertgoing was an activity that a member of the elite in the United States had had the leisure to indulge in at least since the American Revolution. But before midcentury, attending a concert more often than not meant attending a special event that was as much social as musical, an opportunity for people in a community to come together in a ritual space. During the 1850s, increasing numbers of national tours by professional virtuosos, supported by new systems of concert management, enabled people to develop new ways of acting musically that were centered less on amateur performance among friends in the privacy of one's home than on regularly witnessing professional performers in public halls. Young "music lovers," like Lowell, constituted a group that, for the first time in American history, was able to shape its musical experiences entirely around commercial entertainments like concerts, theater, and public exhibitions.

In this chapter, I will outline the ways in which the practices of music lovers not only transformed America's musical life, setting the ground for a late nineteenth-century music business based on listening technologies like the phonograph, but also provided models for cultural consumption that would be adopted and extended in twentieth-century mass culture, particularly by those we today call "fans." For several years, I have studied the diaries, scrapbooks, and letters of people living in the nineteenth-century urban United States in order to learn more about how they understood music. Scattered widely in state and private archives, many of the materials have not been studied as evidence of musical life. Together, however, they offer powerful evidence that, while fandom is often characterized in media studies as a product of mass consumer culture in the twentieth century, the basic practices associated with fandom—idealized connection with a star, strong feelings of memory and nostalgia, use of collecting to develop a sense of self, for example—precede the development of electronic "mass communication" technologies. Music loving suggests that fandom's origins may have less to do with diffuse and private consumption through modern electronic media than with shared modes of participation in older systems of commodified leisure.

Reframing Musical Experience

Cities in the United States had slightly different trajectories for developing new entertainment markets and commodifying musical experience, based on the idiosyncrasies of geographical location, demographics, and religious influences. Boston, for instance, first created markets around making music, including sheet music publishing and instruments sales, thanks to a Puritan prohibition on theater that was not repealed until 1797 and whose effects lingered long after. Overall, however, markets focused on hearing music developed in most eastern cities by the 1850s. Pleasure gardens, theaters and concert halls, taverns, museum stages, and minstrel shows all increased in number between 1840 and 1870 in cities like New York, Philadelphia, Boston, Charleston, and New Orleans. Concert programs, once one-sided announcements of song titles, became, after the Civil War, multipage, stapled documents with advertisements for soap, shoes, corsets, and pianos, alongside the usual list of songs to be performed. Performers themselves became commodities for sale, advertised in circulars and managed by entrepreneurs who carefully manipulated artists' repertoires, schedules, and appearances (Gottschalk 1881: 122).

Along with musical entertainment came a shift in understanding about what music was. Before 1800, music had primarily existed either as a private amateur pastime, made among friends and family, or as an elaborate public ritual, either in street parades or at church services. One could love it, but its embeddedness in social functions made more likely that one loved that which the music enabled. But commodification encouraged an attachment to music's own singular effects. Concerts and public performances, especially, segmented musical experience into distinct phases of production (composition), distribution (performance), and consumption (listening). Understanding musical experience as a thing that one could anonymously purchase and consume must have been an extraordinary idea for people used to having to painstakingly make sounds, through singing or playing, in order to have "music" in the first place. The purchase of instruments and music, the lessons, the rehearsals, the mistakes, the labor—all that was separated out, given to others, and made invisible, so that one could, if one so chose, simply engage in the act of hearing, of audiencing. Not only could people indulge in regular, timed, and relatively reliable music performances but also, by "just listening" to those performances, they were able to encounter music anew.

One part of the appeal of the seemingly endless stream of virtuosos at midcentury, for example, was the extent to which each performer surpassed expectations about what was possible in musical performance. As a critic wrote about Edward Seguin's first appearance in the opera *Andie; or, The Love Test* at Boston's Tremont Theater in 1838, "The moment Seguin opened his mouth, one universal gape of astonishment infected all, such was the wonder produced by his magnificent organ" (quoted in Clapp 1968 [1853]: 376). William Cullen Bryant noted that concerts could even surprise the most jaded of audience members, as happened during a concert by pianist Leopold De Meyer in 1846:

> A veteran teacher of music in Buffalo, famous for being hard to be pleased by any public musical entertainment, found himself unable to sit still during the first piece played by De Meyer, but rose, in the fullness of his delight, and continued standing. When the music ceased, he ran to him and shook both of his hands, again and again, with most uncomfortable energy. At the end of the next performance he sprang again on the platform and hugged the artist so rapturously that the room rang with laughter. (Bryant & Voss 1975: 438)

An important consequence of such encounters, for listeners, was a new and heightened awareness of the personal qualities of performers. In a time when romantic ideas of a core individual self were taking hold and, in romantic relationships, people were striving to achieve an intense "sharing of selfhood" (McMahon 1998: 66), the act of loving music often idealized identification with performers, similar to the communion nineteenth-century romance readers often felt with characters and with authors. Especially after repeated encounters with the same performer, music lovers often began to feel a strong and uniquely charged connection to that performer's unchanging, "inner" self. In fact, the word "star" signified this attitude. First used as theater slang in the 1820s (*Oxford English Dictionary* 2005) and often applied after 1850 to designate the new "system" of theater production that focused on traveling virtuosos rather than local stock troupes, a star was not just an actor or a singer but a unique person whose presence transcended any one role, burning brightly through the artificial masks of the stage.

Many stars of the nineteenth century—Ole Bull, Anna Thillon, Anna Seguin, Marta Alboni—inspired music lovers to understand their listening experiences as part of a continuing and reciprocal relationship with a specific performer. However, the first music star to be widely associated with such feelings of personal connection was Jenny Lind, the Swedish opera singer who contracted with impresario P. T. Barnum in 1850 to tour the United States. Lind had been an opera star in Europe in the late 1840s, famous for her roles, but in her concert tour she was promoted by Barnum as "simply Jenny." In fact, Barnum shrewdly hyped her simplicity, innocence, and humility as a contrast to both the alleged immorality of the theater and her own otherworldly singing talent. As historian John Dizikes put it, "People searched her appearance and especially her face for clues to that inner person [. . .] she would begin hesitantly, nervously, and then: her talent would come to the rescue, her voice, almost as though it existed independently of the body which contained it, would gush out in crystalline splendor and convert a precarious moment into an ecstatic one" (1993: 133).

In diaries and letters, Lind's audience members emphasize her personal character. William Hoffman, a clerk who was in the crowd awaiting Lind's arrival in New York in 1850 and who showed up several times with the crowds outside Castle Garden, hoping to get inside but stymied by the high ticket prices, nevertheless repeatedly copied newspaper reports about her personal qualities in his diary, concluding that "her great powers of benevolence speak for her the most enviable qualities of soul that any being ever could possess" (1850: September 21). Henry Southworth, a twenty-year-old New York City store clerk who, like Hoffman, participated in the welcoming crowds and sought to get a glimpse of her at her hotel, described his experience of hearing her sing in terms of her character: "I cannot express my delight and wonder in words, she is indeed a wonderful woman, she sings with perfect ear and is at home, in everything she does" (1850: September 13). Lind even seemed to heighten auditors' awareness of their own selves. Caroline B. White, in response to hearing Jenny Lind in Boston, wrote, "I have heard her! The wonderful Jenny! And though language itself has been exhausted in her praise—it seems to me too much cannot be said, such a volume of such sounds—singing, clear melodious—can any one listen to them and not feel one's aspirations glow warmer, loftier, holier, than ever before?" (1851: November 22).

Aside from being "star-struck," music lovers were also attracted by the sheer novelty and power of auditory experience. Part of the excitement of attending concert halls was experiencing music with a mass of people; diarists often commented on the fullness (or emptiness) of the house at a performance and of the roar of the crowd at the finish of pieces or in demand of an encore. Likewise, music lovers were enamored of hearing someone confidently project his or her voice or the sound of his or her instrument into a large auditorium, a unique and memorable acoustic situation. Even business directories for cities like Boston and New York touted the magnificence of their halls for audiences. For example, one Boston directory for 1860–61 glowingly described the city's Music Hall, built just six years earlier, in terms of its structural characteristics, including its ceiling "45 feet above the upper balcony," the seventeen unique, semicircular windows "that light the hall by day," the hall's capacity of fifteen hundred people on the floor, and the fact that "the whole has been constructed with special reference to the science of acoustics—a consideration of the utmost importance in a building intended as a music hall" (*Sketches and Business Directory of Boston* 1861: 109).

Concertgoers themselves were careful to note in their diaries the qualities of the halls they had attended, from Lucy Buckminster Emerson Lowell (1845: October 29) noting the "intense perfume" of the straw-filled seats in Boston's new Howard Athenaeum to William Hoffman (1850: November 19), who, after finally attending a Jenny Lind concert, wrote in his diary mostly about the "size and finish" of New York's Tripler Hall. Indeed, music lovers learned the acoustic properties of various halls so as to position themselves to best hear the music coming from the stage. Joseph Sill was thrilled when he was able to obtain a box for a John Braham performance, where, as he commented, "we were so close to him that his softest tones were heard" (1840: December 2). In contrast, Lucy Lowell was none too pleased when she was forced to sit in the balcony of Boston's Apollo Theater where "the orchestra + chorus sounded all blurred" (Lowell 1884: April 30). Henry Van Dyke, writing in 1909, described the ways in which an imagined music lover thought of his seat as a secret treasure, chosen explicitly for its acoustic properties:

The Lover of Music had come to his favorite seat. It was in the front row of the balcony, just where the curve reaches its outermost point, and, like a rounded headland, meets the unbroken flow of the long-rolling, invisible waves of rhythmical sound. The value of that chosen place did not seem to be known to the world, else there would have been a higher price demanded for the privilege of occupying it. (1909: 5–6)

Again and again, listeners talked about hearing a performance as an astonishingly physical experience. Music lovers' profound emotional attachment to stars in part came from attending fully to the physical presence of the virtuosos who performed onstage—from the power and quality of their voices projected from the stage to the dexterity of their bodies as they manipulated instruments. In response to opera, especially, music lovers often expressed overwhelming visceral ecstasy, imagining music "filling their souls" to the point of losing composure, something that was experienced as excitingly dangerous and quite cathartic within the behavioral strictures of middle-class Victorian culture (Rabinowitz 1993). Walt Whitman, in *Leaves of Grass*, drawing on his own fascination with New York opera in the 1840s, described music listening as a kind of sexual communion: "A tenor large and fresh as the creation fills me / The orbic flex of his mouth is pouring and filling me full." Music "convulses" him, "whirls" him, "throbs" him, "sails" him, and "wrenches unnamable ardors" from him. He is "licked," "exposed," "cut," and "squeezed" by waves of orchestral sound (1982 [1855]: 54–55).

Reorganizing Music and Daily Life

Having such an intense attachment to concert performances was sometimes difficult for music lovers, since the desire for musical sound could be satisfied only periodically. Even then, concerts were finite events, and the memories of musical experiences often seemed to recede and disappear, especially after only one hearing. How could one keep heard music—and the feelings created by it—alive over time?

The longing for music was satisfied, in part, by music lovers seeking out as many musical performances as possible. The number of musical experiences one could have in any given week depended on many factors, including the number of theaters and halls in the vicinity, the length of the concert season (typically October to May), and, of course, the availability of cash needed to purchase tickets or subscriptions. But many music lovers, even without money, found ways to experience music. Walt Whitman, when not at the opera, lingered outside churches and halls, listening to the music from the street. Others, like clerk Nathaniel Beekley (1849), sought out music four or more nights a week during Philadelphia's concert season and, in addition, attended both Catholic and Protestant church services on Sundays in order to hear music.

Repeated hearings of the same piece could help to fix the music in one's mind. In the 1850s, it was customary for touring performers to complete a run of shows in the places they visited as long as audiences kept coming, so as to accommodate all who wished to see them and to increase profits. And it was common in the antebellum era for audiences to attend multiple (and often all) performances in the same run, especially if the music was complex enough to merit such attention (Preston 1993: 59–61). George Templeton Strong, for example, regularly attended every performance of pieces that he liked, commenting that "I never can satisfy myself about music till I have heard it more than once and have ruminated on it, marked, learned, and inwardly digested it" (Lawrence 1988: 318). Music lovers engaged in these practices enthusiastically and often lamented in their diaries that they could not hear a piece more often than a run of performances allowed. As Lucy Lowell pined about Wagner's *Ring Cycle*, "O dear how I should like to hear it all over again + again + go to Beyreuth! I wish I could spend next winter in Vienna + go every night anything of Wagner's is given" (Lowell 1884: April 16).

Another way to keep the music alive between performances was to literally reproduce the music through amateur performance. While concertgoing cultivated behaviors and values that were different than those held by amateur performers, the two expressions of musicality tended to reinforce one another: concertgoers often turned to the piano to reproduce the pieces they had heard, and amateur performers found themselves drawn, as audience members, to the virtuosity of the professional stage. This was a phenomenon that instrument and sheet music entrepreneurs knew well. Ads for sheet music began appearing in concert programs as early as the 1850s, touting "full translations" of pieces heard that night in concert. In 1849, the ever-popular Germania Society even distributed the sheet music to one of their original pieces, arranged for piano, to the women in their audiences, with the implication that they would use the music to remember the performance. It was appropriately called "Ladies Souvenir Polka" (Newman 2002: 163).

When not reliving musical experiences in some way, many music lovers worked to extend their audience experiences beyond the concert hall. Those caught up in "Lindmania," for example, vied to capture glimpses of Lind not simply in performance but also outside of performance, arriving in a steamship at the wharf, standing on the balcony of her hotel room, traveling through the streets in her carriage. If they had the resources, music lovers would also travel to sites associated with various performers and composers. The "grand tour" of Europe, a requisite coming-of-age event for wealthy Americans in the 1800s, often turned into a much-saved-for pilgrimage for music lovers. Alice Drake, a young piano student from Colorado, made a voyage to Weimar, Germany, in the 1890s and promptly sought out the house of the recently deceased Franz Liszt, quizzing the house's caretaker, and playing on Liszt's pianos, a thrill she recounted by writing in her diary, "I never tho't I would ever do that!!" (1897: October 26).

In addition to such pilgrimages, music lovers used their personal diaries and journals to extend their musical experiences. Music lovers had, fairly early on, created a new descriptive vocabulary to articulate the feelings they had while concertgoing. Older generations of American audiences had typically experienced music with a mild pleasure. "It was very satisfactory" and "we had a pleasant time" were common phrases for describing concert experiences. In fact, before 1850, people tended to describe their musical experiences with the phrase "we had some music," blandly lumping any sort of musical activity into a descriptive category not worthy of further comment, like the weather. But concertgoers after the 1850s often described their musical experiences with far more personal specificity.

Diaries in the nineteenth century were often used as memory devices, helping writers to remember whom they had met at parties or from whom they had received gifts, for instance, so that they might reciprocate in the future. In terms of music, however, the function was not so much social as psychological, satisfying a longing for more. Some music lovers attempted to fix on paper every moment, every feeling, during a concert to the extent that their diaries were not so much mnemonic tools as stand-ins, indices, for the performances themselves. Thus Lowell could write in her diary after the last concert of the Boston Symphony in 1886, "I feel so desolate at thinking that this is the last, that I shall dwell on each detail, to lengthen out the enjoyment" (1886: May 29).

In all, such recording encouraged self-conscious knowledge and comparison of how it felt to hear and see various performances and performers over time. One could, in effect, "collect" and arrange concerts just as one would collect and arrange phonograph records. Sheet music binders, personal collections of sheet music arranged and bound in leather, were a corollary to this sort of activity; binders—often with the collector's name embossed on the front cover and handwritten marginalia that evaluate or describe the feelings evoked by the pieces—clearly served as a summary of an individual's taste and experience in music. With the growth of the music press at midcentury, including regular reviews and the use of lithography and photography for circulating images of musical stars, scrapbooks supplanted diaries and sheet music binders as music lovers' most useful tool, able to contain descriptive writing, clippings of reviews, and images.

Redefining Normal Participation

What were the consequences of this activity? Music lovers were well aware that their engagement with music was different from that of other audience members. Simply by becoming regular attendees of musical performances of specific forms, or by particular groups, or in particular concert halls and churches, music lovers began to distinguish themselves from others in the audience through their uniquely focused and comparative engagement with the music. Indeed, criticism of early music loving emphasizes the strangeness and potential pathology involved in a singular focus on a performer or performance. William Clapp, for instance, described the mania created by ballerina Fanny Elssler's visit to Boston in 1840 as a disease that trumped every other event in the city:

> It was "Elssler" on every side. She was dreamed of, talked of, and idolized; and some wag having circulated a report that "Fanny" would take

an airing in her barouche, quite a gathering took place on Tremont Street. Boston was not alone in this ovation, for the ladies from Boston to Philadelphia, all wore Elssler cuffs, made of velvet with bright buttons. In every store window articles were displayed flavoring of the mania. Elssler boot-jacks, Elssler bread, etc. etc., were to be seen, showing how violent was the attack of Fannyelsslermaniaphobia. (1968 [1853]: 368–89)

A Boston satirist calling himself "Asmodeus" wrote a pamphlet that thoroughly lambasted the citizens of Boston for their extraordinary enthusiasm about Lind's 1850 concerts:

> For two long weeks, did I hear nought in my rambles, by night or day, in barber shops and work shops, in beer shops and stables, in hotels and private domicils, from Beacon Street to the Black Sea, all the cry was, Jenny Lind and Barnum, Barnum and Jenny Lind! Soon I met my ancient and respected friend Pearce, so full of madness and music that he rushed through the streets with the fearful velocity of an escaped locomotive.
> Hold worthy friend, quoth I, whither so fast?
> He gazed wildly at me for a moment, then shouted as he run—Jenny Lind and Barnum! Barnum and Jenny Lind! (1850: 12)

Clapp's use of the fake medical term "Fannyelsslermaniaphobia" was not unfounded; the activities of music lovers had earlier been recognized by the medical establishment as a pathology called "musicomania." Though it had been known for centuries that music could produce powerful psychological and physical effects, a phenomenon that was used for treatment by medieval physicians (Gouk 2004), in the nineteenth century the effects of music acquired potentially negative connotations. The association of music with "mania" first appeared in the United States in 1833 in the *New Dictionary of Medical Science and Literature*, which described the condition as "a variety of monomania in which the passion for music is carried to such an extent as to derange the intellectual faculties" (Dunglison 1833: 64). Musicomania fell out of use by 1900, and it is not clear that anyone was actually treated for the disease, but during the nineteenth century, the term found its way into everyday discourse as an alternative name for music loving, and references to the condition were sprinkled throughout novels and essays between 1850 and 1870.

The term was even employed by music lovers themselves to jokingly refer to their own concert hopping.

If joking was one response to music loving, a more ominous response was an increasing association of the excessive behaviors of music loving with the divisive caricatures of class politics at midcentury. Depictions of music lovers in the press often featured disorder, with an emphasis on crowd violence, lack of control, and metaphors of savagery or animalism, characterizations that fit with growing middle-class disdain for the social chaos created by immigration and urbanization. As early as 1843, William Cullen Bryant described an audience in such terms, saying, "The concert room was crowded with people clinging to each other like bees when they swarm, and the whole affair seemed an outbreak of popular enthusiasm" (Bryant & Voss 1975: 438). Boston Brahmin Caroline Healey Dall described her experience of a Jenny Lind concert as if she had just visited the cramped quarters of an inner-city tenement:

> No one could conceive a more horrible crowd. Dark windows looked into the offices, and in no way could fresh air be obtained. [...] When I heard the cry for water, air, open the windows &c.—who come as from desperate dying men—in choked voices—I felt what must come. I made several calm attempts to get out, but there was no possible means of egress, and a disappointed crowd were storming without. [...] We saw bonnets torn off—women trampled on, men falling in tiers of five or six. I have seen crowds before, but I never imagined what a suffocating crowd would be. (1850: October 30)

In response—and borrowing from ascendant ideologies of romanticism, as well as "refinement"—idealist middle-class reformers introduced a new way to "love" music in the 1860s. Instead of passionate attachment to a performance, they proposed what might be called a "classical" appreciation: ritualized, reverent, intellectual attention to the unfolding of a composition or work. If antebellum music loving proposed focusing audience attention on performance as a way to challenge the informal socializing of theater culture, this new form of engagement proposed to refine music loving even further by removing the spontaneity and showmanship of live performance that might lead to obsession or spontaneous emotional display. Those promoting this reform found it necessary in a culture that seemingly had been taken over by the excessive spectacles of mass commercialism. True appreciation of art was not about purchasing tickets to experience virtuosic curiosities but rather about encountering the timeless beauty of a composer's work.

Social historians have noted that such a "disciplining of spectatorship," as John Kasson put it, is emblematic of postbellum ideologies of genteel refinement and taste and of the emergence of powerful class divisions in the United States after 1850 (Butsch 2000; Kasson 1990; Levine 1988; McConachie 1992). That this reorientation was based on new class associations is apparent in the changing nature of audience criticism. If the initial criticism of music loving was simply about being too invested in music, by the close of the century accounts of audiences were more often about being too invested in the wrong ways and for the wrong reasons. William Althorp, a classical music reformer and critic, in a long essay in the *Atlantic Monthly* in 1879, specifically compared the approaches of "refined" musicians and "ordinary" music lovers:

> A musician, after listening to a great work, does not, as a rule, care to have it immediately repeated. [. . .] But when the ordinary music-lover hears a piece of music that particularly pleases him, he generally wishes to hear it over again; he will listen to it day in and day out, until he gets thoroughly sick of it, and never wishes to hear it more. He sucks and sucks at his musical orange until there is nothing left but the dry peel, and then throws it away. (1879: 150)

Antebellum criticisms of Elssler or Lind "mania" identified temporarily excessive musical behavior as wildly inexplicable and in a way that left "normal" musical behavior unstated; it was simply understood how one should behave. But in the late 1870s, Althorp was careful to associate excessive musical behavior with lack of discipline and education and to provide his readers with an alternative position, all through metaphorical language that provided cues to social class. He associated the musician with connoisseurship, deference, and judgment, and the music lover with sensualism, immediate gratification, and boorishness. Such distinctions would shape discourses of musical audiences for the next century.

Music Lovers as Fans

"Fan" is a term that came into widespread use only in the early twentieth century, when mass consumerism, based on new systems of marketing and communications, was transforming the industrial West. Media technology not only created a temporal and spatial separation between performers and audiences in the market, but also gave audiences the ability to create affective engagement with performers or products by enabling people to experience, repeat, and study such "texts" in the intimacy of their home, and incorporate them into the fabric of their daily life. That fan studies has become a growing field in media studies is not surprising; the rise of fandom as a self-aware consumer movement (exemplified by fan "clubs" in the 1920s and 1930s) seems to coincide with the hegemony of media entertainment, especially film and music.

However, given the murky etymology and meaning of the term "fan" (Cavicchi 1998: 38–39; Hills 2002: ix–xv), it may be more useful, in thinking about the history of fandom, to start not with the emergence of the descriptive term "fan" but rather with the existing patterns of behavior that the historically contingent term was meant to describe. As I have argued elsewhere (Cavicchi 1998: 4–6; 2004), there is evidence of fan-like practices among people participating in the commodification of urban leisure in the industrial West before 1900, including the readers of mass-produced books, opera lovers, urban theatergoers, and the members of fraternal baseball clubs. Music culture, in particular, is useful for beginning to open up the history of fandom because it was at the forefront of both twentieth-century media technology (in the form of both recording and broadcasting) and nineteenth-century urban entertainment (in the form of commodified performance and mass-published texts) and thus provides linkages between what typically have been perceived as different eras of audience behavior.

Just as fans of the twentieth century were faced with new relationships—with performers, with musical texts, and with each other—created by the advent of recording and broadcasting, music lovers of the nineteenth century wrestled with the shift of such relationships in the development of commercialized music culture. In urban America during the 1840s and 1850s, musical experience became no longer something shared only by a congregation or community in the local rituals of a church service, dance ball, or military muster; it became also a tangible product, made by those who were musically gifted, and easily exhibited and purchased by anyone with cash. The commodification of music in concerts particularly highlighted the process of exchange between performer and audience and the ways in which hearing could become a form of consumption.

Like mass communication technologies, nineteenth-century commercial concerts brought extraordinary access to music for many Americans. However, structurally, such access in both eras was based on an audience anonymity and ephemerality that limited music's ability to signify deeply shared values and experiences. Fans and music lovers represent those who have refused to accept the anonymity and limited involvement of audiences necessitated by the large-scale commercialization of musical experience; they both instead seek to creatively imbue their participation in musical life with a lasting personal connection and depth of feeling. The ways in which modern fans create significant affective involvement in popular culture—including close listening, Internet discussion, pilgrimages, and collecting, among other activities—have numerous parallels in the culture of nineteenth-century music lovers. When the star system unmoored performers from localities and exaggerated their professional skills in the 1840s, music lovers sought to understand stars as authentic people with whom they had an intimate bond. While most people returned to their daily lives after concerts ended, music lovers actively extended their audience role beyond the purchased frame of performance by seeking out music in churches and homes, by attempting to see stars in the street, by making pilgrimages to significant sites, by performing their favorite pieces on home instruments, by collecting sheet music, and by meticulously recording descriptions of their listening experiences.

Not only are individual behaviors parallel, but the functions of those behaviors in their respective contexts are also similar. Scholars have argued that modern fandom is always in some ways an "improper identity" (Hills 2002: xii), often interpreted as a "pathology" (Jensen 1992). According to the frameworks of exchange in the new market economy, music-loving behaviors were likewise abnormal; music lovers did not abide by the equation of a ticket for a performance but sought rather to go beyond and around it, much like the alternative "shunpikes" that had turned up in the 1830s, snaking illegally around toll gates on many states' newly built roadways. Not surprisingly, critiques of music loving were based on lovers' thwarting of the norms of the market: music lovers' rejections of the frameworks of capitalism meant that they had to be sick, suffering from a mania, or unaware of correct social behavior—that is, without "taste."

I don't wish to discount the significant transformations wrought by the mass media in the twentieth century. But as Jonathan Sterne (2003) has shown, even revolutionary inventions like the phonograph became possible in the first place only thanks to previous shifts in the ideological frameworks of science, social class, and the self. In the same way, twentieth-century music fandom became possible with previous changes in the norms and practices of participants in the world of commodified music. Music lovers, as witnesses to the beginnings of the commercialization of popular culture in the nineteenth century, were among the first to assume the role of the audience-consumer and to create the strategies many use today for understanding the world of stars, merchandizing, and spectacle.

NOTE

1 Use of unpublished archival materials in this essay courtesy of the American Antiquarian Society, the Historical Society of Pennsylvania, the Massachusetts Historical Society, the New-York Historical Society, and the Library of the School of Music, Yale University.

WORKS CITED

Althorp, W 1879, "Musicians and music lovers," *Atlantic Monthly* 43(256): 145–53.

Asmodeus 1850, *The Jenny Lind mania in Boston; or, a sequel to Barnum's Parnassus*, Boston.

Beekley, N 1849, diary, octavo vol. 1, American Antiquarian Society, Worcester, MA.

Bryant, WC II & Voss, TG (eds.) 1975, *Letters of William Cullen Bryant*, vol. 2, Fordham University Press, New York.

Butsch, R 2000, *The making of American audiences: from stage to television, 1750–1990*, Cambridge University Press, Cambridge.

Cavicchi, D 1998, *Tramps like us: music and meaning among Springsteen fans*, Oxford University, New York.

Cavicchi, D 2004, "Fans and fan clubs," in G Cross et al. (eds.), *Encyclopedia of recreation and leisure in America*, vol. 1, Scribner's, New York.

Clapp, WE Jr. 1968 [1853], *A record of the Boston stage*, Benjamin Blom, New York.

Dall, CH 1849–51, journal, Caroline Healey Dall papers, Massachusetts Historical Society, Boston.

Dizikes, J 1993, *Opera in America: a cultural history*, Yale University Press, New Haven, CT.

Drake, A 1897, travel diary, Special Collections, mss. 315, Library of the School of Music, Yale University, New Haven, CT.

Dunglison, R 1833, *New dictionary of medical science and literature*, C Bowen, Boston.

Gottschalk, LM 1881, *Notes of a pianist*, JB Lippincott, Philadelphia.

Gouk, P 2004, "Raising spirits and restoring souls: early modern medical explanations for music's effects," in V Erlmann (ed.), *Hearing cultures: essays on sound, listening, and modernity*, Berg, London.

Hills, M 2002, *Fan cultures*, Routledge, New York.

Hoffman, W 1850, diary, BV Hoffman, William, New-York Historical Society, New York.

Jensen, J 1992, "Fandom as pathology: the consequences of characterization," in LA Lewis (ed.), *The adoring audience: fan culture and popular media*, Routledge, New York.

Kasson, JF 1990, *Rudeness and civility: manners in nineteenth-century America*, Hill & Wang, New York.

Lawrence, VB (ed.) 1988, *Strong on music: the New York music scene in the days of George Templeton Strong*. Vol. 1, Resonances, 1836–49, University of Chicago Press, Chicago.

Levine, L 1988, *Highbrow/lowbrow: the emergence of cultural hierarchy in America*, Harvard University Press, Cambridge, MA.

Lowell, L 1880, diary, Lucy Lowell diaries, Massachusetts Historical Society, Boston.

Lowell, L 1884, diary, Lucy Lowell diaries, Massachusetts Historical Society, Boston.

Lowell, L 1886, diary, Lucy Lowell diaries, Massachusetts Historical Society, Boston.

Lowell, LBE 1845, diary, Lucy Lowell diaries, Massachusetts Historical Society, Boston.

McConachie, B 1992, *Melodramatic formations: American theatre and society, 1820–1870*, University of Iowa Press, Iowa City.

McMahon, L 1998, "'While our souls together blend': narrating a romantic readership in the early Republic," in PN Stearns & J Lewis (eds.), *An emotional history of the United States*, New York University Press, New York.

Newman, N 2002, *Good music for a free people: The Germania Musical Society and transatlantic musical culture of the mid-nineteenth century*, PhD dissertation, Brown University.

Oxford English Dictionary 2005, online ed., Oxford University Press.

Preston, K 1993, *Opera on the road: traveling opera troupes in the United States, 1825–60*, University of Illinois Press, Urbana.

Rabinowitz, P 1993, "'With our own dominant passions': Gottschalk, gender, and the power of listening," *Nineteenth-Century Music* 16: 242–52.

Sill, J 1840, diary, collection #600, vol. 2, Historical Society of Pennsylvania, Philadelphia.

Sketches and business directory of Boston, 1860–61 1861, Damrell & Moore and George Coolidge, Boston.

Southworth, H 1850, diary, BV Southworth, Henry, New-York Historical Society, New York.

Sterne J 2003, *The audible past: culture origins of sound reproduction*, Duke University Press, Durham, NC.

Van Dyke, H 1909, *The music lover*, Moffat, Yard & Company, New York.

White, CB 1851, Caroline Barrett White papers, octavo vol. 3, American Antiquarian Society, Worcester, MA.

Whitman, W 1982 [1855], *Leaves of grass*, in J Kaplan (ed.), *Walt Whitman: complete poetry and collected prose*, Library of America, New York.

7

Resisting Technology in Music Fandom

Nostalgia, Authenticity, and Kate Bush's "Before the Dawn"

LUCY BENNETT

A striking development within fandom has been the ascent of digital technology, with it being "empowering and disempowering, blurring the lines between producers and consumers, creating symbiotic relationships between powerful corporations and individual fans, and giving rise to new forms of cultural production" (Pearson 2010: 84). The use of hand-held technology in particular has spurred changing notions of what it means to experience a live event for many fans, a prospect that has also been fostered by the ability to follow an event remotely, yet still feel a sense of "being there" (Bennett 2012b, 2014). This landscape of in situ versus mediated audienceship has been prevalent across different forms of popular culture, from sports events during which fans tweet updates during play (Hutchins & Rowe 2013) to broadcasts of live theater productions in the cinema (Barker 2013). However, this chapter focuses specifically on live music concerts and how technology and fandom are currently converging within them. For many music fans, attending a live concert is a significant event within which they can enact, experience, and display the meanings and values of their fandom (Cavicchi 1998), resulting in the convergence of a personal and collective experience that unfolds live. However, the widespread use of technology has fostered a striking shaping of live music experiences for many attendees, with bright screens held aloft in the air—some in an effort to preserve moments of the live event, others to connect with fans non–physically present.

While fan studies scholarship has developed in tandem with digital technology, exploring the plethora of activities and practices within, this chapter will take a different approach by examining how some musicians and fans purposely reject technology and the implications that arise from this. It will explore the nuances that occur when technology use is rendered absent from a live music setting, or, in other words, when "media refusal" by fans—"a conscious disavowal that involves the recognition that non-use signifies something socially or politically meaningful" (Portwood-Stacer 2012: 1042)—takes place. To achieve this, this study is undertaken through the lens of British musician Kate Bush—a singer-songwriter who has released nine original albums since 1978. Staging her first live concerts since her only tour, which took place in 1979, Kate Bush's 2014 London live show residency "Before the Dawn" consisted of twenty-two dates, which ran from August 26 to October 1, 2014. This highly anticipated sold-out residency was preempted with an online personal request to fans with the musician stating:

> I have a request for all of you who are coming to the shows: We have purposefully chosen an intimate theatre setting rather than a large venue or stadium. It would mean a great deal to me if you would please refrain from taking photos or filming during the shows. I very much want to have contact with you as an audience, not with iphones, ipads or cameras. I know it's a lot to ask but it would allow us to all share in the experience together. Looking forward to seeing you there.
> Respectfully yours, Kate. (Katebush.com)

This chapter will thus be based on a survey with Kate Bush fans, working to unravel and analyze their articulations of experiences without smartphones/technology/cameras during the show and questioning how this guided absence of devices impacted on their immersion in the event. It will argue that in terms of negotiating technology in a contemporary live setting, it is the object of fandom that guides and *manufactures* the definition of what an "authentic" experience constitutes, which also mirrors the core values and taste of the particular fan culture. In this sense, personal requests from musical artists (such as Kate Bush) surrounding the nonuse of technology during concerts can be successful and unifying for some fans (who may remember a pretechnological concert experience) as they direct and act as a marker of a nostalgic, more "authentic" experience that positions technological behavior as disruptive and tasteless. As this study will argue, this nostalgic behavior can be powerfully underscored by a sense of *Heimat* (Sandvoss 2005), an imaginary sense of home and belonging at the core of fandom that reemphasizes notions of taste and value, and works to mark those who do not comply as inauthentic fans.

This study, then, will advance our understandings of the relations between music fandom and technology, demonstrating how, in a contemporary digital vista, nontechnological modes of engagement can be practiced by some fan cultures and be anchored to meanings surrounding authenticity, nostalgia, taste, and belonging. In other words, understanding fan attitudes toward purposeful technological rejection can deliver us a more nuanced understanding of contemporary fandom in general, and give more light to this frequently overlooked practice in a landscape dominated by technology and social media.

The Shaping of Authenticity: Music Fandom and Technology

The use of technology during live popular music concerts is a growing activity (Chesher 2007) having a profound impact on the experiences of many audience members. As Neil Strauss (n.p.) observed at a concert in 1998, "everybody was holding up their hands, and here and there I could see guys holding up their cell phones, playing the music for someone else." Since then, mobile technology has developed further, with Internet and text connections allowing stronger connections with online audiences, alongside smartphones and tablets permitting audience members to film and share moments of the concerts. However, this process, and its impact on the meanings of what an "authentic" live music experience entails for musicians and fans, can be disparate. Whereas some artists, such as U2 and R.E.M., have encouraged mobile phone use as an integral participatory part of the show, others actively discourage it. For example, the Yeah Yeah Yeahs asked audience members, "Please do not watch the show through a screen on your smart device/camera. Put that shit away as a courtesy to the person behind you and to Nick, Karen and Brian. Much love and many thanks! Yeah Yeah Yeahs" (Hann 2013). This debate has continued with greater urgency, and in the domain of theater, with actor Benedict Cumberbatch informing fans after a performance of *Hamlet* in London in August 2015 that what he deems as an "authentic" experience for him *and* audience members could be achieved only through the absence of technology:

I can see red lights in the auditorium. [. . .] It's mortifying, there's nothing less supportive or enjoyable as an actor on stage to experience that, and I can't give you what I want to give you which is a live performance that you will remember hopefully in your minds and brains whether it's good, bad or indifferent, rather than on your phones. (Hewis 2015)

As Burland and Pitts point out, "live listening is made distinctive by its listeners, as each person's connection with the event is shaped by expectation, prior experiences, mood and concentration" (2014: 1). This "shaping" of connection with a live event, then, is what I unpack further in this chapter, most specifically around the notion of authenticity, which is an important element of fandom (Hills 2002) and, as I have demonstrated, can differ between music fan cultures in terms of what is deemed as "authentic" modes of engagement. I will argue that live listening is made distinctive not only by its listeners, but also through the guidance and direction of the musician/object of fandom who can foster *and* mirror what determines the "authentic" values of the fan culture and anchor them to a certain lens. Thus, while technology pervades much activity in fandom, it is not always embraced, but can be refused in powerful ways. For example, as I have shown with my study (2012a) of an R.E.M. fan group that sought to recapture a pre-Internet experience of listening to and purchasing a new album as an "ultimate first listen," some music fans have drawn on nostalgia and rejected technology to shape what an authentic musical experience means and involves, and reclaim what they perceive has been lost. As Boym argues, nostalgia is a "longing for a place but is actually a yearning for a different time [. . . it is] a rebellion against the modern idea of time" (2001: 98). The yearning within nostalgia has often been a central thread of identity for some fan cultures—for example, Ross Hagen found in his study of Black metal fandom that nostalgia for the origins of the genre in Norway served "as a touchstone for fans' sense of subcultural identity as its musical style and fan base expanded and diversified" (2014: 223–24). Cornel Sandvoss also explored similar themes in terms of the imaginary sense of home and belonging within fandom, a "physical, emotional and ideological space" that he describes as *Heimat* (2005: 64). This space offers fans a "sense of security and stability" and can thus be particularly resonant in terms of nostalgic practices within fandom. Nostalgia, then, as Nathan Hunt argues in his analysis of film fan cultures, can be approached as a "mode of interpretation," with the memory narratives circulating in an attempt to "fix or reiterate histories of production as essential contexts for the contemporary reading" (2011: 98).

As I will now move on to explore, Kate Bush's request for an absence of technology during "Before the Dawn" manufactured and underlined nostalgic understandings of what an authentic music and concert experience meant for her and her fans. It positioned the concert as a *Heimatic* space, working in an effort to reinvoke their yearnings for, and sense of home and belonging within, the pre-Internet setting of her previous 1979 tour and "fixing it" as an "essential context" for their concert participation.

Method

In August 2015 I designed an anonymous online survey for attendees of "Before the Dawn" that would address these issues and posted an invitation to participate on Homeground and Unforumzed (both unofficial fan forums) and the Twitter and Facebook networks of Fish People, another unofficial Kate Bush community. The survey was both quantitative and qualitative and received 227 responses. Among the respondents, 59.6 percent identified themselves as male, 40.0 percent as female, and 0.4 percent as other. The survey reached a fairly widespread audience in terms of age, but was more focused on the middle-aged group: there were no respondents aged eighteen or under, 9.7 percent were aged between nineteen and twenty-nine, and 31.3 percent were between thirty and forty-four. The largest amount of respondents, 57.7 percent, were aged between forty-five and sixty-five, and 1.3 percent were older than sixty-six. Respondents came from eighteen different countries, with the United States and United Kingdom dominating. However, the limitations of an online fan study of this nature should be considered. The sample may not have been representative in many ways (for example, reaching only online fans), as the survey and chapter instead aim to uncover a range of responses from specific Kate Bush fans who were in attendance at the concerts.

"A Sea of iPhones and a Sky of iPads": Responses to Kate Bush's No-Technology Request

The first section of the survey that this chapter will focus on is the responses from attendees toward Bush's request, which are encompassed in Table 7.1.

TABLE 7.1. Themes across responses to the survey question, "What were your thoughts upon reading Kate's request?"

Theme	Frequency	Percentage
Agreement with request	183	40.8
Phones/cameras as disruptive	90	20.0
Emphasis on it being a personal request	28	6.2
Will be more immersed in the show now	25	5.6
Respected request	17	3.8
Disappointment	15	3.3
Inability to preserve moments	13	2.9
Typical of Kate Bush	9	2.0
More theatrical than normal concert	9	2.0
Loyalty as a fan	7	1.6
Would not have taken photos/videos anyway	7	1.6
Relief from others' behavior	6	1.3
Efforts of control from Kate	6	1.3
Kate wanting to connect more	5	1.1
People have paid for tickets	5	1.1
Recordings are low quality anyway	4	0.9
Relief from own behavior	4	0.9
Unusual	3	0.7
Will make the show stay special	3	0.7
Kate Bush as publicity shy	3	0.7
Would rather rely on memories	1	0.2
Smartphones weren't around last tour	1	0.2
Kate's stage fright	1	0.2
Kate has done this to sell more DVDs	1	0.2
Inability to connect with those not there	1	0.2
Okay if official DVD released	1	0.2
Traveled a long way for the show	1	0.2
Total	449	100.0

As evident from Table 7.1, agreement was the predominant theme, which arose 183 times across all responses. Within this, the most overwhelming viewpoint centered on phones and cameras at concerts being an unwelcome and intrusive distraction:

> About bloody time—the sea of illuminated screens had been putting me off live music for years.

> I was ecstatic when she requested this. I had been dreading trying to dodge the inevitable tablets and phones that would be in front of me. As I'm only small I was really worried I wouldn't be able to see.

> I thought: "That makes sense—I want a shared experience too." I felt gratitude.

> Relief! I was glad she made the request. I was flying in from the USA to see KT live (a dream come true). I was fearing it would be a Sea of iPhones and a Sky of iPads.

As these responses demonstrate, prior to these concerts some of these fans had not experienced a sense of belonging at other events, with them being "put off live music for years," expressing "fear" and "worry" how they would fit into the technological landscape otherwise common at contemporary live music events. Thus, for some fans, a relief was inherent in the sense of *Heimat* fostered within this space by Bush's request, which offered a "sense of security and stability" and a "profound sense of belonging" that also powerfully generated "emotional warmth" (Sandvoss 2005: 64) around these notions of home: "It was so emotional. A lot of people around me were also in tears, as I was. It wasn't mass hysteria, it was like welcoming a most beloved and long lost friend home. It was a perfect moment of pure joy."

Ninety respondents also articulated technology as intrusive and unwelcome during live concerts, with the repeated term "sea" being used to describe these devices, conjuring an image of inescapable waves across an audience that could possibly wield the prospect of (metaphorically) drowning an attendee. This reaction toward technology may be unsurprising based on respondents being largely older and having experienced concerts without these tools. However, this vantage point is still revealing and can expose the sharp differences within experiences of pre- and post-Internet/digital camera device development and use, and how the meanings and values surrounding authentic engagement with a live concert may differ between age groups and fan cultures. For example, some responses emphasized that during the last Kate Bush tour, in 1979, these forms of technology did not exist, and would not have intruded into the performance. Thus, this sense of returning to a pre-Internet/technological setting and recapturing a nostalgic experience was articulated as a source of motivation and inspiration for some fans, and mirrored by the musician herself:

> I thought her request made perfect sense considering she had not performed live shows in 35 years and it had always been widely reported that she suffered from crippling stage fright. 35 years ago, we didn't have iPhones, iPads or YouTube. To return to the stage after this length of time apart from it and to not only be faced with thousands of faces staring back at you, but also, potentially, thousands of smart phones, iPads and digital cameras held aloft could be quite alarming.

> Didn't want to watch the amazing show through a little 5 inch screen [. . .] what's the point of that. Saw Kate in 1979 in Bristol way before mobile phones etc existed but can still remember it all now.

In these instances, technology use was framed as a new intrusion that did not appear during the 1979 tour, and was similarly not welcome now, a notion that could be viewed as an "essential context" (Hunt 2011: 98) for fostering a sense of *Heimat* at the concerts. This belief was further supported by the theme that attendees would now be more immersed in the show without it, which appeared twenty-five times, demonstrating how, for these respondents, the absence of technology offered a stronger avenue of connection to the event. This fostering of *Heimat*, then, also corresponds to Matt Hills's observations surrounding cult fandom in that "when approaching the fan audience as a target market, the fan culture's values of authenticity must be mirrored [. . .] thus reconstructing the fan culture as a niche market which is isolated from the 'mainstream'" (2002: 12). Bush's request for the concert attendees to "allow us to all share in the experience together," without technology discursively worked to manufacture a sense of "authenticity" at these events that would be reflected in the values of her fan culture—a prospect perhaps partly dictated by the older age of the majority of the fans who were likely to remember pre-Internet concertgoing experiences. This request then worked to reconstruct the concerts as "special," isolated from the mainstream concertgoing experience and the technologies wielded within, conferring a higher and distinct level of "taste" within the construction of these nontechnological habits.

However, although the majority agreed with Bush's stance toward technological tools during the concerts, fifteen respondents highlighted some concerns and disappointment—a prospect that emphasizes the complicated nature of fandom and that even though these individuals may have an affective tie toward Kate Bush (in the sense that they are fans and may feel a strong affinity toward her), not all fans respond in the way that the object of fandom, or fellow fans, may anticipate or hope for. For example, for some individuals the request held meaning not of greater immersion or connection, but rather of disappointment. Some emphasized the money they had paid for the tickets and others expressed sadness at the subsequent inability to preserve moments they were rendered with:

> I could understand her request, but I've waited >30 years to see her and I paid a lot of money [. . .] I couldn't see an issue with discrete photography.

> Initially I was disappointed. This was a once in a lifetime experience (that had cost a lot of money!) and I wanted to be able to have photographs to remember it. However, being a huge Kate fan, I could only respect her wishes.

In this response, a tension between what the fan and the fan's object of fandom wanted is highlighted. These conflicting desires and needs were wielded by the loyalty within the fans, who, viewing it a necessary part of their fandom, felt it a duty to respect the musician's wishes, putting their own desires secondary. However, others did not negotiate her request in the same way and viewed it as an indicator of Kate Bush being too controlling through her wanting to have direction over all outputs of the concerts:

> Characteristic of her as a relatively private person as well as amusement as it was direct proof of how she desires total control over all aspects of her work and she effectively sealed that by issuing that statement.

This response raises important issues surrounding the elements of control from the artist that are inherent within requests of this nature, where audience members are essentially directed to behave in a certain way, regardless of their views and desires. As these survey responses have demonstrated, these requests can be successful and resonant since they strikingly play on issues of meaning and fan loyalty, fostering the notion that a "true" fan would share the values of the object of fandom's request and would desire what is perceived as an "authentic" and immersed experience. In line with this, some respondents emphasized the weight of importance on the request being a personal one from Kate, which added greater significance and fostered feelings of loyalty: "I respected her request and knew that most true Kate fans would do the same."

Thus, notions of authenticity are a key thread and measure of fandom within this landscape, with *true fans* complying with Kate's requests and being able to recognize what an "authentic" experience of the show entails. The next section will move on to unravel the actual experiences of these fans at the concerts, examining the extent to which abstinence from technology use during the show affected their immersion in, and "authentic" experience of, the event, and how these values were imbued with categorizations of fandom.

"When the Lights Were Out It Was Completely Dark": Experiencing the Absence of Technology

To explore how "Before the Dawn" attendees articulated and experienced the request for abstinence from technology use during the shows, and consequently how this impacted on them, the survey asked respondents to describe how the lack of these technological devices during the concerts affected their experience. As evident from Table 7.2, the predominant theme within responses was that the absence of technology at the concerts had greatly improved their concert experience:

> [It was] better. Authentic, connected and fully present.

> It felt so much more "in the moment" and personal.

TABLE 7.2. Themes in response to the question, "In what ways, if any, did your experience of attending a 'Before the Dawn' concert feel different without technology?"

Theme	Frequency	Percentage
The experience was better/improved without technology	157	39.4
Felt more immersed	146	36.7
The experience was no different	59	14.8
I did not have to think about taking pictures	18	4.5
It was more of a shared experience	13	3.3
Wanted to preserve a moment but could not	4	1.0
Felt less involved	1	0.3
Total	398	100.0

These fans described this occurrence as making their experience "authentic" and "personal," with some considering the process as being very "liberating." Appearing commonly was the theme of feeling more immersed in the concert due to the lack of technological devices. This was particularly felt by some as a striking improvement on their experience, with the absence of bright glowing lights of screens being noticeably significant:

> I didn't feel distracted by flashes or screens. I didn't feel like I had to duck out of the way to avoid other people's cameras. I felt totally engrossed with what was happening on stage.

> It helped create a special atmosphere. When the lights were out it was completely dark. You didn't see phone light everywhere.

> I was able to enjoy what was going on on-stage and on-stage only rather than being distracted by selfie loving attention seekers.

> At one point [...] I turned round and saw not a single smart phone light. I felt that the adenine were all better connected to each other and also savouring every moment—knowing we might never see it again, certainly not on the tube home via our smart phone screen!

Thus, these responses conjure a sense that, in line with Kate Bush's direction, the "authentic" experience of the live show involved being engaged fully in the dark, with the absence of the bright screen lights enabling them to maintain concentration on the event. The lack of technology was also cited by some as making it more of a shared experience, with strangers and attendees conversing and connecting with each other more, rather than looking at their devices:

> I do not attend many live concerts now [...] so I only remember shows pre-personal technology. However, complete strangers were talking to each other in London [...] so something very unique happened.

> I've gone to shows for over 35 years, so not using the smartphone was no big deal. Plus the interaction I had with complete strangers was unforgettable.

For some, their abstinence worked to give a stronger sense of unity and collaboration, working together with their object of fandom to enhance the experience of the event, and preserve it as a more special experience that they had to be physically there "in the room" to partake in:

> It felt like a more unique and special experience that was shared with just those people in the room at the time as opposed to the whole of the internet like a normal gig.

> It was great to see how much undivided attention Kate got—and how the audience seemed to come together as a unity that had sworn some kind of pact: No we are not gonna film this.

Another respondent summarized the nostalgic elements threaded throughout these experiences:

Felt like the good old days. Before Twitter and Facebook, I never felt the need to give a running commentary on any show I was at.

In this sense, Kate Bush's request acted as a controlling mechanism through which "liberation" and "unity" were achieved for some fans, pulling themselves away from contemporary technological life and back toward "the good old days"—a prospect that may imbue the sense of home and belonging at the core of fandom and *Heimat*. This shared retreat into a pre-Internet age worked powerfully to deliver a sense of a more "authentic" experience for some fans, and conversely mark the fandom of those who did not comply. Most respondents did not witness people use their phones or cameras during the shows, but those who did were framed as lesser fans:

I saw one person try and very quickly told not to and everyone looked and thought they were disrespectful.

When requested the announcement was cheered and applauded some non fans videoed and when hissed we expected it to happen and I believe most of those doing it were not real fans.

I went to Before the Dawn 3 times and only saw 1 person breaking her request and staff immediately responded. The whole audience appeared to appreciate her request. I know of instances at other concerts where audience members helped police the request by telling offenders to stop what they were doing.

As Sandvoss pointed out, "the idea of *Heimat* is based upon notions of security and emotional warmth, but *Heimat* also always involves an evaluation and categorization of others" (2005: 64). This "textual and social discrimination articulated through taste" (2005: 65) is evident here: notions of *true* and *real* fandom circulate strongly within these responses, anchored closely to the sense of authenticity generated by Bush's request, with those who broke these values deemed to be inauthentic fans, lacking taste and contesting the nostalgic sense of *Heimat* that was being fostered. As Bourdieu explains, taste and the habitus "enables an intelligible and necessary relation to be established between practices and a situation, the meaning of which is produced by the habitus through categories of perception and appreciation that are themselves produced by an observable social condition" (1984: 101). In this sense, taste is a "forced choice" with the habitus working to be an important "form of communication and identity building [. . .] forming a sense of who we are and believe ourselves to be" (Sandvoss 2005: 34). In essence, this is the keystone element within this example of Kate Bush fandom, with the rejection of technology at the concerts being a "forced choice" that successfully worked to enable a sense of *Heimat* and taste that reflected the values at the core of her fan culture, allowing many of the fans in attendance to powerfully enact who they "believed themselves to be."

Conclusion

This chapter has demonstrated that the interplay between live music fandom and technology remains an area worthy of exploration, since, contrary to widespread behavior and technological advancement in music listening, both can sit uneasily with one another in some fan cultures that have a middle-aged demographic. As I have highlighted here, these music fans can be directed successfully to negotiate and resist technology use during live concerts, working to transform this abstinence into a *Heimatic* unifying force, resulting in what is perceived by the majority as a more immersive and "authentic" experience: "like all symbols, authenticity is interpreted by individuals and mediated through interaction with significant others" (Williams 2006:189). It is these "significant others" that are important here though, with not only the majority of fans partaking in this act, but also the object of fandom, who plays a key element in directing and manufacturing this performance of nostalgic resistance, consequently allowing fans to collectively enact a "sense of [their] place" (Bourdieu 1984: 466) that powerfully underlines the key values of taste in their fan culture. Ultimately, the use of technology by fans in live music spaces can be manufactured as a powerful marker of taste and belonging, with these values, of course, changing between different fan cultures and musicians.

These findings lead to further questions and considerations. For example, the quite complex relationship within music fandom toward technology use during live shows and changing attitudes toward it by musicians needs to be considered. How do fans respond to the different approaches by musicians toward the use of technological tools during live concerts? When these differences of views occur, how do fans situate themselves and negotiate them? In addition, the impact of this manufacturing of authenticity surrounding technology and the restriction it may wield upon fans should be explored further. As Matt Hills argues, there can be a "contradictory limit" to the power within fandom in that when it views its own agenda through the lens of the media (and, as I would argue, the object of fandom), it can lose "any possibility of creative textual mutation and thus becomes locked into its own rigidly maintained sets of values, authenticities, textual hierarchies and continuities" (2002: 13). I would also argue that this prospect of rigidity can be especially resonant with regard to nostalgia and the attempted fostering of a *sense* of another time that depends on specific rules being adhered to. More research along the lines of that I have conducted here that requests fans to articulate their experiences of live music spaces, and how the values, authenticities, and taste within may become "rigidly locked" by specific fan cultures and musicians, is required. Consequently, how these notions impact upon the identity of fans in live music spaces that contest these "locks" and do not demonstrate the accepted forms of taste displayed by the fan culture and object of fandom, and, likewise, do not *feel* the sense of *Heimat* during the event, should also be further examined.

WORKS CITED

Barker, M 2013, *Live to your local cinema: the remarkable rise of livecasting*, Basingstoke, Palgrave.

Bennett, L 2012a, "Music fandom online: R.E.M. fans in pursuit of the ultimate first listen," *New Media & Society* 14(5): 748–63.

Bennett, L 2012b, "Patterns of listening through social media: online fan engagement with the live music experience," *Social Semiotics* 22(5): 545–57.

Bennett, L 2014, "Texting and tweeting at live music concerts: flow, fandom and connecting with other audiences through mobile phone technology," in K Burland & S Pitts (eds.), *Coughing and clapping: investigating audience experience*, Ashgate, Surrey.

Bourdieu, P 1984, *Distinction: a social critique of the judgement of taste*, Routledge, London.

Boym, S 2001, *The future of nostalgia*, Basic Books, New York.

Burland, K & Pitts, S 2014, "Prelude," in K Burland & S Pitts (eds.), *Coughing and clapping: investigating audience experience*, Ashgate, Surrey.

Cavicchi, D 1998, *Tramps like us: music & meaning among Springsteen fans*, Oxford University Press, New York.

Chesher, C 2007, "Becoming the Milky Way: mobile phones and actor networks at a U2 concert," *Continuum* 21(2): 217–25.

Hagen, R 2014, "Kvlt-er than thou: power, suspicion, and nostalgia within Black metal fandom," in L Duits, K Zwaan, & S Reijnders (eds.), *The Ashgate research companion to fan cultures*, Ashgate, Surrey.

Hann, M 2013, "Yeah Yeah Yeahs launch pre-emptive strike at phone-wielding gig-goers," *Guardian Blog*, April 10, www.guardian.co.uk.

Hewis, B 2015, "Benedict Cumberbatch urges fans to switch off cameras and phones," *What's On Stage*, August 9, www.whatsonstage.com.

Hills, M 2002, *Fan cultures*, Routledge, London.

Hunt, N 2011, "Nostalgic [re]membering: film fan cultures and the affective reiteration of popular film histories," *Image and Narrative* 12(2): 96–117.

Hutchins, B & Rowe, D (eds.) 2013, *Digital media sport: technology, power, and culture in the network society*, Routledge, New York.

Pearson, R 2010, "Fandom in the digital era," *Popular Communication* 8(1): 84–95.

Portwood-Stacer, L 2012, "Media refusal and conspicuous non-consumption: the performative and political dimensions of Facebook abstention," *New Media & Society* 15(7): 1041–57.

Sandvoss, C 2005, *Fans: the mirror of consumption*, Polity, Cambridge.

Strauss, N 1998, "A concert communion with cell phones; press 1 to share song, 2 for encore, 3 for diversion, 4 to schmooze," *New York Times*, December 9, www.nytimes.com.

Williams, JP 2006, "Authentic identities: straightedge subculture, music, and the Internet," *Journal of Contemporary Ethnography* 35: 173–200.

8

I Scream Therefore I Fan?

Music Audiences and Affective Citizenship

MARK DUFFETT

It's my theory that rock'n'roll happens between fans and
stars, rather than listeners and musicians—that you have
to be a screaming teenager, at least in your heart, to know
what's going on.
—Willis (2011: 77)

Screaming has long been regarded, in the mainstream media, as the
sine qua non of celebrity fandom. Pop music represents one of the
obvious places where it is heard in the public sphere. Not all fans
scream, but those who do are not doubted *as fans* since they express
their position on the "knowing field" of fandom in an emotional
way.[1] As scholars, however, we rarely if ever discuss exclamations
made by fans, instead focusing on their creativity, autonomy, and collective intelligence. Screaming is actively underexamined. It forms
an awkward remainder, something that too easily justifies negative
stereotypes. To borrow a phrase from Katherine Larsen's (2014: 1) discussion of Janice Radway's classic work on romance novel reading, in
some quarters screaming represents a "culturally unsanctioned [fan]
activity." The fact that screaming has become most associated with
celebrity fandom and pop music reflects their perceived status as sites
of emotional excess—sites that remain comparatively unexamined by
aca-fans, shamed by more "mature" fandoms, and lambasted by mass
culture critics.[2] Rather than disappearing in an era of social media,
however, screaming has been amplified and reconstituted.[3] Dedicated
audiences express nonverbal utterances more regularly than researchers have discussed.

Taking popular music as its focus, what follows will develop in two sections. The first considers why screaming has been framed as a problematic activity. The second argues that fan screaming can alternatively be understood as a form of enunciative productivity, an indicator of totemic interest, and a mode of affective citizenship. My discussion will develop in a way that also includes issues of gender.

One might argue that any academic attention to screaming is doomed to chase media misdirection and prioritize a stereotypical fan practice at the expense of others that are more obviously political or transformative. Certainly, repeated media attention to screaming reifies fandom; it forgets other moments in fans' lives. Rather than dismiss screaming, however, I think that we should recognize it as a practice worthy of more analysis. Larsen (2014: 1) has requested that we put the fans back into fans studies. Academic attention to screaming has that potential.

Misunderstanding Screaming

BBC4 recently broadcast a television documentary called *When Pop Ruled My Life* designed to offer insights on music fandom. When it came to screaming, the British broadcaster interviewed fans. Lillian Adams, who loved the Beatles in the 1960s, said that she did not know why she screamed. Taking such claims as the last word, reviewers found an opportunity to stereotype pop fandom. A journalist writing in the *Independent*, for example, said "Beatlemaniac Lillian Adams was one of the screamers (others wet themselves, allegedly)" (Newall 2015: n.p.). This section examines what is problematic about such widespread perceptions. Unfortunately, the legacy of mass culture thinking has shaped assumptions both inside and outside of academia, framing "screaming fans" as victims of commercial manipulation who have lost their critical faculties and can produce only blank noise that has no other function other than advertising their favorite artist. Of course, screaming does draw attention to the artist and phenomenon he or she creates. Any explanation that reduces human beings to drones, however, seems rather suspect. At the core of such thinking is the questionable idea that audiences do not use music but are entirely used by it.

Histories of music tend to contrast pop to compositions in the avant-garde or classical tradition; "serious" music is not regarded as popular culture because it is associated with more sedate audience responses. In *Textual Poachers*, Henry Jenkins (1992: 60) noted that critiques of media fandom often justified themselves by using the notion that dedicated audiences sit "too near" the text and did not assume a sufficient emotional distance to contemplate their object in a rational or artistic sense. In such thinking, fandom is framed in terms of surrendering to a special kind of temptation. If popular music prompts "bodily experience" (Bicknell & Fisher 2013: 3), then commentators can also say that it is both seductive and primal. In one of his famous readings of the "fetish character" of popular music, Theodor Adorno wrote, "Before the theological caprices of commodities, the consumers become temple slaves. Those who sacrifice themselves nowhere else can do so here, and here they are fully betrayed" (2001 [1938]: 39). Adorno frames music consumption as a process in which each individual is blinded by the meanings marketed to him or her and guided down the wrong path, toward a form of self-sacrifice that is, ironically, self-centered. By supposedly getting too engaged in their passions, fans are, furthermore, said to lose their civility. This is why commentators have linked screaming to Dionysian collective chaos such as mobbing and "pandemonium" (see Clark 1966: 80, for instance).

A stage further in this line of thinking is that popular music evokes collective transcendence. Academics writing on religion and popular culture routinely single out music fandom as a spiritual or "proto-religious" phenomenon (see, for instance, Jennings 2014). Such research can associates fandom with "worship," framing it as a practice through which fans relinquish some of their personal autonomy in exchange for affective benefits. Religiosity readings based on the "Orphic manipulation of emotion" (Partridge 2014: 237) imply that music can override the conscious mind to generate screaming as a response that is both "out of character" and central to pop fandom. This casts music fandom as what Fred Vermorel once called "a quite frightening form of possession" (1985: 248). The idea that "Beatlemaniac" Lillian Adams cannot account for her own actions lends apparent "proof" to the notion that screaming—like fandom itself—is something that even direct participants do not understand and is therefore inherently irrational. There is then an assumption that screaming (as the hallmark of fandom) is based on an absence of thinking. Each scream becomes understood as cathartic: expelling something from the body.[4]

Reviewing *When Pop Ruled My Life* in the *Guardian*, Filipa Jodelka affirmed: "Lillian Adams doesn't know why she screamed at Beatles shows, just that that was what everyone did [. . .] hundreds of children [. . .] screaming their lungs out in a puddle of warm piss" (2015: n.p.). In this reading, screaming is portrayed as a "little madness" with something enigmatic at its core. It appears to be an involuntary expostulation: an explosion that releases physical essence from the body (in this case breath)—an idea expressed in the phrase "screaming their lungs out." To use Brian Massumi's language, we might say that screaming is framed—alongside "warm piss" and other excreted residues—as a "nonconscious, never-to-be-conscious autonomic remainder" (2002: 25). Fan screaming has been formulated as the expression of an *opaque wall of desire* that fans dutifully erect between themselves and their icons (see Auslander 2006: 264): a blank expression of affect that reveals little more than blind loyalty and isolation. Screaming is therefore often dismissed as a form of "noise"—something that interferes with rather than contributes to "the music."[5] As part of a relatively sympathetic editorial, Goddard, Halligan, and Spelman, for example, discuss Beatlemania as a kind of joyous and unrestrained "case of noise meeting noise" (2013: 3).

At this point, I wish to restore some silence and remind readers that not every fan screams. The issue is not just a matter of "cold" fandoms or unexcited fans. Since adolescent girls and gay men are most typically thought of as screaming, the assumptions discussed above reflect a gendered imagination. Male audiences members might "shout," but they do not scream, supposedly, and neither do those who are in control of their emotions, including "mature" women. Screaming is perceived as non-masculine, female, or effeminate. Other terms that code fandom as "excessive" in accounts of live music—particularly "hysteria," "knickers throwing," and "incontinence"—also reflect anxieties about unchecked lust.[6] In that sense, screaming is assumed to be a form of unbridled female or gay male desire, collectively expressed in public: the "over-heating" (Larsen 2014: 2) that occurs when fans are overwhelmed by their desires or charged up with excitement and associated anxiety. If the proceeding paragraphs have located screaming as a kind of lobotomy, evacuation, evisceration, or sacrifice—*removing* something from the individual fan as a subject—screaming can be seen here, instead, as a *doubling* or super-imposition. What both the lack-based and excess-focused readings share is the idea that screaming reflects a decrease in the subject's personal autonomy. Such critique is, nevertheless, contradictory. Screaming supposedly reflects a state of worship and a state of chaos, a doubling of the individual subject and her supposed absence, a moment of consumer sovereignty and insanity.

Popular portrayals of "screaming fans" rarely make contact with their historical object, except in a passing way. Academic perceptions of popular music romanticize it as an object but are careful not to look too closely at the cognitive faculties of its audience. It is not just that only some fans scream, but that "screamers" also judge the music of their heroes, even as they express excitement about encountering them as people.[7] Whatever path of reasoning is followed, its development does not admit clear logic. Nevertheless, phrases that I have been discussing here are not just used by critics or even other media and music fandoms in their attempts to claim relative superiority. Instead they have become an almost universal paradigm within which both critics and fans themselves speak, often using the same words and ideas, but expressing them in different registers and from different perspectives. For example, Lady Gaga described the "insanity" of an encounter with fans she had while on tour in Australia to an interviewer from *Vanity Fair*: "The scream was so loud, it was a *roar*. [. . .] [My fans had just been] screaming for two hours, and then waiting for me for two hours—5000 of them. It was *insane*" (Robinson 2010: 139, original emphasis).

Fan Screaming as Affective Citizenship

You have to remember that in the 1960s, too, all these groups were really created to be screamed at by girls. Everybody saw girls as the market they were chasing. There was one time when I was at the Finsbury Empire [in London]. When the Stones started playing, I heard a girl screaming at the back. I looked and I couldn't see it. I walked to the back and I found [manager] Andrew [Loog Oldham] under the seats, screaming: "Ahhh!!!" Very soon, they were all screaming.
—Simon Napier-Bell[8]

Music manager Simon Napier-Bell's description of a 1964 Rolling Stones concert presents a moment that would be easy to interpret as the result of manipulation, pure and simple: the Stones had facilitated a "phenomenon." Any reduction of this process to commercial manipulation, however, hides significant complexity. If the fan screams were not already happening, then they were neither spontaneous nor automatic. Manager and producer Andrew Loog Oldham might not have been as successful had he tried in other circumstances—for example, if the Stones were not anticipated, present, or popular. Screaming reflects an intensity of audience engagement that does not emerge sui generis each time, but is heralded in various ways. It is evidently something that happened well before the arrival of the Stones, before the Beatles, and before Elvis.[9] Their performances are especially remembered because they appeared on a newly adopted medium (television). In the 1960s, pop fan screaming was telecast, was covered by the press, and formed a prominent aspect of marketing. It therefore became the cultural context for music production and consumption. Audiences knew the popularity of performers from media coverage, radio airplay, and record charts, and they were already familiar with past screaming. Just like the girls who screamed for Elvis and the Beatles, the fans who screamed for Mick Jagger had to be "nudged" into "topping" less intense responses such as applauding, whistling, and hollering. It is evident that Loog Oldham *cued* an audience response, rather than created it. He encouraged the audience to break a rule against screaming to which they had previously adhered.

What is "contagious" is not so much the screaming itself, but the willingness of audience members to contradict a taboo that upholds more sedate kinds of female behavior in public (Ehrenreich, Hess, & Jacobs 1992). This offers a powerful sense of enfranchisement; the female fans who scream "own" not just their heroes, but their collective right to emotionally express that sense of ownership. Fan screaming, therefore, in parallel to Judith Butler's (1999) notion of gender, is a performance without an origin. For Butler, absolute gender distinction is a compelling social fiction constantly re-created when individuals approximate each other's performances of gender. Insofar that it has no clear, evident starting point, screaming has a similar quality; indeed, I would suggest, it is a performance of gender—an academically neglected expression of fandom realized *through* a contested performance of gender. We can therefore interpret screaming as personal reaction becoming "social interaction, spectatorial culture [turning] into participatory culture" (Jenkins 2006: 41).

A participatory culture approach might frame such nonverbal expression as part of a range of public activities in which both celebrities and fans are engaged as active players: co-creators who collectively pursue a shared process of cultural production. This replaces notions of emotional manipulation with the idea that screaming arises collaboratively. After conducting interviews, Candy Leonard noted:

> Anticipating a live Beatles' performance, female fans said they would discuss with their friends beforehand whether or not they would scream—not quite daring each other, but conspiring to do something uncharacteristically bold, expressive, and free—something they couldn't do elsewhere. Some said they wouldn't but lost their inhibitions in the contagion of the crowd. (Leonard 2014: 54)

Open discussion before concerts implies that screaming was a benchmark for the girls themselves. Psychologists and others have ascribed emotional causation to screaming, and distinguished different types.[10] In his 1967 book *The Naked Ape*, the well-known sociobiologist Desmond Morris wrote a section on the subject of pop fan screaming. Morris argued that screaming was not natural but "deliberately stylized" so that female fans could "reassure one another of their developing emotional responsiveness" (2007 [1967]: 80). Quite why they needed to reassure each other of their "developing emotional responsiveness" is open to debate, but Morris's interpretation at least opens up the idea of screaming as a networking tool. From this perspective, we might read screaming as a discourse in itself, a form of "enunciative productivity" where "the moment of reception is often also the moment of enunciation" (Jenkins 1992: 278). Candy Leonard (2014: 54) suggested that screaming for the Beatles communicated excitement, a loss of inhibition, a roar of lust, a form of live participation, and a way of expressing thanks to the band. Yet it seems erroneous to assume that we can decipher nonverbal utterances through the same research strategies that analyze words. If screaming actually "says" anything, it expresses emotion *beyond words*, emotion of a pitch and intensity for which words are not adequate.[11] As engaged participants, fans therefore collectively create a unique version of their hero that is sonically expressed as an embodiment of their own affect. Just as this unique symphony is not "noise," neither is it made only as a pretext for conscious discussion; a key issue with participatory culture concepts is that they cannot conceive of such fan activity except as an epiphenomenon or premise for further communication. One solution is to frame the analysis by drawing on Émile Durkheim's notion of totemism.

Durkheim examined totemic religions in Australian aboriginal society. He described how the energy of the collective is expressed in a feeling he called effervescence: "The very fact of assembling is an exceptionally powerful stimulant. Once individuals are assembled, their proximity generates a certain kind of electricity that quickly transports them to an extraordinary degree of exaltation" (Durkheim 2008 [1912]: 166). The sociologist noted that clan rituals are inevitably mediated by totems. Each one—whether a person, plant, animal, or object—is thought to embody divine agency; it has the power to excite people, because it is the focus of collective attention. The totem necessarily occupies a prominent role, symbolizing the power of the collective in an "energetic" sense.[12] Durkheim therefore described it as "a group incarnate and personified" (2008 [1912]: 158). Individual followers touched by the totem experience moments of effervescence as jolts of energy that give them a mood-raising personal boost. This feeling motivates shared beliefs, values, and behavior that maintain the social system. I suggest that totemism helps us see celebrity fan bases as "moral economies" that reproduce themselves and uphold wider shared values; screaming is one way in which such collectively envisaged structures are manifest and thus maintained.

Commercial music and celebrity fandom do not, taken together, seem like an easily recognizable form of religious pursuit. Totemism is, nevertheless, worth considering as a central secular, human, social, and psychological mechanism that can begin to explain some fan phenomena. Durkheim's work does not reduce fandom to a mysterious pathological response (without social context), a product of manipulation (without any "real" reward), or embryonic form of religion (without actually having a theology). Instead it directs our attention to widely circulated yet unspoken assumptions that compound to make fandom possible. Within a totemic context, screams are expressed by those who encounter people they value most highly. Hence the anxiety over screaming: it represents a conventionalized moment when totemic concerns exceed traditional gender taboos *and* endorse industrial agents (stars). Totemic practices, however, cannot be fully reduced to manipulative transactions. The music industry traditionally overproduces candidates in hope of finding acceptable product. It rhetorically uses and takes guidance from fans.[13] Finally, online restructuring now allows listeners to endorse popular musicians who have not (yet) been fully groomed for commercial appeal. An emerging set of YouTube stars, like Sam Tsui, already draw high levels of totemic interest and prompt audience screaming, regardless of whether they decide to join established structures—like record labels, agents, and managers—or simply ignore them (see Moss 2014).

Durkheim's theory is not an empirical reality. It is a conceptual template that can be used to frame fan phenomena and help explain what is happening. Like any theory, it is a tool that is less nuanced than empirical reality. Nevertheless, totemism gives us a working hypothesis for the role of screaming as a form of communication. From a neo-Durkheimian perspective, all fans understand their hero as a totem and believe his or her talent has "won over" a fan base. This explains why screaming is *preceded* by knowledge of the popularity of the performer and can be prompted by him or her at events where the audience is physically present. One Bay City Rollers fan, interviewed by the BBC in the 1970s about why she screamed at their concerts, replied, "Well, during the year we see pictures of them, and received [fan club] letters off them, and it's all building up inside you. And when you see them on stage, you just scream."[14] Screaming thus becomes recognizable as an expression of the "electric charge" of the excitement felt when finding oneself in relative proximity to a socially valued person. It is a way to gain a star's attention, and something that demonstrates the emotional commitment of his or her fan base. The totemic mechanism also suggests that fan screaming may be motivated by a need to express that understanding, in a very urgent and immediate way, to all those around—whether the star, fellow fans, or curious onlookers.[15]

Just as Jürgen Habermas (1989) argued that from 1680 to 1730 London's coffee houses were arenas for the meeting and debate that helped to form Britain's public sphere, so, some have argued, commercial, social media platforms can facilitate participatory culture and foster fan activism (see Jenkins, Ford, & Green 2013: 173). Rather than young girls reassuring each other of their own "developing emotional responsiveness," they are participating in a shared *symbolic economy* that prizes a famous person (or group) over a whole audience, in order to give the thought of a closer relationship immense affective charge. From this perspective, we might equally note that fan screaming is a form of supportive heckling (see Duffett 2009). In that sense, I want to suggest—by reformulating an idea from political studies—that fan screaming may be a form of "affective citizenship." Most theorists use this term to consider the circumstances under which national citizenship gains or loses its emotional resonance (see, for instance, Holland 2006; Coleman & Blumer 2009). I mean quite the opposite: understanding how screaming, as something denoting membership of a fan base, can, in turn, constitute a *political* kind of belonging.

We find it hard to be a fan of anyone who flatly contradicts our values or fails to ignite our interest; the actuality of each phenomenon therefore indicates a meaningful stance on the part of particular fans at a specific point in time. Though not all fans scream, the emotionally engaged "nation within a nation" of "screamers" thus raises a political issue: what certain audiences find exciting others can find appalling; many of the most prominent instances of fan screaming are also the most controversial. The girls who screamed at Elvis expressed public interest in a performer who, in effect, appeared like a disreputable boyfriend—a working-class southerner who adopted Black style and taunted his followers with his body. Audiences who screamed at the Beatles publically approved of working-class lads from a "fringe" city who were known for their surreal humor, rebellious haircuts, and nondeferential attitudes. The girls who screamed for the Stones loved their cavalier attitude. Fans who later got excited over David Bowie endorsed a bisexual crossdresser who likened himself to an alien. The girls who screamed for Boy George openly accepted a gay man as their hero.[16] Gay fans who screamed at Lady Gaga were supporting an LGBT advocate who in turn became an activist for them.[17] Though, of course, high levels of totemic interest can exist for much more "conformist" artists, the wider point is that *there is no abstract screaming, no generalized excitement, and no generic "screaming fans."* Screaming is always *for* someone and not for anyone else. Never fully contrived, it therefore expresses excitement for a particular celebrity in a particular historic context and demonstrates the tacit acceptance of particular shared values. As Candy Leonard (2014: 54) put it, "If the screams were sublimating romantic and sexual desire, there was a subversive element [both] to the behavior and to the unconventional, controversial object of desire."

NOTES

1   I define "knowing field" as an inner territory of emotional conviction (in other words, knowing that one is above a threshold level of affect)—something that is both a personal experience and mutually recognized in different ways by other fans (see Duffett 2013: 161).

2   As anyone familiar with the slang term "squee" (squeal) knows, in text-based sci-fi and fantasy fandom, screaming at celebrity actors is marginalized (Zubernis & Larsen 2012: 55). Equally, in popular music, audience screaming is lambasted by "serious" rock and blues fans.

3   Online screaming can be heard in uploaded videos, deduced from photos, or expressed through emoticons, "OMGs," or other expressions. The latter are interesting because they are conscious inscriptions by fans.

4   Cursory attention to the work of even maverick thinkers like Arthur Janov (1970) and Antonin Artaud ([1935] 1988) reveals screaming is associated with intimate forms of inner, personal expression.

5   Audience screaming contributes to the live sound and appeal of popular music, and performers frequently evoke it as part of the music (Duffett 2009). Musicians also scream on stage. *Their* screaming is framed as intentional, creative, and artistic—qualities largely erased from accounts of the audience.

6   The term "hysteria" linked screaming to mass culture criticism (media culture as brainwashing) and psychoanalysis (hysteria as a gendered pathology) (see Yarom 2005; Blackman and Walkerdine 2000). For a critique, see Duffett (2013).

7   I doubt, for instance, that the fans who screamed at Elvis would have said that all his records were equally appealing.

8   *Moguls: Masters of Pop, Episode 1: Money Makers* was aired on January 15, 2016, on BBC4.

9   Screaming has long accompanied various spectacles, including music hall and theater, and public appearance of screen celebrities. In 1850 at least one newspaper story about the star singer Jenny Lind, for example, said that some of her followers were "screaming at the very tops of their voices" (reproduced in Cavicchi 2011: 151).

10 In an early landmark study, the psychoanalyst Nina Searl (1933) argued that screams of rage may reflect the infant's inability to control whether her or his needs are met. Later researchers have also explored screaming as means of attempting social control, whether based on fear (in fights) or offering encouragement (during sex). Arthur Janov's (1970) primal scream therapy suggested

that lower frequency screams are essential expressions of emotional pain that individuals had repressed.

11 The conscious writing of fan screams in tweets, and other forums, relates to what Matt Hills (2015: 150)—borrowing from discourse psychologist Margaret Wetherell—has called the "affective-discursive": "a kind of collision between the two, rather than a taking apart of the binary." Are the tweeted "OMGs" just gift-exchanged parcels of affect? I suggest they actively re-create totemic relationships *through linguistic practices*, insofar as they spread assumptions undergirding totemic appreciation (e.g., that the celebrity is important not only because he is "cute," but also because he moves lots of people to express their excitement about him).

12 Interviewed by Marc Maron for his *WTF* podcast in 2015, Iggy Pop explained the role of a rock frontman: "The energy's got to move through you and then go out; [you] make it accessible for the other people in the room to receive it."

13 This includes not only managers or A&R staff who *watch* fans, but also those who are fans.

14 *Rollermania: Britain's Biggest Boy Band* was made by STV Productions for BBC Scotland and aired September 15, 2015, on BBC4.

15 This is part of what makes totemism more than a reified social structure. Like the proverbial Haçienda, it "must be built" by the actions of all involved. Perhaps this is also why screaming can sometimes be heard outside of *direct* attention to the star, induced as a kind of orchestrated convention. The pre-concert documentary *Heavy Metal Parking Lot*, for instance, showed metal fans who could festively shout and holler for the camera without requiring the presence of their heroes, Judas Priest.

16 If female fans of openly gay men scream, it does not necessarily *disprove* the idea that screaming is about expressing lust. It does, however, open up further possibilities.

17 "'Tonight, this is my house Russia,' Lady Gaga told a crowd of screaming fans during her performance there in December. 'You can be gay in my house'" (*Sputnik News* 2013).

WORKS CITED

Adorno, T 2001 [1938], "On the fetish-character of music and the regression of listening," in T Adorno, *The culture industry: selected essays on mass culture*, JM Bernstein (ed.), Routledge, New York.

Artaud, A 1988 [1935], "An emotional athleticism," in *Antonin Artaud: selected writings*, S Sontag (ed.), University of California Press, Berkeley.

Auslander, P 2006, "Music as performance: living in the immaterial world," *Theatre Survey* 47(2): 261–69.

Bicknell, J & Fisher, J 2013, "Introduction: making space for a song," *Journal of Aesthetics and Art Criticism* 71(1): 1–11.

Blackman, L & Walkerdine, V 2000, *Hysteria: critical psychology and media studies*, Palgrave Macmillan, Basingstoke.

Butler, J 1999, *Gender trouble: feminism and the subversion of identity*, Routledge, New York.

Cavicchi, D 2011, *Listening and longing: music lovers in the age of Barnum*, Wesleyan University Press, Middletown.

Clark, A 1966, "2000 Beatles fans storm box office here; it's an early augury of show in August at Shea Stadium," *New York Times*, May 1, 80.

Coleman, S & Blumer, J 2009, *The Internet and democratic citizenship: theory, practice and policy*, Cambridge University Press, Cambridge.

Duffett, M 2009, "We are interrupted by your noise: heckling and the symbolic economy of popular music stardom," *Popular Music and Society* 32(1): 37–57.

Duffett, M 2013, *Understanding fandom*, Bloomsbury, New York.

Durkheim, É 2008 [1912], *The elementary form of religious life*, Oxford University Press, Oxford.

Ehrenreich, B, Hess, E, & Jacobs, G 1992, "Beatlemania: girls just want to have fun," in LA Lewis (ed.), *The adoring audience: fan culture and popular media*, Routledge, New York.

Goddard, M, Halligan, B, & Spelman, N (eds.) 2013, *Resonances: noise and contemporary music*, Bloomsbury, New York.

Habermas, J 1989, *The structural transformation of the public sphere: an inquiry into a category of bourgeois society*, MIT Press, Cambridge, MA.

Hills, M 2015, "Fandom as an object and the objects of fandom," *MATRIZes* 9(1): 147–62.

Holland, E 2006, "Affective citizenship and the death state," in I Buchanan & A Parr (eds.), *Deleuze and the contemporary world*, Edinburgh University Press, Edinburgh.

Janov, A 1970, *The primal scream: primary therapy, the cure for neurosis*, Dell, New York.

Jenkins, H 1992, *Textual poachers: television fans and participatory culture*, Routledge, New York.

Jenkins, H 2006, *Fans, bloggers, gamers: exploring participatory culture*, New York University Press, New York.

Jenkins, H, Ford, S, & Green, J 2013, *Spreadable media: creating value and meaning in a networked culture*, New York University Press, New York.

Jennings, M 2014, *Exaltation: ecstatic experience in Pentecostalism and popular music*, Peter Lang, Bern.

Jodelka, F 2015, "*When pop ruled my life*: a loving look at extreme fandom," *Guardian*, May 29, www.theguardian.com.

Larsen, K 2014, "Radway roundtable remarks," *Journal of Popular Romance Studies* 4(2): 1–4.

Leonard, C 2014, *Beatleness: how the Beatles and their fans remade the world*, Skyhorse, New York.

Massumi, B 2002, *Parables for the virtual: movement, affect, sensation*, Duke University Press, Durham, NC.

Morris, D 2007 [1967], *The naked ape*, Vintage, London.

Moss, C 2014, "I went to a YouTube stars convention with 3000 screaming girls," *Business Insider: India*, May 19, www.businessinsider.in.

Newall, S 2015, *"When pop ruled my life*. The fans' story, BBC4, TV review: these super-fans were a scream," *Independent*, May 31, www.independent.co.uk.

Partridge, C 2014, *The lyre of Orpheus: popular music, the sacred and the profane*, Oxford University Press, Oxford.

Robinson, L 2010, "Lady Gaga's cultural revolution," *Vanity Fair*, September, 134–41.

Searl, N 1933, "The psychology of screaming," *International Journal of Psychoanalysis* 14: 193–205.

Sputnik News 2013, "Lady Gaga fires back at Russia in tweet rant," August 6, sputniknews.com.

Vermorel, F 1985, *Starlust*, WH Allen, London.

Willis, E 2011, *Out of the vinyl deeps: Ellen Willis on rock music*, University of Minnesota Press, Minneapolis.

Yarom, N 2005, *Matrix of hysteria: psychoanalysis and the struggle between the sexes enacted on the body*, Routledge, New York.

Zubernis, L & Larsen, K 2012, *Fandom at the crossroads: celebration, shame and fan/producer relationships*, Cambridge Scholars, Newcastle.

9

A Sort of Homecoming

Fan Viewing and Symbolic Pilgrimage

WILL BROOKER

She says nobody wants to believe
You're the same as everyone.
What makes me unique? My dark life.
. . . And you think you're a guest, you're a tourist at best
Peering into the corners of your dark life
—Elvis Costello, "My Dark Life," *Songs in the Key of X*

A back alley in Vancouver. A road tunnel in Los Angeles. A gravestone in Guildford. A mock-up of the Rovers Return pub. Graceland. The study of fan pilgrimages is sufficiently established for us readily to accept the idea that some dedicated followers of cultural texts or icons—in the above cases, *The X-Files*, *Blade Runner*, Lewis Carroll, *Coronation Street*, and Elvis Presley—will travel across the world to often mundane places that fandom has made sacred and special (see, respectively, Hills 2002; Brooker 2005b; Brooker 2005a; Couldry 2000; King 1993). But the idea that watching television constitutes a "symbolic pilgrimage" may still prompt a skeptical response. Such is Roger Aden's assertion in his chapter "Transforming the Panopticon into the Funhouse: Negotiating Disorientation in *The X-Files*" (1999: 149).

Aden makes grand claims about fan viewing, presenting the experience of sitting down to watch *The X-Files* as *symbolic pilgrimage*—a trip without drugs, a journey and return without leaving the easy chair. Fans, according to Aden, leave their structured, everyday environment to enter Agents Fox Mulder and Dana Scully's diegesis—a fictional world that echoes the panoptic control of normal working life, yet allows a playful exploration of these structures and always includes, at the end of the episode, the reassurance of an exit. The show's panoptic environment of surveillance and control is a pleasurably threatening but safe simulation; a "funhouse" where viewers test themselves, scare themselves, and equip themselves with coping strategies for the real structures of social life. Aden has no hesitation in describing this psychological immersion and return from the show's fictional world in the same terms as physical, geographical pilgrimage, relating it to the tripartite structure used by Victor and Edith Turner (after Arnold Van Gennep):

> Each trip to the funhouse is a new yet ritualistic experience for both the agents [Mulder and Scully] and their vicarious partners, the fans. In fact, the show's recurring form mirrors the pilgrim's journey as described by Edith Turner: [. . .] "(1) separation (the start of the journey), (2) the liminal stage (the journey itself, the sojourn at the shrine, and the encounter with the sacred) and (3) reaggregation (the homecoming)." (Aden 1999: 152)

My main intention in this chapter is to explore the validity of terms such as "symbolic pilgrimage" to describe the experience of viewing a TV show. I discuss metaphors of interior journey, then examine the testimonies of my own *X-Files* fan sample in terms of the tripartite structure Aden takes from Van Gennep through Turner, and Csikszentmihalyi's concept of "flow." In the third and fourth sections, I explore two further issues raised by this case study: whether a lack of fellow travelers—a lack of physical, spiritual, or virtual connection with other people—impoverishes the pilgrimage, and what difference it makes when the symbolic pilgrimage is not a trip into the unknown but an immersion in a familiar fiction where the protagonists are old friends. Ultimately, I suggest that instead of treating symbolic pilgrimage as a separate category, we should ask whether all geographical pilgrimage in fact involves a degree of conceptual, inner, symbolic travel.

Traveling without Moving

The whole concept of TV viewers as pilgrims, entering a different state that qualifies as a journey, albeit "symbolic," may initially sound far-fetched. When we consider a *Lord of the Rings* fan making the trip from Britain to the New Zealand film locations, the word "pilgrim" comes more easily, but does a fan sitting in his or her own domestic environment, watching a screen—even though we readily grant the fan the status of an active viewer rather than a passive receiver—really deserve such associations of adventure?

Aden uses the metaphor repeatedly and without qualms: "just what in the series spawns the pilgrimages of X-philes is difficult to pinpoint" (1999: 151), viewers "accompany the agents on their journey" (1999: 153), "fans leave their homes to enter the invisible liminoid aura surrounding *The X-Files*" (1999: 162).

Though this language of physical journey seems unusual when applied to TV viewing, the idea of traveling without moving has various precedents in religion and anthropology. Alan Morinis's study, *Sacred Journeys*, opens with the reminder that it is "questionable to distinguish between terrestrial and 'metaphorical' pilgrimages. This distinction portrays the earthly journey as somehow more real, when, in fact, most cultures subsume physical journeys and other quests into one more inclusive category: the spiritual life is a pilgrimage" (1992: 4). Morinis includes in his discussion of "nongeographical goings-forth" (1992: 2) the "inner pilgrimage" to sacred places within the mind and body, practiced by Hindu mystics (1992: 3), and the celestial "Vrndavana of the mind," the city inhabited by Krishna that devotees can "visit" through perfect prayer.

As already indicated, Aden's notion that fans "travel" while engrossed in the show is tied to Victor Turner's anthropological structure of pilgrimage—yet that structure refers, in both Turner and Van Gennep's work, not specifically to pilgrimage but to a more general "rite of passage." Turner describes *rites de passage*, after Van Gennep, as "rites which accompany every change of place, state, social position and age" (Turner 1969: 94; see Van Gennep 1960: vii). Although the word "passage" of course implies journey, a change of place is only one of the possible transitions connoted by the phrase, and the shifts from one state to another that Turner describes are by no means exclusively physical. When, for instance, he writes in *The Ritual Process* of the ritual subject in Zambian tribal culture as a "passenger," "passing through a cultural realm" (1969: 94), the individual may be going physically no farther than to a shelter a mile from his village, though symbolically the ritual may involve a transit from boy to man, man to chief.

This notion of passage as a spiritual and symbolic state rather than a literal movement can be identified in Christianity, as well as in African tribal culture. Turner notes that "traces of the *passage* quality of the religious life remain in such formulations as: 'The Christian is a stranger to the world, a pilgrim, a traveller, with no place to rest his head.' Transition has here become a permanent condition" (1969: 107). Indeed, in his later work with Edith Turner, *Image and Pilgrimage in Christian Culture*, Turner describes physical travel to a sacred shrine as a second-best, layman's substitute for the "interior salvific journeys" practiced only by "monastic contemplatives and mystics" (Turner & Turner 1978: 7).

Another promising metaphor of interior travel can be found in Csik-szentmihalyi's theory of "flow experience," which shaped Turner's later work and also explicitly informs Aden's study. Flow, in this context, is the pleasurable sensation of losing oneself in an activity—work, a game, a physical or mental challenge—and becoming immersed, with everything perfectly meshing in a harmonious state where goals are set and satisfyingly met. Time contracts or stretches, and the individual merges with the activity, totally absorbed.

This sense of immersion, where the everyday is transcended and the participant enters a different state of being, a form of communion with a text, with a process, and sometimes with other participants, seems to offer a productive approach to the experience of watching television: in particular, the more intense viewing practiced by fans with their favored shows. Aden uses the term in this sense when he describes the "deep sense of involvement" reported by *X-Files* fans as similar to the "flow experiences reported by pilgrims."

However, in applying Csikszentmihalyi's concept of "flow" to television fandom, Aden ignores the fact that Csikszentmihalyi does not merely fail to mention TV viewing in his discussion of flow activities; he deliberately excludes it, denying it any such potential and referring to it only as a negative example, a contrast to more worthwhile practices. Reading is, to Csikszentmihalyi, "the most often mentioned flow activity around the world," and studying a work of art can transport the viewer symbolically to "a separate reality" (2002: 118–19). Sex and eating can be transformed from biological urges into flow experience with the right kind of discipline and discrimination (2002: 101, 114). Even trench warfare and criminal activity such as vandalism or joyriding are, according to Csikszentmihalyi's respondents, potential sources of flow (2002: 68). Yet Csikszentmihalyi refuses to discuss television viewing as anything but a passive, brainless, numbing act. "Watching TV is far from being a positive experience—people generally report feeling passive, weak, rather irritable, and sad when doing it" (2002: 169). In order to apply Csikszentmihalyi's concept to a fan's immersion in his or her favorite show, we have to negotiate this prejudice and find, as I later suggest, a loophole in his damning ruling against television viewing as flow experience.

I Want to Believe

Aden's study is based primarily on a textual analysis of ten episodes from *X-Files* seasons 1 and 4, and interviews carried out in person and by email with fans. The viewer feedback, however, is not extensively used, and fan voices only emerge occasionally through the discussion of theory, narrative, and character. I want to address that here by giving more space to viewer response. My own data are drawn from a survey (thirty questions, inviting lengthy qualitative replies) submitted to thirteen *X-Files* fans, recruited from the *Xfiles* community of LiveJournal.com. While the sample is small-scale, the responses were rich, sometimes running to several pages for each question. These data can, of course, only be suggestive of possible trends, but the fan voices are intriguing nonetheless.

First, we can return to Van Gennep's tripartite structure of a rite of passage. In Aden's application of the theory, this involves a separation from the habitus, the "panopticon-like culture" of postindustrial culture with its "constant surveillance," employment and financial insecurities, and controlling social structures (1999: 160). The second stage of pilgrimage involves an in-between, liminal transit, away from home but not yet at the "promised land," the sacred site that marks the pilgrim's goal:

> Once we are immersed in the liminoid flow of watching *The X-Files*, fans such as myself can begin the rhetorical process of constructing a symbolic community that offers an outpost for transcending the habitus. In this case our construction efforts build a community that exists in between the real and unreal, with faith generating the bonds of connection. (1999: 165)

Aden's two references to the blurred boundaries between real and fictional worlds repeat the theme of ambiguity and liminality, while the viewer's involvement in the fictional world is characterized as "immersion" in "flow." This latter term is, of course, a reference to Csikszentmihalyi's theory of "optimal experience," the state of being pleasurably lost in an activity to the extent that the outside world drops away, and the individual meshes perfectly with his or her goals (1999: 164). It also implies a state of ambiguity and being between, as flow experience, like liminality, seems to contract and expand time, and combines the paradoxes of structure and freedom, work and effortlessness, individual achievement and a sense of community.

Aden's respondents are briefly cited to support his argument that the *X-Files* viewing experience is immersive, which in turn helps indirectly to justify his use of terms like "journey," "trip," and "traveling." Aden's interview subject Sandy emails, "While I'm watching, I'm only involved with the show and don't do anything else" (1999: 164). Other fans tell Aden that they "control their material environments to make the move to the symbolic even easier"—that is, they turn off the lights, "enhancing the distinction between being materially positioned in a living room to being symbolically ensconced in a liminoid flow" (1999: 164). Finally, Aden's subjects shut out interruptions, telling their mothers not to call during the show or ignoring telephones and doorbells so as not to disturb the "flow experience" (1999: 164).

Our initial response to this passage may well be skeptical; a single quotation from Sandy, who doesn't do anything else when the show is on, seems quite a stretch away from providing convincing evidence that watching *The X-Files* qualifies as immersion in liminality. The other half of Sandy's testimony, in fact, suggests that a more halfhearted, absentminded involvement with the show is equally likely: "I watch *The X-Files* by myself, while my husband works on the computer and listens to it."

However, my own respondents went some way toward justifying Aden's characterization of the viewing experience as absorption in flow, and even as a metaphorical "trip." Eleven of the thirteen fans I asked reported that they felt "anticipation" or "excitement" just prior to an unfamiliar episode, comparable perhaps to the enjoyable nerves a traveler might feel before setting off on a journey. Twenty-three-year-old Schally's response was typical:

When the show was airing on television I would often get a little nervous before the second or third part of a multipart episode because those had invariably ended at an unpleasant cliffhanger the week before and I was usually worried about the characters. The season four finale "Gethsemane" absolutely killed me. I was very worried about Mulder and extremely anxious about the upcoming season premier. I used to also get very excited about episodes that had had particularly funny or suspenseful teasers the week before.

The fact that most episodes now are familiar to X-philes, and the difference this makes to their viewing experience, will be discussed below; as will be evident, the respondents often made a distinction between watching for the first time and reacquainting themselves with a favorite installment.

"Trip," of course, has a double meaning of drug-induced trance, and a number of responses suggested that this dual connotation may be appropriate. Only one respondent, forty-one-year-old Steve, stated explicitly that his preparation for watching *The X-Files* involved getting "hammered (ie. indulge in alcohol and drugs)," but Schally spoke of her "cravings" for the show, and Seoirse, a twenty-nine-year-old woman, described it as "like an addiction for me. If I catch an episode on TV [. . .] it starts this cycle of needing to watch at least 6 episodes before I'm satisfied." Maddy Martin, aged twenty-one, talked about becoming "annoyed and fidgety" if she was called away from an episode to work; Katherine, aged seventeen, exclaimed, "I always feel like watching another—they are addictive!"; and Bellefleur, aged twenty-nine, confessed a "withdrawal feeling" during the week while waiting for the next installment. Thirty-year-old Jamie's observation that if the flow of the episode is interrupted, "I tend to lose interest [. . .] it feels as though the 'magic' is lost" also carries overtones of a ritualized trance state.

Some form of preparation ritual is not uncommon among media fans, and this often seems to approach an act of communion, a symbolic activity that removes the participant from the everyday and brings him or her closer to the fiction. To draw two examples from my own research, listening to the soundtrack CD and wearing an authentically "distressed" Capeside T-shirt before an episode of *Dawson's Creek* (Brooker 2004: 572) and dressing up for a *Star Wars* home screening in Queen Amidala lipstick with Leia hair-buns while feasting on "Wookiee Cookies" and "Yoda Soda" (Brooker 2002: 35) are both forms of bonding with the text, taking the fan a little way out of normal structures and arguably into a liminal border zone between the real world and the diegesis, where the viewer eats the same snacks or wears the same outfits as the characters on screen. The *Twin Peaks* cultists who gathered religiously for a new episode with cherry pie and coffee, and the "Dinner & Dynasty" meetings of the 1980s (Fiske 1987: 71) provide further examples of this ritualized viewing; most recently, fans of the BBC time-travel cop show *Life on Mars* (2006) celebrated its season 1 finale by eating 1970s-style Viscount biscuits and spaghetti hoops.

Aden's X-philes described turning out the lights, unplugging their phones, and creating an appropriate environment for undisturbed passage into "flow"; each of my respondents independently testified to a similar routine. Seoirse made this ceremonial aspect explicit: "Before, when there were still new episodes, I would unplug the phone, switch of all the lights and make myself a pot of tea—it's a ritual!" The common practice among these respondents was notable, with six of the thirteen mentioning that they turn off or unplug telephones, and seven preferring to watch *The X-Files* in the dark.

> I usually watch the show right before I go to sleep, Lights off, door shut, so on. (Schally)

> A lot of the people I watch episodes with prefer to watch it in the dark: all lights out and curtains drawn. When the show used to be on TV, I had to ignore my phone, ignore my parents, and I was unable to draw my gaze from the TV screen. (Maddy Martin)

> When it was on the BBC it was a case of turning out the lights [. . .] getting away for the fifty or so minutes of the programme. (Jamie)

In part, this may be an attempt to transform the domestic viewing environment into a kind of home cinema, with the screen as main focus. The preference for dimmed lights or total darkness could also be related to the horror and suspense aspects of *The X-Files*; this creation of a setting particularly conducive to "flow" may be shaped by the genre and the need for an appropriately spooky setting.

Already we can see that the fans' language suggests immersion and journey. Maddy's gaze is fixed on the screen for almost an hour, as if hypnotized, while Jamie speaks of "getting away," clearly conveying the idea of a "trip" and departure from the everyday world. This terminology is particularly appropriate to a show that, in addition to the geographical journeys and emotional quests of its protagonists, frequently returns to the motif of alien abduction.

These experiences of partial to total absorption were typical of the responses I received. "On good episodes," Schally became "completely engrossed in the show." Jamie stated that "the show makes you forget the real world in its opening moments," while Seoirse and Katherine Woodruff were both "completely involved." Kevin, aged fifty-one, entered the story-world through a main character: "I identify with Mulder in particular and so feel totally immersed [. . .] often very moved by it, always thrilled by it."

Those fans who qualified their replies nevertheless felt enough connection with the fiction for it to prompt a dramatic emotional response. Steve reported, "I lose myself, but not to the extent of forgetting the real world," yet added, "I've felt the whole range of emotions, ranging from extreme joy to anger"; and Ceruleanjen, aged twenty-two, stressed that she was always aware of her "real" surroundings as she watched the show, but continued, "if something sad happens I might cry [. . .] nothing out of the ordinary."

Ten respondents echoed Jamie's comment that external distractions broke the spell of *The X-Files*; disruption often riled them to hostility. "I really don't like it" (Schally), "I was never happy about interruption" (Bellefleur), "It has happened—and I'm not pleased when it does!" (Kevin), "It would greatly annoy me" (Chantal), "I hated being interrupted [. . .] I responded with anger" (Steve). Again, these reports tally with Aden's theory of viewers becoming "enmeshed in flow experiences while consuming popular stories."

We should also note the echoes of Csikszentmihalyi's "flow" experience. The sensations described by his research subjects, from mountaineers through chess and basketball players to dancers—"that's all that matters" (2002: 58), "it becomes your total world" (58), "your concentration is very complete" (52), "the concentration is like breathing—you never think of it" (53), "your comrades are there, but you all feel the same way anyway, you're all in it together" (40)—tally closely with the reports from these fans at the moment of closest engagement with their favored show. It seems even more perverse in this context that Csikszentmihalyi takes such an outdated view of television, excluding its potential for active involvement; although he does unwittingly provide a gap where his theory can be levered open to include certain forms of viewing.

Csikszentmihalyi dismissively compares television with a "drug" (2002: 169) that "keeps the mind from having to face depressing thoughts," but then allows that drugs can only produce optimal experience, or flow, when used "in highly skilled ritual contexts, as is practiced in many traditional societies." Unsurprisingly, he declines to consider the possibility that television viewing could bear any similarities to the ceremonial trances of shamans and priests, but this chink in his condemnation offers some space for a reevaluation of ritualistic fan viewing as a source of flow experience.

You're the Same as Everyone—What Makes Me Unique?

So far, the testimonies of my respondents tend to support Aden's characterization of immersive viewing as a transition to a world "between the real and unreal" (1999: 165), "a sacred place where 'real' time and space are excluded" (1999: 164). Another integral aspect of this journey away from the immediate, material surroundings into a liminal state is "connection with a spiritual community of others [. . .] as vicarious participants in the stories" (1999: 166–67). Just as the fans' journey, in Aden's account, does not involve physical movement from the sofa, so the community is also symbolic, and can take place even if the individual is sitting alone. "Despite watching the show by themselves, they feel attached to the community of nonpresent viewers" (1999: 168).

This congregation, an invisible network uniting fellow fans— dependent in part on traditional schedule-based broadcasting, so the viewer can imagine millions of others doing the same thing at the same time—unites individual viewers, according to Aden, in a kind of intellectual elite. My respondents, as members of LiveJournal's *Xfiles* community, were part of a virtual, invisible network that enabled them to communicate with other fans instantaneously, across geographical distance. However, few of them mentioned community as a major aspect of their pleasure in the show. Several stated that they kept their *X-Files* enthusiasm mainly to themselves and felt no close connection with like-minded viewers, whether physically (in real life), virtually (through the Internet), or, in Aden's sense of communion with nonpresent fellow travelers, spiritually. Some expressed regret that the most vibrant and rewarding period in the show's fandom was now lost in nostalgic memory:

> I think it would have been cool to have been one of the ardent online fans back in the show's early broadcast days in the US. I've never really met anyone who has more than a casual interest in the show, which is a shame. (Nina)

The fact that the show is now complete and finished, having reached its final closure—it ran over nine seasons, from September 1993 to May 2002—may make all the difference; when fans watch their DVDs or videos now, they have the convenience of deciding how long their "journey" is and when it starts and finishes, but have lost the sense that they are undertaking it at the same time as a nationwide community, undergoing the same or similar experiences during the same time scale. Katherine, like Nina, mourned this loss: "I would love to talk about it with other people—I'm desperate for fellow Philes!"

Communitas is discussed by Turner as a significant aspect of the transition from everyday frameworks into liminality and back again with an enhanced status or understanding. "In *rites de passage*, men are released from structure into communitas only to return to structure revitalised by their experience of communitas" (1969: 129). His quotation from Martin Buber—"community is the being no longer side by side [. . .] but *with* one another of a multitude of persons. And this multitude, though it moves towards one goal, yet experiences everywhere [. . .] a flowing from *I* to *Thou*" (Buber 1961: 51, cited in Turner 1969: 127)—reminds us of Csikszentmihalyi's respondents describing the single purpose of a group in "flow": "your comrades are there, but you all feel the same way anyway, you're all in it together" (2002: 40).

However, while the lack of perceived connection with fellow fans, even on a virtual or spiritual level, may impoverish the sense of communion to some extent—Nina expresses regret for the loss of an intense sharing, and Katherine is desperate for a bond with others—a pleasurable immersion in liminality, outside normal space and time, does not seem *dependent* on the company of others. Csikszentmihalyi's testimonies of flow experience include competitive activities like chess, public debate, hurdling, and tennis, where the player is usually pitted against an opponent rather than moving as one with a team, and solitary pursuits like rock climbing, solo ocean cruising, music composing, and orchard tending (2002: 53–59). Community is clearly not a requirement of the total immersion and connection Csikszentmihalyi describes.

In my own work on geographical pilgrimages to the *Blade Runner* locations of Los Angeles, my respondents reflected on the lack of potential for community bonding with fellow fans, partly because of the key sites' multiple coding as everyday utilities (the Second Street road tunnel, Union Station) or architectural landmarks (the Bradbury Building, the Ennis-Brown House) and the lack of any organized *Blade Runner* pilgrimage culture. One fan reported that "the group I toured [the Ennis-Brown House] with were all fans of its architect, Frank Lloyd-Wright"; another complained that "I actually tried to shoot a short film at Union Station, but the Grand Concourse was booked solid with weddings and stuff" (Brooker 2005b: 24).

However, these obstacles failed to prevent even these cynical fans from expressing some sense of wonder and immersion: "If a movie is like a dream, then standing in an actual location is like stepping into the dream. There's a weird kind of energy to it" (Brooker 2005b: 25). The feeling of connection is not with other fans, but with the fiction; with Rick Deckard and Los Angeles 2019. It is a need for connection with the *text*, not with fellow travelers, that motivated my respondents to take photographs and shoot digital video from the precise angles Ridley Scott used, in an attempt to capture the fictional space of the film. This is the same impulse we see in the photographs of *Star Wars* pilgrims who painstakingly seek out the exact dune framed for a shot of Tatooine, and place themselves into the fictional world by striking the pose Mark Hamill adopted in the 1977 movie. This, too, is the impulse behind websites that place precisely composed images of contemporary

San Francisco streets alongside screen grabs from Hitchcock's *Vertigo* (1958), pinpointing the location and direction of Hitchcock's camera, and pilgrims' photographs of Vancouver that echo *The X-Files'* shots of a hotel, a bridge, a Skytrain overpass. As Sandvoss writes of pilgrims to Graceland and the *Coronation Street* set, "the emotional significance of visiting fan places lies in the ability of fans to put themselves physically into the otherwise textual universe" (2005: 61).

These pilgrims are not necessarily bonding with others like them; they are bonding with Luke Skywalker, Scottie and Madeleine, Mulder and Scully. Remember in this context how Kevin and Schally described themselves as becoming immersed in the text through an emotional identification with Fox Mulder. Chantal described the characters as "old friends," a term repeated by Nina: "I am sitting down with old friends; I know they are not going to let me down." As already noted, Aden suggests that viewers "accompany the agents on their journeys" (1999: 153); Bellefleur echoes this idea that the characters, rather than other fans, can be a viewer's fellow travelers. "They take the audience on a journey, or Mulder takes Scully on a journey and thus the audience along with her." Fans can achieve a sense of belonging by entering on their own into the familiar world of the text, and a sense of companionship from reuniting with characters they know almost as family.

A Sort of Homecoming

Fan viewing of *The X-Files* has changed since Aden's research. Seven of my thirteen respondents made a distinction between watching new and unfamiliar episodes, which for them was now only a nostalgic memory, and their current practice of re-viewing the show on DVD and video, or catching a repeated episode by chance on TV. In the latter case, the experience was entirely different. Kevin spoke of feeling "just reassured because it's familiar [. . .] I could have a really bad day, and pop in an episode"; Maddy expressed her feelings of "relaxation, assurance, happiness—I am always cheered up." To Chantal, episodes now are "a much more relaxing experience. [. . .] I really miss the excitement of having unfamiliar episodes," and Nina, as already shown, used similar terms: "I feel relaxed and reassured. I am sitting down with old friends; I know they are not going to let me down."

Is "pilgrimage" still the right word for these reassuring, therapeutic, cheering sessions with familiar guides and confidantes? Revisiting one of Mulder and Scully's old journeys evokes a nostalgic trip to the known past, like an evening with old diaries and holiday videos, rather than an expedition into the unknown. Should pilgrimage not involve more sense of effort, struggle, trial, and test, and imply a transit away from the homely toward the sacred? How can an immersion in both physical and emotional comfort, a session with "old friends," be discussed alongside the ordeal of pilgrims at St. Patrick's Purgatory at Lough Derg, where sleep- and food-deprived visitors must repeat nightlong circuits along stony paths, repeating scores of Hail Marys and Our Fathers (Turner & Turner 1978: 119)?

Alan Morinis, while embracing the concept of inner, or nongeographical, pilgrimage alongside more traditional, physical journeys, suggests that a factor in all pilgrimage must be a passage from one pole (which he lists as familiar, known, human, social) to the other (mysterious, divine, ideal, perfect); a movement between the "all-too-known" and the "unknown" (1992: 25–26). These fan testimonies of watching *The X-Files* in its current form—and the same must be true of every show that has passed from the excitement of weekly installments through finale to DVD archive—clearly describe the first pole, the origin point, but with no apparent transit to a destination. Although the experience of an unfamiliar episode—an hour of anticipation, tears, joy, and anger, which encourages the viewers to question what they know, strengthens or challenges their spiritual faith, invites them to sympathize with villains and believe in the inexplicable— could fit within this structure of oppositions, cozy re-encounters with a familiar show would be a more difficult case to argue.

The answer lies in a revisiting of what pilgrimage means. The case of Lough Derg is a particularly extreme example of physical deprivation and committed faith, but the performance of apparently endless stations, devotions, and circuits on jagged rock and in rain, with only lake water and dry bread for consolation, offers its pilgrims a remarkable feeling of comfort. Lough Derg is a center for Irish nationalism, and many of those who make the devotional trip are overseas Irish, connecting, though they have left their everyday environments behind, with a powerful sense of homeland. Turner quotes a 1944 volume on the pilgrimage that stresses the deep pleasures in the physical punishment:

"Most pilgrims develop for this rocky island and its harsh routine an affection that really defies explanation. Again and again they return to it with a gaiety, an uplifting of the heart, a profound sense of relief, in short the very sentiments proper to homecoming after life-long exile" (Curtayne, quoted in Turner 1969: 124).

This experience of pilgrimage as a homecoming—a sense of rejoining a community, even if the individual travels far from home—is, Turner notes, also central to other cultures, such as the Guadalupe pilgrimage with its importance to Mexican ethnic identity (1969: 125); we might consider the Islamic hajj to Mecca in the same context. However, the feeling of belonging to a community is not confined to nation and race. Sandvoss, writing of football supporters and media followers, suggests that fandom "best compares to the emotional significance of the places we have grown to call 'home,' to the form of physical, emotional *and* ideological space that is best described as *Heimat*" (2005: 64).

The association of a sacred place of fandom with belonging helps contextualize the practice and experience of fan pilgrims. The visitors to Graceland in King's 1993 account "have travelled thousands of miles, from Japan, from Europe and now from Russia" but now experience "a feeling of shared purpose" in candlelit vigil and quiet devotion, where Elvis impersonators "greet each other solemnly" (King 1993: 102–3). Similarly, Doss describes Graceland as "the most visible public place where they can comfortably and collectively express their private feelings for Elvis" (1992: 90). The Lewis Carroll Society of Great Britain returns regularly to Charles Dodgson's birthplace in Daresbury and grave in Guildford: though reserved, their testimonies are invested with emotional connection. "One gets a bit closer to the man and his time by being in places associated with him"; "Seeing where it all began, Daresbury Parsonage, was very affecting" (Brooker 2005a: 282).

They depart from their own habitus and the frameworks of everyday life, but those who travel to the homes or final resting places of Presley and Carroll experience their destinations as familiar, safe, places of communion and reassurance. The terms Morinis associates with the two poles of pilgrimage's origin and destination should therefore be adjusted: though the destination point does carry, as Morinis suggests, the values of "perfect ideal," that ideal can also be bound up with the "familiar," the "known," the "human" and "social" (1992: 26).

In Sandvoss's conception of *Heimat*, the feeling of belonging can operate at a conceptual level, as well as in physical space. The latter offers a deeper, more intense experience—offering "the rare opportunity to relocate in space a profound sense of belonging which has otherwise shifted into the textual space of media consumption"—but *Heimat* can also signify a "symbolic, personal space" (2005: 64). So, just as football fans describe both their club (as a concept) and its stadium (the physical place) in the same terms of security, stability, and warmth, so entering the textual world of *The X-Files* can provide what Sandvoss terms a "mobile *Heimat*," less profound than standing where Mulder stood and inserting oneself into the fiction, but nevertheless a sense of returning, of immersion in a place of belonging, that fits the broader definition of pilgrimage.

During this research, I undertook a journey of my own. Despite my own initial resistance to Aden's treatment of TV viewing as metaphorical travel, a revisiting of pilgrimage's connotations—combined with the testimonies of viewers engaged in the same fandom as Aden's respondents—convinced me that this ritualized, immersive TV viewing common to fan practice can qualify as "symbolic pilgrimage."

As a final note, I would go further, and suggest that "symbolic pilgrimage" is more than just a subcategory of or poor cousin to "real," geographical journeys, offering a fainter taste of the same sensations and a shallower sense of connection. In fact, symbolic immersion and psychological leaps of faith are integral to many, perhaps the majority of, geographical media pilgrimages. When a fan visits Union Station, Los Angeles, it takes significant imagination and investment to transform this busy, modern railway hub into the dingy police headquarters of *Blade Runner*. Hills admits that the Vancouver sites of *X-Files* pilgrimage are "banal: a back-street alleyway, a university building, a shopping precinct escalator" (2002: 149). Cavicchi describes Springsteen fans visiting an ordinary house in New Jersey: "No big deal, you know. Could have been anyone's house. (pause) But it was Bruce's house" (1998: 171). Even Graceland, Doss observes, is a "mundane mansion," unremarkable in itself: "well, gee, Graceland's not that grand and Elvis's guitar-shaped swimming pool is awfully teeny" (1992: 23). These places are made special for the most part through their symbolic value, serving as a physical, earthly focus for something greater and intangible. This is what Sandvoss, drawing on Edward Relph, calls "'other-directedness,' places not experienced in and for themselves but in reference to absent codes and symbols" (2005: 58). The alley, the grave, the stadium, the station may seem mundane to non-fans; but once the pilgrim has made the geographical journey, he or she makes an internal leap ("this is where Deckard stood . . . this is where Carroll lies") that completes the connection and enables communion. Just as a fan may "travel" metaphorically without moving to a place of belonging, so fans who travel physically may well, at their destination, still have a symbolic journey ahead of them.

WORKS CITED

Aden, RC 1999, *Popular stories and promised lands: fan cultures and symbolic pilgrimages*, University of Alabama Press, Tuscaloosa.

Brooker, W 2002, *Using the force: creativity, community, and Star Wars fans*, Continuum, New York.

Brooker, W 2004, "Living on *Dawson's Creek*: teen viewers, cultural convergence, and television overflow," in RC Allen & A Hill (eds.), *The television studies reader*, Routledge, New York.

Brooker, W 2005a, *Alice's adventures: Lewis Carroll in popular culture*, Continuum, New York.

Brooker, W (ed.) 2005b, *The* Blade Runner *experience: the legacy of a science fiction classic*, Wallflower, New York.

Cavicchi, D 1998, *Tramps like us: music and meaning among Springsteen fans*. Oxford University Press, New York.

Couldry, N 2000, *The place of media power: pilgrims and witnesses of the media age*, Routledge, New York.

Csikszentmihalyi, M 2002, *Flow: the classic work on how to achieve happiness*, Rider, London.

Doss, E 1992, *Elvis culture: fans, faith, and image*, University Press of Kansas, Lawrence.

Fiske, J 1987, *Television culture*, Routledge, New York.

Hills, M 2002, *Fan cultures*, Routledge, New York.

King, C 1993, "His truth goes marching on: Elvis Presley and the pilgrimage to Graceland," in JA Walter (ed.), *Pilgrimage in popular culture*, Palgrave Macmillan, London.

Morinis, A 1992, *Sacred journeys*, Greenwood, Westport, CT.

Sandvoss, C 2005, *Fans: the mirror of consumption*, Polity, Malden, MA.

Turner, V 1969, *The ritual process: structure and anti-structure*, Aldine de Gruyter, New York.

Turner, V & Turner, E 1978, *Image and pilgrimage in Christian culture*, Columbia University Press, New York.

Van Gennep, A 1960, *The rites of passage*, University of Chicago Press, Chicago.

10

Reimagining the Imagined Community

Online Media Fandoms in the Age of Global Convergence

LORI HITCHCOCK MORIMOTO AND BERTHA CHIN

A central truism of English-language media fan studies is that modern fandoms are "imagined communities" fostered by technologies that enable geographically dispersed people to overcome time and distance in forging virtual communities of affect. As originally theorized by Benedict Anderson (1991), imagined communities arise through the interpellation of both local and expatriate citizens as national subjects under commonalities of language, race, and ideology by means of the transnational reach of "print capitalism" (36). In its fan studies iteration, a theory of imagined communities foregrounds the transborder, transnational reach of the Internet in creating a sense of simultaneous, shared popular cultural experience. In this sense, the emphasis in English-language media fan studies scholarship on online fan communities as comprising people from diverse locations and cultures figures modern media fandom as necessarily transcultural. As we have argued elsewhere, the process of becoming a transcultural fan is not bound by any necessary cultural, geographical, or national difference or similarity, occurring instead "because of a moment of affinity between the fan and transcultural object" (Chin & Morimoto 2013: 104–5). Yet, in fan studies work that uses imagined communities to emphasize distance overcome, we lose sight of the disparities and disjunctures that may characterize transcultural interactions within fandoms both on- and offline. In the process, marginalized and peripheral voices and perspectives are effectively silenced.

Thus, the problems of fan studies' depoliticized use of imagined communities are twofold. First, work that stresses untroubled (and often idealistic) geotemporal convergence in global media fandoms elides the critique inherent in imagined communities as a way of thinking about how and why communities of affect and belonging are constituted. It may be that the online locus of many such fandoms contributes to this depoliticization; absent noticeable signifiers of cultural diversity, English-language online fan communities often flatten difference, particularly when their fannish focus centers on hegemonic Anglo-American media texts. In contrast, research of sports fandoms that coalesce in the physical spaces of stadiums, fields, and gymnasiums has been far more attuned to imagined communities as an inherently critical construct, defined by "the style in which they are imagined" (Anderson 1991: 6). Such scholarship criticizes discourses and practices of community building within fandoms that, in elevating certain constituent commonalities over others, depend as much on exclusion as inclusion (Blackshaw 2008). It is this focus on *how* fan communities are imagined—which culturally specific practices and assumptions are privileged, which are rejected and why—that we would like to see acknowledged in fan studies, particularly when global convergence increasingly exposes media fandoms to an ever greater diversity of texts, cultures, and practices.

Second, the loss of—or, perhaps, missed opportunity for—a transcultural perspective on media fandoms seems symptomatic of an imagined community of English-language media fan studies itself. We are a discipline constituted through not only perceived commonalities of language, culture, and media, but also the exclusion by omission of "other" fan cultures and even disciplinary concerns. Where debates arise over what "we" should be studying, or how "we" should approach it, we discern a centripetal/centrifugal tension between normative community frameworks and those that seek to challenge their assumptions. The ease with which the latter can be—and often is—pushed to the periphery of mainstream fan studies in turn leaves us with an almost empty category of discrete, typically nation-aligned "transcultural fan studies," all too easily dismissed as irrelevant to the real work of the discipline. Yet, particularly in this much vaunted present-day "age of the fan," fans—and fan scholars—hail from a diversity of cultures: of nation and language, but also race, class, gender, sexuality, age, and so on. Inasmuch as we commingle, participate, and not-infrequently clash within global social media-centered fan communities, not to mention English-language fan studies, we see a critical need for media fan studies to adopt a more transcultural perspective that is less about "global fan studies" (Harrington & Bielby 2007: 191), per se, than being rigorously cognizant of what we (re)create when we assert broad generalizations about what fandom is or isn't.

The adoption of a transcultural perspective within fan studies is, of course, easier said than done, at least at first glance. Anecdotal evidence suggests a widespread perception that lack of fluency in other languages and popular cultures all but precludes engagement with them, a perception that is reinforced by the material contexts of existing work.[1] Scholarship of non-Western and non-English-language fans and fan cultures is frequently, if unintentionally, segregated from mainstream English-language fan studies, corralled into area-specific anthologies, special journal issues, and academic conference panels in such a way that they become all too easy to overlook. This is arguably exacerbated when transcultural fan studies scholars contribute to this ghettoization in failing to articulate our work with the broader concerns of English-language fan studies.

We contend, however, that such perceptions equally reflect the way fan studies scholars conceive of "transculturalism" as necessarily implicated in trans*national* media flows and consumption. As Sandra Annett has observed, although transculturalism is "the cultural dimension of transnationalism [. . .] there is often slippage between 'nation' and 'culture'" (2014: 9). Understood as something that *may* be nation-centered, but may not be as well, a transcultural orientation enables us to conceive of extranational subject positions that assert themselves to varying and always shifting degrees at the levels of both the individual fan and fandom generally. By recognizing fans as more than the sum total of a singular affective interest or national belonging, and fan communities as inherently transcultural sites characterized as much by conflict as concord, we open up a space for the possibility of understanding fan studies as a fundamentally transcultural enterprise.

In what follows, we contribute to a growing body of scholarship that draws attention to the problems inherent in generalized and uninterrogated assumptions about fandoms and fan cultures (Sandvoss 2009; Stanfill 2011; Jenkins 2014; Wanzo 2015; van de Goor 2015) in making the case for a critical fan studies that is attuned to the transcultural contexts of, and implications for, fans and fan communities in the age of global media convergence. With Annett, we do not fix transculturalism at the level of definition. Instead we deploy it strategically to discuss how transnational fans and fan communities intersect with more familiar sites of inquiry, as well as how fans and fan scholars closer to home imagine the communities of English-language media fandom.

"Fan" and "Fandom" in Transcultural Context

Within English-language media fandoms, communities of a certain critical mass tend to understand the "fan" in implicit terms. These are determined in large part by those fans whose practices and preferences have been forged over time in established spaces such as LiveJournal communities or fan-run conventions and fan clubs, who have attained a certain level of social and cultural capital within them and thus hold sway over how they are defined. This is the generalized fan favored by—among others—those gatekeepers whose often self-appointed role within fan communities is maintaining certain standards of behavior, practice, and even fannish object. Given their mediating role between insider/outsider, such fans are also often the face of fandom that finds its way into English-language fan scholarship, where references to implicitly understood, ill-defined "fans" and "fandom" abound. It might be argued that such generalizations are a holdover from the earliest days of English-language fan studies, when VCR-fueled transnational media exchange was in its infancy, pre-Internet fan communities were still heavily localized, and circulation of English-language scholarship was confined to relatively closed academic communities.

Nonetheless, this generic fan fails to reflect the actual diversity of inherently transcultural media fandoms. Nor are such transcultural fandoms a new or even recent development. Ien Ang's (1985) groundbreaking study, *Watching Dallas*, explored how Dutch viewers made meaning of the otherwise ostentatiously American television show *Dallas* against a backdrop of ambivalence toward the United States. In a fan studies context, her work foregrounds the need for research of fans outside an Anglo-American habitus as a means of challenging not only the hegemonic "fan" of English-language fan studies, but also our assumptions about how familiar texts might change when viewed against other cultural backdrops. This is a need that has not diminished in the intervening years. The popularity today of American and British television shows in Mainland China, for example, has had a material effect on overseas distribution practices, often streaming online concurrently—and legitimately—with the United States and/or United Kingdom where once they had been confined to the rare terrestrial broadcast or DVD. Such immediate access to this media in turn enables Chinese fans to participate in online show-centered fandoms in real time. Chinese fans react to narrative developments and extranarrative star and production news, and participate in the creation of transformative works, in many of the same online spaces as other fans around the world. Where language is sometimes a barrier to one kind of communication (albeit less frequently than one might think), Chinese fan artists post their works to sites such as US-based Tumblr and DeviantArt, as well as Japan-based Pixiv.net, often to the acclaim of fans from around the world. In this sense, they are as fully members of a given media text's fan community as the more recognizable "fan" of English-language scholarship. As such, these fans' presence begs the question of what it is they make of (and do with) media texts, and how it might not simply differ from, and clash with, the norms of the imagined fan community, but inflect that community as well.

Indeed, the heavily visual sites where online fandoms today proliferate are populated by a diversity of transnational media fans who, armed with online dictionaries and copy/paste functions, learn to navigate them well enough to participate in them. Neither is this a unidirectional, West-to-rest flow of media and fandom. Japanese terminology, for instance, has become common in certain kinds of English-language fanfiction (Chin & Morimoto 2013: 103), while in some fan communities, words like *nakama* (indicating a close associate) and phrases such as "*sempai* noticed me" take on fresh significance almost independent of their Japanese origins. Western fans of South Korean popular culture or Japanese anime and manga equally use the Internet to participate in those fan cultures to degrees of involvement ranging from lurking on official and unofficial fan sites to acting as local intermediaries for West-residing fans and to incorporating the media and fan practices of the originating culture into their own popular cultural repertoires. And certainly, this kind of intensified participation in online (and offline) global media fandoms encourages a sense of transcultural fan community belonging among globally dispersed individual fans.

Particularly when such fans are able to participate in a real-time fannish moment—the online release of a new film trailer, or an overseas celebrity junket played out in photographs posted to news, entertainment, and fan websites—the sense of camaraderie produced by this shared and intensely affective experience, regardless of perceived language and cultural barriers, cannot be overstated. When, for example, *Sherlock* star Benedict Cumberbatch traveled to Japan for the second of two junkets to promote *Star Trek into Darkness*, his activities—including a television interview in which he was outfitted in a traditional Japanese summer kimono—were followed avidly by fans both in Japan and abroad. Among resulting Internet memes was art produced by fans in Japan, China, Thailand, France, the United States, and elsewhere featuring the fan-dubbed "Yukata!Batch" in all his kimono-clad glory. The junket might have been intended for Cumberbatch's and the *Star Trek* franchise's Japanese fans, but it played out as a globally shared fan experience.

At the same time, it is this very simultaneity and distance overcome that equally produces misunderstandings and conflicts within fan communities. The same copy/paste function that enables Western fans of anime to seek out and enjoy Japanese anime-centered fan art, for example, allows them to copy and repost that art instantly, with or without permission from the original artist. The resulting transcultural conflict, born of incompatibilities in the community standards and practices of distinct fan cultures within a broader fan community, has the potential to both foster discussion and deepen existing schisms. Thus in the early 2000s, for example, non-Japanese fans who understood Japanese fan art as there for the taking, so long as one acknowledged the artist (reflecting, among other things, a "fair use" framework that underpins American transformative works), clashed with Japanese artists who, coming from a more clandestine shadow economy of fanworks, insisted that "that will be same [*sic*] as stealing to us" (Online Fanarts Protection 2006: n.p.). As a result, many Japanese fan artists reacted by locking their fan art behind password-protected walls. Fast-forward to 2013, when one of the American fan artists who contributed to the above-mentioned "Yukata!Batch"-themed artwork has adopted these Japanese artists' stance toward the reposting of her art in reaction to similar practices by Russian fans more recently arrived in transcultural fan communities.

This is to say, the distinct cultural backdrop that differentiated Ang's Dutch *Dallas* viewers from the show's American audience in the 1980s still exists today, albeit in spatiotemporally intensified online fan communities that at once belie the cultural hybridity of online fan communities, and are often punctuated by incompatibilities between (fans') cultural assumptions and expectations. Particularly given the proliferation of avenues for global media dissemination (both official and unofficial), lowered barriers to entry for online participation in fan communities, and changing technoscapes of online fandoms themselves, there is thus a critical need to recognize and engage with the transcultural dimensions of the online fan communities we research. As online media fandoms migrate from relatively lockable, often moderated communities such as bulletin boards, Yahoo! groups, and Live-Journals to more rhizomatic social media platforms such as Twitter and Tumblr,[2] and fan conventions increasingly attract attendees immersed in the transfandom mélange of online fan cultures (Hills 2015, quoted in Greco 2015: 160), so must we recognize that normative "fans" and "fandom" are increasingly untenable objects of research.

Fandom in/as Contact Zone

Online fandom began in earnest for us both at the beginning of the new millennium, in the moderated, members-only confines of the *X-Files* Yahoo! group, I Want to Believe (IWTB). This was where we first met and became acquainted through both shared fandom and the happy coincidence of being PhD students working in media fan studies. We were each transnational migrants and transcultural media fans, Bertha as an Australia-educated Malaysian expatriate living in the United Kingdom, and Lori as an on-again-off-again American expatriate in Japan by way of a childhood spent in Hong Kong. In this sense, neither of us was ever the normative "fan" of either English-language scholarship or fandom, an affinity that helped draw our attention to how the "fan" and her "fandom" were being imagined by both fans and scholars alike.

Indeed, how our small *X-Files*-centered community was imagined by a core group of fans was foregrounded when, in September 2001, two commercial airplanes hit the twin towers of the World Trade Center in New York. This was an event that, for several of us, became inextricably linked to our online fan activities when a Lower Manhattan–residing member of the group began reporting on IWTB about what she was witnessing outside her window, before some of us had made it to a television to see what was happening for ourselves. Early conversation about the event on IWTB was characterized by intensely personal stories—the above-mentioned fan's trauma over experiencing it firsthand, and another fan's loss of a close personal friend in the tower collapse. Within the week, though, certain strains of discourse began to assert themselves over others. In particular, "fans" were exhorted by some fellow fans to display "our" patriotism openly and actively, while online discussion of where "we" might go from there was dominated by a handful of strident American voices inclined toward a military response. Our mutual horror at the lives lost notwithstanding, those fans with different perspectives on the causes and potential responses to, if not effects of, the attack were effectively silenced by a hegemonic community ethos that demanded agreement or, lacking it, acquiescence to a nationalistic American interpretation of what had happened, and what should happen next; never mind that many members of the community were neither Americans nor based in the United States.

This anecdote may seem unusually fraught with "real-world" upheaval, yet fandom is always performed against a backdrop of real-world events, constraints, and subjectivities. Our experience exemplifies the ways intercommunity and transcultural conflict often play out within fandoms. Even when the stakes are (arguably) lower, centering on issues such as racial (mis)representation and misogyny in media, or gendered, racial, or sexual derision aimed at fans from within fan communities, what frequently get privileged are consensus and decorum: hewing to unwritten rules that benefit the few in the name of the undifferentiated many. The assumption that all fans necessarily agree with and are governed by such rules or, conversely, that there exist agreed-upon rules of engagement for disputing them—*this* is how fan communities are in fact imagined.

Mary Louise Pratt (1991) argues that dissent and difference are as characteristic of increasingly transnational and transcultural communities as accord and consensus. For Pratt, communities may be imagined, per Anderson, as essentially homogenous sites of mutual affinity, but in practice they are "contact zones [and . . . those] social spaces where cultures meet, clash, and grapple with each other, often in contexts of highly asymmetrical relations of power" (34). Following from Pratt, Henry Jenkins (2014) recently has observed, "digital fandom is increasingly becoming [. . .] a 'contact zone' between participants with very different historical experiences of race" (98)—a sentiment with which we are in agreement, and would suggest extends to other cultural and social contexts as well. Thus, for example, within an American context alone, where white American fans are in no way compelled to pay attention to or otherwise acknowledge racial representation in the American media around which a given fandom arises, African American fans are often unavoidably implicated in a love/hate calculus with media they may love, but that has not been created with them in mind. For them, fandom is not solely or simply a "mode of social organization that has the potential to move from being a subculture (that is, a social group based on common interests) to a community (that is, based on shared geography, kinship, or history)" (Coppa 2014: 78). Rather, fandom for these fans is also a *culturally generalizable* African American experience of "anxious waiting for a troubling representation to appear" (Wanzo 2015) both on-screen and within media fandom, often at odds with the communal possibilities of "fandom."

Within the contact zones of online fandom, the normative fandom of shared affinities and even aspirations is, in its intrinsic transculturality, always already a site of difference, and even potential danger, for fans who do not hew to the cultural norms of the imagined community. Fans and scholars alike imagine English-language online fandoms as sites of often-irreverent play, where meanings may be inverted and texts parodied and transformed even past the point of recognition. Yet what happens when this play is imbued with irrevocable gravity for a marginalized culture within a given fan community?

The hashtag #BlackLivesMatter was coined by Alicia Garza, Patrisse Cullors, and Opal Tometi in the wake of police officer George Zimmerman's 2013 acquittal in the death of African American teenager Trayvon Martin (Garza 2014: n.p.). Subsequently, activists deployed it to draw attention to the phenomenon of institutionalized police brutality in black communities throughout the United States in a movement that continues as of this writing. In 2015, the hashtag was appropriated by non–African American fans to ostensibly "playful" ends in a *Teen Wolf* Wikia-produced vid titled "Blue Jeeps Matter," created to mourn the loss of Stiles Stilinski's blue Jeep, "Roscoe." The vid opens with a faux gravitas-laden eulogy, overlaying episode footage of the car being destroyed in an accident:

> What happened this week in Beacon Hills is a tragedy that none of us will soon forget. We at *Teen Wolf* Wikia want you to know that you all are in our thoughts and prayers at this difficult time. We urge you not to dwell on the horrific death of our fallen friend and avoid recriminations against the individual who appears to be responsible. Instead, we implore you to remember just how much having this special friend enriched all our lives. (2015: n.p.)

Possibly created in response to MTV's own #RIPRoscoeTheJeep hashtag, the vid, opening monologue, and hashtag-derived title (which subsequently appeared as the hashtag #bluejeepsmatter on a news banner image at *Teen Wolf* Wikia) are clearly intended to be tongue-in-cheek, congruent with the kind of playfulness foregrounded in fan and scholarly conceptions of fandom.

Yet, its creator's intentions notwithstanding, the intended playfulness of the vid was lost on some fans within the transcultural contact zone of online *Teen Wolf* fandom. As African American *Teen Wolf* fan Cloama wrote on her Tumblr,

> It's wild, I tell you. It's really wild. I gave myself a moment to enjoy fandom. I'm chilling, enjoying femslash week, digging on some gifsets, loving the inclusion of all ladies in fic and art [. . .]. Then teenwolfwikia makes a Blue Jeeps Matter vid and that shit spreads like gingivitis over here on tumblr. It's so horrid. It's so bad. It's so disrespectful. Can I have one day where I can chill and read about two lady supernatural creatures having sex and cuddling after fighting evil forces without y'all blowing up the fucking spot with your bullshit????? Can I live? (2015: n.p.)[3]

Cloama's feelings are further elaborated in tags to this post, where she states, "fandom is not made for me," noting, "whenever I try to tailor it to my interests it still blows up in my face" (Cloama 2015: n.p.). Her frustration is made palpable in language that, rather than reinforcing a stereotype of dour and humorless racial critique, in fact transforms the playful language of fan-speak ("having sex and cuddling after fighting evil forces") to serious ends. This is to say, through her fannish fluency she claims a subjectivity no different from that of any other "fan," then foregrounds her actual distance from such normative fandom through an intensely personal response to the racialized violence the vid's playfulness overlays (and even enacts).

Other fannish appropriations of #BlackLivesMatter have had similarly distancing effects; as Zina H. writes in response to an unapologetic likening of activists' use of the hashtag to fan activism that critiques masculine representation in DC comics fandom:

> I've never felt safe in the DC fandom as a black person (so much racism from people who never tried to do better and still were beloved) but geez, when I see people taking a movement about my people being killed at shocking numbers so they can proselytize all over the place about how male sexualisation in Grayson is the real evil, I'm just reminded that fan spaces really aren't safe spaces for black people. (2015: n.p.)

Not restricted to race, there are myriad such frictions within fan communities, the result of different degrees of access to and identification with power, and vulnerability to textual misrepresentation or violence mirrored in fandoms. And it is where such experiences, generalizable at the intracultural level, are expressed in terms of frustration or outright anger within the contact zone of the imagined fan community that we may discern Pratt's observation of "internal social groups with histories and lifeways different from the official ones [. . .] insisting on those histories and lifeways *as part of their citizenship*" (1991: 39) in that community. Migrations from and incursions into heretofore-bordered (fan) spaces have become increasingly marked by ongoing and often heated contestation of "accepted" community standards. When dissent is voiced by marginalized fans, they typically are met with variations on a familiar refrain of how "toxic" fandom has become, and exhortations (even demands) to be "civil," "moderate," or "nice" as part and parcel of how "the fandom" should behave—the fandom equivalent of journalists and commentators who, in the wake of #BlackLivesMatter disruptions of American politicians' speeches, urged African American decorum over dissent.

We see such skirmishes as characteristic of the transcultural nature of online fandoms today, rather than markers of toxicity and the breakdown of fan communities. And it is when fans begin to recognize themselves not as the norm to which all must hew, but as individuals with histories and subjectivities different from those of fellow fans, that the potential of a transcultural orientation is realized. As white, queer *Sherlock* fan UrbanHymnal explained of her decision to shelve a fanfiction writing challenge that would have seen Sherlock Holmes and John Watson translated to the cross-dressing world of the early 1980s television show *Bosom Buddies*:

> I think a lot of the concern around the idea *is* genuine. The truth is many trans women are portrayed in media as nothing more than "men in dresses" trying to trick people. Comedy is especially bad about doing this and I was fully aware of this trope when I picked the show. It is, in part, what I hoped to work against.
>
> In part I had hoped to take something that could be seen as being trans phobic and turn it on its head: what if Sherlock was just as comfortable in heels and a dress as he is in his Belstaff and suits? What if this leads to discussions of gender representation? What if John learns something about himself during the case and by talking to Sherlock about gender and sexuality? What if I did all that and still kept it lighthearted and fun without it ever portraying Sherlock as being odd or John as being malicious in his confusion? Regardless, I think if I were ever to approach this idea in full, I would want to devote a lot of time to it and get quite a bit of feedback from people who are transgender, something I just wouldn't have time for with this current challenge. (UrbanHymnal 2015: n.p.)

Rather than hiding behind good intentions, UrbanHymnal acknowledges the potential for harm in an idea that, within the context of the normative "fan community," might not be perceived as inflammatory (indeed, her post here is in response to a fellow fan encouraging her to write the story regardless of criticism she has received). She implicitly acknowledges here both the transcultural diversity of her fandom readership and her own need to delve deeper into an unfamiliar culture before she attempts to write it.

It is in this recognition of fan communities as both imagined, in Anderson's sense of the word, and reimaginable through thoughtful engagement within online contact zones that we locate the possibility of critical, transcultural fandom and fan studies. As we have asserted elsewhere, we are uninterested in moral dualisms that pit "good" fandom against "bad" fandom (Chin & Morimoto 2013: 98); rather, we are interested in the question of "what happens when"—what happens when nonnative English speakers participate in Anglo-American-dominated English-language fandom? What happens when nonwhite fans, regardless of geographical location, voice their concerns over racial representation within predominantly white online media fandoms? What happens when the walls separating fans and producers (or fan-scholars) begin to crumble, thrusting us all into yet another kind of contact zone? Fandoms *are* imagined communities, and as such they—like fan studies itself—are reimaginable to reflect more closely their inherent transcultural diversity and complexity.

Conclusion

In the introduction to this chapter, we asserted that English-language fan studies are ourselves an imagined community, defined as much by where we choose to focus our attention and how we define "fans" and "fandom" as by shared scholarly concerns. There exists a growing wealth of scholarship on fandom in both non-Western and non-English-speaking contexts, as well as the transcultural dimensions of more familiar fannish activity. Yet, these remain overwhelmingly outside the aegis of "mainstream" English-language fan studies, isolated by double-edged journal issues and anthologies that at once enable scholars seeking such scholarship to find it, while at the same time enabling others to overlook them entirely, on the basis of their perceived disconnectedness and inapplicability to discussion of Anglo-American media and fandoms.[4] Indeed, the idea that specialized knowledge of foreign languages and/or popular cultures is a prerequisite for engagement with transcultural fans and fandoms pervades fan studies culture, to the extent that scholars of transcultural fandoms are effectively dependent on the kindness of allies to engage with and disseminate our work.

Those of us working in non-English-language, non-Western fan studies have a responsibility to articulate our work with the broader concerns of fan studies, identifying intersections of object and theory in such a way that we are active participants in a global(izing) conversation. At the same time, a transculturally oriented fan studies must acknowledge the ways that fans and fandoms have been imagined in English-language scholarship. As is the case in the majority of work on so-called transcultural fans and fandoms, the subjects of Lori's research ("Japanese female fans") typically require at least two descriptors in order to situate them within a broadly conceived fan studies. Contrast this with, as but one example, recent work in general issues of journals such as *Transformative Works and Cultures* and *Journal of Fandom Studies*—the flagship publications of our discipline—in which references to generalized "fannish" practices, "fans," and "fandom" abound. The effect, however unintentional, is an implicit privileging of one kind of fannish identity and experience (Anglo-American, typically imagined as white, middle-class, and heterosexual, although seldom stated in so many words) as the de facto object of fan studies proper—the centripetal norm.

As such, the first step toward a more transculturally oriented fan studies is to identify exactly who it is we are discussing in our research in the same way we do other—and othered—fans. Only through our transparency about the subjects of fan studies will we be able to discern the ways we imagine the discipline, the better to begin incorporating other voices and experiences of fandom in an age of global convergence.

NOTES
1 A lack of fluency in other languages and cultural contexts may hinder attempts at conducting research. More often than not, however, it becomes the raison d'être for not engaging in fan culture beyond that which is familiar.
2 This doesn't mean that these social-media-based sites aren't deleted or locked when convenient to fans. Rather, they represent more personal pages and identities than the communal ones of Yahoo! Groups, LiveJournal, and forums.
3 All quotes from fan blogs and personal identifiers are used with permission.
4 See Gatson and Reid (2012) and Kustritz (2015).

WORKS CITED

Anderson, B 1991, *Imagined communities: reflections on the origin and spread of nationalism*, Verso, London.

Ang, I 1985, *Watching Dallas: soap opera and melodramatic imagination*, Methuen, London.

Annett, S 2014, *Anime fan communities: transcultural flows and frictions*, Palgrave Macmillan, New York.

Blackshaw, T 2008, "Contemporary community theory and football," *Soccer & Society* 9(3): 325–45.

Chin, B & Morimoto, LH 2013, "Towards a theory of transcultural fandom," *Participations: Journal of Audience & Reception Studies* 10(1): 92–108.

Cloama 2015, "It's wild, I tell you," August 21, cloama.tumblr.com.

Coppa, F 2014, "Fuck yeah, fandom is beautiful," *Journal of Fandom Studies* 2(1): 73–82.

Garza, A 2014, "A herstory of the #BlackLivesMatter movement by Alicia Garza," October 7, www.thefeministwire.com.

Gatson, SN & Reid, RA 2012, "Race and ethnicity in fandom," *Transformative Works and Cultures* 8, doi.10.3983/twc.2012.0392.

Greco, C 2015. "Fandom as an object and the objects of fandom: Interview with Matt Hills," *MATRIZes* 9(1): 147–62.

Harrington, CL & Bielby, D 2007, "Global fandom/global fan studies," in J Gray, C Sandvoss, & CL Harrington (eds.), *Fandom: identities and communities in a mediated world*, New York University Press, New York.

Jenkins, H 2014, "Fandom studies as I see it," *Journal of Fandom Studies* 2(2): 89–109.

Kustritz, A 2015, "Transnationalism, localization, and translation in European fandom: fan studies as global media and audience studies," *Transformative Works and Cultures* 19, dx.doi.org/10.3983/twc.2015.0682.

Online Fanarts Protection 2006, ofp.yu.to.

Pratt, ML 1991, "Arts of the contact zone," *Profession*, 33–40.

Sandvoss, C 2009, "Popular culture and globalisation," in BS Turner (ed.), *The Routledge international handbook of globalization studies*, Routledge, London.

Stanfill, M 2011, "Doing fandom, (mis)doing whiteness: heteronormativity, racialization, and the discursive construction of fandom," *Transformative Works and Cultures* 8, doi:10.3983/twc.2011.0256.

Teen Wolf Wikia 2015, "Blue Jeeps matter," August 6, www.youtube.com.

UrbanHymnal 2015, September 4, urbanhymnal.tumblr.com.

van de Goor, SC 2015, "'You must be new here': reinforcing the good fan," *Participations: Journal of Audience & Reception Studies* 12(2): 275–95.

Wanzo, R 2015, "African American acafandom and other strangers: new genealogies of fan studies," *Transformative Works and Cultures* 20, dx.doi.org/10.3983/twc.2015.0699.

Zina H 2015, September 4, stitchomancy.tumblr.com.

PART III

Temporalities of Fandom

11

Do All "Good Things" Come to an End?

Revisiting Martha Stewart Fans after ImClone

MELISSA A. CLICK

At its height, in 2002, Martha Stewart Living Omnimedia (MSLO) was a $295 million a year business (Carr 2003: C5) built on the reputation of Martha Stewart's own good taste and her penchant for "good things." Droves of eager fans consumed Stewart's advice for tasteful living through a number of formats, including books, magazines, television, radio, newspaper, and the Internet. Shaken by Stewart's conviction in 2004 for lying to federal prosecutors over the sale of her shares of ImClone stock, though, MSLO has struggled in the years since to regain its financial success, reporting annual losses every year since 2003, with the exception of 2007, when sales were boosted by an unusually large payment from Kmart (Andrews 2013). When I first wrote about fans' reactions to Martha Stewart's conviction and imprisonment over her involvement in the ImClone scandal (Click 2007), I argued that studying changes in fans and media texts would engender a better understanding of how and why fans' feelings change over time. Demonstrating the potential in such an approach, I used focus-group interviews with a range of people in Stewart's audience (from fans to anti-fans) to show that audiences' sympathetic feelings were rooted in their beliefs that Stewart was mistreated by the legal system and the media because she was a successful woman. Years later, and in the wake of MSLO's continued changing fortunes and circumstances, I have the opportunity to build on this earlier work. Taking up Matt Hills's (2005) call for fan scholars to explore "cyclical fandom," or the movement of fan objects in and out of fans' lives over time, here I revisit some audience members to whom I first spoke over ten years ago, alongside others who have similarly long histories with Martha fandom.

My current analysis engages recent research that aims to expand fan studies' boundaries by examining fans and fannish attachments from new perspectives, including fan responses to the ends of beloved media texts (Harrington 2013; Williams 2011) and exploration of fannish identifications over the life course (Harrington & Bielby 2014; Hills 2014). Such scholarship compels a longitudinal and holistic focus on the processes and purposes of fandom. For instance, Williams's examination of fan response to moments of transition, including the endings of television series and the loss of beloved characters, underscores how much there is still to learn about fans' varied reactions to loss and how we must develop a deeper understanding of how "fandom is related to self-narrative, identity, and a sense of ontological security" (2015: 197). Studies like Bennett's (2006), Katz's (2014), and Scodari's (2014) highlight how much more we know about youthful fans than aging ones, and demonstrate the importance of generation and life experiences for the development of a complex and nuanced understanding of fandom.

This scholarship aligns with Hills's (2014) call for fan studies scholarship to see fandom not as a fixed experience singularly focused around one text or grounded in one community, but as a practice that encompasses a dynamic set of skills and competencies that can be transferred through a range of lifelong engagements. Hills asserts that the practice of "[f]ixing audiences into static categories—being a 'fan' of X or an 'anti-fan' of Y—misses the variability in shifting audience-text relations" (17). Seeking a phenomenology of fandom, Hills encourages scholars to consider the variability of fandom and to consider how fans move in and out of fandoms, and maintain multiple fannish attachments over time.

In what follows, I continue my exploration of the changes members of Stewart's audience have experienced since Stewart's imprisonment for her involvement in the ImClone scandal, and I draw upon a set of interviews with thirty-five Stewart fans: ten with whom I had previously conducted interviews, and twenty-five who are new to my project. A few weeks after Stewart's post-prison, live program *The Martha Stewart Show* premiered, in October 2005, I reinterviewed four fans whom I had originally interviewed in June 2003, hoping to capture their impressions of Stewart's comeback attempt. I conducted two additional reinterviews between March and July 2013 with six fans I had originally spoken to in October 2002 and April 2004. The twenty-five participants I interviewed in the remaining five focus groups (conducted between March and July 2013) were new to my study, but had already established relationships with and opinions of Martha Stewart. Instead of observing longitudinal fluctuations in these participants, I solicited their recollections of their feelings about Stewart.

Twenty-one of the thirty-five interviewees described themselves as fans of Martha Stewart whose interest in her remained continuous through her imprisonment, and eight indicated that their fan identity had changed, growing either more or less interested in Stewart. Alongside their pseudonyms and quotes below I indicate fans' self-report of change or continuity in their interest in Martha Stewart, and also their age. Those who reported little to no change in their fandom are designated as a "continuous fan," those who reported a decline in their fandom are designated as "no longer a fan," and those who reported an increase in their fandom are designated as "recently became a fan." Even though a majority of the (twenty-three) fans I interviewed reported continuity in their identities as Martha Stewart fans, they still recounted a number of ways in which their fandom had grown, changed, and receded. Below, I describe the three main forces that influenced fans' feelings about Martha Stewart—life transitions, textual changes, and cultural changes—and demonstrate how each contributes to their fluctuating interests in Martha Stewart.

Fandom, Life Transitions, and Homekeeping

Many of the interview participants reported that their feelings about Martha Stewart ebbed and flowed in step with life changes like the kind Harrington and Bielby (2014: 129) have described as "age-graded life transitions." As their words demonstrate, fans' changing lives created needs that they felt were readily fulfilled with engagement with Stewart's media texts. When fans moved away from particular stages into new life transitions, their interest in Stewart declined, creating space for new attachments to other media texts to develop.

The kinds of changes that impacted fans' interest in Stewart are connected to the fact that Stewart appeals to many female fans by offering information about how to perform a range of domestic tasks that Stewart describes as "homekeeping," including tasks for enjoyment and gendered tasks expected of wives and mothers. Nellie (thirties, continuous fan) explains her belief that Stewart teaches women to take pleasure and pride in domestic tasks:

> [Martha Stewart] brought us women—or women of a certain age—back to these ideas of making béchamel [. . .] my generation would have been like, "why am I going to do that? I'll go buy alfredo at the store." And she brought back a sense of pride to that sort of thing, and like, there's no shame in that, that you can still be a feminist or still be a strong woman and make yourself something.

Amelia (thirties, continuous fan) shared that Stewart offers information about homekeeping that she would have received from her mother, who had recently died: "So there are things, like [. . .] how did my mom do that? And now she's not here to ask, I feel like you can to Martha Stewart, literally." Catherine (fifties, no longer a fan) asserted that Stewart gave her useful information to help her maintain a home and raise kids while she was focused on her career, "I was working [. . .] I was not a homemaker with kids [. . .] so all of a sudden, this person had the answers, and this is what it's supposed look like because I have no idea." Thus, Martha Stewart's media messages became useful to these fans as they grew into and aspired to successfully accomplish a number of feminine tasks involving homekeeping and caregiving.

While they gravitated to Martha Stewart to learn about tasks of interest to them, fans also suggested that their age and stage in life aligned with their interests. Lillian (thirties, continuous fan) described that her interest in Stewart was connected to reaching "a certain age where domesticated tasks matter to you." For Lillian, this age was also connected to the milestone of owning her own home, when she found Stewart integral to setting up her kitchen: "When I bought my house and remodeled my kitchen, *all* of my kitchen utensils are Martha Stewart Macy's turquoise and red." Evelyn (forties, continuous fan), who described herself as a lifelong subscriber to Stewart's magazines, revealed how her investment in Stewart's magazines progressed alongside her life transitions. She described that she "planned my whole wedding using magazine pages torn out [of *Martha Stewart Weddings*] in 1999." Later, after her two sons were born, she "graduated to *Martha Stewart Kids*" and used Stewart's *Everyday Food* for "planning meals that are quick and kid friendly and sort of healthy, but with ingredients you can find at [the neighborhood grocery store]."

Life events that build new family structures, like weddings and childbirth, drove many interviewees to Martha Stewart. Katie (seventies, no longer a fan) first noticed Stewart's book *Weddings* (1987), "right about the time my kids were getting married so I was reading that. And I thought [it was] terrific." Amelia's (thirties, continuous fan) mother gave her a stack of *Martha Stewart Weddings* magazines when she became engaged: "My mom and I sat down and *poured* over *Martha Stewart Weddings*. And [she] had kept years of backlog to revisit." Having children was another milestone that many fans, like Evelyn above, mentioned as significant to their interest in Stewart. Maura (thirties, continuous fan), for instance, recounted that although she had been a fan of Stewart since college, her interest intensified after the birth of her daughter, in part because she had more time to watch television: "when I was on maternity leave I was able to watch her show almost daily, and then DVRed it until it was canceled." Pearl (fifties, recently became a fan) similarly relayed that her interest in Martha Stewart "coincided with the time in my life when I might have been looking for more things like that. You know, the kids are young and you're doing stuff."

While life changes drew many to Stewart, some fans reported that age—both their own and that of their family members—made Stewart less useful. Like many fans, Catherine (fifties, no longer a fan) indicated that her interest in Stewart corresponded with the birth and growth of her children, but reported that now that her children are older, her interest in Stewart has waned: "I used to be a big fan of Martha Stewart. And I think it was because my kids were little, I was organizing my house [. . .] so she was providing lots of useful information, and now I'm not needing that information so I've stepped away a little bit." Fiona (fifties, no longer a fan) similarly connected her reduced interest in Stewart to her current life stage, "Maybe back then, in that amount of time, there's stuff [. . .] I was learning from her shows. Now I simply just don't have [. . .] the interest. I mean, my house is set up. I'm not looking for new fashion ideas for my house, you know?" Katie (seventies, no longer a fan), who recalled being "just blown away" by Stewart when she first encountered her in the 1990s, had recently moved into a retirement community when I spoke with her for the second time. She shared that because she is in a "stage in life where I don't buy anything anymore" she is less interested in Stewart's ideas and thus "just really [has not] been aware of her in the last ten years."

Martha Stewart's media texts were useful to these fans, whether setting up a new house, getting married, or having children, because they offered the information they felt they needed to succeed at the feminine tasks required by the age-based transitions they experienced. Suggesting that their own life stages may have more impact on their fandom than an attraction to Martha Stewart, some fans' interest in Stewart declined once they no longer felt the need or desire to perform these feminine tasks. This demonstrates Hills's (2014: 10) assertion that entering a fandom may not always be a transformative, life-altering moment; instead "it may just as well form part of a routinised, habituated way of interacting with pop culture." The ease with which many fans cast off their interest in Stewart suggests that leaving fandoms may be an equally routine part of cyclical fandom.

ImClone: Endings and New Beginnings

While changes in fans' lives had a clear impact on their feelings about Martha Stewart and her media offerings, the interview participants also indicated that they believed Stewart, and her messages and products, had changed over time and as a result of her imprisonment. While Stewart's success had been built on her ability to consistently offer novel recipes, craft ideas, and homekeeping methods through new TV episodes, magazine issues, radio programs, and licensed products, her five-month incarceration impeded her ability to produce new content, and also fractured her expert persona. Her fans, as their comments below indicate, were tasked with making sense of these changes and the new media Stewart would produce post-prison, as well as deciding whether they continued to be interested in Martha Stewart. Their evaluations and conclusions underscore Harrington and Bielby's (2014) point that fan objects also change over time, and illustrate Williams's (2015) assertion that fan engagements are continuously impacted by the changing nature of media texts.

Most fans felt that Stewart's media offerings had changed because of her prison time, which ended her television program, *Martha Stewart*

Living (1991–2004), and temporarily removed her presence from her magazine of the same name. Hannah (thirties, continuous fan) shared when I reinterviewed her in 2005 that she and her partner had canceled their subscription to *Martha Stewart Living* when Stewart went to prison: "When she was in jail, the quality of her magazine, I think, went downhill big time. And we actually stopped our subscription. [. . .] But we just bought the Halloween issue and it was back to her old quality, I think." Catherine (fifties, no longer a fan), also a reinterviewee, shared that her feelings about Stewart's magazine had dwindled because she felt it lacked innovation: "It was my favorite magazine. But after a while it's all the same. It didn't change that much, it's the same."

Longtime fan Evelyn (forties, continuous fan) watched Stewart's post-prison television program, *The Martha Stewart Show*, but did not feel like it contained the range of topics she enjoyed in Stewart's previous program: "One of the things that was sort of captivating to me about the magazine and the old show was that kind of balance between cupcakes with fun ways to arrange candy on top and a trip to a furniture maker in North Carolina who is the only one who can re-cane antique chairs." Evelyn lamented the lack of topic variety in Stewart's newer show, "The [post-prison] TV show [. . .] seemed much more like fast ideas for Halloween costumes made out of things in your drawer, which is also useful, but just one-note to me." Joyce (sixties, no longer a fan) also suggested that Stewart's post-prison messages felt different than those created before Stewart was involved in the ImClone scandal:

> It seems like when she went to jail, somehow or another her business got away from her. It was no longer, "this is how Martha likes to do it, and these are things that Martha likes to do" [. . .] she was no longer putting out a personal product. [. . .] I saw her as someone who was becoming just a corporate entity and not a person creating something that other people would like.

Just as some fans were put off by the changes in Martha Stewart's media offerings, others insisted that her media offerings had not changed and were drawn to Stewart's new television programs. Beth (thirties, continuous fan) suggested that Stewart's involvement in the ImClone scandal was a minor, quick incident with no lasting impact: "And reflecting on what she does now, whether it's on the *Today Show* or her magazine, it is seamless. It happened and she went to prison, and then beyond that—blip, she's done!—and kept going." Rose (sixties, continuous fan) stated simply, "I don't think she's changed." Amelia (thirties, continuous fan) emphasized that "I don't watch a ton of the television shows, but I do read *Martha Stewart Living*, *Everyday Food*, [and . . .] *Whole Living*. And I didn't notice any change in any of those publications or around that time."

Frances (thirties, continuous fan) enjoyed the post-prison *Martha Stewart Show* and felt it offered a new perspective on Stewart: "I think it seemed, a little warmer. I liked her banter back and forth between people [. . .] it did make her more personable a little bit." Lauren (forties, continuous fan) also emphasized that the new show made Stewart seem more relatable: "The fact that it was live, and there wasn't a way for her to go back and be a perfectionist about it [. . .] it was definitely sort of more human because it was in the moment." Alternately, Hannah (thirties, continuous fan) described her enjoyment of discovering a less personable Stewart on the prime-time *The Apprentice: Martha Stewart*, believing it offer a glimpse of her pre-prison stern persona, "She's very hardcore [. . .] like, the [episode] from last week where the woman was like, 'Oh, I'm going to cry. We did so bad.' And [Stewart] was like [sucks in a breath, preparing to imitate Stewart], 'women don't cry in business. If you cry you are fired.' And [my partner] and I were like, 'ooooh! *That's* Martha Stewart.'"

While it is apparent that the frequency and character of Stewart's media texts and licensed products have changed since Stewart emerged from prison in 2005, it is difficult to evaluate definitively their quality. However, it is important to note that Stewart fans' continued interest in her was connected to their evaluations of her post-prison offerings, especially in comparison to what they came to expect before. As Whiteman and Metivier (2013: 291) suggest, such evaluations are likely commonplace in all fandoms, given that most fan objects regularly face "myriad smaller endings," such as the conclusions of episodes or the endings of characters' romantic relationships. Thus, making sense of "the continuity of loss" (2013: 292) is a regular component of most fan cultures. Taking note of these regular practices of loss and (re)evaluation enables us to acknowledge the complexities of fandom that Hills (2014: 19) theorizes, including "the somewhat occluded, temporal question of just how fan objects are selected or arrived at," as well as how they are discarded. Below I discuss a number of other shifts and transitions, in the culture at large, that may have had and continue to have an impact on Stewart's financial success.

Changing Options, Changing Interests

Aside from age-based transitions in fans' lives and fans' responses to changes in Martha Stewart's media texts, many interview participants also discussed cultural changes in the US economy and the media industry that impacted Stewart's audience broadly and established new media forms and competitors. Changes like these are difficult to identify when focused on only one text or fan community, especially without a longitudinal focus. Deller's (2014) exploration of two online fan communities at two time points ten years apart uses a longitudinal perspective to demonstrate how cultural changes external to fan texts and communities can be influential. Deller found one online community to have remained relatively stable and found the other to have changed substantially. While she indicates that the average age of the fan communities and the success of the musical artists around which the communities were formed contributed to each community's health, she attributes part of the change to the emergence of Web 2.0 and social networking, which made some formerly popular websites obsolete and made contemporary fan activities difficult to locate and observe. While fan studies scholarship has largely disregarded the ways that cultural changes may influence fannish attachments, the viewpoints of the Martha Stewart fans I interviewed demonstrate the necessity of considering broader cultural influences in the context of cyclical fandom.

Changes in the US economy were mentioned by a number of fans. For instance, Katie (seventies, no longer a fan), whose attention had been captured by Stewart in the 1990s, pointed out that when Stewart first became popular in the 1990s, "people had money [. . .] they were living sort of high on the hog and buying lots of things. I just think that the time was right for [Martha Stewart]." Accentuating this point, Joyce (sixties, no longer a fan) asserted that Stewart's contemporary audience "is dwindling" due to the economic downturn the United States began experience in 2008:

After the recession [. . .] as we get more and more divided in this country by income, and as people feel more hopeless about if they can get good jobs or hang on to them, [. . .] fewer people are going to be interested in what she has. You know, they might want to look at the magazines but they're not going to buy the products or do the crafts or have the Halloween parties.

Abby (fifties, never a fan) agreed with Joyce's point: "People are really worried about, do they have jobs? Do they have health insurance? Is there enough money to like, pay the bills and basic stuff, not like, 'I'll just get cupcakes for the kids.'"

Alongside discussions of the US economy, many speculated about the impact that changes in the media industry had on Stewart's media texts and also on their interest in them. Evelyn (forties, continuous fan) expressed concern over the magazine industry and reflected on publishing's significance to Martha Stewart's empire and image: "I think one of the things that's worrisome about the brand, as a huge fan and consumer is that, you know, magazines are going away. Magazines were the core at the beginning—with books—of her identity and her business, and magazines are disappearing left and right. Really established, really great magazines are disappearing, and so hers are [also] disappearing." Others, like Joyce (sixties, no longer a fan), discussed changes in the television industry: "When Martha Stewart started, there was print, magazine, broadcast TV, and I think cable TV too, but there weren't all the networks there are now, [and] you couldn't watch things on the Internet." Amplifying Joyce's argument by suggesting that Stewart predated many of the contemporary cable networks focused on home life, Beth (thirties, continuous fan) described Martha Stewart as "kind of the first Food Network and HGTV all in one."

Nellie (thirties, continuous fan) discussed the increase in media offerings, and thus competition, from the height of MSLO's success (before ImClone) to Stewart's attempts to rebuild her image post-prison: "Now that she has gone away and come back [. . .] there are so many other people that are in that market doing that sort of thing [. . .] there are other websites that are good. There are other shows that are good. So we're all going to go somewhere else, because now the market's been opened." Olivia (forties, never a fan) indicated that Stewart's influence on daytime television programming has likely reduced her novelty and exclusivity because many shows now incorporate aspects of Stewart's programs: "Every show now, like Ellen DeGeneres, or the *Today Show* [. . .] they always have a piece where you go into the kitchen and you make something."

Adding yet another twist to the interview participants' discussions about how television has changed since Stewart's program began, Catherine (fifties, no longer a fan) argued that contemporary approaches to domestic work and decorating make Stewart's personality-driven approach seem dated: "The reality shows have taken over. So it's 'we'll take this space and redecorate it for you, and you can watch' [. . .] that was basically what Martha Stewart did, too, but the approach is just so different [. . .] it's not really about the person and their personality [. . .] as much." Given the range of new formats and personalities present in contemporary television, Abby (fifties, never a fan) presumed that Martha Stewart is uninteresting to contemporary audiences: "She's drab. She's boring. She's not playful. She's flat. She has no music in the background. It's dull. I mean, baking cookies with her isn't fun. Baking cookies with Ellen DeGeneres is. We don't want to bake with [Stewart] anymore! Go away!"

The Internet and social media specifically were also frequently mentioned in conversations about the changes in the media environment Stewart had once dominated. The growth of blogs focused on the home was mentioned by Amelia (thirties, continuous fan), who said, "Well, think about how much, with the Internet and blogging, being a domestic goddess has blown the eff up [. . .] it's saturated the market. There are so many brands, so many ideas. What Martha Stewart did, every blogger ended up doing their version of that, I think." Likewise, Beth (thirties, continuous fan) asserted that the growth of blogs has drawn younger women's attention away from Martha Stewart: "I think if you would get a bunch of twenty-one-year-olds in the room and ask them about Martha Stewart, their perceptions will be very different. Because now there's so many opportunities, whether it's reading *Young House Love* or blogs, or. . . ."

Likewise, the social bookmarking site Pinterest was regularly mentioned in group interviews. Catherine (fifties, no longer a fan) described the site as "the next step to Martha," and Nora (forties, never a fan) suggested that "Pinterest has started this whole new thing for this generation." The overarching sentiment in these discussions about media was summed up by Fiona (fifties, no longer a fan), who described not only a proliferation of media options, but also audiences' greater power to choose when they want to access media and what media they want to use: "I just think that social media, and the Internet in general, whether you're interacting with other people and Pinterest kind of stuff, or searching for movies, or shows, or whatever, you can find it all right there. You don't need TV channels to set your programming for you, you can figure out what you want to watch yourself."

Even if these interview participants had not reported changed feelings about Martha Stewart due to life transitions and milestones, or reactions to changes in her media offerings and licensed products, the cultural changes they discussed would have been, on their own, powerful influences on audiences' feelings about Stewart. Less noticeable when focused on present dynamics, cultural factors like economics, changes in the form and content of media messages, and new delivery options such as blogs and Pinterest become visible when viewed over time. These larger transitions are, nonetheless, critically important for understanding how fans and media texts are impacted by cultural trends and changes.

Concluding Thoughts

Hills's (2005) call for a new attention to "cyclical fandom" and Harrington and Bielby's (2014) call for examinations of "fandom across the life course" challenge fan studies to produce fuller accounts of the practices and purposes of fandom through fans' narratives, produced over time and through moments of transformation. Harrington and Bielby outline four age-based topics that have received some coverage in fan studies—life milestones, the aging self, changing age norms, and changing fan objects—and these topics have proven useful in making sense of how life transitions, changing media texts, and an evolving cultural landscape impacted fans' connections to Martha Stewart and her media messages. While Hills (2014) reminds us that people move in and out of fandoms over time and can be fans of multiple objects simultaneously, Harrington and Bielby (2014: 138) remind us that long-term engagements intertwine fans with the media they enjoy: "long-term fans' *existence* is gradually transformed into *texistence*—the self that unfolds over time in ongoing dialogue with the media object that helps define and sustain it." While it may not always be possible to disentangle people's life trajectories from their fannish attachments, without focused attention on fans' narratives over time, we cannot begin to develop a fuller understanding of fandom.

My interviews with Martha Stewart fans show that fans come to and leave media texts in concert with the expectations and interests of their life stages, the continuities of loss regularly experienced as texts evolve and decline, and the larger cultural changes that shape the world around them. Not unlike many beloved media properties, Martha Stewart's magazines, television programs, and licensed merchandise have experienced enormous transition since the height of their popularity in 2002. My previous work (Click 2007) demonstrated that fans' perceptions that Stewart had been mistreated in the media and the legal system through her involvement in the ImClone scandal galvanized many fans' and antifans' support of Stewart. In the years since Stewart's release from federal prison, as the company has returned to a semblance of stability, fans have ebbed and flowed in response to the rebranding of Stewart's media texts. All the while, fans' own lives, and the world around them, have continued to change, influencing their interests and abilities.

There is much work to be done to produce a phenomenology of fandom—both in the analysis of individual cases and in the construction of theories and models. Perhaps there are demographic, psychological, behavioral, or generational patterns that mark why some fans continue their interest in a fan object while others leave it? Perhaps different kinds of media texts produce different kinds of attachments? The answers to these questions cannot be found by looking only at fan response to solitary moments related to particular media texts or fan communities; they will be found only longitudinally and in and through fan engagements, just as fans experience them.

WORKS CITED

Andrews, S 2013, "The golden goose lays an egg," *Vanity Fair*, August 16, www.vanity-fair.com.

Bennett, A 2006, "Punk's not dead: the continuous significance of punk rock for an older generation of fans," *Sociology* 40(2): 219–35.

Carr, D 2003, "For the press, a case that is an irresistible draw," *New York Times*, June 5, C5.

Click, MA 2007, "Untidy: fan response to the soiling of Martha Stewart's spotless image," in J Gray, C Sandvoss, & CL Harrington (eds.), *Fandom: identities and communities in a mediated world*, New York University Press, New York.

Deller, RA 2014, "A decade in the life of online fan communities," in L Duits, S Reijnders, & K Zwaan (eds.), *The Ashgate companion to fan cultures*, Ashgate, Burlington, VT.

Harrington, CL 2013, "The *Ars Moriendi* of US serial television: towards a good textual death," *International Journal of Cultural Studies* 16(6): 579–95.

Harrington, CL & Bielby, DD 2014, "A life course perspective on fandom," in CL Harrington, DD Bielby, & AR Bardo (eds.), *Aging, media, and culture*, Lexington, Lanham, MD.

Hills, M 2005, "Patterns of surprise: the 'aleatory object' in psychoanalytic ethnography and cyclical fandom," *American Behavioral Scientist* 48(7): 801–21.

Hills, M 2014, "Returning to 'becoming-a-fan' stories: theorising transformational objects and the emergence/extension of fandom," in L Duits, S Reijnders, & K Zwaan (eds.), *The Ashgate companion to fan cultures*, Ashgate, Burlington, VT.

Katz, S 2014, "Music, performance, and generation: the making of boomer rock and roll biographies," in CL Harrington, DD Bielby, & AR Bardo (eds.), *Aging, media, and culture*, Lexington, Lanham, MD.

Scodari, C 2014, "Breaking dusk: fandom, gender/age intersectionality, and the 'Twilight Moms,'" in CL Harrington, DD Bielby, & AR Bardo (eds.), *Aging, media, and culture*, Lexington, Lanham, MD.

Whiteman, N & Metivier, J 2013, "From post-object to 'zombie' fandoms: the 'deaths' of online fan communities and what they say about us," *Participations* 10: 270–98.

Williams, R 2011, "'This is the night that TV died': television post-object fandom and the demise of *The West Wing*," *Popular Communication* 9(4): 266–79.

Williams, R 2015, *Post-object fandom: television, identity, and self-narrative*, Bloomsbury, New York.

12

The Lives of Fandoms

DENISE D. BIELBY AND C. LEE HARRINGTON

Death ends a life, not a relationship.
—Mitch Albom, *Tuesdays with Morrie* (tweet from actor
Cory Monteith's former agent following Monteith's unex-
pected death; twitter.com/slimyagent)

Death is not uncommon in the lives of fandoms. Although fandoms typically form around an interest that is present and ongoing, endings do
occur: actors pass away, television series conclude, and film franchises
run out of story, at which point fandoms are confronted with the reality
that their central focus has ceased to be. While not usually anticipated
by fans when they form a fandom, the fact of absence, as in many other
realms of life, does not go unacknowledged. In their introduction to the
first edition of this anthology, Gray, Sandvoss, and Harrington observed
that while research reveals the ways fandom is now integrated with
modern life, there remains a need for scholarship that "further[s] our
understanding of how we form emotional bonds with ourselves and others in a modern, mediated world" (2007: 10). We know a lot about what
fans gain through participation in fandom because of analysts' near-
singular focus on fans' enjoyment and pleasures (including pleasure as
antipathy). In contrast, we know far less about how fans interrelate with
one another or their community as a whole when the basis for their
enjoyment disappears.

Our particular interest here is understanding how fandoms experience loss and grief, and practice commemoration. Our focus is not on
fandoms that have ceased to exist, or on how fan communities dissolve
following a loss, although that would be a logical next stage of inquiry.
Rather, we are interested in how a fandom's loss is acknowledged and
incorporated; in short, how the loss is processed and understood by fans

as members of a social community. If shared interests bring fans together, how does disruption of those interests affect the life of a fandom?

To explore this question, we examine the effect of loss that is traumatic for fandom: the unexpected death of a well-liked actor in a popular, on-going franchise. Celebrity deaths regardless of cause are not insignificant cultural events; for example, they dominate Google's year-end lists of top searches (Kelly 2015). We selected actor deaths as the means for examining fandom disruption because, of all the possibilities for exploring the aftermath of absence, an actor's unexpected passing is particularly profound due to the multiple ways the absence can rupture the storyworlds and communities in which the actor is embedded. To examine the impact of this kind of loss on fandom, we chose to focus on actor Cory Monteith from the Fox TV show *Glee*. His recent death generated intense media coverage, he was in the midst of a long-term narrative arc within his storyworld, and the narrative resolution of his reel- and real-life death was perceived as unsatisfying by *Glee*'s fandom. The reasons for this outcome comprise our analysis. We recognize that loss can result in other kinds of outcomes, as we see among US soap opera fans grieving the slow death of a beloved genre or online gamers whose fan objects can be "forever deleted not with a bang, but an error message" (Lowood 2009: 121). We take these differences into account, and our interest is in achieving a more comprehensive and systematic understanding of the experience of loss and adaptation in the lives of fandoms.

Below, we briefly review scholarship on loss, grief, and collective memory. Next, we examine Monteith's death to better understand fan communities' response and adaptation to tragic loss; as will become clear, we are particularly interested here in fans' commemorative practices. We conclude by addressing implications of loss to the persistence of fandom.

Change in the Lives of Fandoms

I'm still tremendously bitter; I probably always will be.
—*Glee* fan commenting on the show's finale (cometsweepandleonidsfly.tumblr.com)

Scholars have increasingly taken note of the relevance of *change* to fans' lives. We raised this as a core issue in our discussion of the impact of age-related structures on the development of fan identities, practices, and interpretive capacities (Harrington & Bielby 2010). By emphasizing that lives are embedded in developmentally and socially determined life stages, we clarified the relevance of the life course to how fans experience fandom. Other work contributes to this emergent conceptual framework, such as Katz's (2014) auto-ethnography exploring the generation-defining relationship between aging adults and their music, and Hills's (2014b) analysis of the significance of becoming-a-fan stories to age-related self-continuity as a fan. This nascent scholarship considers personal change within the larger context of aging and the life course. Still other scholars have noted the relevance of changing social contexts to fan experiences: Click (in this volume) observes shifting affiliations among Martha Stewart's fans after her legal troubles; Williams (2015) explores how TV fans discursively accommodate the cancellation of a series; and Deller (2014) studies the impact of evolving technologies on online fan communities. Yet even as these works highlight change, we need to better understand how fans respond *emotionally* to change. How are we to better understand the effect on a fandom of the loss of its interest object?

Understanding Personal Loss

Personal loss is best understood through the expression of grief, defined as "the term that applies to our *reactions* to loss, to all of those reactions whether they are physical, behavioral, psychological (cognitive or affective), social, or spiritual in nature" (Corr & Corr 2007: 131, emphasis added). Mourning, often confused with grief, is the personal, interpersonal, and "social, public, or ritualized *responses* to loss" (2007: 131, emphasis added). Grief and mourning have in common the experience of absence; they need not include the permanency of death. When absence does stem from death, shifting epistemologies have generated new understandings of healthy grieving (Staudt 2009). The twentieth century was dominated in the West by a neo-Freudian "get over it" model, wherein the purpose of grief was to move past the loss. The emergent twenty-first-century epistemology emphasizes maintaining connections with the object of loss, with the process of grief understood to be negotiating loss over time (Klass, Silverman, & Nickman 1996).

This emergent approach offers opportunities to redefine the self, redefine social roles, and reconstitute communities.

Grief has been characterized as a "pining," the emotional urge to search for a lost object (Parkes & Prigerson 2010: 6, 50). The "highly specific 'search' component" of pining shows grief "to be an inevitable part of love" (2010: xv). This clarification is especially relevant to fandom in light of Grossberg's (1992) foundational research that recognized the essence of fan behavior as based in *affect*. Fandom is socially constituted by fans' emotional investments determined according to their sensibilities. Fans' personal "mattering maps" (1992: 82) differentiate one fan's interests from another's and reveal fans' emotional investments to themselves and to others. For observers, mattering maps thus present not only the terrain of fans' interactions with one another but also how that landscape constitutes the social community whose activity collectively defines a fandom.

Loss, Grief, and Collective Memory

Loss and grief at the collective level are important to social memory as a constituent of communities. Collective memory "defines the relationships between the individual and society and enables the community to preserve its self-image and transfer it over time" (Zandberg 2015: 111). Research on collective memory has come to serve many purposes, including affirming identity within nations and delineating the boundaries of middle-range collectivities like social institutions and communities. Within each context, the temporality of the human experience "of pastness" (Wallerstein 1991: 78) is essential. "Communities [. . .] have a history—in an important sense [they] are constituted by their past—and for this reason we can speak of a real community as a 'community of memory,' one that does not forget its past" (Bellah et al. 1985: 153). So important is memory to community that communities actively and presently engage in origin stories: "In order not to forget that past, a community is involved in retelling its story, its constitutive narrative" (1985: 153).

Scholars of collective memory typically address societies writ large, but their principles apply equally to the social communities constituted by the mattering maps of fandoms (see Garde-Hansen 2011: 123). For example, Kuhn's (2002) study of the first "movie-made generation"—the men and women who grew up in the 1930s—reveals the crucial role of memory in defining the existence of a film-going fandom and in shaping the self-narratives that identify one as a member of that community. Her scholarship (alongside that of others) underscores the important role of personal *and* group memory against the backdrop of larger sociocultural narratives to the shared experience that defines a fandom as a collective identity that exists over time. Underexplored, however, are the ways in which the collectivity of self-narratives that constitute fandom are socially constructed, and how that, in turn, forms the fabric of social memory that sustains fandom across time. Hills (2014b), in his research on "becoming-a-fan stories," raised an aspect of this when he considered the effect of a fandom's *pre*existence on the dynamics of fandoms. In observing the downside of scholars' failure to recognize the capability of fans to transfer their interest from object to object, Hills called attention to "an insistent academic focus on identifiable, established and habituated fan communities" (2014b: 15). Although his focus was the scholarly blind-spots that constrain our ability to recognize fans' capacity for developing new interests, their aptitude for variation in intensity and focus over time, and their ability to cycle through object attachments, our interest is in the *reverse*—the factors that account for the effect of change in an object of interest on the continuity or discontinuity of fan engagement at the group level.

To clarify the reciprocal dynamic we bring into play here, we rely upon work by Bellah and his colleagues (1985) that emphasizes the necessity of attending to a social community's collective expression of its personal and social memory—its commemorative actions, practices, and forms—to better understand the constitutive elements that sustain a fandom over time. How are individual expressions of grief expressed, and how do those individual expressions interrelate at a collective level?

Fandom Disruption: Celebrity Death

Experience: that most brutal of teachers. But you learn, my God you learn.
—C.S. Lewis. R.I.P. Cory [Monteith], you are forever missed. (Fan post at this-is-an-open-letter-tumblr.com)

What types of loss or absence cause the most trauma for fandoms? Recent scholarship on death and media emphasizes Western expectations for a satisfactory textual death, the expectation of not just an *ending*, but a *closure* that achieves coherence, finality, and narrative resolution (e.g., Harrington 2013; Mittell 2015). We argue that the type of celebrity (actor) death explored here has the potential to complicate survivors' (fans') grief in several specific ways. First, it entails multiple deaths or endings—at the very least, that of the actor and (separately) that of the character she or he portrayed on-screen. Second, there is a temporal lag between real- and reel-life endings, problematizing fans' grieving process in that they are simultaneously experiencing grief for the real-life death and anticipatory grief for the expected reel-life ending (Corr & Corr 2007), which extends the pining process discussed earlier (i.e., searching for a lost object). Finally, the reel-life death is necessarily mediated, in the hands of a creative team tasked with the unwelcome responsibility for narrative (and ultimately real-life) closure for a grieving public.

The recent death of Paul Walker (1973–2013) offers an instructive (albeit brief) example of a loss widely considered to be well-handled by a creative team, and widely perceived as satisfying by fans. Walker ("Brian O'Connor") costarred with Vin Diesel ("Dominic Toretto") in *The Fast and the Furious* film franchise, which takes viewers inside the world of Los Angeles street racing and its criminal elements. Walker died in a car accident before the latest installment of the franchise was completed, challenging the production team for how to incorporate his death into both the installment and the overall narrative of the franchise. By all accounts, the resolution was brilliant. From a production perspective, the creative team used flashbacks, body and stunt doubles, and CGI to complete the movie and memorialize Walker. From a narrative perspective, the film's ending—which had O'Connor deciding to spend more time with his family—was a fitting tribute to both Walker and O'Connor. The last scene of the film was an extended driving-into-the-sunset, with aerial shots indicating the together-then-divergent paths of Diesel/Toretto and Walker/O'Connor, with Diesel's car headed down one road (life?) and Walker's another (death?). The film resonated with fans (Griggs 2015) and with critics (DeFore 2015), earned record profits (Box Office Mojo 2015), and allowed for the franchise to continue with Walker/O'Connor still "alive" in the fictional community.

In contrast, the passing of Cory Monteith (1982–2013) has been broadly perceived by both critics and fans as poorly handled, thus potentially generating greater trauma among Monteith/*Glee* fans than seemingly experienced by fans of Walker/*The Fast and the Furious*.[1] A more complicated death than Walker's—in that it represented the death of Monteith, the death of his character ("Finn Hudson"), the death of "Finchel" and "Monchele" (the monikers given to his reel- and real-life romantic relationships with *Glee* costar Lea Michele), and the finale of *Glee*—Monteith's passing held potential for an even more problematic grief process for fans. As *Glee*'s lead male, Monteith's character was the window into the social dynamics of a midwestern (US) high school and its collection of social outcasts and rebels who composed the school's musical glee club. Along with costar Michele ("Rachel Berry"), Monteith was the center of the storyworld cast around which subplots of aspiration, defeat, and social difference played out. Finn's appeal was his "everyman" journey of self-discovery after being blackmailed into joining the club. The foundation Monteith (and Finn) provided the show collapsed when Monteith died, leaving the trajectory of Finn's (and of Finn and Rachel's entwined) story arc unresolvable. Subsequent efforts by the show's creators to redirect the narrative away from Finn and Finchel were poorly received by fans and industry critics, and the series limped its way to a finale after six seasons. We examine this outcome in more depth below.

Adaptation in Fandom

Forever remembering Cory Monteith and believing that his
legacy is more important than celebrity.
—Fan comment on rosesandcynicism.tumblr.com

Monteith's death left a complicated story both on- and off-screen due to *Glee* producers' poorly received narrative choices, the significance of Monteith's death to his real-life girlfriend and costar, and the unpublicized reasons for his (relapse back into) substance abuse. While any one of these factors could be the basis for an individual fan's pining, in the aggregate something else can come into play that is brought about by the social dynamics of a fan community—the effect of compound factors upon the fandom as a whole, which then layers onto an individual fan's personal reaction. Each factor, alone and in the aggregate, left most of the fandom (at both individual and group levels) bereft in different ways for how to find (much less achieve) resolution, revealing the powerful importance of adequate narrative closure for audiences.[2]

A little background: the entire run of *Glee* (2009–15) revealed little apparent set-side drama. When show leads Monteith (Finn) and Michele (Rachel) became an item off-screen, they were quickly consecrated as one of Hollywood's golden couples, trailed by paparazzi recording their every move. During the early months of their relationship in 2011 the actors kept their romance under tight wraps, but the possibility was shipped hard by Finchel fans and watchfully anticipated by industry insiders and savvy viewers.[3] Once firm evidence of a rumored real-life Finchel leaked out (dubbed Monchele), Twitter and Tumblr exploded.[4] Before Monteith confirmed the romance in 2012 the couple's fans reveled online in what they called "Monchele riots,"[5] visual celebrations that accompanied their "retweets" and "likes" and often trended in the (unsponsored) most popular Twitter topics whenever evidence of the couple was posted. Then, after a year and a half of coupledom, and in the context of Monteith's past struggles with addiction and seemingly successful rehabilitation (Malcolm 2011), Monteith died in a Vancouver hotel room from "mixed-drug toxicity involving heroin and alcohol" (British Columbia Government 2013).

Both Monteith, by himself, and Monchele, the couple, were enormous fan favorites. Monteith was well-liked by fans, the industry, his fellow cast members, and production staff, and was regarded as the "glue" of *Glee*.[6] The loss of Monteith and Monchele simultaneously compounded the effect of each loss separately. Michele's tweet acknowledging Cory's passing was the single most retweeted message of 2013 (Conniff 2013), followed in second place by retweets of the message confirming Paul Walker's death. While Lea Michele's personal loss and grief were even further devastating to fans (Nahas 2013), our focus here is not on her. Rather, it is on how fans' shock following Monteith's death was exacerbated by their perception of *Glee* producers' erasure of his character from the show's canon and, because of that, of Monteith's contribution to the show's success. Because of the importance of Monteith, of the character of Finn, and of Monteith's portrayal of the character to the overall architecture of the show, what follows underscores how the depth of the cultural imperative for satis-factory narrative resolution applies equally to unexpected disruptions of the unfolding narrative, and also the degree to which fans hold show cre-ators accountable to that standard. In Monteith's case, the show's fandom perceived that *Glee*'s creators failed to fulfill their tacit contract with its audience—that of honoring fans' sense of affective ownership (see Ford 2015)—in ways that could have better aligned the double real-life loss of Monteith and Monchele with the show's canon for Finn and for Finchel. In short, in the case of *Glee*, and in the minds of the fans, the show's cre-ators failed to facilitate adequate closure.

From the pilot onward, the show's narrative had established Finn as a tent-pole character. However, fans perceived that after Monteith's death the producers essentially erased Finn from the canvas and deleted him as a crucial propellant in the canon of Finn's romantic partner, Rachel (played by Michele).[7] Here's how: when the show returned for its fifth season, following Monteith's death, it aired a two-part tribute to The Beatles that had begun production after his passing. This was followed by a single tribute episode to honor Monteith and Finn by having Finn (inexplicably) die off-screen, with the glee club gathering to mourn his death. After this, Finn was not mentioned until a brief inclusion in the sixth season (and series) finale, an episode that—according to fans—conclusively revised the narrative canon. The integral story arc Monteith had shared with Michele was retroactively rewritten by having Rachel omit recognition of Finn's contributions to her career success and hav-ing her marry a former antagonist who had been dropped from the narrative three years earlier. Only a few professional critics marked the demise of this once-lauded series, most expressing relief that it was end-ing rather than mourning its departure. But even then, they invariably praised Monteith's portrayal of Finn as *Glee*'s core:

> [W]hen Monteith tragically passed away during the summer of 2013, "Glee" lost its heart. And that's when I stopped watching. [. . .] Because without Finn, there was no "Glee." That's how good Monteith was at his job. (Bell 2015)

That the show's producers inadequately (in fans' eyes) acknowledged the importance of Monteith's death to the narrative only rankled the fandom even further. With this core aspect unsatisfactorily resolved, the fandom expressed anger, bitterness, and betrayal in ways familiar to grief experts (Parkes & Prigerson 2010: 91–92). However, this loss is more complicated than most real-life losses—again, it's the loss of an actor, a character, and on- and off-screen relationships, all simultaneously. Fans attribute their dissatisfaction to *Glee* creator Ryan Murphy—in the minds of some, he "murdered" the fan community:

> You just thought *Glee* was an inspirational show about the inherent worth of all people. [. . .] But nope. It wasn't. It was a six season long revenge fantasy. The "special" characters Ryan identified with—those who were labeled high school losers—end up as winners the world revolves around. [. . .] Glee: where high school losers become winners and high school winners become irrelevant or overlooked; left out or left behind. In the end all the masks come off. (cometsweepandleonidsfly.tumblr.com)

Mused another:

> People expected what after these last two seasons? [. . .] I'll always be glad I met wonderful people here, I'll always be thankful for Cory who brought me joy when I very much needed it [. . .] from now on I live by the rule: anything RM productions = run away and don't look back. (twitter.com/micro_tats)

Dissatisfaction with the narrative also left some fans wondering how much the show's increasingly negative portrayal of Finn contributed to Monteith's drug relapse. This speaks to the significance of pining and suggests its relevance to the importance of adequate closure, which here entails searching for a reason for the relapse and looking for someone to blame in order to achieve resolution. The fact that the cause is unknowable (read: unpublicized) to many fans only magnifies their search for attribution:

> [I]t's like Ryan meant from the very start to make [Finn] the icon of "some will lose" and [Ryan] never waivered from piling it on as high as it could go. They forced him into a relentless and non-stop drum beat of acting out LOSER-LOSER-LOSER-LOSER-LOSER for his entire period

on the show. I will wonder forever how much that fucked with his mind, especially knowing RM always says he writes characters based on his impressions of who the actors are as people. (cometsweepandleonidsfly. tumblr.com)

Here, because fans are dealing with an inexplicable and unresolved loss in both reel and real life, memory and commemoration play crucial roles in finding a semblance of narrative closure:

> All I wanted from the last day of Glee filming was for someone . . . any-one . . . to acknowledge Cory and the fact that, gone for a year and a half or not, he was a big part of the show (and really, the *heart* of the show). (breathofmidnightair.tumblr.com)

Lacking adequate closure, ongoing reminiscences and commemorations remain active on social media.[8] Although professional critics haven't been targeted by fans, no amount of discussion about *Glee*'s finale has lessened the intensity of this fandom's bitterness. Instead, fans remain in close contact via social media and mark the contribution Monteith made to their lives through creative GIFs (fan edits) of his sense of humor, his scenes on *Glee*, or his scenes in his films, with AU (Alternate Universe) GIFs and fan fiction that rewrites the show's finale to portray Finn and Rachel in the show's canon, to recapture Finn and Rachel as they were, or to celebrate Monchele and Finchel. Particularly poignant forms of commemoration have been fans' donations to Monteith's favorite charities and outreach to his grieving mother, who, in response, posted her appreciation.[9]

Conclusion: Closure, Commemoration, and Collective Memory

We have examined how a fandom responded to the loss of an actor pivotal to the text in which he was embedded. Although anchored in distinct circumstances and reflecting particular frames of accommo-dation, Monteith's death reveals in clear ways the importance of con/textually related aspects of loss to fandom adaptation. After Monteith's death, the fandom's loss(es) were perceived (by most fans) as mishandled by the show's creators. By revising *Glee*'s narrative canon and that of its central couple as they did, the show's creators seemed to exacerbate fan trauma rather than facilitate narrative and psychological closure. Because this outcome left the fandom with inexplicable and unresolved losses in reel and real life, fans' expressions of memory and commemoration—which might be thought of as "banal commemoration" (see Hills 2014a; Vinitzky-Seroussi 2011)—have come to play an important recuperative role in their adaptation to Monteith's death and to the creative choices made by the show's writers and producers. These commemorative efforts validate fans' emotional investments in what was once (they felt) a text worth committing to, and memorialize a valued life lost. But these expressions have also grown to accomplish something else. As they increasingly emphasize not only the relationship the fandom once had with Monteith when he was alive but the one it *continues to have* with him now that he's gone, their meaningfulness has deepened in the two years since Monteith's passing, because they now also express a relationship that has become temporally restructured—one rooted in a past that brings significance to the present. The emerging temporality of the fandom's relationship with Monteith is reinforced by anniversary remembrances from his former cast mates, industry colleagues, and Lea Michele herself, and its growing strength was revealed when #2YearsWithoutCory trended in second place on Twitter World Wide on the anniversary of his death (Yagoda 2015).

For Paul Walker, in contrast, the loss of his popular character was perceived by critics and fan audiences as satisfactorily integrated into the film franchise's narrative, in part due to the director's responsiveness to the desires of the fandom to keep Walker's character intact and grant him a respectful send-off. Although Walker's death altered production of *Furious 7*, the film's director (James Wan) shared the intense pressure he felt for a satisfactory resolution and reached out to the fandom to accept the creative license he took to complete the film. Vin Diesel has spoken publicly of how emotionally satisfying he finds the *Furious 7* installment. In contrast, it took a full year after Monteith's death for *Glee* creator Ryan Murphy to admit what was perceived by many fans—that he had "stepped away" from the show following Monteith's death, a revelation underscored after the show's finale by cast members who offered postmortems on the series (Bacardi 2015; Barnes 2014). Murphy's belated comments (Ausiello 2014) about the creative difficulties Monteith's death presented only deepened fan discontent over final canon revisions for Finn and Finchel.

While every celebrity death is a tragedy on its own, the outcomes for fandoms can be very different. Indeed, the contrasting grief trajectories surrounding Walker's and Monteith's deaths reveal that the particulars of how each loss was resolved *textually* have been crucial to whether the fandom has accepted or rejected the revised narrative outcome. To more fully understand the importance of fans' textual memories to their adaptation to loss, we return to our earlier discussion of the interplay between social history and community for insight into how collective memory operates at the communal level, and how it can be shaped under divergent circumstances. In the case of traumatic loss, acknowledging what came before matters centrally to a community's identity, and the erasure of an important presence does not translate into "it never existed" or "it should be minimized," as was seemingly attempted by *Glee*'s creators. Just as Walker's widely applauded narrative closure can account for his fandom's continuing interest in the *Furious* franchise, the on-screen handling of Monteith's passing may account for the fact that while *his* fan community remains, the *show*'s fandom has dissipated now that the series is over. Long-term consequences for *Glee*'s legacy are unclear at this point. Commemoration of positive events reinforces desirable images of collective identity, but commemoration of difficult pasts complicates commemoration by foregrounding the trauma and embedding the disruption in cultural memory that cannot be ignored (e.g., Saito 2010).

Two decades ago, Dayan and Katz (1992) observed that mass media play a decisive role in generating collective memories at the national level. But there is an important difference in the basis for collective memories that emanate from social communities that are fandoms compared to those that are not. Fandoms consist of media consumers entrusting aspects of their emotional selves to an artistic creator, and they are thus partly at the mercy of his or her creative logics, impulses, whims, and sensibilities. As fandoms become more central to the experiences that constitute our lives in a mediated society (Gray, Sandvoss, & Harrington 2007), the expectations of fans have become more sensitive to the boundaries of the tacit contract between cultural consumers and producers:

Television shows don't have to make us happy to be wonderful. [. . .] But if there is going to be pain, it has to feel warranted. It must be necessary to the story that is being told. [. . .] The relationship between fans and the powers-that-be is a tricky one. [. . .] Is there, however, a certain amount of respect and consideration that is due to the millions of people to make a show possible? (Barbash 2015: n.p.).

Finally, there is little scholarship to guide our understanding of how fans' experience of loss at the individual level and that of fandom at the collective level are linked. This chapter suggests the relevance of studying local or group-level dynamics that result from triggering events that instigate recognition of a collective experience (Fine 2010). In that regard, our work raises issues associated with the complex and dynamic relationship between fans and creative personnel, who are increasingly called upon to negotiate responsibility and control not only with those for whom they work in the industry but with audiences' interests, tastes, preferences, and, most important, affective investments as well.

NOTES

1 We note that the fandoms for *Glee* and *The Fast and the Furious* are likely to be quite different from one another. While our analysis focuses on how production (creative) decisions engendered a particular response within the *Glee* fandom, an alternate analysis might reasonably focus on the nature of the text itself in shaping fan response to an actor's death. We thank an anonymous reviewer for this insight.

2 Due to space limitations we are able to present only the dominant response of the fandom; there are, of course, alternative (more positive) perspectives and reactions among *Glee* fans.

3 See, for example, a post at moncheles.tumblr.com in response to an anonymous "ask" about when Cory and Lea "briefly dated in early glee days." Moncheles.tumblr sent in reply this link from a year earlier: moncheles.tumblr.com.

4 See the *E! News* clip of Monteith trailed by a reporter probing about his rumored relationship with Michele, posted November 30, 2011, with reader replies at allcory.tumblr.com. See this reply post for exuberant reaction to the news: nohappyendingtheresjustnothing.tumblr.com.

5 Example of a typical image used by fans to signal their celebratory mood at a sighting: glee.wikia.com.

6 See, for example, celebrities' tweets in coverage by CBS News (Moraski 2013), and the quotations from *Glee* director Adam Shankman to CNN (Almasy 2013) and from Monteith's now-disgraced costar Mark Salling to *People* (Miller 2014).

7　Fans regarded Finn as the core of the show: "There has been a continuous and concerted effort to attempt to convey that Finn's death didn't change anything in the story at all: that everything within the narrative and the narrative world is exactly the same and fine and no different than it would be if the character was still there. . . . Telling the story in [this way] unravels the integrity of the fabric of the fictional story, leaving it tattered and torn" (cometsweepandleonidsfly.tumblr. com). Writing about the impact of Monteith's death, one critic said, "And he was Finn Hudson, Glee's main testament to the life-changing power of music, argu-ably the show's primary message" (Hoffman 2013: 13).

8　For examples, see "A Finchel/Monchele blog because I simply love them. . . . Cory, I'll miss you forever" (allcory.tumblr.com); "This tumblr is All Cory Monteith. I am currently in celebration of Cory's life, his work, and his humanity. You can send me any messages you want to share. I can't promise that I'll answer every anon message but I can faithfully promise that I will sincerely read all of them. If you come unanon, we can talk more. Or you can tweet me at twitter.com/ AllCory" (savethedateforourwedding.tumblr.com); "Cory Forever: remember-ing, missing and loving Cory Forever!! I reblog just about anything having to do with Cory Monteith . . . STILL MISS CORY SO VERY MUCH. BE WELL ALL!!!" (smk0057.tumblr.com); "It doesn't matter if we are 'moved on' or not, or whenever we have kids. They're going to know about the Awkwardly Tall Canadian Drum-mer who stole our hearts and have a place for him in our hearts. Because we're going to keep reblogging photosets, and make posts every May 11th and July 13th. Because no matter how much we fought to see which ship is the best or who is the better character, etc. We have one thing in common, we all miss him" (morrte-ithrps.tumblr.com).

9　"I didn't think I could bear another birthday without Cory buzzing up to my condo . . . as a pizza delivery man, Chinese food delivery man, UPS delivery man, police, management . . . you name it . . . but today he sent all of you. Thank you for all your support and love today . . . and always. He is certainly is [sic] in our hearts" (Ann Mcgregor post on moncheles.tumblr.com).

WORKS CITED

Almasy, S 2013, "'Glee' star Cory Monteith found dead in hotel in Canada," *CNN*, July 15, www.cnn.com.

Ausiello, M 2014, "*Glee* boss Ryan Murphy reveals game plan for 'satisfying' final sea-son (who'll be back?!); plus—inside the 'painful' Rachel romance debate," *TVLine*, April 15, tvline.com.

Bacardi, F 2015, "Kevin McHale says Cory Monteith's death made it hard for Glee to come back—watch now," *E!*, May 6, www.eonline.com.

Barbash, T 2015, "Grey's Anatomy postmortem: do fans have rights?" *Community. ew.com*, April 27.

Barnes, N 2014, "*Glee*: Ryan Murphy reveals he 'stepped away' from *Glee* following Cory Monteith's shock death!," *Unreality Primetime*, June 24, primetime.unrealitytv.co.uk.

Bell, C 2015, "Remembering Cory Monteith, the heart of 'Glee,'" *MTV News*, March 20, www.mtv.com.

Bellah, RN, Madsen R, Sullivan, WM, Swidler, A, & Tipton, SM 1985, *Habits of the heart: individualism and commitment in American life*, University of California Press, Berkeley.

Box Office Mojo 2015, "Furious 7," May 3, www.boxofficemojo.com.

British Columbia Government 2013, "Cause of death confirmed for Cory Monteith," news.gov.bc.ca.

Conniff, K 2013, "This is the most retweeted tweet of 2013," *Time*, December 12, www.time.com.

Corr, C & Corr, D 2007, "Historical and contemporary perspectives on loss, grief, and mourning," in D Balk (ed.), *Handbook of thanatology: the essential body of knowledge for the study of death, dying, and bereavement*, Routledge, New York.

Dayan, D & Katz, E 1992, *Media events: the live broadcasting of history*, Harvard University Press, Cambridge, MA.

DeFore, J 2015, "*Furious 7*: Film Review," *Hollywood Reporter*, March 16, www.hollywoodreporter.com.

Deller, RA 2014, "A decade in the life of online fan communities," in L Duits, K Zwaan, & S Reijnders (eds.), *The Ashgate research companion to fan cultures*, Ashgate, Farnham.

Fine, GA 2010, "Group cultures and subcultures," in JR Hall, L Grindstaff, & MC Lo (eds.), *Handbook of cultural sociology*, Routledge, New York.

Ford, S 2015, "Social media ownership," in R Mansell & PH Ang (eds.), *The international encyclopedia of digital communication and society*, 1st ed., John Wiley, Indianapolis.

Garde-Hansen, J 2011, *Media and Memory*, Edinburgh University Press, Edinburgh.

Gray, J, Sandvoss, C, & Harrington, CL 2007, "Introduction: why study fans?," in J Gray, C Sandvoss, & CL Harrington (eds.), *Fandom: identities and communities in a mediated world*, New York University Press, New York.

Griggs, B 2015, "Paul Walker fans choke up at Furious 7 finale," *CNN*, www.cnn.com.

Grossberg, L 1992, *We gotta get out of this place: popular conservatism and postmodern culture*, Routledge, New York.

Harrington, CL 2013, "The *ars moriendi* of US serial television: towards a good textual death," *International Journal of Cultural Studies* 6(6): 579–95.

Harrington, CL & Bielby, DD 2010, "A life course perspective on fandom," *International Journal of Cultural Studies* 13(5): 429–50.

Hills, M 2014a, "*Doctor Who*'s textual commemorators: fandom, collective memory and the self-commodification of fanfac," *Participations* 2(1): 31–51.

Hills, M 2014b, "Returning to 'becoming-a-fan' stories: theorising transformational objects and the emergence/extension of fandom," in L Duits, K Zwaan, & S Reijnders (eds.), *The Ashgate research companion to fan cultures*, Ashgate, Farnham.

Hoffman, L 2013, "Cory Monteith was invaluable to *Glee*: where does the show go now?," *Vulture*, July 14, www.vulture.com.

Katz, S 2014, "Music, performance, and generation: the making of Boomer rock and roll biographies," in CL Harrington, DD Bielby, & AR Bardo (eds.), *Aging, media, and culture*, Lexington, Lanham, MD.

Kelly, H 2015, "What you really Googled in 2015," *CNN*, January 3, www.cnn.com.

Klass, D, Silverman, PR, & Nickman, S 1996, *Continuing bonds: new understandings of grief*, Routledge, New York.

Kuhn, A 2002, *Dreaming of Fred and Ginger: cinema and cultural memory*, New York University Press, New York.

Lowood, H 2009, "Memento mundi: are virtual worlds history?," paper presented at iPRES2009—Sixth International Conference on Preservation of Digital Objects, www.escholarship.org.

Malcolm, S 2011, "Cory Monteith's turning point," *Parade Magazine*, June 24, www.parade.com.

Miller, M 2014, "Mark Salling: Cory Monteith's death leaves a 'big hole' in *Glee*'s final season," *People*, November 24, www.people.com.

Mittell, J 2015, *Complex TV: the poetics of contemporary television storytelling*, New York University Press, New York.

Moraski, L 2013, "Cory Monteith: stars react to "Glee" actor's death," *CBS News*, July 15, www.cbsnews.com.

Nahas, A 2013, "Cory Monteith's tragic death: Lea's broken heart," *People*, August 5, www.people.com.

Parkes, CM & Prigerson, HG 2010, *Bereavement: studies of grief in adult life*, Routledge, New York.

Saito, H 2010, "From collective memory to commemoration," in JR Hall, L Grindstaff, & MC Lo (eds.), *Handbook of cultural sociology*, Routledge, New York.

Staudt, C 2009, "From concealment to recognition: the discourse on death, dying and grief," in MK Bartalos (ed.), *Speaking of death*, Praeger, Westport, CT.

Vinitzky-Seroussi, V 2011, "'Round up the unusual suspects': banal commemoration and the role of the media," in M Neiger, O Meyers, & E Zandberg (eds.), *On media memory: collective memory in a new media age*, Palgrave Macmillan, New York.

Wallerstein, I 1991, "The construction of peoplehood: racism, nationalism, ethnicity," in E Balibar & I Wallerstein (eds.), *Race, nation, class: ambiguous identities*, C Turner (trans.), Verso, London.

Williams, R 2015, *Post-object fandom*, Bloomsbury, New York.

Yagoda, M 2015, "#2YearsWithoutCory: Twitter pays tribute to Cory Monteith two years after his death," *People*, July 13, www.people.com.

Zandberg, E 2015, "'Ketchup is the Auschwitz of tomatoes': humor and the collective memory of traumatic events," *Communication, Culture & Critique* 8(1): 108–23.

13

"What Are You Collecting Now?"

Seth, Comics, and Meaning Management

HENRY JENKINS

"What are you collecting now?" asks Chet (modeled after comic book artist Chester Brown), in a scene early in Seth's 1996 graphic novel, *It's a Good Life, If You Don't Weaken*, while the fictionalized "Seth" starts pulling books off his shelf and replies, "I've got some GREAT stuff to show you!" (17).

Chet's question conveys much. First, it indicates that the act of collecting (gathering, researching, appraising, showing "great stuff") is a normative part of their lives together. But, second, the question implies that the objects of their collecting passions are variable, both within the individual (Seth makes new discoveries) and between them (Seth and Chet collect different stuff). What Seth ends up sharing with Chet—and with the readers of this graphic novel—is his discovery of Kalo, an obscure gag cartoonist who becomes the focus of Seth's obsessive search for more—more work, more information.

It's a Good Life, like Seth's other works, is a collecting story—a story by, for, and about collectors. Seth's characters are obsessed with "stuff," "paper" collectibles (comics, books, posters, other printed ephemera) in particular: they devote their lives to acquiring, grooming, displaying, discussing, exchanging, and appraising stuff.

In *Cult Collectors*, Lincoln Geraghty (2014) protests the lack of critical attention directed toward collectors and their practices, as compared to other fan activities. This absence of studying collector culture perhaps reflects an ongoing discomfort among academics with forms of consumption that cannot easily be reread as forms of cultural production. Early fandom studies research (Jenkins 1992) sought to clear away negative stereotypes from popular media representations—including those that linked fandom to collecting—in order to prepare ground for an alternative and more empowering understanding. But graphic novels may be one place where collecting has been explored rather than dismissed. Understanding the kinds of stories comics tell about collecting may inspire new insights about the relationship between fandom, collecting, and consumer culture. With artists like Seth, it may be more productive to theorize *with* rather than *against* such representations; these artists are asking complex questions about how people construct their identities through consumption within works intended to be read by others who share their lifestyles and passions.

Seth himself never uses the word "fan," consistently focusing on collectors. I respect that word choice throughout. Yet, what Seth's characters consume (especially old comics, classic movies, and pulp magazines) and how (as part of their identities, in conversation with others, with passion and mastery) would make them fans by most definitions.

Like other fan practices, collecting is often understood through a Marxist lens as hyperconsumerism or through a Freudian lens as fetishism and narcissism. For the moment, I want to bracket both interpretations not as wrongheaded but as blinding us to other levels on which collecting operates. I want to tap cross-disciplinary research, especially in anthropology, on material culture, stuff, things, objects, junk, or ephemera. As Daniel Miller explains:

> Whatever our environmental fears or concerns over materialism, we will not be helped by a theory of stuff, or an attitude to stuff, that simply tries to oppose ourselves to it; as though the more we think of things as alien, the more we keep ourselves sacrosanct and pure. [. . .] Instead, this book tries to face up to stuff: to acknowledge it, respect it, and expose ourselves to our own materiality rather than to deny it. (2010: 5–6).

Comics are a rich medium for thinking about "stuff." At the most basic level, comics *are* stuff, material objects that are collected and appraised. Comics are also undergoing transitions as they shift from disposables (stuff designed to be discarded) toward collectibles (stuff intended to be archived) and as they shift from a "junk" medium to a respectable art form. Comic artists have often had to become collectors and curators, simply to get access to their "aesthetic ancestors" (Heer 2010; Gardner

2012). Comics as a medium have particular affordances that encourage their readers to scan the landscape and pay attention to mise-en-scène, where the artist may well be fabricating or duplicating material objects. Reading such comics taps visual literacies and social skills we use in reading people's belongings (bookcases, for example) as signs of who they are and what they value. In short, comics *are* stuff; comics *tell us about* stuff; and comics *show us* stuff.

Seth as a collector/storyteller respects what anthropologists have argued about consumer culture more generally—that its practices and processes are meaningful, in the sense that they are full of meaning. Grant McCracken (2005: 4) writes, "Goods help us learn, make, display, and change choices required of us by our individualistic society. They are not shackles but instruments of the self." Unlike previous generations, our most meaningful stuff does not consist of heirlooms and legacies but rather elective purchases. One might imagine a highly mobile society to be relatively unencumbered with stuff. However, curiously, as North American society becomes more mobile, there is also a tendency to hold onto reminders of the places where we have lived and the people we have known. We use our selection and display of stuff to signal how we see ourselves, our place in the world, our connections with others, and our relations to the past. We come to regard our stuff as "belongings," a term that implies both ownership and emotional connection. Such choices enter every consumer purchase, but the stakes become clearer when we deal with those goods we collect (whether goods we carry with us from childhood or those from earlier generations). Such goods were not built to last, yet they are things we refuse to let go of.

Every object, it seems, has a story, and part of how we connect with the past is to insert ourselves into these continuing narratives about the production and circulation of stuff. Philipp Blom (2002: 191) writes, "Every collection is a theatre of memories, a dramatization and a mise en scène of personal and collective parts, of a remembered childhood and of remembrance after death. It guarantees the presence of those memories through the objects evoking them." Both collections and stories are ways of managing memory. G. Thomas Tanselle (1998: 12) reminds us, "Objects not only stimulate us to discover how they came to exist and what their original function was; they also tease us into probing their subsequent status and adventures." Such questions generate stories about quests and searches as collectors pursue desired objects. And, in that context, the exchange of collected objects becomes one and the same with the exchange of stories. Mieke Bal (1994: 103) tells us that "collecting is an essential human feature that originates in the need to tell stories, but for which there are neither words nor other conventional narrative modes."

Seth's obsessions as a collector run through *It's a Good Life*. The protagonist's stream-of-consciousness narration often talks about things in his environment that remind him of classic cartoonists and where the illustrations show characters salvaging in dime stores and used bookshops. Seth's fascination with the history of Canadian broadcasting yielded *George Sprott 1894–1975* (2009); a key character in *Clyde Fans: Book 1* (2004) is defined through his collection of vintage postcards; *Wimbledon Green* (2005) offers a tall tale about "the greatest comic book collector in the world." And Seth's own bibliophilic tendencies inform his small press book, *Forty Cartoon Books of Interest* (2006). "To know me is to know that I am a collector," Seth begins the book, acknowledging that, above all, he wants to share his "finds" with his readers. In *Seth's Dominion*, Luc Chamberland's 2015 documentary about the artist and his work, Seth showcases his home as yet another "art project": "I am just trying to make it the world I want to live in."

Longing without an Object

In part 3 of *Clyde Fans* (still a work in progress, being published in fits and starts in Seth's *Palookaville*), Simon, the more introverted of the two Matchcard brothers, recalls an old wooden box his brother Abe passed along to him when it no longer had a lid and was thus perceived to be worthless. The box once contained "the little trinkets that are important in a boy's life," childhood "treasures" the adult Simon no longer fully recalls: "Time has mostly erased its contents from my memory [. . .] but somehow that box still looms large in my daydreams." And Simon maintains a futile fantasy: "Sometimes I imagine that if I could just remember those objects, find them again and place them back in the box in just the right order, then (like a magic recipe) it would open up that time barrier and I'd be on the other side . . . in a better moment." Simon shakes his head: "how utterly, utterly stupid" (Seth 2002: 19–20).

Simon is a collector; he has been systematically acquiring and cataloging old picture postcards—in particular, photo manipulations depicting outlandishly large objects or animals. No one collects in general; collecting is always particular. His brother Abe is *not* a collector, though Seth slyly connects him with another set of decaying papers: "all the invoices, the purchase orders, the receipts buried in old filing cabinets or tied up and stacked in warehouses, fragile pieces of paper scattered over the province. Yellow bits of scrap with my name signed on them. Those fragments prove to the world out there that I once existed" (Seth 2004: 30). So, what makes one pile of papers a collection and the other an archive? Abe struggles to grasp what motivates his brother's collecting: "I suppose we all, somewhat arbitrarily, pick something to give our lives meaning" (Seth 2004: 57).

Understanding nostalgia as an unfulfilled and "utterly, utterly stupid" fantasy of returning to a better world has been the dominant frame since Susan Stewart published *On Longing* in 1984. She writes, "Nostalgia is a sadness without an object" (23). Like the contents of Simon's box, what we seek through nostalgia cannot be recovered (and was never ours to begin with); it remains an ideological and sentimental illusion. For Stewart, the collection (which she compares with Noah and his Ark) involves the creation of a "hermetic" or "self-enclosed" world that protects the contents (and the collectors themselves) from the ravages of time by removing them from circulation and use (151).

Speaking about his own collecting impulses, Seth told one interviewer:

> I have no illusions about the superiority of the past. People have always been miserable and life has always been difficult. However I can honestly say that I don't think much of this present time. Certainly, here in North America, things couldn't be cheaper, uglier, or more vulgar than they currently are (well, they could, and probably will be—in the near future). [...] While I personally have no desire to live through the Depression or World War II, I do think that culturally the quality of many things were superior, especially design. [...] You cannot look at a popular medium-priced radio or clock from that period and compare it with the same popular medium-priced item from today, and not come away convinced that things are just shittier today. (quoted in Miller 2015: 70)

We can see Seth's collecting stories as a way of working through his own "muddled" thinking about the relationship between past and present: "If I were to create a utopia, it would not be the past. It would be something incorporating favorite elements from the past—aesthetics from the past, ideas from the past" (quoted in Hoffman & Grace 2015: 219). In other words, it would be a collection.

Gathering Dust

"Am I nostalgic? Can you feel nostalgic for an era you never lived in?" (Miller 2015: 70), Seth asks in his interview with Bryan Miller quoted previously, before concluding that he sees his own childhood era as a moment of transition between the midcentury modern culture he loves and the contemporary junk culture he holds in contempt—speaking of the 1960s and early 1970s, when "the last vestige of that old world [. . .] were still hanging around everywhere" (70). Such impulses, he suggests, motivate his collecting:

> Mostly I collect as a way of exploring the past. By buying the cultural objects (especially books, movies, and records) of the past you begin to get a deeper understanding of the times. There are so many surprises to be found. It's a constant process—there are so many layers of the past to dig through. [. . .] I just love the objects of the past and looking for them (and possessing them) brings me the most happiness in life. I like nothing better than looking through some dusty pile of magazines in an out-of-the-way store with the hope that something great is at the bottom of that unpromising pile. (Miller 2015: 69)

For the most part, Seth is searching for objects from before he was born. But, like other collectors, he also seeks to "recapture the feelings of childhood" by recovering some "totem" that once slipped through his fingers. He says, "Recently I tracked down a wrist-radio on eBay that I owned as a child. Holding it in my hands again was a beautiful moment" (Miller 2015: 70). The core metaphors here are archaeological: digging and sorting through dust, "holding" an old object in "my hands." Both speak to the idea of memories made material. On the one hand, materiality makes memory more enduring—a form of prosthetic memory. Yet, the idea that the object will last is also partially an illusion, since all material culture is always in some state of decay.

Dust is something that breaks off as the object breaks down; we can't hold onto the past because it is coming apart in our hands. The protagonist in *It's a Good Life* talks about the "evocative sadness for the vanished past" that emerges from "the decay of old things": "It's the difference between a dilapidated old farmhouse and a pristine deco hotel lobby. Somehow that lobby doesn't convince you of the reality or the beauty of yesterday." Listing what makes him sad, the protagonist cites "those little bits of broken glass at the bottom of the box when you're unpacking your Christmas ornaments" (42). Dust and rust (something new emerging through the decomposition process) add aesthetic value, much as scarcity increases a collection's value. Dust is also something that hides, masks, covers over, and obscures these objects' true value, until they are rediscovered. Seth's protagonist describes aging plastic flowers by saying, "[Y]ou can barely make out their colours under all that dust" (41). Dust can be brushed aside. The object can be polished and put on display. We can rescue treasures from the dustbin of history. Things break down, and, in the process, they become indistinct and meaningless. This is where the anxiety of collecting lies: the desire to arrest or reverse this process, to preserve objects from normal wear and tear, and to place them in a meaningful context where they can be appreciated and protected by generations to come.

Without collectors, what survives seems random. Seth's *George Sprott* gives us several examples. On the one hand, the recordings of Sprott's long-running television program get trashed as no longer having any material value for the television station. Yet, many of his personal belongings are salvaged by collectors who value them only because they are incidentally connected to something else from the past. "Owen Trade, Collector" annotates his holdings, primarily focused on CKCK Television's horror show host, Sir Grisly Gruesome, but including objects belonging to other on-air personalities. Trade sees himself as protecting Sprott's "legacy": "I Googled George the other day and got only one hit. Nobody under 40 even knows his name any more" (n.p.). But, does it remain George's legacy if he is recalled on terms very different from his own? Trade's collection involves a process of de-sentimentalization, where objects previously

bearing Sprott's private memories get attached to some other narrative—
the history of the company where he worked, the story of a disrespected
rival, or simply the collector's own experiences.

Seth's comics often acknowledge that the past (both the world and
our memories of it) recedes "beyond our reach." Collectors sift through
the debris and hold onto things to which they can ascribe meaning. The
fantasy is that someone can read the collector's spirit from the accumulated objects. The opening of *Clyde Fans* shows Abe, after his brother's
death, wandering around the spaces they once shared, seeking to read
his cryptic and reclusive brother from the things he assembled:

> Simon prepared this place for me. [. . .] Somehow he put some of himself
> in every object in here. [. . .] The piles of books he left—almost like a
> planned a course of study for me. [. . .] And as I read each book, I linger
> over the thought that he turned these pages before me. [. . .] Only by
> infusing this whole place with the spirit of his lonely struggle could I ever
> come here and understand him. (2004: 54)

A collection consists of objects you can put your hands on as opposed to
memories, which recede from your reach. Walter Benjamin, in his 1969
essay "Unpacking My Library," makes a similar connection: "One only
has to watch a collector handle the objects in his glass case. As he holds
them in his hands, he seems to be seeing through them into their distant
past as though inspired" (60–61).

Collecting as Meaning Transfer

So far, we've described a process of meaning transfer: that is, memories,
associations, and sentiments are transferred onto collected objects. By
holding these materials in our hands, brushing off the dust, the collector
brings order to what Benjamin (1969: 60) calls the "chaos of memories."
Grant McCracken (1988) has described the various rituals of meaning
transfer ("rites of passage") consumers perform to develop a sense of
ownership over the readymade goods they purchase and integrate them
into their own life. By rituals, McCracken means shared social practices
through which meaning is manufactured and managed. He identifies
four basic sets of rituals:

- Exchange rituals refer to practices determining how we acquire objects. His examples are those surrounding gifts—When are gifts given? Who is obligated to give a gift? What kinds of obligations do gifts create? What values determine the choice of gifts? And so forth. As we deal with collector culture, exchange might also refer to the ethics of how collectors make their finds and deal with each other.

- Possession rituals determine how we personalize and develop attachments to things once we have acquired them: "[C]onsumers spend a good deal of time cleaning, discussing, comparing, reflecting, showing off, and even photographing many of their new possessions" (85). Such behaviors are the most visible aspects of collecting culture—as, for example, Seth showing off new "finds" to Chet.

- Grooming rituals have to do with how we preserve valued materials from wear and tear; this seems especially important as we think about the fragile materiality of paper. Much of what I've said about dust and hands speaks to this dimension, as do ongoing debates about how much value should be ascribed to objects that are pristine and untouched.

- Divestment rituals shape how we get rid of things that are no longer meaningful, a process that has to do with the mental frames we place around objects we collect.

Here, I will focus on exchange and divestment rituals, but all four categories are useful for thinking about Seth's collecting stories.

Exchange Rituals: Quests, Searches, and Finds

What makes Wimbledon Green "the greatest comic book collector in the world"? A folk hero for consumer culture, Green represents a particularly hyperbolic version of the collector's capacities for consumption, acquisition, and discrimination. Bruce of Comic Ark tells us, "He could determine a comic's publication date just by the position of the staples" (15); another notes his ability to distinguish the particular scents of different publishers' newsprint (77); and Waxy Combs shares that Green could "grade" a comic's condition at a hundred yards (91). Like Uncle Scrooge or Richie Rich, Green can land anywhere and ferret out hidden treasures. Harvey Epp of The Comic Cellar explains, "[Green was] a real picker—working the Goodwills and back alleys and yard sales. [. . .] He was a genius at finding things. He just knew where to look. [. . .] You've never be able to do that today—the books just aren't out there anymore" (22–23). Green is the world's greatest comics collector not because he possesses the world's greatest collection, but because he has the skills and instincts of a great collector.

Seth similarly characterizes his own collecting practices in *Forty Cartoon Books of Interest*. Surrounded by massive bookcases, Seth describes the "thrill of the hunt," since comics, often devalued by others, can "turn up anywhere at any time." He explains, "[N]ow-a-days, sadly, most of my collecting is done on a computer. But for most of those years it was done the old-fashioned way. Bookstores. Thrift Shops. Rumages. Paper shows. University Sales. [. . .] [S]ome of the happiest times of my life have been spent rooting about in these places" (n.p.). What interests Seth about the "old-fashioned way" is the possibility of making a true "find."

In "Nothing Lasts," Seth (2014) describes how he acquired the childhood nickname "Back Issues." Young Seth tells his bemused classmates that he can look up an obscure horror actor by digging through his old monster magazines. Seth digresses into a long rumination about the "unavailability of information in that era," as opposed to the "labyrinth of internet connections" (n.p.). There were few if any answers to be found at his local library to such pressing questions: "[C]ontext was hard to come by. [. . .] Answers came by serendipity alone." Instead, he "mentally filed away" the pursuit of such information, "awaiting the day an answer would arrive, usually much later, and most likely by sheer chance" (n.p.). He learns, like many other collectors, to grab materials when he can find them. For Seth, web culture's easy answers devalue his collecting skills. As Seth told one interviewer, "When you discover something off the beaten path, you can kind of make it your own" (Hoffman & Grace 2015: 175).

Being a gifted collector requires acts of discrimination. The collector should be able to appropriately value (in both the economic and cultural sense) what he or she find. The fictionalized comics critic Art Stern explains of Wimbledon, "The other customers of the store seemed shallow and crass. Men of poor taste seeking out old comics in a vain attempt to buy back their childhoods. Or empty speculators hoping to cash in on some collecting trend. Most of them quite lacking in knowledge. [. . .] Not Wimbledon Green. [. . .] He really seemed to know things. To understand!" (42–43). But Stern's admiration for Green's "high standards" ends in disappointment when he stumbles upon his idol sitting in a fast-food joint, eating "greasy chicken," and reading through "crummy superhero comics" with "a look on his face [. . .] of a pig in shit" (43). A collector's reputation rests on his or her discriminating tastes; a collector's touch should be dusty, but not greasy or crummy.[1]

Each time you acquire an object, you place your reputation at risk: a collector is defined by what he or she collects, and the collector is shamed when his or her purchases are not respected or valued by others. Collecting stories are often drenched with flop sweat as the collector-storyteller asserts his or her mastery and expertise in the face of uncertainties about the status of his or her activities. In "Nothing Lasts," Seth describes his own anxiety about how his contemporaries would react if they knew he was still reading comic books as a teenager, showing his elaborate preparations to ensure that he can swoop in, grab what he wants, and buy it to minimize the risks of being seen with his purchases. Seth contrasts his timidity with the boldness of a "more popular boy" who walked into the store, a girl on each arm, and proudly walked out with a bundle of comics. Why do some collectors, thus, draw stigma, where others walk away untainted by their desires?

Seth is also strongly interested in the social relations among collectors. As Bart Beaty (2011) notes, Seth, along with Chester Brown and Joe Matt, constitute a particular artistic community, based at least for a time in Toronto. These artists not only are friends in real life but also depict their friendships in many of their works. For Beaty, these interlocking acts of self-fashioning contribute to a process of reputation building, but I am interested in what such moments suggest about the ethics of collecting. Throughout *It's a Good Life*, Seth and Chet pool their knowledge, tap each other's expertise, and share resources (informational and economic). This collaborative relationship between Seth and Chet contrasts sharply with the Coverloose Club in *Wimbledon Green*, an organization that exists simply so the leaders can blackball their competitors. Here, the collectors engage in endless grudges—rivals but never friends. They are all pursuing the same objects and willing to do anything and everything to get them.

If *It's a Good Life* uses collecting to demonstrate the strong homosocial bonds between Seth and Chester, Joe Matt uses collecting in *Spent*

(2007) to suggest the opposite—the ways different expectations about how collectors should treat each other generate frictions. The book opens with Joe and Seth rummaging through a used bookstore. Joe stumbles onto a rare volume of the *Birdseye Center* comic strip: "I've been looking for that book for years," Seth proclaims, anticipating that Joe will bow to his prior claim, but Joe holds his ground. Seth is still grumbling as they exit the store: "[Y]ou deliberately bought that book just to piss me off! [. . .] You wouldn't even know about it if I hadn't shown you my old newspaper clippings!" (10–11). Almost a hundred pages later, the two are still bartering over this particular book, and Joe has intentionally purchased other stuff he knows Seth wants—"every man for himself" (92).

If such interactions seem juvenile, in *Fair Weather* Matt (2002) depicts similar ethical lapses in his childhood collecting practices, such as taking advantage of a price guide to cheat a less savvy pal out of his most valuable titles or selling out a friend's secrets in hopes of convincing another collector to sell him a coveted comic. If Seth uses *Wimbledon Green* to construct a folk tale about the world's greatest collector, Matt often depicts himself as the world's scummiest collector. In this same spirit, Seth modeled unsavory collector Jonah in *Wimbledon Green* after his own familiar persona. For example, Ashcan Kemp characterizes Jonah as an example of collectors as "self-deluded fops [. . .] pining for a time before they were even born." While Jonah prides himself on his sensitivity, he is "a rather hard hearted individual with no real sympathy for others" (65). Jonah is a shoplifter who steals other people's prized objects, justifying himself as "a preservationist—freeing these comics from the wrong owners" (68).

Divestment Rituals: Putting Away Childish Things

McCracken's divestment rituals involve "letting go" of collected objects, shedding parts of ourselves as we toss the things that embody them. If choices about what to save reflect sentimentalization and aestheticization, divestment requires depersonalization and desacralization, shifting mental frames.

Clyde Fans depicts the moment when Simon becomes disenchanted with his collection. Nagged by Abe, Simon restlessly flips and sorts through his postcards, using these grooming practices to limit engagement. But Abe accidentally overturns a box. Simon brushes it off: "It's not important, Abe. Just old paper" (81–82). Abe promises to set things right—"nothing ruined"—but, for the slumped-shouldered collector, nothing much matters any more. The fascination has passed; he is just going through the motions. I use the term "disenchantment" above advisedly, because it conveys the sense of sympathetic magic that collectors sometimes ascribe to their objects and hints at the sense of "breaking a spell" prior to divestment.

In "Nothing Lasts," Seth documents when and how he abandoned meaningful objects from his childhood. For example, as young Seth lost interest in model building, those "models that had fallen from favor" landed in his dresser drawer. "Each time I opened or closed the drawer something would break. The damage only got worse as I crammed more and more models in there. Eventually, the drawer was filled only with shattered pieces" (2013: n.p.). In another passage, he recalls his "best loved" stuffed animals: "Each toy invested with a life of its own, emotionally animated as only a child can. Their faces remembered better than any childhood friend, recalled clearer than any teacher from that time" (2013: n.p.). Yet, one day the adolescent takes his plush friends out of the attic, hangs them from a tree, and shoots them "all to pieces" with a pellet gun: "It wasn't a meaningful act, just something to pass the time. Still, I can think of no more fitting event to signify the end of my childhood" (2013: n.p.). Divestment of objects is closely linked with closing off a chapter in one's life—a rite of passage. Seth shows us two ways that divestment occurs: gradually (models breaking down into shards of plastic) and dramatically (shooting the stuffing out of his plush).

Chester Brown, Seth's collector friend, tells yet a third story in *The Playboy* (1992). His guilt-ridden character struggles with his addiction to pornography. Chester, as an adolescent, purchases and then systematically destroys one porn magazine after another—ripping up the pages, burning the magazines in the family fireplace, burying them in the woods far from his home—only to replace them yet again. Brown refuses, at least in the context of this particular narrative, to label his habits collecting, even as he increasingly demonstrates his own growing expertise (displayed here in part by the artist's loving re-creations of specific covers) and even as he taps collector networks to acquire the issues he fetishizes.

How do we understand these depictions of collecting as a source of shame in a context where, as artists, Seth, Matt, Brown, and the others are placing these same habits on such bold display? What happens when we see these men, who are afraid to be seen in public buying comics, stripped naked in the pages of their publications? Underground comics have long been celebrated for their refusal of self-censorship; the artists claim to set no limits on what they can and will share with their readers. Matt depicts himself eating his own snot, taking a crap, smelling his underarms, jerking off, and spending all of his money to purchase obscure View-Master slide sets. We can read such images as a disgusting yet "honest" display of our common humanity; there are aspects of how we relate to our bodies and our stuff that we do not talk about in public.

This is why it matters that the kinds of collecting stories we have been discussing here are stories constructed *by* and *for* collectors. Some of these representations come precariously close to negative stereotypes about fans and collectors elsewhere in the culture; Seth and the others depict collectors as engaging in emotionally immature behaviors, as socially isolated, as coping with professional failures. Yet, they show us these collecting practices as representations of self and not of the Other, and they do so alongside a broader range of representations of what it means to collect. Collecting, here, is normalized, even as we are encouraged to reflect on both its constructive and destructive dimensions. They often depict themselves as having little control over their collecting fever and having little to no self-awareness. Yet, as artists, they are the ones selecting what to place on the page. Their readers are encouraged to recognize themselves within such representations—even if they are amplified for comic effect.

All of this is complicated, messy, contradictory . . . and that is perhaps its power. Such representations force us to think through how well these stereotypes fit our own life narratives. These collectors' shared shame and self-pity means that they are drawn into closer identification with each other, but, at the same time, that they hold each other at arm's length. Their relationships are sometimes depicted as mutually supportive and other times as competitive and bullying. As such, these creative projects have much in common with recent efforts in fandom studies to reconsider the ways shame, guilt, and embarrassment shape fan culture—determining how deeply, how openly, fans are willing to express their desires or how they react when producers engage with their culture in a more direct way (Zubernis & Larsen 2012). Even where these texts continue to circulate the stereotypes that disturbed us early in the development of fandom studies, they do so with a different degree of self-consciousness and with a different degree of distance. It matters enormously whether it is William Shatner telling his fans to "get a life" or whether fans and collectors are talking among themselves about those aspects of their cultural experience that generate shame.

NOTE

1 Here is where other cultural scholars turn to Pierre Bourdieu (1984)—cultural and social capital, habitus, discrimination and class distinctions, every taste masks a distaste, etc. But those articles have already been written (see Fiske 1992).

WORKS CITED

Bal, M 1994, "Telling objects: a narrative perspective on collecting," in J Eisner & R Cardinal (eds.), *The cultures of collecting*, Reaktion Books, London.

Beaty, B 2011, "Selective mutual reinforcement in the comics of Chester Brown, Joe Matt, and Seth," in MA Chaney (ed.), *Graphic subjects: critical essays on autobiography and graphic novels*, University of Wisconsin Press, Madison.

Benjamin, W 1969, "Unpacking my library: an essay about book collecting," in *Illuminations*, H Zohn (trans.), H Arendt (ed.), Schocken Books, New York.

Blom, P 2002, *To have and to hold: an intimate history of collectors and collecting*, Overlook, Woodstock, NY.

Bourdieu, P 1984, *Distinction: a social critique of the judgment of taste*, Harvard University Press, Cambridge, MA.

Brown, C 1992, *The Playboy*, Drawn & Quarterly, Toronto.

Chamberland, L 2015, *Seth's Dominion*, National Film Board of Canada.

Fiske, J 1992, "The cultural economy of fandom," in LA Lewis (ed.), *The adoring audience: fan culture and popular media*, Routledge, New York.

Gardner, J 2012, *Projections: comics and the history of 21st century storytelling*, Stanford University Press, Palo Alto, CA.

Geraghty, L 2014, *Cult collectors: nostalgia, fandom and collecting popular culture*, Routledge, London.

Heer, J 2010, "Inventing cartooning ancestors: Ware and the comics canon," in DM Ball & MB Kuhlman (eds.), *The comics of Chris Ware: drawing as a way of thinking*, University Press of Mississippi, Jackson.

Hoffman, E & Grace, D 2015, "Interview with Seth," in E Hoffman & D Grace (eds.), *Seth, conversations*, University Press of Mississippi, Jackson.

Jenkins, H 1992, *Textual poachers: television fans and participatory culture*, Routledge, New York.

Matt, J 2002, *Fair weather*, Drawn & Quarterly, Toronto.

Matt, J 2007, *Spent*, Drawn & Quarterly, Toronto.

McCracken, G 1988, "Meaning manufacture and movement in the world of goods," in *Culture and consumption: new approaches to the symbolic character of consumer goods and activities*, Indiana University Press, Bloomington.

McCracken, G 2005, "Living in the material world," in *Culture and consumption II: markets, meaning, and brand management*, Indiana University Press, Bloomington.

Miller, B 2015. "An interview with Seth" [2004], in E Hoffman & D Grace (eds.), *Seth, conversations*, University Press of Mississippi, Jackson.

Miller, D 2010, *Stuff*, Polity, Cambridge.

Seth 1996, *It's a good life, if you don't weaken*, Drawn & Quarterly, Montreal.

Seth 2002, "Clyde Fans part three," *Palookaville* 16.

Seth 2004, *Clyde Fans: Book 1*, Drawn & Quarterly, Toronto.

Seth 2005, *Wimbledon Green: the greatest comicbook collector in the world*, Drawn & Quarterly, Toronto.

Seth 2006, *Forty cartoon books of interest*, Buenaventura Press, Oakland.

Seth 2009, *George Sprott 1894–1975*, Drawn & Quarterly, Toronto.

Seth 2013, "Nothing lasts, part one," *Palookaville* 21.

Seth 2014, "Nothing lasts, part two," *Palookaville* 22.

Stewart, S 1984, *On longing: narratives of the miniature, the gigantic, the souvenir, the collection*, Duke University Press, Durham, NC.

Tanselle, GT 1998, "A rationale of collecting," *Studies in Bibliography* 51: 1–26.

Zubernis, L & Larsen, K 2012, *Fandom at the crossroads: celebration, shame, and fan-producer relationships*, Cambridge Scholars, Cambridge.

14

Sex, Utopia, and the Queer Temporalities of Fannish Love

ALEXIS LOTHIAN

Looking Backward: Fan Cultures in Queer Times

At one point in my life as a scholar of queer culture and
theory, I thought the point of queer was to be always ahead
of actually existing social possibilities. [. . .] Now I think
the point may be to trail behind [. . .] to be interested in
the tail end of things, willing to be bathed in the fading light
of whatever has been declared useless.
—Freeman (2010: xiii)

Elizabeth Freeman's description of queer scholarship as a lingering, insistent drive that holds on to ideas, loves, identities, and communities long after their expiry from official discourses and profitable markets will resonate with many fans, scholarly and otherwise. Writing for the second edition of a book whose 2007 first edition coincided with my own emergence as a scholar of both queer and fan studies, I find Freeman's passage rich in parallels between the fields. In 2007, as Henry Jenkins wrote in his afterword, fandom was the future, the vanguard of Web 2.0—though the very ubiquity of formerly marginal participatory cultures also meant that fandom as a distinctive subculture was at risk of having no future at all. Fan practices have indeed become inseparable from the ever more fragmented mainstream over the past eight years, as many of the contributors to this collection document. Yet, as Kristina Busse elaborates in her introduction to a 2015 *Cinema Journal* dossier on feminism and fan labor, the brave new world of the "new industry-fan model" has not proven worthy of celebration for everyone—and especially not for the most marginalized, feminine, and queer fan practices (111). Trailing behind the emergence of new economies of capitalized sharing, marginal fan subcultures offer alternate narratives for the recent history of gender, sexuality, and media economies. This essay explores the queerness of sexually explicit fan fiction, not just in terms of erotic representation but also in its production of imaginative times and spaces. To look queerly at fannish temporalities is to attend to moments in which they refuse narratives of development and progress by which particular moments in media and LGBT history are seen as passing into irrelevance; reconfigure norms of gender and sexuality; and use the affective technology of fannish love to build spaces that both reproduce and subvert dominant economies.

If our current moment is one of unprecedented visibility for creative fandom, this is even more the case for US-based LGBT people and communities. As of 2016, same-sex marriage is a federally recognized right; gay and lesbian people can serve openly in the military; emerging televisual superpowers Netflix and Amazon have LGBT characters at the center of their flagship shows, *Orange Is the New Black* and *Transparent*; trans women Laverne Cox and Caitlyn Jenner have graced the covers of *Time* (2014) and *Vanity Fair* (2015) respectively. A narrative of progress, from homophobia and misrepresentation into a bright inclusive future, seems self-evident. Yet this is precisely the story that Freeman and other queer studies scholars warn us not to take at face value, no matter how often we are told that "our problems are solved now that our market niche has been discovered" (Freeman 2010: xvi). In this context, to insist on "trail[ing] behind," as Freeman does, is to refuse the overwhelming force of assimilation, focusing instead on moments, experiences, and analyses whose apparent outdatedness risks dismissing the truths they uncover. Juana María Rodríguez writes that queer temporalities and possible futures in excess of liberal progress narratives become available to thought and feeling through the power-laden, nuanced ways that sexual acts and desires function as "social world-making" (2014: 183); the writing and reading of fans' sexual fictions is such a world-making practice.

Freeman writes of being "compelled" by "embarrassing utopias" (2010: xiii). This association of embarrassment and outdatedness with utopia reflects the histories of both fan and queer studies. For while utopian perspectives, taking fans' responses to popular culture as blueprints for social change, characterized the early years of fan studies scholarship—named in the introduction to this volume's first edition as the "Fandom

Is Beautiful" perspective (Gray, Sandvoss, & Harrington 2007)[1]—a description of scholarly work is these days more likely to be called "utopian" as a challenge to insufficiently critical analytics. Queer studies' critiques of heteronormativity have long had a utopian thrust, described by Lauren Berlant and Michael Warner as "radically anticipatory, trying to bring a world into being" (1995: 344). Yet as gay inclusion into normative culture has increased, queer studies scholars have focused on dystopian aspects of the present, especially the ways in which successes for more privileged members of lesbian, gay, bisexual, and transgender communities can obscure continuing oppression of the most vulnerable, especially LGBTQ people of color (Reddy 2011). The possibility of utopia for marginalized and racialized queer subjects recedes into an imaginable but inaccessible future—what José Muñoz calls the "not yet here" (2009: 1)—that can be invoked without necessitating an earnest, literal belief that utopian possibilities could truly be enacted. Fan fiction creators have, however, turned earnest literalism into a variety of art forms—making sexual and emotional fantasies narratively real with an explicit detail that can be delightful, arousing, awkward, or embarrassing, depending on the reader's perspective. This need not be incompatible with the insights of critical queer studies.

The queerness of fan practices has been most extensively chronicled with regard to slash fan fiction, which depicts sexual and romantic relationships between same-sex media characters. This transformation of heterosexual source texts into queer erotic visions has fascinated generations of cultural critics. I came to fandom in the early 2000s after reading about slash in a feminist magazine, looking for the queer pleasures it described. And I found them—alongside a politicized community attentive to the power dynamics that structure sex, gender, disability, class, and race. While fan studies has often located politicized understandings of fans' practices in the writings of cultural studies academics who may celebrate or condemn, I became part of a subcultural network that avidly produced its own theories, critiques, and contradictions.[2] Indeed, my participation in online fandom would shape my emergence as a queer cultural theorist committed to intersectional feminism and critical race analysis almost as much as the graduate studies I began a few years later. The queer fannish forms of being and belonging I came to know have only rarely become part of scholarly conversations about consumer practices in the digital age or about LGBT cultural production, for they have remained marginal to the rapidly changing universes of participatory culture. Yet queer fannish world making continues, entangling realms of fantasy and imagination with material social practice.

I will make my argument by way of two works of fan fiction published in 2008, at the beginning of its ascendancy to mainstream attention and a time when my own engagement with queer fandom was at its height.[3] Speranza's "Friendly" and Toft's "Healing Station Argh," both celebrated works by prolific authors in a large slash fandom (Stargate Atlantis's McKay/Sheppard pairing), offer meta commentaries on fannish time, space, and queerness that are intellectually and erotically compelling. My choice to focus on a fandom whose moment of dominance has passed is in part an effort to quell the anxious compulsion to remain ahead, a feeling common to the temporalities of scholarship, technology, and capitalism alike. Inhabiting the temporality of repetition, return, and lingering attention that characterizes fans' constant turning back to favored texts, I uncover some queerly utopian moments that persist in the products of fannish love.

Welcome to the Tower: Slashing Queer History and Community

Scholarly discussions of slash fan fiction have often been rhapsodic, describing the genre as a site for the liberation of gender and sexuality. In 1986, Patricia Lamb and Diana Veith hypothesized that women (white, middle-class, American, and heterosexual, though none of these categories are marked) were drawn to Kirk/Spock (K/S) slash because the sexual imagining of two male bodies allowed for a "vision of a new way of loving" that would transcend the gender inequalities in which heterosexual relationships were mired (254). They quoted Joanna Russ—feminist science fiction author, lesbian, and K/S writer—stating that slash was an answer to women's question "what if I were free?" (Lamb & Veith 1986: 254). This early essay's tone of breathless discovery appears in many subsequent scholarly works on slash. P. J. Falzone describes Kirk/Spock slash as "liberating the characters [. . .] from the heterosexist norms of commercial media production" (2005: 249); Sharon Hayes and Matthew Ball assert that slash "thumbs its nose at the insidious heterosexism underpinning most forms of literary expression" (2010: 223); Ika

Willis describes slash as "challenging [. . .] queer-eradicating impulses" and "refusing to submit to [. . .] effacement of homosexuality" (2006: 161). Though the substance of their arguments differs and incorporates much more complexity than my brief quotations, these authors all posit the act of writing slash as a practice of freedom, a blow struck against heteropatriarchy and for new sexual and social possibilities. It is unsurprising that other scholars stepped forward to offer critiques of this utopianism, from Sara Gwenllian Jones's reminder that many of slash's seemingly inventive structures can be found in cult television itself (2002) to Christine Scodari's exposé of slash fans' misogynistic response to their beloved characters' female love interests (2003) and Kyra Hunting's exploration of the ways some *Queer as Folk* fans used the tropes of slash fiction to write heteronormativity back into the narrative of a show that brought queer cultural politics to American TV (2012).[4]

Here I want to offer an account of slash that sidesteps the question of whether it is subversively queer or hegemonically heteronormative. To ask this question, no matter how nuanced the answer, is to remain caught in the idea that we could somehow ascertain the moral or political utility of all slash with respect to a predetermined progressive agenda. Given the extent to which mainstream political discourse has reduced queer politics and culture to a march of progress toward social and representational assimilation, it is especially important not to flatten any site where diverse and complex understandings of gender and sexuality appear. Kristina Busse and I (2008) sought to detail some of these complexities by examining the breadth of political standpoints to be found in the "genderfuck" genre of fan fiction. This chapter expands on some of the insights initiated there, arguing that the changing LGBT mainstream makes the queer challenges of fan fiction more necessary than ever, even as it also demands attention to the contexts and histories of fans' sometimes-contradictory queer practices. The stories I discuss draw from a TV series that lacked any queer representation or LGBT awareness; yet they draw from wider cultural and intertextual contexts for their queer references, underlining in the process that viewing fan productions purely in the context of their canon is insufficient.

The 2008 story "Friendly," by Speranza, demonstrates intimate entanglements between queer histories and communities and slash fandom. As Russ (1985), Hunting (2012), and others have observed, it is common—though by no means universal—for slash fan stories to feature male/male sexual activity without any reference to the lived experience of gay or same-gender-loving men. Science fiction and fantasy media sources make this particularly easy, since the author can simply assert that sexual norms differ in the imagined world. "Friendly" goes against this trend, focusing on realistic elements of its setting (a US-backed, military-led expedition) rather than speculative ones (the mission sent explorers to the Pegasus Galaxy, where they occupied an ancient city built by alien ancestors of humanity). The story's premise is that queer explorers would be unable to live openly under military discipline—Don't Ask, Don't Tell is not explicitly mentioned but is an obvious inspiration—and that they would need some outlet for their erotic energies. As the story unfolds, we learn that gay male members of the expedition have created a secret place in the city of Atlantis: an abandoned tower by the sea, whose promenade, pier, and many empty rooms recollect the cruising zones, docks, and bathhouses of the urban gay men's public sex cultures documented by queer historians and memoirists George Chauncey (1994) and Samuel R. Delany (1999). The existence of this space for fucking and socializing succors a "fragile community" whose hub is Rodney McKay, Atlantis's chief scientist and half of the fandom's main slash pairing. The story follows John Sheppard, military commander of the expedition and the other half of McKay/Sheppard, as he discovers this group and persuades Rodney to induct him—which he does first by kissing him and then by giving him a public blowjob, offering material for potential blackmail in order to prove that John will not betray his comrades. Rodney assures John that "every gay man in Atlantis will have this image on their hard drive by morning, but most of them know the value of a strong password" (Speranza 2008). And it appears that they do, for the story ends as John and Rodney's secret relationship deepens within the security and comfort of their hidden queer network.

The story, especially read a few years after its publication and after the demise of Don't Ask, Don't Tell, is a fantasy of queer history as much as of its main characters' love. Speranza encourages us to imagine the lives of forcibly closeted gay men not as an oppressive situation we should be campaigning to change, but as a circumstance rife with possibilities where the closet itself can be productive of vitality, pleasure, and love that would be erased by a move toward visibility. This fantasy of a queer past is also a fantasy of fandom. For the network of visitors to the tower is cemented through images of illicit love they create and share online—through their participation in their own McKay/Sheppard fan community, in fact. They must remain underground, as slash fans have sought to maintain anonymity for fear of reprisals over copyright or of the damage to social status that public knowledge of their homoerotic fiction could cause. My colleagues and I (Lothian, Busse, & Reid 2007: 105) connect Delany's writings on public sex with slash fans' interactions, suggesting that similar forms of "radical intersubjective contact" could take place through shared sexual fantasy rather than bodily touch; "Friendly" extends and fictionalizes that comparison. This is not, it turns out, an interpretation I make alone. In comments to the published story, several fans read Speranza's imagined tower as an analogy to the fan-created online Archive of Our Own, of which Speranza was among the founders. "Friendly" was the first story she posted to the archive, and one commenter found it to be "perfect" for that purpose, adding "Welcome to the tower—it's beautiful here" (Martha in comments to Speranza 2008).

The analogy between the Archive of Our Own and Speranza's fictional tower of queer sexual community is instructive both for what it reveals and for what it hides. The creation of the Archive was a moment when a group of activist fans took their subcultural sense of community into the public sphere, seeking ownership over their own transformative works (Lothian 2013; Brooker 2014). Speranza's imagined queer space might be based on histories of public sex, but it could not become public in the way that the Archive is without the lifting of the regulations that make its seductive secrecy necessary in the first place. And in practice, though the lifting of Don't Ask, Don't Tell regulations might make such spaces conceivably possible, celebration of the legislative change through published pictures of gay and lesbian soldiers coming home to husbands and wives suggests a seamless integration into mainstream discourses of family and state that is a far cry from Speranza's depiction of communal sexual fraternizing on military bases. As a utopian fantasy, the tower elides not only the complications that its illegality and illegitimacy would create, but also some of the elements that are most important for queer historians. Not only do there seem to be no women or genderqueer people among the queers of Atlantis, there is also no conflict or hierarchy among the queer tower's denizens; race and class conflicts are absent as they never were in the communities to which Speranza alludes. In "Friendly," those who enter the tower will encounter only others who have been approved by its preexisting denizens; but urban spaces of public sex, as Delany (1999) insists, were defined by the messiness, unexpectedness, and capacity for conflict of the truly public. The analogy of the Archive and the tower hints at a desire on the part of fans to be similarly safe, perhaps, from the ever-increasing messiness and publicity of online life, as social media permeate everyday life and online existence is no longer restricted to those with greatest access to technology. Fans' interest in understanding the Archive as the tower highlights continual and ongoing discomfort with the mainstreaming of fan practices, along with a desire to turn back to and live within a queer past that is all the more enticing for never having quite existed.

The Ostentatiously Moralizing Dildo: Sexual Fantasy as Social Justice

In naming the queer community described in "Friendly" as a utopian fantasy and critiquing it for evading some of the conflicted messiness of lived queer history, I do not mean to dismiss the importance or the complexity of utopia and fantasy. The idea of sexual fantasy has been most extensively explored within psychoanalytic theory, where it is a structuring element in the operation of desire (Laplanche & Pontalis 1968). Feminist thinkers have sought to understand how processes of identification in sexual fantasy and its cultural representations reverberate in political and social structures, perpetuating or challenging sexual degradation (Penley 1991). Joanna Russ named slash fan fiction as a collective outpouring of "sexual fantasy," stating that her "autonomous nervous system" did "nip-ups [. . .] upon merely reading the premise" of K/S (1985: 81) and remarking that "only those for whom a sexual fantasy 'works,' that is, those who are aroused by it" can fully analyze that fantasy's significance (89). Scholars writing on slash have tended to focus more on the possibility of political significance in slash's implicit media critique than on the eliciting of bodily thrills—though the tones of excitement in slash scholars' analyses hint at, and sometimes explicitly state, the same "nip-ups" that fans discussing their own writings take for granted.[5] Yet those thrills of arousal deserve and require attention, not only for what they might reveal about individual experiences of desire but also for what their collective expression reveals.

The story to which I now turn places the arousing affects of sexual fantasy front and center, having been written within a context designed to do just that. The Kink Bingo challenge, which ran from 2008 until 2013, invited fan writers to create transformative works based on a dizzying array of kinks (from animal play to watersports and everything in between) with the explicit goal of diversifying representations of erotic activity in fandom and diminishing the shaming of unusual preferences. Stories written for Kink Bingo cover a vast range of genres, fandoms, and formats, but are required to engage with their assigned kink in earnest—the story may be comic, but the writer must give the fantasy the respect it is due, finding a way to make it "work." "Healing Station Argh," which combines loving comic parody of fandom tropes with detailed group sex scenes, was written for a Kink Bingo assignment of "pegging," the practice of women topping men in anal sex. Toft uses the speculative elements of *Stargate: Atlantis* to elaborate extensively on this basic idea. Like "Friendly," the story depicts fan practices as ways of participating in a queer world, calling attention to particular elements of what their authors view as central to slash fandom's queer spaces and possibilities. For Speranza, this was autonomous community, existing in independent opposition to a commodifying gaze. For Toft, it is the power of sexual fantasy—and laughter.

"Healing Station Argh" builds a fantasy world around a sexual practice that is commonly taboo in non-porn media by creating a fan community for *Stargate: Atlantis*'s characters to join. *Healing Station Argh* is an invented TV show, similar to *General Hospital*, which Toft imagines to have aired decades before the Earth-based expedition arrived. *Stargate: Atlantis* featured only two regular characters who were depicted as hailing from the galaxy in which the show took place; of these, Toft casts Ronon Dex (Jason Momoa) as having been *Healing Station Argh*'s star doctor, while pregnant Teyla Emmagen (Rachel Luttrell) enjoys the rerun episodes with the pleasure of a longtime fan. Both these characters were played by actors of color within a largely white cast, and their position as native guides to the colonists from Earth struck frequently racist tones. Within media fandom's racially unmarked (presumptively white) spaces (Stanfill 2011), it is a common observation among fans of color and race-conscious white fans that white men get the majority of erotic attention in fan fiction (TWC Editor 2009); *Stargate: Atlantis* fandom was no exception. While "Healing Station Argh" still focuses significantly on the relationship between two white men, John and Rodney, both its driving sexual fantasy and the action of the plot depend on Ronon and especially Teyla. Depicting Ronon as a TV star and Teyla as a TV viewer was both amusingly unexpected and a more serious reversal of the racializing logic that places them technologically behind their Earth-based teammates; Teyla holds the position both of fan and of prime mover in the story's development.

The plot of Toft's story, unashamedly contrived to maximize the number and configuration of sex scenes, is that in viewing *Healing Station Argh*, our main characters discover that the primary Pegasus method of birth control was the use of the comedically named "wangkum," a double-ended dildo that women use to penetrate men. John, Rodney, and Teyla watch together as Ronon's on-screen girlfriend takes out a "sculpture [. . .] with a bulb on one end" and performs its function on camera. The two men are thrown into a panic of awkward arousal, while Teyla calmly asks if the scene "disturbed" them, commenting that "the style of production has not dated as well as [she] had thought." Remarking that "most [Earth] movies contain sex," she goes on to consider that *Healing Station Argh* was "a little ostentatiously moralizing, but the show was broadcast on many more conservative worlds, and children might be watching" (Toft 2008). Teyla's mocking concern for the backward customs of the US-led Earth expedition, and Toft's delight in turning around the reader's expectations, is clear. As the story goes on, the wangkum shifts gear from comedy to titillation, inviting readers to inhabit the fantasy world Toft has set up: Teyla inducts John and Rodney into the use of the device through group sex with herself and Ronon, in the process leading John to recognize his homosexuality and accept Rodney's love as part of a four-way partnership.

When Teyla describes the on-screen dildo use as "ostentatiously moralizing," the comedy comes from the deep incongruity we experience between what "moralizing" television usually means and what has been described. But this story too, while filled with explicit sexual fantasy, has an ethically prescriptive aspect. It offers readers the utopian prospect of a sexually open world, where a pregnant woman of color can be the center and subject of a sexy, joyous fantasy rather than subjected to gendered violence and denied reproductive choices—the latter being Teyla's actual fate during her on-screen pregnancy in the show itself. The story also identifies fannish practice, the lingering love for an old TV show that leads it to new audiences, as the instigation for this severing of sexual pleasure from racialized gender oppression. Had the Atlantis expedition not fallen headfirst into *Healing Station Argh* fandom, after all, they would have remained ignorant of the erotic universe the wangkum opened up. "Healing Station Argh" in fact hinges on precisely the kind of openness to difference that the tower in "Friendly" elided: the presence of otherness in the form of the Pegasus Galaxy, the space that the principal characters of *Stargate: Atlantis* are attempting to colonize. While "Friendly" was about setting up a space of one's own, lingering in the light of a queer past imagined as somewhat more straightforward than it actually was, "Healing Station Argh" makes its characters admit that the world they live in has complicated, unsettling histories. We still experience moments of utopia that are attained through a fannish lingering in the past—but it is not John and Rodney's past, nor a past familiar to the audience. Instead it is a continuing history of the subaltern characters of the show, which the main characters had previously overlooked due to their privilege. That such an encounter could take place without extensive conflict is perhaps the most utopian of the fantasies in which the story trades. Fans' reconfigurations of dominant media do not always push away from media's racism and sexism, but they have a powerful capacity to do so.

Looking Forward: Transformative Works as Queer Sexual Futures

Both "Healing Station Argh" and "Friendly" invent fictional analogies for fans' creative networks, and in doing so offer a suggestive narration for what practices of creative production grounded in collective fantasy could build. They connect fantasy as sexual desire to the expansive, political definition of fantasy that Judith Butler has articulated, in which "fantasy is what allows us to imagine ourselves and others otherwise

[. . .] when it is embodied, it brings the elsewhere home" (2004: 29). Fan works establish multiple possibilities for imagining their media sources otherwise. Embodied and brought home through communities of writers and readers, they may do transformative work in several senses of the word. The two stories I have explored transform the characters and setting of *Stargate: Atlantis* in the legal sense that the Organization for Transformative Works has popularized; but they also both set their sights on a larger transformation, hoping to perpetuate queer visions of sexual community or women of color's erotic subjecthood. Fan fiction can participate in this kind of transformation by taking the media that provide raw material for so many fantasies and rewriting them such that powerful and compelling fantasy moments can be shared with others. "Healing Station Argh" in particular puts fantasy to work in the ways that Juana María Rodríguez describes, building on Butler, as a way to "inhabit the imagined elsewhere of a radical sexual sociality [. . .] as a way to conjure and inhabit an alternative world" (2014: 26). Highlighting the work of fantasy for a group that is often marginalized even within queer studies, Latina femmes, Rodríguez writes that fantasy "has functioned as [. . .] a place to confront the racially gendered scripts that have been used to define us, and make something else of them" (2014: 184). She reads fantasy as a necessity for transformative work: a means of reconfiguring what is given, of eroticizing homophobic, misogynistic representations and living them anew within the context of queer community.

This chapter's lingering on the queerness of fannish love has sought to make some older ideas in fan studies new again, suggesting that the utopias and fantasies of fannish creativity contain transformative possibilities that linger past their apparent outdatedness. For, while work on contemporary digital culture faces a constant struggle to maintain contemporaneity in a rapidly changing technological landscape, and while fan communities' size, habits, and members change even faster, scholars' and fans' everyday digital practices do not move constantly forward into the new. We linger in the most appealing of the worlds we have encountered, returning to texts that resonate with the sexual, social, and political fantasies that move us most. Davina Cooper uses the term "everyday utopias" to describe subcultural communities that "perform regular daily life, in the global North, in a radically different fashion" (2013: 2). The examples from which she draws are not explicitly "utopian" projects, in that they do not lay claim to having come up with the ultimate alternative ideal world. But they do set out to do things differently and to make things work in a different way from the world as it is, "bring[ing] about (or seek[ing] to bring about) new forms of normalization, desire, and subjectivity" (Cooper 2013: 4). The queer fannish sexual fantasies I have described in this essay operate as everyday utopias in this sense.

Though they are necessarily imperfect, "Friendly" and "Healing Station Argh"—and many other stories, pieces of art, vids that I could have chosen—reward the return of attentive readers with the felt, fantasized experience of a different way of being: a world in which gendered and racialized power structures attach to sexual practice in ways that are different from the ideologies that dominate readers' realities. Through their existence as *fan* works, parasitic on the economies of media production where the possibilities for representation of marginalized people rely on the bottom lines of profits and marketing strategies, they can articulate possibilities that will remain unspeakable even in the most optimistic view of queer media progress. Making it worthwhile for readers to linger in transformed versions of unfashionable and outdated media worlds, they can operate even outside the idea of progress itself. Transformative works are not direct paths to radical or alternative futures, queer or otherwise. But as we return to the worlds they create, we may put ourselves in the way of transformation.

NOTES

1 See Coppa (2014) for an affirmative restatement of the "Fandom is Beautiful" perspective.

2 As I discuss in more detail elsewhere (Lothian 2013), my use of the term "subculture" does not refer to fandom as a whole but rather seeks to name the amorphous but powerful senses of self-consciousness about shared community norms within particular networked counterpublics.

3 For analyses of some of the various encounters between fan subcultures, wider audiences, and media producers at this time, see Brooker (2014).

4 If my summation of slash scholarship here appears to flatten a thirty-year history into sameness, it is because the scholarship itself has a tendency to represent slash as appearing in an eternal present.

5 Examples of fans' perspectives can be found in the discussions quoted in Green, Jenkins, and Jenkins (2006) and Lothian, Busse, and Reid (2007: 107).

WORKS CITED

Berlant, L & Warner, M 1995, "What does queer theory teach us about X?," *PMLA* 110(3): 343–49.

Brooker, W 2014, "Going pro: gendered responses to the incorporation of fan labor as user-generated content," in D Mann (ed.), *Wired TV: laboring over an interactive future*, Rutgers University Press, New Brunswick, NJ.

Busse, K 2015, "Fan labor and feminism: capitalizing on the fannish labor of love," *Cinema Journal* 54(3): 110–15.

Busse, K & Lothian, A 2008, "Bending gender: feminist and (trans)gender discourses in the changing bodies of slash fanfiction," in I Hotz-Davies, A Kirchhofer, & S Lepannen (eds.), *Internet fiction(s)*, Cambridge Scholars Press, Cambridge.

Butler, J 2004, *Undoing gender*, Routledge, New York.

Chauncey, G 1994, *Gay New York: gender, urban culture, and the makings of the gay male world, 1890–1940*, Basic Books, New York.

Cooper, D 2013, *Everyday utopias: the conceptual life of promising spaces*, Duke University Press, Durham, NC.

Coppa, F 2014, "Fuck yeah, fandom is beautiful," *Journal of Fandom Studies* 2(1): 73–82.

Delany, SR 1999, *Times Square red, Times Square blue*, New York University Press, New York.

Falzone, PJ 2005, "The final frontier is queer: aberrancy, archetype, and audience generated folklore in K/S slashfiction," *Western Folklore* 64(3/4): 243–61.

Freeman, E 2010, *Time binds: queer temporalities, queer histories*, Duke University Press, Durham, NC.

Gray, J, Sandvoss, C & Harrington, CL 2007, "Introduction: why study fans?," in J Gray, C Sandvoss, & CL Harrington (eds.), *Fandom: identities and communities in a mediated world*, New York University Press, New York.

Green, S, Jenkins, C, & Jenkins, H 2006, "'Normal female interest in men bonking': selections from the *Terra Nostra Underground* and *Strange Bedfellows*," in H Jenkins, *Fans, bloggers and gamers*, New York University Press, New York.

Hayes, SL & Ball, MJ 2010, "Queering cyberspace: fan fiction communities as spaces for expressing and exploring sexuality," in B Scherer (ed.), *Queering paradigms*, Peter Lang, Bern.

Hunting, K 2012, "*Queer As Folk* and the trouble with slash," *Transformative Works and Cultures* 11, journal.transformativeworks.org.

Jenkins, H 2007, "Afterword: the future of fandom," in J Gray, C Sandvoss, & CL Harrington (eds.), *Fandom: identities and communities in a mediated world*, New York University Press, New York.

Jones, SG 2002, "The sex lives of cult television characters," *Screen* 43(1): 79–90.

Lamb, PF & Veith, D 1986, "Romantic myth, transcendence, and Star Trek zines," in D Palumbo (ed.), *Erotic universe: sexuality and fantastic literature*, Greenwood, New York.

Laplanche, J & Pontalis, J-B 1968, "Fantasy and the origins of sexuality," *International Journal of Psycho-analysis* 49: 1–18.

Lothian, A 2013, "Archival anarchies: online fandom, subcultural conservation, and the transformative work of digital ephemera," *International Journal of Cultural Studies* 16(6): 541–56.

Lothian, A, Busse, K, & Reid, RA 2007, "Yearning void and infinite potential: online slash fandom as queer female space," *English Language Notes* 45(2): 103–12.

Muñoz, J 2009, *Cruising utopia: the then and there of queer futurity*. New York University Press, New York.

Penley, C 1991, "Feminism, psychoanalysis, and popular culture," in L Grossberg, C Nelson, & PA Treichler (eds.), *Cultural studies*, Routledge, New York.

Reddy, C 2011, *Freedom with violence: race, sexuality, and the US state*, Duke University Press, Durham, NC.

Rodríguez, JM 2014, *Sexual futures, queer gestures, and other Latina longings*, New York University Press, New York.

Russ, J 1985, "Pornography by women, for women, with love," in *Magic mommas, trembling sisters, puritans & perverts*, Crossing Press, Trumansburg, NY.

Scodari, C 2003, "Resistance re-examined: gender, fan practices, and science fiction television," *Popular Communication* 1(2): 111–30.

Speranza 2008, "Friendly," October 6, archiveofourown.org.

Stanfill, M 2011, "Doing fandom, (mis)doing whiteness: heteronormativity, racialization, and the discursive construction of fandom," *Transformative Works and Cultures* 8, journal.transformativeworks.org.

Toft 2008, "Healing Station Argh," August 31, archiveofourown.org.

TWC Editor 2009, "Pattern recognition: a dialogue on racism in fan communities," *Transformative Works and Cultures* 3, journal.transformativeworks.org.

Willis, I 2006, "Keeping promises to queer children: making space (for Mary Sue) at Hogwarts," in K Busse & K Hellekson (eds.), *Fan fiction and fan communities in the age of the Internet*, McFarland, Jefferson, NC.

PART IV

The Fan Citizen

Fan Politics and Activism

15

The News

You Gotta Love It

JONATHAN GRAY

This chapter began while I was conducting interviews with *Simpsons* viewers about parody and satire (see Gray 2006). While discussing *The Simpsons'* news parody, one of my interviewees talked at length about her love for politics and the news. She watched, by her estimate, three to four hours each day of Canadian parliamentary access television, and was a voracious news consumer. Yet quite impassionedly, and with more than just Canadian humility, she insisted that a great deal of this was entertainment for her:

> Don't get me wrong: I do know every MP in Canada, and when it's an election, I'll tell you their opponents too. I can tell you what they believe, how well they debate, and how ugly or handsome they are. But I don't just watch "to be a good citizen" and do my "Canadian duty" [laughs]. Really, I, it's entertainment. I love it. I really *love* it. It's my soap opera. There are, are villains, and good guys, you can cheer some on, and get involved. If I did all this just to vote, that would be excessive. I watch because it amuses me.

At the time, her comments were off-topic, so I rushed her along. But I remained fascinated by what was clearly a news *fan*, and by someone so impressively involved in Canadian polity, yet who talked of it in very un-Habermasian ways. This chapter marks a return to the site of news fandom, as I explore the love and passion for a genre that is given plenty of academic consideration, but rarely if ever as a fan object. "Serious" news and fandom are typically described with wholly different theoretical tool kits, but here I examine their points of contact to suggest a more profound marriage among news, politics, and fandom than many would deem either existent or appropriate. To perform such a marriage between the news and an idea of fandom may seem either unholy or odd to some readers. Certainly, there is much established work to suggest that they are fundamentally different. Thomas Patterson defines what in America is frequently called "hard news" (or what others might call "real" or "political" news) as "coverage of breaking events involving top leaders, major issues, or significant disruptions in the routines of daily life, such as earthquakes or airline disasters. Information about these events is presumably important to citizens' ability to understand and respond to the world of public affairs" (2000: 3). Amid the many concerns regarding contemporary infotainment and dumbed-down, "soft" journalism (e.g., Kerbel 2000; Patterson 2000; Postman & Powers 1992), and amid endless accusations of news bias, a very clear notion of news appears. News should, so goes the rationale, offer objective facts and reporting on current events, and other information relevant to the practice of citizenship, hailing its viewers as intelligent, cerebral individuals in search of rational debate and thought. Ingrained in the First Amendment of the US Constitution and in its protection of the press is the reflection that the free flow of information and opinions is vital to democratic citizenship and participation in civic society, and hence that the news acts as the very doorway to the public sphere, or agora. Indeed, Habermas's notion of the public sphere (1989)[1] is perhaps the most academically invoked ideal for news and media practice. Particularly important to this ideal is Habermas's call for *rational* discourse: borrowing from a long line of post-Enlightenment thinking (see Marcus 2002), Habermas believed in the emotional as irrational, and thus in the need to separate heart from mind in this public sphere. Especially in the wake of Lippmann's (1922) and others' fear of propaganda and emotional appeals polluting the news and, through it, democratic society, entertainment and the emotional have been seen as incommensurate with hard news, and as poisonous to its realm.

In contrast to the news as a supposedly somber, rational, informational genre would seem to lie the very concept of fans. By definition, fans have an avid like or love for something. Hills (2002) plumbs psychological depths to offer the elaborated idea that fans are those who have made of their beloved text a transitional object, in Winnicott's terms (1974), imbuing it with special personal and/or communal symbolic value, and Hills, along with many others (e.g., Brooker 2002; Harrington & Bielby 1995; Jenkins 1992; Lewis 1992), has shown how fandom is a site of intense pleasure and often of play. In other words, fans have a remarkably emotional relationship to their beloved text. But Habermas (1989) documented the degree to which emotion, and particularly emotive forms of political communication, refeudalizes the public sphere, acting as an obstacle to a meaningful and active deliberative democracy in which all citizens are open to engage with all contributions to the public sphere. Hard news and fandom, then, would seem to be at loggerheads, as any ideal news program (ideally and supposedly the preeminent genre of political communication) would act as a paragon of (masculine) rationality, while the play, emotions, and entertainment of fandom mark it and the objects of fandom definitively as the (supposedly) emotional, feminine, bodily, and less civilizing.

But what about news fans? By news fans, I mean not merely those who consume a lot of news, but those who construct fan-like relationships to certain news programs or texts, characters, and journalists, and those who speak of and relate to the news in fan-like ways. Furthermore, where infotainment detractors may well *expect* to see fan cultures surround soft news, here I am interested only in fans of hard news—congress or parliamentary access channels, and reports on stories of obvious and direct civic importance.[2] In other words, what happens with and what can we learn from instances when the rational, uplifting, cerebral content of hard news encounters the emotion, enthusiasm, and excitement of fans?

As should be clear by now, I ultimately intend to suggest a confusion and a thorough mixing of rationality and emotion. But before we see this blurring in action, it is important to set the stage by beginning a deconstruction of the binaries between news and fandom, between elite ideals for news consumption and elite ideas of how the (fan) masses consume, and between rationality and emotion.

The Emotional News Consumer

The notion that the news does or should serve primarily an informational purpose has been easier to sustain when many studies of the news have focused either on its production or on idealized discussion of what the news *should* do. When we turn to audience theorists and researchers, though, we encounter many different uses for the news. In particular, Roger Silverstone discusses television's, and especially television news', role as a transitional object that creates for its viewers a sense of onto-logical security. The news, he notes, "holds pride of place as the genre in which it is possible to see most clearly the dialectical articulation of anxiety and security—and the criterion of trust—which overdetermines television as a transitional object, particularly for adult viewers" (1994: 16). The news tells us of how horrific the world is, but then controls this chaos with its perky newscasters, highly polished look, human inter-est stories, and relaxed banter with weather and sports reporters; after suggesting that the world might fall apart, it rocks us to sleep at night, assuring us that everything will be okay, dear. In this way, Silverstone suggests, the news has become one of the primary coping mechanisms for living in a world replete with risk and fear.

Meanwhile, both Silverstone (1994) and Morley (2000) examine the news' role in managing our sense of home and belonging. As a prime instance of what Hartley calls television as "cross-demographic com-munication" (1999), television news brings all sorts of ideas, people, and places across the threshold of our front doorstep, telling us of the world "out there." By doing so, the news, and our use of it, becomes a key site for the negotiation not only of the idea of the family home but also of neighborhood and national home (Morley 2000). Hence, television news acts as a command center for many projects of identity and per-sonal security that are deeply emotional, and not at all coldly "rational," and yet that allow us to place ourselves in our house, neighborhood, nation, and world. Indeed, it is particularly noteworthy that both Sil-verstone and Hills draw from the same theoretical well—that of Win-nicott's object-relations theory (1974)—to explain, respectively, the news and fandom.

The likelihood that news reception and fan reception come from and draw on similar mental faculties is given further support by the recent neuropolitical science of George Marcus (Marcus 2002; Marcus, Neuman, & MacKuen 2000). Marcus takes aim at the age-old belief in the separation of mind and heart, and at political and media theo-rists' concern that the heart, passions, and emotion might invade the rational deliberative zone that is the mind. Drawing from Lakoff and

Johnson's work on the power of metaphors (1980), he shows the dangers of conceiving of heart and mind as distinct, independent, and antagonistic, and instead he consults neuroscience to paint a very different picture. Rational thought, he proves scientifically, *requires* emotions; indeed, neuroscience shows that much of our rational decision making is performed by our brain's emotional center, or is at the very least made wholly possible by our brain's emotional faculties. Thus, Marcus rebukes the common assertion that democracy is in danger, with entertainment and emotional appeal solely trivializing serious issues; rather, he argues, "rationality is a special set of abilities that are recruited by the emotion systems in the brain to enable us to adapt to the challenges that daily confront us" (2002: 7), and, therefore, "emotion is required to invoke reason and to enable reason's conclusions to be enacted" (2002: 31). Emotion, after all, is what makes us care to think rationally in the first place, and it is emotion that drives us to work for change or for conservation. Emotion lets us deliberate, and then encourages us to act on that deliberation. Consequently, Marcus calls for "a sentimental citizen" (2002), gifted with "affective intelligence" (Marcus, Neuman, & MacKuen 2000), and he flips common assumptions to suggest that a wholly "rational," "cerebral" electorate is one unfit to govern.

Drawing on the ideas of Marcus and others, Liesbet Van Zoonen (2005) examines how fan cultures display numerous traits of an ideal citizenship. Van Zoonen realizes the boldness of this idea, given many critics' belief that "[s]upposedly, entertainment brings audiences consisting of fans into being, whereas politics produces publics composed of citizens. Audiences and publics, fans and citizens, are thus constructed as involving radically different social formations and identities" (2005: 56). But she then observes numerous close parallels between fans and the ideal citizens of a deliberative democracy. First, she notes that "fan groups are social formations that are structurally equivalent to political constituencies" (2005: 58), groups united by a shared sense of values and a proclivity and willingness to act upon those values to some degree. Therefore, she observes an "equivalence of fan practices and political practices" (2005: 63), which leads her to ask provocatively, "Maybe, then, the only difference between fans and citizens is located in the different subjectivities on which they seem based; affective relations in the case of fans, cognitive processes in the case of citizens. Is this difference bona fide, though?" (2005: 63).

Van Zoonen is careful not to suggest a complete equivalence between fans and (ideal) citizens, but nevertheless denies the tenuous distinction as being based on affectivity rather than cognitive, rational thinking. She is also careful not to suggest that fan engagement could in any way be seen as a desirable *alternative* to political involvement; certainly, while some fan cultures are driven by deeply political motives, we must avoid seeing, for instance, a campaign to reinstate a favorite love interest on a television show as on a par with a presidential campaign. However, Van Zoonen sees great potential in fan cultures and their structuring logic for modeling meaningful citizenship. Fandom, she notes, "is built on psychological mechanisms that are relevant to political involvement: these are concerned with the realm of fantasy and imagination on the one hand, and with emotional processes on the other" (2005: 64). Fantasy, and a *desire* for change, along with the emotional investment required to work toward it, is a prerequisite to any and all political movements. Van Zoonen points to political rallies and conventions as some of the more obviously fan-like events in civic life, and realizes the need for such fan-like elements to motor both politics and citizens.

Clearly, then, we can see how politics and the news overlap with fan behavior and practice in many ways. Van Zoonen, Marcus, Morley, and Silverstone all show not only how the political is deeply affective and how it succeeds in part by offering emotional appeal but also how it must matter to the individual and must be consumed emotively to some degree if it is to become meaningful to its viewers. Hence, these writers suggest that fandom and political citizenship and an ideal consumption of the news are by no means foreign to each other. Meanwhile, we could also consult the wealth of fan studies literature to point out how highly literate, rational, and cerebral many fans are. If, though, as Van Zoonen argues, fandom offers models for political citizenship, this would seem to suggest that fans of the news itself might prove a particularly rich example of fandom and the political uniting to improve citizenship.

News Fandom: Ever the Twain Shall Meet

The beginning of November 2005 brought plenty of serious news to American readers and viewers. Vice President Dick Cheney's chief of staff, Scooter Libby, had been charged with leaking classified information; Hurricane Wilma had hit Florida; an earthquake in Pakistan had killed thousands; Harriet Miers had withdrawn her nomination for the US Supreme Court, quickly followed by President Bush's nomination of Samuel Alito; Asian bird flu fears were arising; and civil rights hero Rosa Parks had died. Thus, multiple issues ripe for discussion were on the table, ranging from the state of civil rights today to governmental response to natural disasters to the future balance of power in the Supreme Court. During a two-week span at the end of October and beginning of November, I explored several sites for the discussion of this news and the reporting of it. I consulted all of the news threads on Television Without Pity (www.televisionwithoutpity. com), a site known for fan discussion of all things televisual, and I monitored three of the most popular news and politics blogs that allow room for discussion, one typically liberal—Daily Kos (www.dailykos. com)—and two typically conservative—Right Wing News (www.righ-twingnews.com) and Little Green Footballs (www.littlegreenfootballs. com). I read through pages upon pages of commentary to see how this news was discussed both by people who identified themselves as fans of a particular news program and by posters whose frequency of visits and posts to a particular news thread, combined with the ways in which they discussed the news, coded them as either fans or at least fan-like.

This methodology was not intended to be wholly scientific; rather, it, like this chapter, was rudimentary and exploratory. In a cyberspace and blogosphere as vast as the Internet provides, accurate sampling is impossible, as can be the act of ascertaining accurate poster demographics upon which such sampling could be based. Ultimately, my methods represent an attempt to take a brief peek at how professed or obvious fans of the news talk about the news; deeper ethnography could undoubtedly reveal more, and I hope others take me up on this challenge for future work. Meanwhile, here I conflate individuals with different objects of fandom, ranging from a certain presenter to a party to a news program itself. Important differences exist among these subgroups, but, with very few exceptions, these posters have access to these political "realities" only through the textualized form of the news. Hence, just as, for instance, two fans, one of a character on a reality show and one of the show itself, both experience their object of fandom through reality television, and thus could be described as reality television fans, so too can these various subgroups be talked of here generically as news fans.

Perhaps most immediately surprising was the remarkable level of *play* with the news and its newscasters exhibited by these posters, even while they made serious points. For instance, a poster on Daily Kos (hereafter DK) dubbed prime-time cable news debate program host Chris Matthews "Tweety" in a post about press reaction to the alleged Libby leak, entitled "Tweety is schizophrenic":

> One day he's all over the story, the next day Bush reacts with "nobility" to Libby's resignation. Yeah, it's so noble to let a perjurious, leaking aide resign instead of firing him, while keeping another perjurious leaking aide stay on the job. Maybe Tweety takes his meds for some shows and not others?

Or, on Television Without Pity (hereafter TWoP), after opening a post by asking, "Does [prime-time cable news journal host] Keith Olbermann have no friends? Does his assistant secretly hate him? Is his producer blind? Because the man's clothes? They BLIND me," and continuing with fashion advice, a poster concludes by adding, "Also? I expected everyone else to report the standard Rosa Parks the tired seamstress story, but I expected more of Olbermann, to report the fact that Parks was a wonderful activist and organizer way before she even got on the bus." Another poster, on Little Green Footballs (hereafter LGF), discussing the Democrats' call for a closed Senate to debate intelligence that led to the invasion of Iraq, states, "Yes, our intelligence stunk at the start of the war, I'm entirely in favor of investigating it until the cows come home. And it may just force a more open and honest accounting by Dubya of why we went in and why we now see additional justifications," before adding, "But geesh, the grandstanding ignorant sluts of the Democratic rump, unbefreakinglievable."

What we see in all three above-quoted remarks is an interesting mix of deliberative, "rational" opinion and emotive, playful elements far more fan-like (or, in the last case, anti-fan-like) by nature. At one moment, for instance, Olbermann's fashion sense is being discussed, then his coverage of Rosa Park's death, with a point that addresses both the content and form of the news article in a smart, "rational" manner. Certainly, quotations like these abounded, to the point of being standard. Another poster at DK, for instance, addresses other posters' comments that Bush has effectively ended the marriage between liberalism and Catholicism in America:

> My spouse and I attend regularly, we teach catechism, and Bush can kiss my rosy, red butt. Go see Pax Christi and National Catholic Reporter, then read Fr. Andrew Greeley and Sr. Joan Chittister, and you'll find reports of the death of liberals in the Catholic church are greatly exaggerated.

Significant evidence is marshaled to support the poster's view, and he shares this with others, contributing to the wealth of this public sphere, but his summation of his regard for President Bush and his conservatism takes the emotive form of "Bush can kiss my rosy, red butt." Or, one final example of this overlapping of emotionalism and rationality comes from a highly detailed attack on irascible right-wing ideologue and debate show host Bill O'Reilly's reporting of illegal aliens. The TWoP poster engages in close analysis of O'Reilly's words to note that

> he denies ever describing illegal aliens as "biological weapons." He swears to his audience that he "never said anything like that," and claims to be the victim of "smear merchants." And, yes, technically, he never said the words "biological weapons." However, a caller on his show did use those words. The charming caller described illegal aliens as biological weapons because of the alleged diseases they carry, and likened them to the 9/11 terrorist attacks. And Bill responded by agreeing with the caller, saying, "I think you could probably make an absolutely airtight case that more than 3,000 Americans have been either killed or injured, based upon the 11 million illegals who are here." And yet he cries that he is the victim of malicious lies.

However, in opening the post, the writer responds to an ongoing discussion about O'Reilly's views on spanking children as a punishment by opining, "O'Reilly's spanking fetish confirms my suspicion that he's secretly an ass freak."

Name calling such as this is rampant, as, for instance, liberal discussion on DK often reverts to describing conservatives as "wingnuts" and painting crude caricatures of uneducated rednecks, while conservative discussion on LGF and Right Wing News (hereafter RWN) lashes out at the "moonbats" who, as one poster at RWN states, "hate America" and "have no ideas for the future [and] no ideas for the nation." Particularly in such crude, childish forms, it would be easy to point to such statements as prime examples of where emotions destroy rationality, and indeed if one standard is to mix rational discussion with emotional play, sadly another is to merely curse and rage. Some such posts should hardly be looked to as helping deliberative democracy. When this same poster at RWN, for instance, chides liberals for possessing ideas that have already "failed in the Soviet Union," the laughable equation of Soviet communism to the Democratic Party platform is worrying. This therefore illustrates a dire risk of fannish involvement with the news, for fans can at times adopt preformulated reading positions that seek to find only reaffirmation of already held beliefs (see Johnson, this volume; Sandvoss 2005), which when applied to news consumption and political debate stands to harm the vitality of the public sphere. Certainly, the bulk of one-line posts that read, as does one at DK, "dumb-ass Republican hicks" in response to breaking news could hardly be seen as contributing greatly to public political discourse.

However, in the many instances when such emotional outburst and/ or play *is* mixed with rational, thoughtful discussion, we should not be so quick to write off the emotional. One could, perhaps, see the emotional here as the assumed passkey to community discussion—a display of "hip factor" to show that one belongs. But in many other ways, these sites are not fan communities in a traditional sense—there is little friendly banter, off-topic asides about struggles in life, supportive advice (see Bird 2003), or, as TWoP calls them, "meet markets." The dictates of a political discussion board, as is shown, do not preclude emotionalism, but they clearly limit it. Thus, it seems unlikely that posters would feel the need to offer elaborated emotional passkeys. Or, alternatively, we could see the emotional as variously motivating the commentary, or adding a human element to an otherwise cold, uninviting discussion. After all, it is in these emotive moments that the poster's feelings are most evident, and hence they are the moments when we are invited to connect to the comment as something human, something more than disembodied typeface on our computer screen. They are moments that color and code the commentary as felt and as lived, and hence that call to us as readers. As much fan theory shows, the fan's emotional play with texts frequently gives life and meaning to those texts—the Velveteen Rabbit principle that Jenkins discusses (1992: 50). While we must avoid thinking that *only* fans turn texts into rich symbolic products (see Gray 2003), fandom and fan-like feelings are a key mode by which many viewers can approach the world's saturation with texts, and assign personal or communal meaning and value to any given text. In reading these news fans' discussion of topics, I was watching a similar process at work, whereby the emotional investment with the story or newscaster framed and made possible the ensuing rational debate.

Above, I have quoted numerous examples of motivation to post out of anger or disappointment (themselves both key emotions in the fan's repertoire), but, amusingly, many newscasters attracted love and adoration too. CNN reporter Anderson Cooper proved particularly popular with TWoP posters, as amid thoughtful discussion regarding his previous on-the-spot reporting on Hurricane Katrina's aftermath, some posters worried about why he was currently off the air, with one joking, "He's at my house getting hot baths and massages. No more hurricanes for my man!" Keith Olbermann also had his share of fans, with the previously quoted discussion of his clothes coming in the middle of numerous TWoP posts expressing significant admiration for the man, yet playful concern for his wardrobe, his hair, and even his "womanly hips." NBC reporter Brian Williams, Tim Russert (host of NBC's famed political interview program *Meet the Press*), and Bill O'Reilly all had vocal fans too. However, while I am left with only their postings to judge from, the expressed basis of fandom was not merely looks or sense of humor, but reporting vigilance. Cooper's fans talked glowingly of how informative and challenging his reports from New Orleans had been, as did Williams's fans. O'Reilly's fans felt his combative style broke through many guests' rehearsed veneer, thus offering more of the story. Olbermann's fans praised his sly wit and ability to see other, less-remarked-upon sides of various issues. And Russert's fans felt his economy of reporting gave them, as one poster observed, "more news and more ideas per minute than many of the other schleps out there." Therefore, rather than fantasies of hot baths with Cooper or of making over Olbermann being on the opposite end of a scale from attending carefully to what the newsmen were reporting, in many cases the news fans showed the ability for fan-like engagement and civic duty to work together.

Furthermore, while these fans were hardly writing Russert fanfic or arranging O'Reilly cons, their fandom proved productive in its own ways. To begin with, in a deliberative democracy, to post one's political beliefs and reactions to news stories and the perceived quality or reporting (or lack thereof) and to enter into political dialogue with others are already productive, and contributive to civic discourse. Thus, their mere presence online is often automatically productive, and a key reason behind many excited appraisals of the blogosphere's potential to reenergize politics (e.g., Gillmor 2003). But beyond posting, several posters share their letters either to news stations, newscasters, or politicians. Also, one DK poster, whose posts frequently appeared on the site, suggesting an active news viewership, included the transcript of a phone call he made to conservative pundit Sean Hannity's talk radio program. Other entries at the blogs, too, showed remarkable footwork, as, for example, one DK poster compiled a list of all one hundred senators' reactions to Harriet Miers, and another RWN poster offered a painstaking line-by-line refutation of an excerpted article from DK. Finally, many posters wrote of offline political activity, making it clear that these websites had by no means become virtual agoras far removed from flesh-and-bone reality.[3]

Taking the News to Heart

While I hesitate to offer any grand conclusions based on a limited study, the activities of these news fans are nevertheless revealing. First of all, we (and political communication scholars in particular) must acknowledge that news fans exist, and in significant numbers; thus, clearly, entertainment, fiction, and supposedly "low" culture are not alone in inspiring such audiences. Beyond mere existence, though, remains the issue of the nature and meaning of their activity. Most democratic political theorists dream of an electorate who continually update themselves with news and opinions, who discuss this news and these opinions with others, and who take politics and policy seriously. Here, I found many such individuals. And yet far from being somber, rational conversationalists, these individuals were emotionally involved, exhibiting many of the emotive, playful qualities of fandom in the ways in which they consumed, processed, and discussed the news. Many were savvy viewers, keen to critically evaluate, and yet they also cared, ranted, had fun, and got angry. Ultimately, though, rather than read this as an indictment of these viewers, I pose that we instead indict the unrealistic and unhelpful desire for a politics without emotion. Habermas is still right to point us toward some of the dangers of emotive citizenship, but opening the door to emotion does not necessitate *giving up* on rationality. *Of course* we still require some balance, and so we would be foolish to believe that either all emotions or all political fandoms are necessarily a good to be cherished. As Sandvoss (2005) points out, fans can at times overload a text with meaning, rendering it "neutrosemic"—a potentially worrying development if the fan object is a political party or the nightly news. Similarly, a fan polity could restrict the free flow of ideas if fans became as rigidly sure of their facts and politics as, say, a Yankees fan is sure of his team's divine superiority. Finally, too, the excesses of Fox News' emotive and heavily biased format illustrate the dangers of incorporating too much emotion on the *production* end. Skeptics of emotion in politics, in other words, still have much to justifiably concern them. But at the same time, an absolute rationality would leave no room for caring, for personal or communal drive, nor for belief, engagement, or enjoyment, all of which are basic requirements for an active electorate.

Such emotions risk overlooking important realities, but this is where, why, and how fandom can help the news. With so many texts out there, fandom allows us to chart paths of value and meaning through this semiotic wilderness, and becomes a way of coping, a way of being able to move forward. While this is true of fandom and entertainment and/or fiction, it is also true of fandom, politics, and the news, for we also need paths through the wilderness of facts, policies, movements, issues, and spin before us. Some such paths are unhealthy, but perhaps it is by examining them in light of fan engagement that analysts will find better ways to account for them, and, ultimately, to challenge them. However, while both fears of the emotional and reverence for the rational are age-old, and at times justified, it is often emotions—and fandom, as a particular nexus of emotions—that point us forward, not just backward. This long-standing distrust of emotions and enjoyment is partially behind the pathologization and disapproval of fandom, but perhaps then by seeing fandom at times in, behind, allowing, and *driving* rationality, we might learn better to value not only emotions in politics but also fandom more generally, not as a magic tonic for citizenship—for that it is not—but as a constitutive element of it, for worse and for better.

NOTES

1 Dahlgren neatly defines the public sphere as "a space—a discursive, institutional, topographical space—where people in their roles as citizens have access to what can be metaphorically called societal dialogues, which deal with questions of common concern: in other words, with politics in the broad sense" (1995: 9).

2 I do not wish to brand other news as unimportant, however, for as Glynn (2000) and Hartley (1999) have argued, "soft" or tabloid news also offers its viewers political, meaningful commentary.

3 More deviously, leading on from Hills's arguments in this volume regarding fan-academic practice, we might even pose that our own universities' media and journalism departments contain some of the most active news fans of all.

WORKS CITED

Bird, SE 2003, *The audience in everyday life: living in a media world*, Routledge, New York.

Brooker, W 2002, *Using the force: creativity, community, and Star Wars fans*, Continuum, New York.

Dahlgren, P 1995, *Television and the public sphere: citizenship, democracy, and the media*, Sage, Thousand Oaks, CA.

Gillmor, D 2003, "Moving toward participatory journalism," *Nieman Reports* 57(3): 79–80.

Glynn, K 2000, *Tabloid culture: trash taste, popular power, and the transformation of American television*, Duke University Press, Durham, NC.

Gray, J 2003, "New audiences, new textualities: anti-fans and non-fans," *International Journal of Cultural Studies* 6(1): 64–81.

Gray, J 2006, *Watching with* The Simpsons: *television, parody, and intertextuality*, Routledge, New York.

Habermas, J 1989, *The structural transformation of the public sphere: an inquiry into a category of bourgeois society*, T Burger (trans.), Polity, Cambridge.

Harrington, CL & Bielby, DD 1995, *Soap fans: pursuing pleasure and making meaning in everyday life*, Temple University Press, Philadelphia.

Hartley, J 1999, *The uses of television*, Routledge, New York.

Hills, M 2002, *Fan cultures*, Routledge, New York.

Jenkins, H 1992, *Textual poachers: television fans and participatory culture*, Routledge, New York.

Kerbel, M 2000, *If it bleeds, it leads: an anatomy of television news*, Westview, Boulder, CO.

Lakoff, G & Johnson, M 1980, *Metaphors we live by*, University of Chicago Press, Chicago.

Lewis, LA (ed.) 1992, *The adoring audience: fan culture and popular media*, Routledge, New York.

Lippmann, W 1922, *Public opinion*, Macmillan, New York.

Marcus, GE 2002, *The sentimental citizen: emotion in democratic politics*, Pennsylvania State University Press, University Park.

Marcus, GE, Neuman, WR, & MacKuen, M 2000, *Affective intelligence and political judgment*, University of Chicago Press, Chicago.

Morley, D 2000, *Home territories: media, mobility, and identity*, Routledge, New York.

Patterson, T 2000, "Doing well and doing good," Kennedy School of Government Working Paper no. 01–001, www.ssm.com.

Postman, N & Powers, S 1992, *How to watch TV news*, Penguin, London.

Sandvoss, C 2005, *Fans: the mirror of consumption*, Polity, Malden, MA.

Silverstone, R 1994, *Television and everyday life*, Routledge, New York.

Van Zoonen, L 2005, *Entertaining the citizen: when politics and popular culture converge*, Rowman & Littlefield, New York.

Winnicott, DW 1974, *Playing and reality*, Penguin, Harmondsworth, UK.

16

Memory, Archive, and History in Political Fan Fiction

ABIGAIL DE KOSNIK

Real-World Politics in Fan Fiction

Scholars have established that media fans frequently engage with political issues, for example by producing feminist and queer versions of mass media productions (see Russ 1985; Penley 1992; Lothian, Busse, & Reid 2007) and by employing slogans, costumes, and themes appropriated from popular culture in public demonstrations (Gray 2012; Jenkins 2010). This essay analyzes another way that fans explicitly engage with politics: by writing stories that situate fictional heroes in the midst of real-world social justice movements. Fan fiction stories that transmute popular characters into avatars of specific political issues invite fans to become deeply emotionally invested in news reports, proposals for new legislation, the platforms of elected officials, and the actions of voter organizations. In other words, what I call "political fic" potentially transforms the sphere of real-world politics from a dry, dull, remote, and abstract space into a universe as exciting, and as inviting of participation, as any fantastical fictional realm—a sphere worthy of fandom.

The political fics discussed in this essay deal with two issues that have figured prominently in national political discourse and campaign rhetoric in recent years: the Occupy movement, which began in 2011 in response to the global financial crisis, and the DREAM Act, a piece of legislation that would grant civic rights to undocumented immigrants, which has been a topic of debate since 2001. By delving into how these fics incorporate politics into their narratives, I aim to establish the relationship of the genre of fan fiction to the archive of history, and to foreground the valuable role that fan productions can play in reframing the stakes of real-world policy debates for media users.

Battlestar Galactica and Occupy

The first political fic I will discuss is a story based on *Battlestar Galactica* (*BSG*), a science fiction television series (Syfy 2003–9; the series was a reboot of a 1978–80 ABC show). Two main *BSG* characters are the upstanding Lee Adama and rule-breaker Kara Thrace, two ace pilots in a space fleet embroiled in a long war against a fleet of AI (artificial intelligence) beings called Cylons.

A fan author named embolalia posted a story titled "The Way It Should Be" to a *BSG* LiveJournal community in February 2012, a few months after the start of Occupy Wall Street and the proliferation of Occupy encampments in cities around the United States and the world. "The Way It Should Be" transmutes space pilots Lee and Kara into young people participating in the Occupy movement. In the story, Lee is a college student from a wealthy family, and Kara is a crafty street kid. The two meet at an Occupy camp in their city's largest public park. Kara educates Lee about the perspectives and experiences of the poor, and Lee inspires Kara to turn into an activist leader. Lee and Kara become two prominent voices of Occupy (just as on *BSG*, Lee and Kara are two primary leaders of the fleet), and succeed in raising the public's awareness of and sympathy for the movement, but when a police raid disperses the camp, Lee and Kara run to evade arrest. Hiding in an alley from the police, Lee asks Kara, "So what do we now?" Kara replies, "Fight 'em til we can't."

Kara's final line, which is the final line of the story, is taken from *BSG*'s season 2 closing episode, titled "Occupy," in which Kara encourages her fellow humans to resist their planet's takeover by a Cylon army: "Fight 'em til we can't," *BSG* Kara grimly instructs the people standing with her as they watch the Cylon occupation force march past. The repetition of this one line of dialogue in embolalia's story invites a host of comparisons between the real world and the world of *BSG*: neoliberal capitalism is like a race of robots intent on destroying humankind; Occupy's struggle for greater economic equality against the overwhelming dominance of capitalism is like the human space fleet's war to preserve humanity against a vastly more powerful enemy army; and Occupy's members, and all opponents of neoliberal capitalism, must show the same depth of resolve and commitment that Kara expresses when the Cylons begin their occupation—since *BSG*'s humans are embroiled in battles that will likely be long and painful, they must have the will to fight until they can fight no more. In *BSG*, humankind is the collective protagonist, and the technologically superior Cylon race is the antagonist; in "The Way It Should Be," the "99 percent"—as many Occupy participants and sympathizers called themselves, referring to Joseph Stiglitz's statistic that 40 percent of US wealth is held by 1 percent of the nation's population (2011; see also Weinstein 2011)—is the root-worthy hero, and the immensely privileged 1 percent, along with the vast techno-networks of neoliberal capital that support and safeguard its superiority, is the villainous entity that seems unconquerable but must somehow be overcome.

Superman and Immigration Reform

My second example of political fic is not a single story, but a group of works created by fans of the DC Comics superhero Superman. Over the past decade, Superman has become a popular symbol in activist writing, performance, and art related to immigration reform, especially the DREAM (Development, Relief, and Education for Alien Minors) Act, which was initially introduced in the US Senate in 2001. If passed, the DREAM Act would grant conditional legal status to undocumented immigrants in the United States who arrived in the country as minors and graduated from an American high school (or earned a GED), and would grant permanent residency to these residents upon their completion of two years of higher education or military service.

In 2003, regional Mexican band Los Hermanos Ortiz released a Spanish-language corrido (ballad) on their album *Puro Norte* called "Superman Es Ilegal," which includes these lyrics (translated into English by Jerry Kammer): "He came from Krypton in his ship. And from the looks of it, he isn't American, just another undocumented like me. So, Immigration man, he shouldn't work. Though it hurts to say it, Superman is illegal" (Kammer 2011). In December 2010, East Los Angeles journalist Erick Huerta wrote an essay for *Zócalo Public Square* about his experiences as an undocumented immigrant that includes the following paragraph:

> I guess I should be inspired by Superman, arguably the most accomplished of all "illegal aliens." Literally, in his case, as he came from another planet

as an infant because his parents wanted to give him a better life when his home world was annihilated. He landed on earth and was raised in the Midwest by a loving couple to become a symbol for truth, justice and the American way. Last time I checked, he was still working at the Daily Planet, getting by under the name of "Clark Kent." I hope that the e-verify system doesn't catch up with him someday; where would ICE deport him?

Then, in DC's *Action Comics #900*, published in April 2011, Superman announces that he intends to speak before the United Nations "and inform them that I am renouncing my U.S. citizenship" because "I'm tired of having my actions construed as instruments of U.S. policy" (DiChiara 2011), an announcement that prompted a strong reaction from conservatives who would have preferred that Superman remain the iconic defender of "the American way" (Jenkins & Shresthova 2012; Appelo 2011). A spate of commentary and artworks followed the publication of *Action Comics #900*, including articles questioning Superman's official nationality in the *Los Angeles Times' Hero Complex* column (Anthony 2011) and in the *National Review* (Krikorian 2011); comedian Hari Kondabolu's (2011) "Superman Is Undocumented" video; artist Neil Rivas's (2012) exhibit "Illegal Superheroes," which depicts twenty-six superheroes on "WANTED" posters whose fine print reads, "Super heroes who enter this country without proper authorization are breaking the law [. . . and] are subject to deportation at any time"; and artist El Random Hero's 2011 fancomic showing Superman explicitly supporting the DREAM Act (Superman says at a press conference, "I came to this country as an infant through no fault of my own. And much like the DREAM Act students . . . I am a super achiever").

In addition, I have found nine works of fan fiction, published on Fanfiction.net or on LiveJournals between 2006 and 2014, that portray Superman as an undocumented immigrant in the United States. The fanfic "Infinite DCU [DC Universe]: Superman" by InfiniteUniverse10 tells the story of a teenaged Clark Kent being blackmailed by the US government into becoming a type of defense weapon for the country. Though Clark's adoptive mother, Mrs. Kent, protests, Clark says:

> "Ma . . . first and foremost I'm an illegal alien. They could have me deported . . . from Earth. Or just put [me] in jail for life. [. . .] My powers

are growing stronger and stronger every day. I'm a possible adversary for them and for the planet and as much as I hate it."

He looked up into his mother's eyes. "I'm going to have to be their Superman."

The fanfic "Bureaucratic Nightmare" by ShayneT presents a comedic version of what would happen if the US government discovered Superman's undocumented status. After suffering through a court case with Immigration and Naturalization, an audit by the Internal Revenue Service, and numerous restrictions placed upon his flights by the Federal Aviation Administration, Superman announces that, despite his love of Metropolis, "I find myself forced to move to Mexico City for the immediate future," for the reason that, the narrator states, "[t]he Mexican government had been willing to waive the birth certificate requirement for a driver's license in return for his promise to help on certain public works projects." In a more tragic register, the fan story "I Love You (It's Just a Minor Technicality)" by BabyDee depicts a disheartened Superman on the brink of deportation. Superman agonizes, "For as long as I can remember, I've lived in Kansas. I grew up here! I graduated from school! [. . .] And I can't give up being Superman. I'm making a difference."

These fanfics aim to make the plight of undocumented immigrants relatable to readers by combining well-known elements of the Superman universe with elements extracted from current debates over immigration policy, which include undocumented people's views on the challenges, from the quotidian to the existential, that they routinely face in the United States.

Tactical Media, Transmedia, Inter(in)animation

While these fanfics were not written or published, as far as I can discern, as components of specific political campaigns or events, I assert that political fics do political work, and form a type of tactical media.

In *Tactical Media*, Rita Raley analyzes a cadre of new media art projects developed since the turn of the millennium that critique and challenge the "dominant semiotic regime" (2009: 6). Raley writes, "[Tactical media] projects are not oriented toward the grand, sweeping revolutionary event; rather, they engage in a micropolitics of disruption, intervention, and education" (1). Political fics, like tactical media (I am citing Raley's descriptions of tactical media here), "replicate and redeploy" the "existing semiotic regime"; they mark the "temporary creation of a situation in which signs, messages, and narratives are set into play and critical thinking is possible," and bring about "the substitution of one message for another, the imposition of an alternative set of signs in the place of the dominant" (6). The differences between *BSG* as received by television viewers and *BSG* as it appears in "The Way It Should Be," and the differences between Occupy as it is characterized in official news sources and as it characterized in the same fic, potentially unsettle the meanings of narratives that readers may think they thoroughly comprehended. The new arrangement of both *BSG* and Occupy signifiers in embolalia's story can, however temporarily, displace the originals and set preexisting terms into play, generating unexpected substitute meanings. Raley points to tactical media projects' indeterminate future, "their opening to the unexpected" (6), their alliance with "speculation, uncertainty, and the aleatory" (6), and their "requir[ing] a certain openness, a surrendering to chance or the 'postmodern roll of the dice'" (8, citing Critical Art Ensemble). The goal of all tactical media is to keep "the postmodern roll of the dice" going, so that the future, the endgame, remains undecided. Political fics urge readers to question what current events *mean*, and to ponder what *may* happen—to not believe that present political or social problems, such as the financial crisis, are predestined to resolve in ways that reward previous winners, and instead to view such events as potential game changers, events that may bring about unexpected outcomes.

Political fic works specifically by *transmediating* texts. All fanfic possesses three defining characteristics of transmedia works, as outlined by Jenkins (2011): seriality, radical intertextuality, and multimodality. For understanding political fan fiction, the most important of the three attributes of transmedia is radical intertextuality. In radical intertextuality, says Jenkins, there is a "connection of multiple texts with each other for the purposes of building out a world or an experience," as when, with respect to the DC or Marvel universes whose characters often appear in one another's comics, "when we read across the [comic] books, they add up to something bigger than any individual book" (Jenkins 2011: n.p.).

In political fanfic, radical intertextuality manifests as a mingling of two archives by a fan author—a reality archive and a fiction archive. The authors of Superman-as-undocumented-immigrant fanfics merge elements from news stories, first- or secondhand experience, and/or everyday discourse about US immigration policy with elements from comics, movies, and TV shows, and in doing so, they cause the two archives to change each other. Political fics constitute a special category of "crossover fanfic": crossover fics blend two fictional universes and depict interactions and relationships between characters that never "meet" in official fictions. Although Superman cannot "really" crusade for immigration rights, and undocumented people cannot "really" become Superman or witness Superman representing them to the government and American public, political fics effectuate a "crossover" of reality and fantasy, and produce a mutual inflection.

The operation of radical intertextuality in political fic is best described by a term that Rebecca Schneider explores in her book *Performing Remains*: inter(in)animation:

> John Donne used the world "interinanimates" in his 1633 love poem "The Extasie" in which he tells of lovers lying as still as stone statues while their souls intertwine, redouble, and multiply. Here, the live and the stone are inter(in)animate and the liveness of one or deadness of the other is ultimately neither decidable nor relevant. [. . .] Fred Moten has recently used the term "interinanimates" to suggest the ways live art and media of mechanical and technological reproduction, such as photography, cross-identify, and, more radically, cross-constitute and "improvise" each other. (2011: 7)

Schneider's objects of study here are live reenactments, and she is interested in the relationship of past events to performances that take place in the present. Schneider's key insight is that, in reenactment, the past and the present *bring one another to life*. There is movement *between* past and present, and that movement is what Schneider calls inter(in)animation: "a constant (re)turn of, to, from, and between states in animation." Past *and* present transform one another in the reenactment, each changing in the commingling; neither is what Schneider calls (citing Judith Butler) "sedimented" (7). The past seems different when it is enacted again (but with differences, never *exactly* again) in new bodies, and the present is suffused with styles, movements, and qualities of being from the past. Past and present enliven one another in live reenactment, and also, says Moten (2003), in multimodal transmedia—so, in addition to the binary of living/dead disintegrating, the binary of live/recorded also dissolves in the concept of inter(in)animation. Just as the past and the present, and the live and recorded, can inter(in)animate one another, reality and fiction inter(in)animate one another in political fic.

Living Reality

I propose that, in political fan fiction, reality and fiction infuse one another with liveness in three ways. The combination of reality and fiction in political fic makes *unreal* events and characters—both real and fictional—*real*; makes *absent* events and characters *present*; and brings *past* or *dead* events and characters into the *now*.

What is unreal about news events? Jean Baudrillard, whose warnings that reality has been overtaken by hyperreality are by now quite familiar, writes that when masses of people receive information about real-world events through media, even a global event such as the 1991 Gulf War, "[W]hat we live in real time is not the event, but rather [...] the spectacle of the degradation of the event and its spectral evocation (the 'spiritualism of information': event, are you there? Gulf War, are you there?) in the commentary, gloss, and verbose *mise en scène* of talking heads" (Baudrillard 1995: 48). Baudrillard claims not that events do not occur, or that journalists manufacture news, but rather that we who receive Occupy and immigration debates as information are not convinced of their reality. Even as we are updated "in real time" about an event, what we "live in real time is not the event" but the spectacle of the event, the evocation of the event. However, Baudrillard says, we *wish* we did *feel* that events were real; we wish we were suffused with their actuality—it is as if we call out to events in the hopes of verifying their existence: "event, are you there?" Baudrillard points to our dissatisfaction that news often does not register as real, as part of "real life," when we take it in as mediated information.

Political fic authors battle the unreality of actual events. By merging the fictional with the real in their stories, authors aim to *transfuse* the interestingness, the attention-worthiness, and the liveliness of fictional characters and events *into* actual people and situations. The Occupy movement may become more real to *BSG* fans through "The Way It Should Be" because the fanfic maps Kara and Lee's conflicts and hopes onto the struggles and aspirations of Occupy participants, and might lead *BSG* fans to be open to transferring their emotional investment in the fictional characters to the actual protestors, and thereby to the larger event of Occupy. "The Way It Should Be" creates the potential for Occupy to *come alive* for *BSG* viewers, for whom fictional characters Kara and Lee, and the fictional human fleet's war for survival, are already deeply compelling and full of life. *BSG* fans who read "The Way It Should Be" can become intellectually interested in, emotionally attached to, and desirous of following, *both* Kara and Lee's story as it takes place in the "Occupy universe," and the "story" of Occupy as it unfolds in actual time and space. The reality bestowed upon Occupy through political fic is not the same type (or level, or degree) of reality as that experienced by people who actually dwelled in the Occupy encampments, but it is the reality that Baudrillard says we wish for, a reality that is verified when we call out to an event, and the event answers back that yes, it is there, it exists. Political fic authors give news events a way of "answering back" to us. In political fic, events answer back *through* fictional characters and fictional situations in whose reality fans already know how to believe, and about which fans already know how to care.

The second way in which political fan fiction can infuse real events with liveness is through making remote happenings *present*. In *Digital Performance*, Steve Dixon argues that artworks, both mediated and live, work well to convey a sense of presence to audiences:

> [F]rom a subjective, perceptual standpoint liveness in itself has nothing to do with the media form. [. . .] Put simply, for the spectator, liveness is just "being there," whatever performance form (live, recorded, telematic—or their combination) is being watched. [. . .] [A]ll art is concerned with presence, or presentness, be it painting, poetry, net-art, recorded media, or live performance. The Rembrandt portrait (both the original *and* its reproduction), Jane Austen's words in a battered paperback, the images on the monitor, and the live performer on stage are all equally "present" to us when we engage with artworks. (2007: 127–29; 132)

Dixon claims that both live and mediated artworks can convey presence to audiences. Building on Dixon, I argue that for many, mediated artworks are more present than actual events occurring in the world in remote locations. Mediated artworks are full of liveness and presence when we experience them; what lack liveness and presence are "absent" (that is to say, distant) real events. I propose that many important political events in the world transpire without ever being "present" to many people, simply by the fact of the events taking place "elsewhere."

Rallies that support the passage of the DREAM Act, for instance, may take place in cities all over the United States, but are often spatially confined to the steps of city halls or to the plazas of university campuses, sites that the majority of people do not have reason to visit regularly. In addition, news coverage of events related to immigration rights is often scarce. Studies by the Pew Research Center's Project for Excellence in Journalism from 2007 to 2010 show that the percentage of news stories about immigration issues that appeared in major media outlets (including newspapers, cable and broadcast TV, websites, and radio) varied from 0 percent to 16 percent in any given week (Pew Research Center: Journalism & Media Staff 2008; Jurkowitz 2010), but that the higher percentages were primarily driven by short periods of coverage of specific issues (such as the failure of the Comprehensive Immigration Reform Act, which contained the entirety of the previously introduced DREAM Act, in the US Senate in 2007, and the passing of Arizona SB 1070 in 2010). Despite the relevance and importance of immigration issues to the US economy and to Americans' daily lives, physical events and media representations of events pertaining to immigration may be largely absent from many people's perceptions and experiences.

Fanfic is a genre of artwork that, like all of the genres of artwork mentioned by Dixon (paintings, novels, screen images, and live performances), has the power to transmit the presence of characters, plots, and settings to audiences. Dixon (2007) writes, "in purely semiotic terms, there is no significant difference between the image of, for example, a woman waving a revolutionary flag as described in a novel, painted on a canvas, screened in a cinema, or standing live on a stage" (132), and I take this to mean that the reader *feels* that the woman waving a revolutionary flag is *there*, before her or with her. Because of this power of making present that all effective art possesses, political fics about Superman as an undocumented immigrant make immigration issues present to readers alongside the hero himself.

Superman's coming to presence in fans' lives through comics, films, television series, fanfics, and other media is essential to fans' being able to enter into a fictional "world"—the world of Superman. This relationship between presence and virtual worlds is a common thread in the effects research branch of mass communication studies. This thread is summarized by Dennis Beck et al. (2011), who explain that there are two types of presence described in mass communications scholarship: sentient presence (SP), which "is the sense of 'being there' with animate objects (people, cartoon characters, anything that pretends to have feelings and possesses intelligence at some level)," and non-sentient presence (NSP), which "is the 'sense of being there' within an environment" (8). Beck et al., like Dixon, employ the phrase "being there" to indicate that media users feel themselves to be present with characters or in worlds. I argue that SP and NSP can also be understood as "co-presence": users can experience virtual worlds as a "being here" (Superman and his universe are *here*, with and surrounding fans as they read Superman fics) as well as a "being there" (as fans read Superman fics, they temporarily inhabit the universe of Superman, and feel transported *there*).

A third way in which political fan fiction injects liveness into actual events is by bringing past events into the now, or maintaining the currency of current events. Fans are typically spurred to action and production by liveness and immediacy: for example, fans produce most fanfic about a television series while the series is still airing, or in anticipation of and shortly after movie premieres (see De Kosnik et al. 2015). Also, Louisa Stein (2002) writes that live news events can spur fans into greater participation in, and production for, fan communities. Stein describes how, in the wake of 9/11, members of a fan site dedicated to the television series *Roswell* created heartfelt visual and textual responses to the tragedy using *Roswell*'s characters, imagery, and themes. This proclivity for producing fan work roughly in time with "live" events makes fans ideal agents for maintaining the relevance of media commodities.

Schneider (2012) takes up Karl Marx's observation that labor is required to awaken "dead capital" (capital that is "not in immediate use") and reflects on the importance of labor to both generating *and preserving* value. Schneider states, "Living labor brings dead capital (back) to

life, recirculates value through the 'dead' by means of a liveness understood as labor" (158). In this article, Schneider is writing about examples
of fan activism, specifically, the "zombie marches" enacted by Occupy
Wall Street participants in 2011 (in which people supporting Occupy
dressed as zombies and walked, zombie-like, on Wall Street as a critique
of the seemingly all-devouring and unstoppable monstrousness of the
US financial sector). Schneider reads the Occupy zombie marches as
commentaries on Marxian notions of all capital's dependence on the living to ward away deadness. I extend Schneider's argument to all media
productions, both fictional and real, since information of all sorts is also
the product of living labor, and thus tends to "die off," lose its liveliness
and relevance, and become the forgotten past. Information, like other
commodities, requires the constant reinvestment of living labor in order
to be reanimated and to remain animate, living, contemporary, still happening, still unfolding.

Above, I described fans' tendency to want to produce fan works in
response to "live" media events. But fans also *keep* media events *alive*.
Fan labor can sustain audience interest in media texts between television seasons or movie franchise installments, and long after shows are
canceled or after movies leave theaters. Jenkins writes about how transmedia works sustain audiences' interest in source texts: "Redundancy
between media burns up fan interest and causes franchises to fail. [Fans]
offering new levels of insight and experience refreshes the franchise and
sustains consumer loyalty" (Jenkins 2008: 96). The same is true of real-
world happenings: fans' consistent output of stories related to real-world
crises can stoke "fan interest" in the event and repeatedly bring it "back
to life," staving off the deadness—irrelevance, forgottenness, pastness—
that threatens all news.

Fanfic in the Archive of History

Journalistic reports in major media outlets, police and court records,
and statements and policies issued by institutions such as universities,
corporations, and government offices all enter political events into the
archive of history under the banner of "official" documentation. "Bot-
tom-up" accounts of social movements, including citizen journalists'
stories, blog entries, social media posts, and fan productions, form a

different historical archive of the political. Political fic memorializes real-world events as media texts that circulate through the same global networks as the culture industries' productions, such that both (fictional media and news of actual demonstrations and debates) can be reconfigured to share, exchange, reinforce, and multiply specific narratives and affects. The archive of history now contains cultural forms that hybridize science fiction and global crises and interleave popular entertainment genres and public protests.

Fans continue to develop techniques for explicitly addressing policy debates not in the languages of empiricism and argument, but in the languages of "fantasy and spectacle," which, Stephen Duncombe (2007) states, "have become the lingua franca of our time" (9). In his book *Dream*, Duncombe calls upon progressive politicians and thinkers to more actively engage voters by making their messages more narratively interesting and affecting. Duncombe challenges progressives to "build a politics that embraces the dreams of people [. . . ,] a politics that understands desire and speaks to the irrational; a politics that employs symbols and associations; a politics that tells good stories" (2007: 9). Fan authors enter the political arena, and encourage others to enter, by writing about the harsh realities of policy in the playful register of dreams, desire, symbols—that is, by telling "good stories" about important real-world issues. Employing what Duncombe terms a "spectacular vernacular" (9) to creatively comment on current political events, fans produce works that simultaneously enlarge archives of fictions and augment the archive of history.

WORKS CITED

Anthony, T 2011, "Superman: American patriot, illegal immigrant or both?," *Hero Complex—Los Angeles Times*, May 15, herocomplex.latimes.com.

Appelo, T 2011, "Superman renounces U.S. citizenship as Warners, DC Comics bids for global audiences," *Hollywood Reporter*, April 28, www.hollywoodreporter.com.

Baudrillard, J 1995, *The Gulf War did not take place*, Indiana University Press, Bloomington.

Beck, D, et al. 2011, "Synthesizing presence: a multidisciplinary review of the literature," *Journal of Virtual Worlds Research* 3(3): 3–35.

Bennett, L 2012, "Fan activism for social mobilization: a critical review of the literature," *Transformative Works and Cultures* 10, journal.transformativeworks.org.

De Kosnik, A, et al. 2015, "Watching, creating, and archiving: observations on the quantity and temporality of fannish productivity in online fan fiction archives,"

Convergence: The International Journal of Research into New Media Technologies 21(1): 145–64.

DiChiara, A 2011, "Superman renounces American citizenship," *Examiner*, April 28, www.examiner.com.

DiDio, D (ed.) 2011, *Action Comics #900*, DC Comics.

Dixon, S 2007, *Digital performance: a history of new media in theater, dance, performance art, and installation*, MIT Press, Cambridge, MA.

Duncombe, S 2007, *Dream: re-imagining progressive politics in an age of fantasy*, New York University Press, New York.

El Random Hero 2011, "Superman for the Dream Act," *Just a Random Hero*, May 25, justarandomhero.blogspot.com.

Gray, J 2012, "Of Snowspeeders and Imperial Walkers: fannish play at the Wisconsin protests," *Transformative Works and Cultures* 10, journal.transformativeworks.org.

Huerta, E 2010, "The double life of an undocumented student: pressure from family and the law bear down," *Zócalo Public Square*, December 5, www.zocalopublic-square.org.

Jenkins, H 2008, *Convergence culture: where old and new media collide*, New York University Press, New York.

Jenkins, H 2010, "Avatar activism," *Le Monde diplomatique, English Edition*, monde-diplo.com.

Jenkins, H 2011, "Transmedia 202: further reflections," *Confessions of an Aca-Fan: The Official Weblog of Henry Jenkins*, August 1, henryjenkins.org.

Jenkins, H & Shresthova, S 2012, "Up, up, and away! The power and potential of fan activism," *Transformative Works and Cultures* 10, journal.transformativeworks.org.

Jurkowitz, M 2010, "WikiLeaks puts Afghanistan back on media agenda," Pew Research Center, August 3, www.pewresearch.org.

Kammer, J 2011, "Superman meets his match: Los Hermanos Ortiz," Center for Immigration Studies, April 28, cis.org.

Kondabolu, H 2011, "Hari Kondabolu—Superman is undocumented," *YouTube*, www.youtube.com.

Krikorian, M 2011, "Superman, illegal alien," *The Corner—National Review*, April 28, www.nationalreview.com.

Lothian, A, Busse, K, & Reid, RA 2007, "'Yearning void and infinite potential': online slash fandom as queer fandom space," *English Language Notes* 45(2), 103–11.

Moten, F 2003, *In the break: the aesthetics of the Black radical tradition*, University of Minnesota Press, Minneapolis.

Penley, C 1992, "Feminism, psychoanalysis, and the study of popular culture," in L Grossberg, C Nelson, & P Treichler (eds.), *Cultural studies*, Routledge, New York.

Pew Research Center: Journalism & Media Staff 2008, "Every now and again—a study on news coverage of immigration," www.journalism.org.

Raley, R 2009, *Tactical media*, University of Minnesota Press, Minneapolis.

Rivas, N 2012, "U.S. Department of Homeland Security Immigration & Customs Enforcement Department of Illegal Superheroes," *ICE DISH*, www.icedish.org.

Russ, J 1985, "Pornography by women for women, with love," in *Magic mommas, trembling sisters, puritans, and perverts: feminist essays*, Crossing Press, Berkeley.

Schneider, R 2011, *Performing remains: art and war in times of theatrical reenactment*, Routledge, New York.

Schneider, R 2012, "It seems as if . . . I am dead: zombie capitalism and theatrical labor," *Drama Review* 56(4): 150–62.

Stein, L 2002, "Subject: 'off topic: oh my God, US terrorism!' *Roswell* fans respond to 11 September," *European Journal of Cultural Studies* 5(4): 471–91.

Stiglitz, J 2011, "Of the 1%, by the 1%, for the 1%," *Vanity Fair*, May, www.vanityfair.com.

Weinstein, A 2011, "'We are the 99 percent' creators revealed," *Mother Jones*, October 7, www.motherjones.com.

17

Between Rowdies and Rasikas

Rethinking Fan Activity in Indian Film Culture

ASWIN PUNATHAMBEKAR

Let us begin by examining two recent moments of fan activity surrounding Indian cinema. On October 8, 2005, A. R. Rahman, the renowned film music director, performed in Bangalore as part of a worldwide tour. The entire concert was managed by fans who volunteered their services for everything from ticket sales to stage construction to crowd management. As part of their effort to gain recognition as the "official" Rahman fan club, they also decided to present Rahman with a gift—a montage, composed of thumbnail images of all his album covers, which formed the contours of his face. Faced with the prospect of buying expensive software, these fans (who run a design company called 3xus.com) went on to develop their own software. After many sleepless nights of painstaking coding, they finally got to meet Rahman and present the gift. A few days later, they learned that Rahman liked the gift and had displayed it in his studio in Chennai. This story of fan activity went largely unreported in mainstream media.

Little more than a month later, Amitabh Bachchan, the enduring superstar of Hindi cinema, was hospitalized and had to undergo surgery. Not only did media outlets cover every detail of Bachchan's hospital stay and subsequent recovery, but many instances of "fan devotion" were also recorded. Citing several examples of fans organizing prayer sessions in cities worldwide, Chopra writes, "fans routinely gather outside Mr. Bachchan's home in suburban Mumbai for a *darshan*, or sighting, but that is the least of it: some have sent him paintings of him done in blood, presumably their own" (2006: 1).

It is perhaps not surprising that mainstream media coverage of Bollywood ignores fan activity except when it seems obsessive or pathological—"paintings in blood" certainly makes more sensational copy when compared with a group of highly educated, technically skilled fans who discuss Rahman's music on an Internet newsgroup. Indeed, when one raises the question of fan activity surrounding cinema, the standard response, among academics and film journalists/critics, is to point to Tamil and Telugu film cultures where fan associations devoted to former stars like M. G. Ramachandran and N. T. Rama Rao have played pivotal roles in these stars' political careers. As the editor of *Filmfare* explained, "you'll find crowds outside Bachchan or Shahrukh Khan's house. But never that level of passion as you'd find in the south. There is no organized fan activity around Bollywood. No one asks Shahrukh to float a political party or threatens to commit suicide just because his film flops!"[1]

In this chapter, I argue against framing fan activity in Indian film culture in terms of devotional excess or in relation to political mobilization in south India. I suggest we shift our attention away from the cinema hall and heroes like Amitabh Bachchan to the realm of film music and the figure of the music director. This move will force us to take into account how cinema, as an object, is constituted in fundamental ways through convergence with other media. In other words, developing fan activity surrounding film music as an entry point entails rethinking the history of cinema's publicness as a history of cinema's intersections with various "new" media (radio, TV, Internet, and mobile phone), and thereby adds to the mapping of different cinematic spaces that projects such as "Publics and Practices in the History of the Present" (www.sarai. net) have initiated.[2] Such a reconceptualization of cinema's publicness will also help us steer away from treating fan activity as epiphenomena of formal politics and transitions in the political sphere proper. This is necessary not only to chart the way fan activity operates in relation to Bollywood but also to acknowledge and begin accounting for fan activity in south India that may have no connections whatsoever to political parties and electoral campaigns. Following this, I argue for a reassessment of the figure of the fan and the need to dismantle the binary of *fan-as-rowdy* versus *fan-as-rasika* and, instead, locate the "fan" along a more expansive continuum of participatory culture.[3] I conclude the essay by situating it in relation to academic calls for fan studies to "go global," and posit that it is just as critical, if not more, for studies of media globalization to focus on fan activity. In fact, examining fan communities that cohere around film culture in India might make valuable contributions to our understanding of the emergence of Bollywood as a global culture industry.

Music Directors and Fan Identification: The Case of A. R. Rahman

Among other elements that distinguish a popular Indian film from, say, a Hollywood film, the one that is cited most often is the presence of at least five or six songs with seemingly no direct connection to the narrative. Songs, often choreographed into elaborate dance sequences, have been an integral part of popular Indian cinema ever since sound was introduced. As Majumdar further explains, "film songs and song sequences have their own circuit of distribution, both official, or industrial, and unofficial [. . .] they permeate the aural environment of India's public spaces, from markets and festivals to long-distance buses and trains" (2001: 161). The commercial value of film music has also meant that music directors have occupied a key role in the industry from the very beginning.[4]

Music directors have been central to developments and transformations in practically every aspect of the process—lyrics, expansion of orchestras and introduction of instruments from around the world, singing styles (the transition from actor-singers to playback singers), and, from the perspective of producers, responding to and shaping audience tastes (Arnold 1991). In fact, since the early 1940s, producers have been giving prominence to music directors. Film songs became a central component of prerelease publicity of films, and advertising began emphasizing the music director. Arnold points to a practice that continues to this day: major producers began to select commercially successful music directors to work on their new productions (1991: 206). Having their names displayed prominently on posters, billboards, and gramophone record sleeves, and radio shows such as the nationally popular *Binaca Geet Mala* (on Radio Ceylon), led to the construction of what Majumdar terms "aural stardom" (2001).[5] Over the years, songs came to be associated with music directors (and playback singers) just as much as with actors/actresses lip-synching on the screen.

A. R. Rahman started his musical career as an advertisement jingle composer and emerged as a music director in the 1990s—first in Tamil cinema and post-1995 in the Bombay-based Hindi film industry. While translations of his work for Tamil-language films such as *Roja* (1992, dir. Mani Ratnam) and *Bombay* (1995, dir. Mani Ratnam) were highly successful nationwide, it was with *Rangeela* (1995, dir. Ramgopal Varma) that Rahman made his mark as a "national" music director. Rahman's nonfilm projects have also been highly successful—for instance, his 1997 album *Vande Mataram*, released to coincide with the fiftieth year of Indian independence, sold millions of copies worldwide.

There are at least two things to keep in mind that set Rahman apart from other important music directors. First, projects such as *Vande Mataram* (1997) that involved Rahman in music videos, promotions via MTV, Channel [V], and other music shows on satellite television established him as the first music director in India to have a strong *visual* presence in addition to the aural stardom conventionally associated with music directors. In fact, Rahman figures prominently in posters advertising "Bollywood tours" worldwide—his performativity, in other words, extends beyond recorded sound.

Second, his rise coincided with the Bombay film industry attracting mainstream attention in transnational arenas, in main part due to the Indian diaspora's close ties to cinema. This led not only to an expanded audience and fan base but also to visibility generated in "world music" circles (Talvin Singh's music from the Asian Dub Foundation in London, for example) and to composing music for international projects such as *Bombay Dreams* (2002) and the stage version of *Lord of the Rings: The Return of the King* (2006). The multiple boundaries that Rahman (and his music) traverses—linguistic (Tamil-Hindi-English), religious (Hindu converted to Islam), regional/national, diasporic, and global—are strongly reflected in the online fan community.

The Rahman fan community is an online newsgroup that was formed on January 1, 1999, and today involves nearly eight thousand five hundred members from twenty-six different countries (arrfans.com). This is a space that brings together, for instance, fourth-generation Tamil Malaysians, second-generation Indian Americans, Indians in Gulf countries like Dubai, middle-class youth in urban India, and a growing number of non-Indian fans.[6] Embedded as citizens in disparate ways, each fan brings her or his own linguistic/regional background, experiences of varying racial/ethnic politics, religious affiliations, and different registers of knowledge and affiliation with India and "Indian" culture to bear on her or his engagement with Rahman's music (and Indian cinema in general).

The primary activity that defines this group is a detailed discussion of Rahman's music. This involves translating and evaluating lyrics, the use of different instruments and musical arrangement, songs' place in the film narrative, song picturization (and choreography), playback singers, and so on. Like other fan communities around the world, Rahman fans also monitor print publications, radio and television shows, and different websites for news and trivia about their star. The community includes people who work with Rahman on a professional basis, who have played a key role in getting this fan community recognized as Rahman's official fan club. Over the past two years, fans based in different cities around the world have begun meeting offline to extend discussions conducted online, to help organize Rahman concerts, and, in some cases, to form informal bands and perform Rahman songs.

Enabled by the Internet, constituted by individuals from different parts of the world, driven by an interest in film music that reaches across the world, the Rahman fan collective clearly is formed at the junction of many border-crossing dialogues. It is important, therefore, to also note how interactions are influenced by broader technological, economic, and political changes. For instance, the past decade has witnessed the film and music industry, new media companies, and the Indian state engaging in attempts to curb "nonlegal" media practices that include sharing of films and film music. Relying on stereotypical notions of "rowdy" fans who operate in the shadowy bylanes of cities like Bangalore and Kuala Lumpur, media organizations and nation-states tend to view fans' appropriation of music as a deviant act and rely on a "prohibitionist approach that seeks to protect intellectual property at all costs" (Ford 2006: 3; Liang 2005).[7] Treating spaces like the Rahman fan community as online extensions of neighborhood stores that sell MP3 collections for a fraction of the cost of a CD tells us little about how fans broker consensus on what constitutes "legal" sharing and appropriation of Rahman's music. Examining the many discussions Rahman fans have had on intellectual property, CD pricing mechanisms, availability of Rahman's music in different parts of the world, legality of sharing background music from films for which Rahman has composed the score, monitoring FTP sites that circulate Rahman's music, and so on is crucial if we are to understand how online fan communities have emerged as a crucial node in a larger realm of "porous legality" (Liang 2005) that defines Indian cinema's circulation around the world.

What I wish to suggest here is that, over the years, the Rahman fan community has emerged as a "zone of engagement" (Tsing 2005) where individuals, media technologies and institutions, and broader cultural and political forces participate in the construction, contestation, and negotiation of Indian cinema's place in a transnational cultural sphere. However, before we examine the formation and social dynamics of such zones, we need to rethink our understanding of fan activity surrounding Indian film culture. It is this problematic that the rest of the chapter will tackle.

Beyond the Cinema Hall: Reconceptualizing Publicness and the Fan

Sivathamby provided what is perhaps the earliest articulation of cinema and the public sphere in India. He argued that "the cinema hall was the first performance centre in which all Tamils sat under the same roof. The basis of the seating is not on the hierarchic position of the patron but essentially on his purchasing power. If he cannot afford paying the higher rate, he has either to keep away from the performance or be with all and sundry" (1981: 18). As Srinivas notes, this "formulation can be read as pointing to the democratic possibilities of cinema" (2013: 20). While there was a certain mode of policing this "democratic" space (e.g., seating codes, from the "Gandhi class" all the way up to "dress circle"), this does "permit us to conceive of the cinema hall as a kind of public institution that had no precedence in India" (Srinivas 2013: 20).

Following this early formulation, scholars have approached the problematic of cinema's publicness by focusing on a range of filmic and extra-filmic sites with varied theoretical lenses: (1) Indian cinema as a "site of ideological production [. . .] as the (re)production of the state form" (Prasad 1998: 9), (2) Indian popular films as social history (Virdi 2003), (3) Indian cinema in terms of spectatorship and democracy (Rajadhyaksha 2000), (4) Indian cinema in terms of censorship (Mehta 2001; Vasudev 1978), and (5) Indian cinema in terms of stardom (Majumdar 2001). While these studies grapple with the idea of how cinema relates in complex ways to the civic and the political, fan practices have not been the focus of systematic research. The two notable exceptions here are Srinivas's pioneering work on fan associations in Andhra Pradesh (2003) and Dickey's work in Tamilnadu (1993).

Dickey locates fan activity at the intersection of the formal realm of politics and civil social activity (conducting charity work, organizing blood donation campaigns, and performing other "social services"). Building on scholarship on Tamil cinema that has examined the relationship between the construction of stardom and the politics of mobilization (Pandian 1992), Dickey provides a very useful ethnographic account of this aspect of fan activity in Tamilnadu. She does, however, ignore the possibility of fan activity that might not necessarily be "public" in the sense of there being a neighborhood fan association that meets on street corners, at tea shops, or outside cinema halls. Indeed, her analysis circumscribes fan activity in Tamilnadu as that defined by working-class (often lower-caste) male youth in visible, public spaces.

In his pathbreaking work on the Telugu film industry, and viewing practices in the state of Andhra Pradesh more broadly, Srinivas complicates Dickey's analysis and theorizes fan activity as being structured by a dialectic of devotion and defiance (2000), as a struggle between fan expectations and the industry's careful management of the star persona to derive maximum mileage from fan activity. Focusing on one major star, Chiranjeevi, Srinivas situates the formation of fan clubs in Andhra Pradesh in relation to a broader history of subaltern struggles (dalit/untouchable movements, for instance) and forces us to consider fan practices as a domain of political activity that does not fit within classical liberal accounts of citizenship and political representation, but one that has clear links to a politics of mobilization around linguistic/regional identity (Srinivas 2000).

While he has written that we also need to understand the political nature of fan associations beyond their "linkages with the politics of linguistic/identity nationalism," he maintains that fan activity is political mainly because it "develops around the notion of spectatorial rights." He writes,

The cinema exists because of my presence and for me. Further, the "I" at the cinema is always a member of a collective: *we make the film happen.* Anyone who has watched a Chiranjeevi or Rajnikanth film knows exactly what I am talking about. Not only do these stars address spectators in rather direct ways (including by looking at the camera) but seem to perform according to "our" demands. (2003: n.p., original emphasis)

Even as he exhorts us to examine the various "webs of public transactions" involving cinema, and to rethink what constitutes the "political" beyond the narrow sense of the term, Srinivas's analyses remain bound by one particular, highly visible mode of fan activity and the film industry's perception and management of such activity. He goes on to say that "much work needs to be done across the spectrum of activities and organizations that fade into the cinema hall at one end and the political party at the other" (2003: n.p.).

In the light of Indian cinema's flows worldwide, the question of who constitutes the "we" in the cinema hall and what "our" demands might be complicates the notion of "spectatorial rights" (Rajadhyaksha 2000). For it would be difficult to maintain that a third-generation Tamil Malaysian fan of Rajnikanth is positioned as a spectator in precisely the same way as a fan in Tamilnadu or, for that matter, Japanese fans who watch subtitled prints. The notion of spectatorial rights also does not help us explain the kind of activity that fans of A. R. Rahman are involved in, as we saw earlier. While opening up an important line of inquiry, Srinivas's analysis needs to be extended in at least two directions.

The first question we need to address is this: Are the two poles of the spectrum—the cinema hall and the political party—useful analytic categories to begin with? If we were to consider film music, a component of films that circulates in the public realm much before and long after the film itself does, we would be forced to consider the radio, the television, the Internet, and cell phone networks as sites constitutive of the publicness of cinema as much as the cinema hall itself, if not more.

Consider the story of Rameshwar Prasad Bharnwal, a resident of Jhumri Tilaiya in the state of Bihar, who has mailed nearly three *lakh* (300,000) request cards to radio stations for nearly two decades, and at least ten cards a day to *Binaca Geet Mala* when the show was broadcast on Radio Ceylon (Krishnan 1991). Bharnwal, a member of a radio listeners club that discusses films, film songs, and requests to be mailed, recalls sending nearly one hundred requests for popular songs of the time. Shows such as *Binaca Geet Mala, Chitrahaar,* and *Showtheme* (on state-regulated Doordarshan), *Videocon Flashback* (on [V]), and *movie zones* (on sites like IndiaFM.com) are all key nodes in a mediated public culture shaped not necessarily in the cinema hall, by the screen. I propose that a focus on fan activities that emerge at the intersection of film and "new" media opens up the possibility of rewriting the history of Indian cinema's publicness as a history of media convergence, and as a history of fan activity that does not necessarily "fade into the cinema hall at one end and the political party at the other" (Srinivas 2003: n.p.).

The second question concerns the image of the fan that we derive from a focus on the space of the cinema hall and its surroundings, or fan associations of stars like Rajnikanth and Chiranjeevi: obsessive, male, working-class, and rowdy. The "excessive" behavior that marks viewers in the front benches of cinema halls, what Liang (2005: 371) calls the "protocols of collective behavior"—whistling and commenting loudly, throwing flowers, coins, or ribbons when the star first appears on the screen, singing along and dancing in the aisles, and so on—is routinely cited as what distinguishes fans from the rest of the audience. Furthermore, the publicness of fan associations' activities—celebrating a star's birthday or one hundred days of a film, organizing special prerelease functions, adorning street corners with giant cutouts of the star, decorating theaters where the film has had a successful run, and so forth—and press coverage of such activities have further served to both marginalize and circumscribe fan activity as undesirable, vulgar, and at times dangerous. As Srinivas, drawing on Dhareshwar and Srivatsan's analysis of rowdy sheeters, writes,

> The fan is a rowdy not only because he breaks the law in the course of his assertion or his association with criminalized politics—the fan becomes a rowdy by overstepping the line which demarcates the legitimate, "constructive," permissible excess, and the illegitimate [. . .] as far as the "citizen" is concerned, the fan is a blind hero-worshipper (devoid of reason) and a villain. The rowdy/fan is an agent of politics which is delegitimized. (2000: 314)

Fans, in other words, are imperfect citizens in aesthetic, sociocultural, and political terms. Middle-class constructions of norms of excess are, without doubt, designed in part to maintain hierarchies of cultural production and taste. I would further argue that the *fan as rowdy* is constructed in semantic and social opposition to the idea of the *fan as rasika*—rowdy fans of the actor Rajnikanth as opposed to *rasikas* (connoisseurs) of the renowned Carnatic musician M. S. Subbulakshmi, for instance.

Where, then, do we position film music fans, like the members of the radio club in Jhumri Tilaiya, who wrote hundreds of letters to Ameen Sayani, the famous anchor of *Binaca Geet Mala*, expressing their admiration of singers like Talat Mahmood and Geeta Dutt? In what terms do we describe the desires and attachments of thousands of "respectable" English-speaking middle- and upper-middle-class men and women who constitute the primary readership for magazines like *Filmfare*? How do we account for shows on Channel [V] or MTV-India that were designed to tap into urban youth's "obsession" with Hindi cinema? And finally, how do we make sense of online lifeworlds of fans in diverse locations worldwide who design websites devoted to film stars, maintain blogs, write detailed reviews, create ways and means to share music, and come together as online and offline communities on the basis of shared attachments to film culture?

I argue, therefore, that we need to move away from meanings derived out of experiences based in the cinema hall and/or linkages to political parties, and place the "fan" along a more expansive continuum of participatory culture (Abercrombie & Longhurst 1998). Yes, there are rowdies and *rasikas*. However, denying the existence of several other sites and modes of participation, and continuing to relegate fan activity to the fringes of a transnational public culture shaped so strongly by cinema, will not only sustain cultural hierarchies but also mean turning a blind eye to the many important ways in which cultural and political identities are being shaped in "new" media spaces today. Let me clarify right away that I am not advocating an exhaustive mapping of different modes and levels of intensity in being a "fan"—that would be both impossible and theoretically pointless. I propose that we treat the "fan" less as a subject position taken up by individuals in different locations, and more as a dynamic construct that is industrial, textual, and social. In other words, I am suggesting that we begin to examine how the "fan" (and fan activity) operates within a certain circuit of cultural production, in this case the convergence between film and "new" media in the Indian context. How do media producers who develop "interactive" content for new media understand "fans," and how is this understanding translated into practice? In what ways do "new media" texts invite and structure fan activity? What does an examination of an A. R. Rahman fan community tell us about the many new and complex relationships among cinema, new media technologies, and social lives?

This shift toward examining the "fan" as a construct that is not eternal and essential but, rather, is shaped equally by industry practices, textual properties of film-based content that flow across multiple media, and social interactions in identifiable fan communities is vital if we are to appreciate and understand the centrality of spaces of participatory culture such as the Rahman fan community to the larger problematic of the emergence of "Bollywood" as a global culture industry.

Conclusion: Fan Studies Meets Global Media Studies

I began this chapter by introducing a fan community that has cohered around a film music director, A. R. Rahman. Building on a brief description of the formation and activities of the Rahman fan community, I have argued that a focus on fan activity surrounding film music will help us rethink the history of cinema's publicness as a history of media convergence, and also to stop considering fan activity solely in relation to political mobilization. By focusing attention on fan activity, I also seek to add to studies that have pushed film scholarship beyond formalist concerns with the text and opened up other entry points into understanding our experience with cinema (Hughes 2003; Liang 2005).[8] Following Stephen Hughes, I would even suggest that once fan activity is "taken as a necessary part of film history, we must rethink how we construct Indian cinema as an object of study" (2003: n.p.). In this concluding section, I wish to situate this chapter in relation to calls for fan studies to "go global," and what it means to focus on Bollywood now.

Scholarly literature on fan activity has emerged primarily from Anglo-American contexts and experiences. This literature has moved from talking about fans as infringers/poachers (Jenkins 1992) to analyzing how fans today operate as lead users, surplus audiences, grassroots intermediaries, the "long tail," performers, content generators, and even future talent for media companies (Jenkins 2006). As Jenkins argues in his recent work, fan participation has become an integral component of contemporary media culture, and both academics and industry professionals are interested more in terms of models of participation (2006: 246). Given how media flows from other parts of the world have influenced Anglo-American media texts, industries, and audience expectations over the past decade, it is not surprising that scholars who study fan activity are calling for fan studies to "go global," to begin to include accounts of fan activity in "non-Western" locations. Furthermore, given "Western" media's current fascination with Bollywood, and the gradual development of Bollywood as a legitimate area of inquiry in academic locations in countries like the United Kingdom and United States, extending fan studies into a new and fascinating realm of non-Western popular culture would certainly seem timely. But I would argue that fan studies "go global" with great caution lest the faulty assumption that "non-Western" media are still tethered to the boundaries of their respective nation-states be reinforced. As several scholars and commentators have pointed out, simply because a circuit of media flow does not include countries like the United States or the United Kingdom does not make it less global.

To begin with, radio shows like *Binaca Geet Mala*, videocassettes of film songs that circulated throughout South Asia, the Middle East, and many countries in Africa, satellite TV channels that beam Indian films and film-based programming around the world, and, now, Internet portals dedicated to Indian cinema are all evidence that, historically, the cultural geography of fan activity surrounding Indian cinema has always been global. Fan communities that cohere around various aspects of Indian cinema also tell us that we need to think beyond the "national" as the most important scale of imagination and identity construction (Curtin 2003). Over the past decade, it has become clear that the creation of Bollywood properties—films, music, apparel, web portals, mobile games, and so on—is an enterprise that takes place in many locations around the world, and involves people with affiliations and stakes that crisscross varied regional, national, and diasporic boundaries. Bollywood, in other words, cannot be understood in terms of a "national" cinema industry limited to the boundaries of the Indian nation-state or restricted in its imagination by rigid definitions of "Indianness." By continuing to limit Bollywood to notions of "Indianness," we risk neglecting attachments that do not follow lines of ethnicity or nationality. We need to recognize that a focus on transnational fan communities (Rahman fans, for example) will help us better understand how media circulate and get hinged to varied aspirations around the world, and, crucially, how Bollywood, from a "non-Western" location, has begun claiming the status of a "global" culture industry.

NOTES

1 Personal interview with Shashi Baliga (editor, *Filmfare*), November 14, 2005. Also see kollywood.allindiansite.com.
2 See www.sarai.net.
3 The term *rasika*, derived from an aesthetic theory (*rasa*) of performance, connotes a highly developed sense of appreciation of various art forms. *Rasika* can be roughly translated as "connoisseur." The term is most commonly associated with religious devotion, and classical music and dance forms.
4 Film music records account for 61 percent of the ten-billion-rupee music industry in India. See www.contentsutra.com.
5 Majumdar argues that "it is necessary . . . to theorize an aural conception of stardom to account for the dual pleasures and recognitions in song sequences, a concept of stardom in which even the absence of glamour and the invisibility of playback singers can be regarded as defining features of their star personas" (2001: 171).
6 The moderator of the group informed me that over the past two years, over 50 percent of new subscribers have been non-Indians.
7 See, for example, in.rediff.com.
8 Also see www.sarai.net for an overview of projects that map transformations in media and urban life in India.

WORKS CITED

Abercrombie, N & Longhurst, B 1998, *Audiences: a sociological theory of performance and imagination*, Sage, Thousand Oaks, CA.

Arnold, A 1991, *Hindi filmi geet*. PhD dissertation, University of Illinois at Urbana-Champaign.

Chopra, A 2006, "Amitabh Bachchan has a cold," *New York Times*, February 12, www.nytimes.com.

Curtin, M 2003, "Media capital: towards the study of spatial flows," *International Journal of Cultural Studies* 6(2): 202–28.

Dickey, S 1993, *Cinema and the urban poor in South India*, Cambridge University Press, Cambridge.

Ford S 2006, *Fanning the flames: ten ways to embrace and cultivate fan communities*, white paper, Convergence Culture Consortium, MIT.

Hughes, S 2003, "Pride of place," *Seminar* 525, www.india-seminar.com.

Jenkins, H 1992, *Textual poachers: television fans and participatory culture*, Routledge, New York.

Jenkins, H 2006, *Convergence culture: where old and new media collide*, New York University Press, New York.

Krishnan, M 1991, "Jhumri Tilaiya: abode of audio addicts," *Sunday Observer*, January 26, 56.

Liang, L 2005, "Cinematic citizenship and the illegal city," *Inter-Asia Cultural Studies* 6(3): 366–85.

Majumdar, N 2001, "The embodied voice: song sequences and stardom in popular Hindi cinema," in PR Wojcik & A Knight (eds.), *Soundtrack available: essays on film and popular music*, Duke University Press, Durham, NC.

Mehta, M 2001, *Selections: cutting, classifying, and certifying in Bombay cinema*, PhD dissertation, University of Minnesota, Minneapolis.

Pandian, MSS 1992, *The image trap: MG Ramachandran in films and politics*, Sage, New Delhi.

Prasad, M 1998, *Ideology of the Hindi film: a historical construction*, Oxford University Press, New Delhi.

Rajadhyaksha, A 2000, "Viewership and democracy in the cinema," in R Vasudevan (ed.), *Making meaning in Indian cinema*, Oxford University Press, New Delhi.

Sivathamby, K 1981, *Tamil film as a medium of political communication*, New Century Book House, Madras.

Srinivas, SV 2000, "Devotion and defiance in fan activity," in R Vasudevan (ed.), *Making meaning in Indian cinema*, Oxford University Press, New Delhi.

Srinivas, SV 2003, "Film culture: politics and industry," *Seminar* 525, www.india-seminar.com.

Srinivas, SV 2013, *Politics as performance: a social history of Telugu cinema*, Permanent Black, New Delhi.

Tsing, A 2005, *Friction: an ethnography of global connection*, Princeton University Press, Princeton, NJ.

Vasudev, A 1978, *Liberty and license in Indian cinema*. Vikas, New Delhi.

Virdi, J 2003, *The cinematic ImagiNation: Indian popular films as social history*, Rutgers University Press, New Brunswick, NJ.

18

Black Twitter and the Politics of Viewing *Scandal*

DAYNA CHATMAN

When ABC's prime-time drama *Scandal* premiered in April 2012, it became the first commercial network television drama to feature a Black woman in a lead role in nearly forty years,[1] and the first such drama to be created and co–executive produced by a Black woman, Shonda Rhimes. Featuring a relatively racially diverse cast of actors, *Scandal* was not positioned by ABC as a "Black program" targeted at Black American audiences.[2] In fact, the network has made every effort when talking about the series to highlight the diversity of the audience for the show and downplay the fact that the show is the highest rated scripted drama among Black Americans (Vega 2013). Nonetheless, by virtue of their active engagement in talking about the show on Twitter and other online spaces, many Black American viewers articulate a sense that *Scandal* is "their show," since like other forms of Black media, it at times serves as a "medium for expression of racial humor, information, entertainment, or values" (Harris-Lacewell 2004: 10) that are recognizable as shared among Black communities.

Actress Kerry Washington portrays *Scandal*'s main protagonist, Olivia Pope, a confident, successful public relations consultant whose clientele are distinguished political figures in Washington, D.C. Olivia will go to almost any length to "fix" her clients' problems, including destroying evidence at crime scenes and manipulating innocent people in order to misdirect attention, but the one moral flaw that has faced scrutiny from some viewers since the series debuted is her affair with President Fitzgerald ("Fitz") Grant, a married white man. In their criticisms of Olivia's relationship with Fitz, some critics and activists (see Desmond-Harris 2012; Maxwell 2013) assert that the show perpetuates and refashions various "controlling images" (Collins 2000)—mainly that of the Mammy and Jezebel—and in so doing undermines activism aimed at promoting television representations that distance Blacks from racist and sexist tropes and stereotypes. These criticisms of *Scandal* often fail to address the varied interpretive lenses through which viewers make sense of the program. Black television viewers take interest in whether media texts break away from or reinforce stereotypes (see Coleman 2000; Inniss & Feagin 1995), but these same media texts can become significant spaces of resistance, pleasure, cultural politics, and identity construction. It is thus necessary to interrogate the affective relationships and constructive dialogue that result from Black Americans' engagement with television and consider what their primary concerns are with respect to the representations they consume.

Extending prior studies that have explored Black women's fandom around *Scandal* (see Clark 2015; Warner 2015a), in this chapter I examine Black Americans' live Twitter commentary during the airing of the season 3 premiere episode "It's Handled," and consider what this commentary indicates about the state of concerns over contemporary representations of Black womanhood. With few exceptions (e.g., Bobo 1995; Coleman 2000; Cornwell & Orbe 2002; Inniss & Feagin 1995), cultural-studies-oriented reception studies have frequently failed to examine Black audiences. Black Americans who live-tweet *Scandal* on a weekly basis provide an in situ picture of their opinions, reactions, and interpretations of the text in real time, and in so doing open a window into the politics of viewing the series. I conceptualize "politics of viewing" as a discursive struggle whereby individuals collectively engage in "a critical politics" (Hall 1996: 444) in which representations are not simply judged on the basis of "negative" or "positive" stereotypes, but instead are interrogated in ways that illustrate their simultaneous grappling with the pleasures of media consumption, concerns over potential influences of representations, and whether television producers and networks or viewers themselves should be held accountable for representations deemed detrimental to out-group perceptions of Black Americans. Although a politics of viewing has likely always been articulated in various spaces, I argue that social media platforms, blogs, and other online media of communication afford Black Americans new counterpublic spheres in which to wrestle with interpretations of texts, and seek to collectively define and police the boundaries of what is acceptable to watch and take pleasure in.

Black Americans have built counterpublic spheres within Black churches, barbershops, hair salons, radio, and other media, in order to exchange interpretations, share individual experiences that resonate with or are implicitly understood by the group, make sense of the political world, and strategize over how to address issues of public concern (Harris-Lacewell 2004; Squires 2000). Twitter has been adopted by some Black Americans as a counterpublic sphere used to discuss issues of representation, social equalities, and racism and to engage in activism. Activists leading the Black Lives Matter movement, for instance, have wielded Twitter to circulate images, critiques, and hashtags (e.g., #IfTheyGunnedMeDown) to bring attention to bias within news media coverage of Black victims of gun violence and police brutality. The use of Twitter by Black Americans for the purposes of collective action and building racial solidarity through sharing ideas and experiences, exchanging jokes, and engaging in the consumption of media texts as a community of invested spectators has resulted in the emergence of what some call "Black Twitter." Black Twitter manifests as a community constructed through their use of social media and shared communication practices and performative techniques (Brock 2012). Black Twitter is not monolithic; rather, there "are millions of Black users connecting, and engaging with others who have similar concerns, experiences, tastes, and cultural practices" (Florini 2014: 225). I situate live-tweeting *Scandal* as one instance in which Black Twitter manifests as a community.

Scandal Fandom and Anti-fandom

Through the practice of live-tweeting *Scandal*, Black Americans become more than just television viewers who make meanings and pleasures through the act of watching (Fiske 1993); they transition from "viewers" to the position of "fans." Henry Jenkins contends that regular television viewers differ from fans because the latter translate their "viewing into some kind of cultural activity, by sharing feelings and thoughts about the program content with friends, [and] by joining a 'community' of other fans who share common interests. For fans, consumption naturally sparks production, reading generates writing, until the terms seem logically inseparable" (2006: 39). The act of live-tweeting television itself is a cultural activity whereby individuals invest time and energy to talk about a text and engage with others doing the same. With this in mind, I situate those who live-tweet *Scandal* as constitutive of a fandom.

Within the context of *Scandal*, it is necessary to include anti-fans in the discussion of commentary about the show because they are active in the Twitter conversation and therefore contribute to the politics of viewing the text. Gray (2005) describes anti-fans as those who have an affective relationship to a particular text that is rooted in feelings of dislike, displeasure, or outright hatred. Anti-fans are productive; just as a defining feature of fandom is the production of texts such as fan art, fan fiction, commentary, and so on (Fiske 1992), anti-fans also create and circulate texts that express their feelings and opinions about a particular program. *Scandal* anti-fans, for instance, generate tweets each week that voice annoyance that their Twitter timelines will be inundated with commentary from fans of the show and express criticisms of the Olivia/Fitz relationship through creating image memes of the characters.

For the purposes of this chapter, I examine only those anti-fans who situate themselves—by virtue of their comments—as non-viewers of *Scandal*. However, I observed at least three types of anti-fans: those non-viewers who circulate their dislike for the series at moments when they know fans will be watching, those who "hate-watch" the show in order to deride it, and those who are fans of the show, but do not like Olivia Pope as a character. The last type of anti-fan is made visible when viewers tweet their support of First Lady Mellie Grant (#TeamMellie) instead of Olivia Pope (#TeamOlitz). Although it may seem that this last category of anti-fan represents not anti-fans at all, but instead fans who have developed a particular allegiance to a character or story line, I view them as anti-fans, but in a limited capacity. *Scandal* anti-fandom has arisen in opposition to the show predominately because of the Olivia/Fitz story line and the depiction of Washington's character as a mistress. Fans of the show who are #TeamMellie often voice the same criticisms of the show as anti-fans and articulate the same reasoning for their dislike of the Olivia/Fitz narrative. Therefore, I view fans who are against this story line through the same lens as anti-fans.

Method

For this study of *Scandal* fandom and anti-fandom, I used "participant viewing," a methodological approach developed for observing live-tweeting practices (Driscoll et al. 2013). The methodology combines micro-level participant observation and macro-level data collection. Before the season 3 premiere of *Scandal* on October 3, 2013, a list of keywords and hashtags was assembled based upon knowledge of the past seasons' trending topics and observations of tweets made days before the broadcast. These keywords and hashtags were added to a custom tracking program that was then connected to the filter function of Twitter's streaming API.[3] On the day season 3 premiered and for several episodes during the first half of that season, I watched *Scandal* live while observing and tweeting about the show, and I transcribed plot points that generated discussion, hashtags that began to trend during the show, images and other forms of content that were circulated, and so on. These transcriptions were then immediately used to input new keywords and hashtags that could be retrieved by filtering tweets from Twitter.

Given the macro-level data collection, the number of tweets acquired was substantive—for the season 3 premiere episode nearly 125,000 original tweets were captured. In order to create a manageable dataset that could be analyzed systematically, a software program (Navicat) was used to retrieve tweets randomly based upon certain moments in the live broadcast that generated the most traffic. The content of these tweets was examined for keywords and phrases, which were then used to retrieve a second randomly selected sample that was coded for themes and subject to textual analysis. In this chapter, I present some of the results from this process.

I have attempted to mediate concerns about taking comments out of context as best as possible through observing *Scandal* in real time with fans, matching commentary with moments in the plot, thematically grouping and examining patterns of interpretations, and drawing upon my own knowledge of the program, as a fan. Because the focus of this research is on the commentary exchanged publicly on Twitter, and not concerned with individual fans, I do not use any identifying information such as Twitter profile names. In addition, I have not substantially edited the tweets beyond inserting words to increase clarity, and removing account names; the names of those associated with the production of *Scandal* (e.g., writers, actors, ABC, etc.), however, are included. The tweets cited throughout this chapter are used as examples of themes that emerged within the collected corpus of tweets.

There are some inherent limitations to the data used in this study. Unlike fan websites, or even comment sections and status updates from other social network sites like Facebook, which can allow for more free-flowing and in-depth expressions of fans' interpretations of and reactions to their favorite programs, Twitter's 140-character limit provides a unique challenge. Tweets on their own offer only snippets of a conversation, often without significant context. This is why my participation in viewing *Scandal* and observing threads of commentary during the live-tweeting helped to provide some of the context that would normally be missing.

Fans' and Anti-fans' Discussion of *Scandal*

In the opening scenes of "It's Handled," the season 3 premiere episode, the news media speculate that Olivia is Fitz's mistress and White House aides are seen scrambling to figure out how to handle the rumor. In the next sequence, her father, Rowan Pope, who works for a covert arm of the government that specializes in making people "disappear" when they are a threat to national interests, whisks Olivia away in a limousine. Upon arrival at a private airport hanger, Rowan attempts to convince her that the best way to handle the situation is to abandon her life and work in D.C. and begin anew someplace else. He is not polite in his efforts to sway her; an animated Rowan rapidly spews his opinions of his daughter's poor decisions, as she stands docile, with her head lowered. Rowan harshly says to Olivia about the breaking scandal: "You've gotten yourself into a lot of trouble, Olivia, and I'm here to fix it. You raised your skirt and opened your knees and gave it away to a man with too much power. You're not rare; you're not special. Your story is no different from a thousand stories in this town."

Rowan's words echo throughout the episode as several characters directly and indirectly admonish Olivia's sexual relationship with Fitz. For instance, Vice President Sally Langston angrily upbraids the president for "sleeping with whores," and the White House Chief of Staff, Cyrus Bean, devises a plan to "play the ambitious slut card" as a means of shifting blame for the affair to Olivia after he discovers she has risen to success through romantic relationships with powerful, older men. Fitz's wife Mellie later calls Olivia a "whore" as they are gathered to discuss a plan for shifting the conversation about Fitz's affair. The use of the word "whore," implicit in Rowan's remarks, and explicit in other characters' comments, became key to fans' and anti-fans' discursive struggle over both how to interpret the Olivia/Fitz story line, and what to make of Rhimes's decision to characterize Olivia in this manner.

Fan Politics of Viewing: Olivia Represents So Much More

Many of the fans live-tweeting the season 3 premiere episode did not offer their views on Rhimes's use of "whore" to characterize Olivia. When fans did have something to say about it, however, comments were directed inward at the text as they often took issue with particular characters hurling the term at Olivia, as indicated by tweets like the following:

> #Scandal How many women of colour have had it up to here with Mellie calling Olivia a whore? Who does this bitch think she is?

> Sally! Olivia Pope is NOT a whore. She has more Prada than you have faith. #Scandal

These fans, in the moment of watching the program, are not concerned with passing judgment on whether the characterization of Olivia as a whore is "good" or "bad," or might have ideological, political, or social ramifications outside of the television context. Instead they are immersed in the act of watching the narrative unfold, and as they do so they voice their pleasures and/or (in the case of certain characters and plot points) displeasures.

Kristen Warner suggests that in order to understand the affective response of Black women fans toward Olivia and *Scandal*, one must consider that Black women on television "are rarely allowed to be main characters in stories about choice, desire and fantasy" (2015b: 17). *Scan-*

dal affords these viewers a romantic fantasy that they can experience remotely and use to escape the day-to-day demands and cultural expectations of society (Ang 1985; Radway 1991). It would be imprudent to think that fans who raise no critical objections to *Scandal*'s characterization of Olivia are apolitical in their consumption of the text. As Bobo's (1995) exploration of Black women's cultural readings of films such as *The Color Purple* illustrate, sometimes subversive readings of a text can occur as viewers actively tease out the parts of the narrative that give them pleasure and those that do not. As indicated by a number of comments, Black fans of *Scandal* perceive Olivia to be a complex character, and some find the romance between she and Fitz thrilling to watch—even if it is perceived as inappropriate, it elicits multifaceted feelings (Warner 2015b).

Although the majority of texts from fans I examined did not critique the show's characterization of Olivia as a "whore" in "It's Handled" or in other episodes, some *Scandal* fans were critical and questioned why she was characterized as such:

Olivia is a whore? Oh Shonda NOOOO!!! #AskScandal #Scandal

But [why] she got to be a whore, though? #scandal

These examples illustrate moments when some fans are jarred by the narrative choices of Rhimes as the primary writer and producer for the series. These fans question the description of Olivia as a "whore," but do not direct their comments to Rhimes by including her Twitter user name in their tweets (@shondarhimes); however, others did, and often included Washington, other actors, program writers, and ABC's publicity staff. In their tweets, fans commented on what they perceived to be an "obsession" with the word "whore"—as it reappeared several times during season 3:

Can't believe that @shondarhimes has reduced the powerful female lead of her show to be called whore repeatedly, such garbage writing.

Do you @ScandalWriters get a kick out of having Mellie call Liv whore? It seems that way. It is not funny or cool to the fans. #Olitz.

@shondarhimes Sigh, and now we see why Olivia Pope is written so hor-
ribly and called a whore on a weekly basis. #ShondaNotHere4Olivia

Other fans implored those associated with the production of the show
to stop using the word:

@darbysofficial @shondarhimes can we please cease referring to Olivia
as a whore?

@kerrywashington @scandalwriters @shondarhimes Stop using the word
whore! she is a educated beautiful, intelligent, business woman

Fans who voiced outrage at the use of the word often called it an "ugly"
term and questioned why it was being used by Rhimes. The general tenor
of fans critical of the discourses used in reference to Olivia's relationship
with Fitz appeared to be that of frustration. For them, the issues were,
first, that Olivia is a dynamic character who cannot be reduced to the
label "whore" and, second, that the use of the word itself is a problem.

Non-viewing Anti-fans' Politics of Viewing: Washington and Black Women Deserve Better

The primary criticism lodged against *Scandal* by anti-fans who do not
watch the show is that Washington's character perpetuates the image of
a Black woman as a "side chick." Boylorn (2014) describes the side chick
as the twenty-first-century manifestation of the Jezebel archetype—a
seductress who purposefully, and without shame, "steals" men from
other women. "Side chick" is a racially coded term used almost exclusively to refer to women of color engaged in romantic relationships with
men who already have wives or girlfriends. Within the confines of this
form of relationship, Black women "are limited to booty calls and late
night texts, are expected to play their position (never interfering with
a mans 'real relationship')" (Boylorn 2014: n.p.). The nature of the relationship is such that Black women—both the girlfriend and the "side
chick"—are devalued and at the disposal of Black men.

For non-viewer anti-fans, the reasons why the depiction of Washington's character touches a nerve are not always articulated. However,

when reasons are given they tend to revolve around two points: first, the expectation that Washington would be given a "better" character to portray and, second, the potential influence the show's narrative of infidelity will have on Black women. With respect to the first point, as illustrated by the tweets that follow, anti-fans voice frustration that an actress of Washington's caliber is playing the role of "side chick":

> Random: I cannot get down with #Scandal because it reduces a powerful, capable, intelligent woman too incapable of avoiding side-piece status.

> My Blackness will not allow me to watch Scandal. It's crazy that in order for a Black actress to blow up she has to play a side chick

> Kerry Washington deserves better than being the most famous side-piece on TV #Scandal.

> Kerry Washington would be far more interesting to me on TV if she were the president's wife and not his side piece. I just can't watch.

These anti-fans see the role of Olivia Pope as a disservice to Washington, and thus a missed opportunity to go beyond an overused archetype.

Although anti-fans tend not to directly mention Shonda Rhimes as the creator, producer, and primary writer for the show, or ABC as the distributor of the show, in their tweets, I would suggest that these parties are implied within some of the comments like those offered above as examples. As the first network drama—and at the time of the third season still the only such drama—to feature a Black woman in a lead role, there were expectations that the program would provide a different type of portrayal than that found in other genres in which Black women have been visible, mainly situation comedies and reality television. These expectations likely stem from the presence of Rhimes as the creative figurehead for the program. As a Black woman making television, Rhimes is inevitably subject to what Mercer calls the burden of representation: "if there is only one Black voice in the public discourse it is assumed that that voice 'speaks for' and thereby 'represents' the many voices and viewpoints of the entire community that is marginalized from the means of representation in society" (1994: 91). By virtue of being one of the

few Black women working in the television industry creating and producing content, Rhimes is seen by some Black Americans as having an
obligation to craft characters and stories that are oppositional to the discourses embedded in television programs that make use of stereotyped
archetypes. Therefore, from the perspective of these non-viewer anti-
fans, Rhimes's use of Washington to portray a character who represents
a trope habitually portrayed in television programs with Black women
makes her complicit in reinforcing an image that is harmful to the Black
community.

The potential social impact of the depiction of Olivia Pope as Fitz's
"side chick" is the second reason Black anti-fans provide for their displeasure with *Scandal*. Anti-fans express concern that the show glorifies
cheating and that Black women viewers will look up to Olivia as a role
model. For example, anti-fans tweeted the following:

> I hope girls don't seriously want to be like Olivia Pope. She's basically the
> other woman. Don't ever become the side chick. #Scandal

> it's crazy how females watch Scandal and want to be the side chick
> whyyyy haha

> Watching #Scandal you shouldn't want to be the side chick . . . Just saying!

What these comments suggest, is that Black women are easily influenced
by the images that they consume. Anti-fans, by virtue of expressing the
hypothetical societal ramifications of *Scandal*, situate themselves as
doing a public service by pointing out the consequences of condoning
and not confronting the show's depiction of infidelity. Such anti-fans
vocalize their belief in the effects that media can have on others, but
likely do not see themselves as being susceptible to the same effects by
virtue of their awareness of the power media wield. Essentially, Black
anti-fans' articulated concern for Black women fans of the program is
rooted in the third person effect (Perloff 2009)—they perceive Black
women as vulnerable to influence by media, but see themselves as relatively unaffected.

Black women fans of *Scandal* who live-tweet the show are cognizant
of the discourse circulated about them by anti-fans. Addressing these

anti-fans indirectly, fans voice being exasperated by the "side chick" conversation, commenting:

> Let us pray that everyone can, this season, keep their misogynistic ass musings to themselves #Scandal

> The only bad thing about #ScandalIsBack is the whole oh y'all aspiring to be sidechicks and down with swirl guaranteed to happen EACH WEEK

Fans actively speak in reference to anti-fans' commentary by offering counterarguments, as illustrated by the following:

> Kerry Washington is a role model. Not Olivia Pope. No one "looks up" to her character so stop w/ the all the side chicks watch Scandal bs.

> LMAO! Folk can be calm & collected about the contradictions in Walter White, but Olivia is a societal problem. Lol

In addition, fans also assert the multidimensionality of Olivia as a character, emphatically commenting, for instance, "And at this point if you are still reducing Scandal to the side chick plot you are a simpleton there are so many LAYERS!"

The viewing experience for Black fans, especially Black female fans, of *Scandal* is such that they are frequently prompted—by the proliferation of tweets from anti-fans—to justify the pleasure they derive from watching a show that in the view of some does not promote a "positive" image, and therefore does not fit within the framework of Black respectability politics. Respectability politics emerged in the early twentieth century in Black Baptist churches across the United States and asserted that it was the responsibility of every individual in the Black community to self-regulate and self-improve their behavior "along moral, educational, and economic lines" (Higginbotham 1993: 196). The aim of such politics both then and now has been to distance Blacks from the images perpetuated by racist stereotypes. Politics of respectability call on Black people to monitor their public behavior because it is viewed as having "the power to either refute or confirm stereotypical representations" (Higginbotham 1993: 196). Historically, discourses of respectability have tended to hold Black women accountable for the rise and fall of the entire race, since they were viewed as primarily responsible for raising families. Therefore, Black women had the responsibility to model moral behavior in public and private in order to ensure that the next generation of Black children grew up as respectable citizens.

In light of this background, anti-fans' criticism of Black women watching *Scandal* equate their fandom with actively "condoning" cheating and consequently undermining efforts to dismantle stereotypes about Black women and, by extension, the entire Black community. Such criticisms are born from an awareness of the panoptic gaze of others and how that gaze informs attitudes about Black Americans. Anti-fans, through their commentary, attempt to police Black women's consumption of the text in an effort to control public perception of the Black community. However, Black female fans of the series take issue with the presumption that because they watch *Scandal* they are doing potential harm to themselves or others in their community. Many actively reject the politics of viewing that are asserted by anti-fans as illustrated by the fact that they continue to watch the program, talk about it, and derive meaning and pleasure from it, and are willing to stand up against anti-fan criticism.

Conclusion

The season 3 premiere of *Scandal* generated important conversation among viewers and non-viewers of the program. Anti-fans voiced a politics of viewing that articulated disappointment in decisions made to portray Kerry Washington's character in a stereotyped way, and concern over the potential influence of *Scandal*'s representation of Black womanhood. Ultimately, however, rather than explicitly directing their criticisms to those involved in the production of the show, anti-fans place the burden of responsibility on *Scandal*'s Black female fans, asserting that by virtue of continuing to watch the program they are complicit in glorifying the image of Black women as "side chicks." In so doing, these anti-fans view Black female fans as thwarting efforts to dismantle public perception of Black women as immoral.

For their part, some Black fans' politics of viewing *Scandal* were rooted in the pleasure in the act of watching, reacting to, and discussing the show with other fans, and not about assessing or criticizing the program's depiction of Black womanhood. Instead, *Scandal* surfaced as a text in which they could escape and immerse themselves in the fast-paced plotlines and tawdry romance between Olivia and Fitz. For other fans, their pleasure in viewing was temporarily suspended during scenes in which Olivia was called a "whore." These fans' politics of viewing demonstrate the negotiation between pleasure and representational politics as they actively interrogate Olivia's characterization on the show, and direct their criticisms to Rhimes and others associated with crafting the program.

The findings that are presented here are in no way representative of the entirety of the viewing audience for *Scandal* in general, or Black American viewers and fans specifically. Instead, this chapter represents a snapshot of a particular segment of viewers and non-viewers who actively engage with the show by discussing and reacting to it online. My conceptualization of the politics of viewing—a discursive struggle over representations that takes place within counterpublic spaces that manifests online—is still in its early stages of development. However, a primary point I want to make is about the utility of the online space in which such politics are fought over. It has been argued that politics that manifest online are not politics, but instead exist passively as the mere circulation of content, opinions, and information. Jodi Dean is particularly critical of politics circulating as content online, asserting that such politics manifest as messages often with no direct receiver and as such cannot facilitate political resistance. To Dean, instead of engaged debate there is simply a multiplicity of voices that add to the flow of communication, "hoping that sufficient volume (whether in terms of number of contributions of the spectacular nature of a contribution) will give their contribution dominance of stickiness" (2005: 53). I concede that within the context of this study critical readings, opinions, and criticisms, as related to the politics of viewing *Scandal*, were often not directed toward specific individuals or parties, particularly those who could address concerns about the show as a cultural text. However, I would argue that the messages sent by both Black fans and anti-fans of the show are targeted; they are directed at a community of viewers and non-viewers who are present on Twitter during the broadcast of the program. Black fans and anti-fans tweet to an imagined, yet real, audience and often in doing so engage in the building of Black political thought through the act of "every day talk" (Harris-Lacewell 2004). In the twenty-first century, on-line debates like those over *Scandal*, are part of the common, everyday mediated practices that, while outside the sphere of politics proper, can be important to the deliberative process that constitutes the "critical work of constructing meaningful political worldviews" (Harris-Lacewell 2004: 2). Thus, Black fan and anti-fans' online struggle over representations of Black women on television should not be dismissed as politically inconsequential, but rather must be situated along a continuum of practices of ideological development, which serve as the building blocks for political consciousness and action.

NOTES

1 The first network drama to feature a Black woman in a lead role was NBC's *Get Christie Love!*, which aired for a season in 1974.

2 Programs that have predominately Black casts, feature storylines about Black cultural experiences, and are viewed by mostly Black audiences are often described as "Black programs."

3 The data collection process for this research could not have happened without the contributions made by Kevin Driscoll, François Bar, Alex Leavitt, and others from USC Annenberg School for Communication and Journalism. This research was also funded as part of the Norman Lear Center's Media Impact Project.

WORKS CITED

Ang, I 1985, *Watching Dallas: soap operas and the melodramatic imagination*, Methuen, London.

Bobo, J 1995, *Black women as cultural readers*, Colombia University Press, New York.

Boylorn, R 2014, "One the glorification of the side chick," *Gawker*, October 4, gawker.com.

Brock, A 2012, "From the Blackhand side: Twitter as cultural conversation," *Journal of Broadcasting & Electronic Media* 56: 529–49.

Clark, N 2015, "Connecting in the Scandalverse: the power of social media and parasocial relationships," in JV Pavlik (ed.), *Digital technology and the future of broadcasting: global perspectives*, Routledge, New York.

Coleman, RRM 2000, *African American viewers and the Black situation comedy: situating racial humor*, Garland, New York.

Collins, PH 2000, *Black feminist thought: knowledge, consciousness, and the politics of empowerment*, Routledge, New York.

Cornwell, NC & Orbe, MP 2002, "'Keepin' it real' and or 'sellin' out the man': African-American responses to Aaron McGruder's *The Boondocks*," in RM Coleman (ed.), *Say it loud! African-American audiences, media, and identity*, Routledge, New York.

Dean, J 2005, "Communicative capitalism: circulation and the foreclosure of politics," *Cultural Politics* 1: 51–74.

Desmond-Harris, J 2012, "'Scandal' exploits black women's images?" *The Root*, October 13, www.theroot.com.

Driscoll, K, Ananny, M, Bar, F, Guth, K, Kazemzadeh, A, Leavitt, A, & Thorson, K 2013, "Big bird, binders, and bayonets: humor and live-tweeting during the 2012 U.S. presidential debates," paper presented at the Association of Internet Researchers conference, Denver, CO, October 23–26.

Fiske, J 1992, "The cultural economy of fandom," in LA Lewis (ed.), *The adoring audience: fan culture and popular media*, Routledge, New York.

Fiske, J 1993, *Television culture*, Routledge, New York.

Florini, S 2014, "Tweets, tweeps, and signifyin': communication and cultural performance on 'Black Twitter,'" *Television & New Media* 15: 223–37.

Gray, J 2005, "Antifandom and the moral text: Television Without Pity and textual dislike," *American Behavioral Scientist* 48: 840–58.

Hall, S 1996, "New ethnicities," in K Chen & D Morley (eds.), *Stuart Hall: critical dialogues in cultural studies*, Routledge, London.

Harris-Lacewell, MV 2004, *Barbershops, bibles, and BET: everyday talk and black political thought*, Princeton University Press, Princeton, NJ.

Higginbotham, E 1993, *Righteous discontent: the women's movement in the black Baptist church, 1880–1920*, Harvard University Press, Cambridge, MA.

Inniss, LB, & Feagin JR 1995, "*The Cosby Show*: the view from the black middle class," *Journal of Black Studies* 25: 692–711.

Jenkins, H 2006, "Star Trek, rerun, reread, rewritten: fan writing as textual poaching," in *Fans, bloggers, and gamers: exploring participatory culture*, New York University Press, New York.

Maxwell, B 2013, "Olivia Pope and the scandal of representation," *Feminist Wire*, February 7, www.thefeministwire.com.

Mercer, K 1994, *Welcome to the jungle: new positions in black cultural studies*, Routledge, London.

Perloff, RM 2009, "Mass media, social perception, and the third-person effect," in B Jennings & D Zillman (eds.), *Media effects: Advances in theory and research*, Lawrence Erlbaum, Hillsdale, NJ.

Radway, J 1991, *Reading the romance: women, patriarchy, and popular literature*, University of North Carolina Press, Raleigh.

Squires, CR, 2000, "Black talk radio defining community needs and identity," *Harvard International Journal of Press/Politics* 5: 73–95.

Vega, T 2013, "A show makes friends and history," *New York Times*, January 16, www.nytimes.com.

Warner, KJ 2015a, "ABC's *Scandal* and black women's fandom," in E Levine (ed.), *Cupcakes, Pinterest, and lady porn: feminized popular culture in the twenty-first century*, University of Illinois Press, Urbana.

Warner, KJ 2015b, "If loving Olitz is wrong, I don't wanna be right," *Black Scholar: Journal of Black Studies and Research* 45: 16–20.

19

Deploying Oppositional Fandoms

Activists' Use of Sports Fandom in the Redskins Controversy

LORI KIDO LOPEZ AND JASON KIDO LOPEZ

Sports teams have long been called upon to stop the offensive and derogatory practice of using Native Americans as mascots, particularly when those mascots rely upon outdated and problematic stereotypes (King & Springwood 2001; Taylor 2013). Amid the hundreds of name-change battles that are being waged across the country, the refusal of the NFL's Washington Redskins to change their name stands out in a number of ways. First, the insistence of the professional football team in using a dictionary-defined slur makes it nearly impossible to defend the name as potentially reverent or respectful.[1] The team offers a clear example of the way that naming and the use of mascots reflect histories of oppression—in this case, the history of Native American genocide and the selling of scalps known as redskins. But the Redskins are also an important case to examine due to their tremendous size and visibility. Representing the US capital, the Redskins are a national franchise with an audience of millions, including the nearly eighty thousand ticket holders who occupy FedExField during games, as well as the viewers who tune in to national telecasts of NFL games every season. Indeed, football is the most popular sport in the United States, and broadcasts of NFL games are the most popular programs on television (Bibel 2014).

While the Washington Redskins serve as an exemplary case of an offensively named sports franchise, owner Daniel Snyder offers an equally exemplary case of holding firm and resisting change. In May 2013, he said in an interview with *USA Today*, "We'll never change the name. It's that simple. NEVER—you can use caps" (Brady 2013). Snyder has stood strong amid an outpouring of criticism and anti-Redskins activism. Since 2013, this has included the stripping of their legal trademark by the US Patent and Trademark Office, the refusals of over forty news organizations to use their name in the media, as well as outspoken condemnation from over ninety Native American tribes and organizations, fifty US senators, and a list of notable celebrities and influencers that includes President Barack Obama (ChangetheMascot.org n.d.). Yet Snyder insists that their fans support the name staying the same, claiming it is a symbol of pride that reflects their history of honoring Native Americans.

Given the extremely offensive nature of the team's name and stubbornness of the team's owner, Native American activist groups have taken up the cause of getting the Redskins name changed. Indeed, the burden seems to fall to them since organized efforts to change the name have not been seen to originate from Redskins fans. This raises the question of what relationship Native American name-change activists have to sports fans more broadly, including fans of the Redskins, the NFL, and sports in general. In this chapter we examine how the controversies surrounding this particular Native American mascot provide an important site for considering the ways that activists can potentially work with, around, or in spite of sports fandoms.

Our research is based on interviews with representatives from the Oneida Nation and the National Coalition Against Racism in Sports and Media and analysis of their actions and strategies. This includes in particular a close reading of the eight radio spots from the 2013–14 Change the Mascot campaign and the media coverage that followed those spots. Although much media studies research finds fans to be the ideal candidates to enlist as allies in the battle for social change, sports fans are a unique kind of audience that demands new theorizing as to their relationship to activism and social justice organizing. By examining what forces push up against the fans, and by breaking from fan studies' dominant framing of fans as progressive political actors to instead examine an instance in which fans are the object upon which progressive activists must act, we aim to broaden the field's picture of fan politics and activism. We argue that sports fans must be understood as participating in "oppositional fandoms," or fandoms that are temporarily defined by their position in opposition to another fandom. This positioning creates a mobile and dynamic set of affective identifications that can be a double-edged sword for social justice activists—serving as a potential opportunity for fans to meaningfully engage with social justice issues, as the dominant view in fan studies goes, while also risking digging in against change. This investigation also reminds us that activists must pay particular attention to the environments in which fandoms are being engaged in order to solicit political support effectively, as not all fandom environments are created equal. What we ultimately see through this case is that despite the bad reputation of many sports fandoms, sport cultures can in fact provide a potentially transformative context for shifting the national discourse on significant social justice issues.

The Power of Fan Activism

Scholarship on fan activism often theorizes and celebrates the potential for fans to use their affective relationships and fannish undertakings in service of social justice activism, or intentionally working to rectify a broader injustice or inequality that extends beyond the realm of the fan object. Fan-based activist organizations such as Racebending.com, Nerdfighters, the Harry Potter Alliance, the Browncoats, Lady Gaga's Little Monsters, and the Colbert Nation have all demonstrated the ways in which fandom can provide a useful set of skills for collectively agitating toward political causes (Lopez 2011; Kligler-Vilenchik et al. 2012; Jenkins 2014; Cochran 2012; Bennett 2014; Burwell & Boler 2008). As Henry Jenkins and Sangita Shresthova (2012: n.p.) argue in their introduction to an edited journal issue on fan activism, "insofar as a growing number of fans are exploring how they might translate their capacities for analysis, networking, mobilization, and communication into campaigns for social change, we support expanding the field of fan studies to deal with this new mode of civic engagement." These investigations of activist collectives echo the progressive and celebratory orientation of early fan scholarship, where studies of active readers argued that fans have the ability to rewrite and repurpose even the most sexist or racist components of a beloved text (Radway 1984; Jenkins 1992). While such studies remind us that fandoms have long been seen to offer a productive site for marginalized audiences such as women and queer folks to build community and develop their voices, here we expand our consideration to include the way that activists are also working with and against fandoms.

We must also note the many fandoms that are rooted in racism, or that organize to promote racist ideologies and actions (Wanzo 2015). Prominent examples of these are in the complaints of fans who are upset at the casting of African Americans in roles that were presumed to be for white actors, such as Amandla Stenberg as Rue in *The Hunger Games*, Idris Elba as the Norse god Heimdall in *Thor*, Michael B. Jordan as the Human Torch in *Fantastic Four*, and many others. Hate-based fandoms such as those of White Power music have also been seen to organize around the promotion and spread of racist ideologies (Corte & Edwards 2008). These examples remind us that fandom itself is a politically neutral endeavor; any collective of engaged individuals can organize their cooperative efforts toward a cause that is larger than their own specific fandom. As such, it is important to theorize the ways that activists are negotiating their desire for progressive social change in relation to these fandoms.

Although we rarely see coordinated efforts such as these emerging from sports fans, they are nonetheless commonly considered to fall within the category of "bad fandoms." A naïve characterization might simply condemn the sports fan as simple-minded, brutish, or prone to emotional outbursts, while more extreme criticism has often posited a connection between sports fandom and violent, misogynistic, racist, or homophobic attitudes and behaviors. Indeed, much scholarship on sports fandom has served to uphold the latter, with scholars exploring the way that sports fans' enjoyment of the sport can be tied to violence and may even increase as player aggressiveness increases (Bryant, Zillmann, & Raney 1998). Others have found that reveling in violence on the field can lead to violence off the field (Lanter 2011; Roberts & Benjamin, 2000). The conception of sports fans as violent is especially concerning when it is combined with problematic attitudes toward disenfranchised populations such as people of color, women, and queer communities (Love & Hughey 2015; Cleland 2014; Kian et al. 2011). While these findings are indeed worrisome, we caution that they should not be taken to represent all sports fans—as with all fan collectives, sports fans are obviously heterogeneous and need not be roundly condemned. Yet they do offer a powerful and common representation of sports fans.

This conception differs from the other "non-bad" fandoms mentioned above and offers an important site for further exploring the relationship between fans and activists. While many fandoms might seem particularly useful to activists in the fight for social justice, sports fans are not often viewed this way. This offers an opportunity to explore how it could still be the case that activists can engage with sports fans as they work toward their cause. In examining the way that activists have approached the Redskins controversy, we can more clearly understand the strengths and drawbacks of deploying sports fans toward activist causes.

The Change the Mascot Movement

The football team that is now the Washington Redskins originated as an NFL franchise called the Boston Braves in 1932. To avoid confusion with the Braves baseball team they soon changed their name to the Redskins, and in 1937 they moved to their current home in Washington, D.C. Their history has been rife with racial controversy, starting with the fact that the claimed Indian ancestry of their original owner, William Henry Dietz, has long been contested. More significantly, the Washington Redskins were the last NFL team to integrate. Owner George Preston Marshall was a famously outspoken racist, and he refused to draft any African Americans to the team until the government stepped in and threatened to cancel their stadium's lease in 1962 (Smith 1987). Although they eventually began to diversify their roster, protests against the racist epithet embodied by their name and logo have fallen on deaf ears since as early as 1973. Indeed, notable protests by Native Americans demanding a name change have been documented every decade since, most often when the Redskins rose to national prominence by playing in a Super Bowl. Their battle is just one of many, as there have been hundreds of struggles over Native American sports mascots and team names waged across the country at all levels, including professional, college, and high school teams (Davis-Delano 2007; Hofmann 2005).

This is the context into which Native American activists reinvigorated a battle over the name in 2013. It was a conversation initiated decades ago that had been fought, and continued to be fought, by many different organizations and political entities—including the National Congress of American Indians, the National Coalition Against Racism in Sports and Media, the American Indian Movement, and others. Here we focus primarily on the strategies of the Oneida Indian Nation and their campaign called Change the Mascot, which was inspired by the actions of high school students in nearby Cooperstown who petitioned to change their mascot to something other than Redskins. Sensing that the success of these young activists reflected a shifting political climate with regard to this persistent issue, members of the Oneida Indian Nation began organizing around the single issue of changing the name of the Washington Redskins. Many activists believed that if they could cut off the head of the snake—the most visible offender, the biggest franchise— others across the country would be forced to follow suit, or at least be weakened in their defenses.

The crux of the activists' strategy was to follow the Redskins along on their road games and buy radio slots in every city. Radio advertisements were relatively cheap in comparison to national television spots, and they could be flexible in shaping their message as the season progressed. These sixty-second spots incorporated responses to relevant issues within the sports world, tying together issues that were already being discussed in news media to the demand for a name change. For instance, in August 2013, Philadelphia Eagles wide receiver Riley Cooper was caught on tape using a slur against African Americans. Change the Mascot immediately incorporated the response of NFL Commissioner Roger Goodell into their radio advertisements, commending Goodell for doing the right thing in saying that "racial language is obviously wrong, insensitive, and unacceptable." The radio ad then transitioned to the voice of Oneida Nation Leader Ray Halbritter, who states that with the Eagles playing the Washington Redskins in the next game, Goodell has the opportunity to now denounce the name Redskins by using the same words he used to describe the Eagles player. As the message concludes, "we do not deserve to be called Redskins, we deserve to be treated as what we are, which is Americans." This strategy proved effective in garnering wider media coverage, as a *Washington Post* article commented that "at least four national programs this week transitioned pretty quickly from comments about Riley Cooper to comments about the Redskins' team name" (Steinberg 2013). A new radio spot was created for each away game, so after Washington's opener in Green Bay, Wisconsin, activists moved on to Oakland, Dallas, Denver, and Minneapolis. Their carefully crafted messages included discussions of the hurtful nature of the epithet, the support for change from the country's leading voices, the racist history of the team, and the history-making nature of their campaign. These media-centered actions were also supplemented with protests that were often staged in conjunction with other Native American organizations. For instance, during the Vikings game, in a state with thirteen Indian tribes, a number of Native organizations came together in a massive game-day protest with between four and five thousand participants that drew national media coverage (Cox 2014).

Alongside their radio spots, Change the Mascot also created a number of videos to convey their message. One was called "Proud to Be" and shows contemporary and historical images of Native Americans while a narrator lists words such as "proud, forgotten, Indian, Navajo, Blackfoot, Inuit, Sioux, underserved, struggling, resilient, rancher, teacher, doctor, soldier, unyielding, strong, indomitable." It ends with the statement, "Native Americans call themselves many things. The one thing they don't . . ." before fading to an image of the Redskins helmet. The two-minute video was released on YouTube days before the Super Bowl in 2014, and was labeled by the *Huffington Post* "the most important Super Bowl ad you didn't see" (Irwin 2014). The video did end up being shown on television four months later, when a California tribe called the Yocha Dehe Wintun Nation paid for the advertisement to run in seven major cities during halftime of the NBA finals, where it was exposed to over fifteen million viewers. Publicity for this video has also flourished online through social media, and the version posted to YouTube by the National Congress of American Indians has over three million views.

Environments of Sports Fandom

The strategies deployed by name-change activists reflect a complicated understanding of sports fans and the role that they might play in organizing around this cause. First, we can consider the fact that Redskins fans themselves have not been seen taking up a leadership role in challenging the racism of their team's name or branding. Although there are dozens of groups and pages on Facebook devoted to fans who want to keep the Redskins name the same, it is difficult to find much solidarity around a slogan such as "love the team, hate the name," which would reflect a fan's participation in name-change activism.[2] When asked if they had any football fans as part of their name-change movement, one name-change activist simply stated that they did not. This does not mean that such fans do not exist—and with such a large regional fan base, it is safe to assume there are indeed fans with widely varying positions on the name—but the lack of fan participation is striking for two reasons. First, we can see that it does not align with much of the previous research on fan activism that shows how the passion of fans can meaningfully be redirected toward social justice causes when it comes to the treatment of a favored franchise. Moreover, in this particular case, converting fans into name-change activists could be a potentially powerful move. Snyder's desire to keep the name is strong, but it seems clear that preserving the name would be unwise in the face of his team's own fans calling for change. All football franchises are simply businesses, and businesses must respond to consumer demands. This would seem to be an opportune moment to utilize fans as consumer-activists and leverage their buying power into a political demand that must be addressed. Yet this has not happened.

On the contrary, the narratives that are consistently propagated position activists as being in opposition to fans, with frequent media coverage of the hostile interactions between activists and fans. For instance, an episode of the *Daily Show* in 2014 was framed as "controversial" because it invited Redskins fans to actually speak to Native Americans, and was rumored to descend into yelling and name calling. The segment that aired was edited so that it remained lighthearted (albeit uncomfortable), cutting away from what news reports later said became so intense and threatening that one person called the police (Williams 2014). This narrative is upheld in conversations with activists, who admit nervousness around staging any events near FedExField. One activist stated:

> A reporter friend of mine once said to me, the way you're going to end this is show up at the stadium on a game day. We've always been like, the fans are great. He's like, the fans aren't great—they're gonna be drunk and throw a bottle at you. [. . .] At the height of this, [the stadium] was a powder keg. If we would have shown up there it would have been a riot.

Both the suggestion of the reporter and the activist's response are telling with regard to the assumptions being made—the sports fans are expected to respond with violence that would endanger the safety of the activists.

Although this assumption about how such an interaction would play out may be unfounded, it is important to consider the environment in which sports fandom takes place and how it facilitates or limits the potential to turn sports fans into activists. In many ways, sports fandom is similar to other types of fandom that take place within rowdy social arenas such as comic conventions or live musical concerts. These carnivalesque environments offer spaces for play and experimentation with one's identity, such as face painting or donning a costume that frees the fan to behave in ways that might otherwise be deemed unacceptable (Lamerichs 2014). These are also spaces of heightened emotion, where random screaming can lead to a collective cheer among the crowd, or where one could be moved to tears of joy or frustration. Yet sports fandom often incorporates additional elements that lead to a particularly combustible set of factors. First, as noted in the reporter's suggestion, there is a lively culture of alcohol consumption that surrounds sports fandom.[3] When coupled with the heightened emotional climate of a space where passionate fans are celebrating or bemoaning their team's performance, the culture of drinking alcohol can lead to serious consequences—in fact, the prevalence of alcohol-fueled disorderly conduct, assaults, arrests, and ejections is one reason for the banning of alcohol sales at most collegiate football games throughout the country (Glassman et al. 2007; Rees & Schnepel 2009). In the environment of the sports arena, it is not uncommon to witness what Foster, Hyatt, and Julien (2012) call the "dysfunctional fan" who engages in confrontational behaviors such as getting in fights with other fans or drinking to excess, as well as fans who engage in the negative rhetorical practices of complaining, obsessing about performances, verbally confronting other fans, and otherwise being obnoxious. They argue that such behaviors must be attributed not only to individual personalities, but to the institutional and social setting of sports fandom itself.

But the aspect of sports fandom that seems most relevant within the strategies of Change the Mascot activism is the structure of pitting one contingent of fans against the other. As Vivi Theodoropoulou (2007) argues, sports fans can often be considered anti-fans in the sense that their love for their own team is often positioned against their hatred of a rival team. While Theodoropoulou focuses on the existence of long-standing rivalries between two teams, here we consider that many sports matches—including football, baseball, basketball, soccer, and others—are premised on opposition. Even in the absence of a specific long-standing rivalry, at every single matchup fans enter the stadium positioned in opposition to fans of the competing team. This kind of oppositional fandom marks a particularly dynamic form of anti-fandom that is structured by the competitive structure of sports like football, which pit the object of one's fandom temporarily against a distinct enemy and its contingent of fans. We define oppositional fandom as a temporary positioning of one's fandom in direct competition to an opponent, as we commonly see within sports fandoms. This opposition serves to deepen one's identification and allegiance (to one's own team), but is also characterized by a larger fandom of the competition that unites the two opponents (to the sport, or to sports itself). Lloyd Sloan (1989) notes not only that fans' affective responses to the emotion of the game parallel those of the athletes, but that the fans themselves become winners and losers depending on the outcome of the game. In this sense, an attack on a fan's sports team feels like a personal attack because fandoms are divided into binary oppositions of "us" versus "them," and each fandom must defend themselves against the other (Boyle & Haynes 2000). When we take this oppositional fandom into consideration, we can even more clearly see the volatility of the specific environment of the football stadium on game day—fans who are passionate about their own team's success, who have perhaps overindulged in judgment-impairing beverages, and who are in an environment that is commonly populated by disruption and emotional outburst are also congregating in a space where they are primed to see opposition as a direct threat. It is not a coincidence that we often see news stories about violence between fans breaking out in the stadium. Furthermore, as Cornel Sandvoss (2003) notes, many sports fans mistakenly view their fandom as apolitical. An incursion of politics could certainly be seen as a threat not only to themselves and the team, but to their entire conception of sports. Amid this environment of fandom, any critique of the Redskins franchise that is directed toward Redskins fans could simply be lumped together as another form of opposition that must be resisted and repulsed at all costs—perhaps even through violence. Thus, despite the fact that turning Redskins fans against their own name or their owner's decisions would clearly strengthen the name-change movement, the particular environment of the stadium on game day may not be conducive to changing minds.

Utilizing Oppositional Fandoms

Yet this does not mean that sports fans are a lost cause when it comes to political engagement. On the contrary, all of the reasons why it might be ineffective to solicit support for the name-change at FedExField during Redskins home games might strengthen the potential to activate fans of the other thirty-one NFL teams during away games. Indeed, we can see that the lessons learned from considering the environments of fandom as well as the strengths of oppositional fandom have both been strategically utilized by name-change activists in order to bolster their movement. Despite the fact that one fan base is positioned against the other fan base, both are united under the banner of the sport they are watching. Thus, even sports fans who boo one other on game day can be seen to identify with one another in some sense; at its root, their opposition to one another is inspired and sanctioned by a larger shared fandom.

We can see an understanding of this aspect of oppositional fandom in the use of radio advertisements in cities to which the Redskins traveled. The strategy of following the Redskins around the country can be seen as a deliberate appeal to the oppositional fandoms of local football fans. Fans of the Green Bay Packers throughout Wisconsin, for instance, would have been particularly susceptible to taking up an anti-Redskins position on the week that the Washington Redskins were coming to town. Opposition to the Redskins, which would make annoyance with the team's racist name an even easier sell, would be a natural position to take up in that moment. The same would be true for Raiders fans in Oakland two weeks later, or Cowboys fans in Dallas the week after that. Amid a climate where it was estimated that 71 percent of the country overall did not support a name change (ESPN 2014), activists recognized they were fighting an uphill battle and that gaining any political ground was important. This means that convincing any NFL fans that the Redskins name was racist could be considered a gain, even if the ultimate goal of changing the name was not necessarily a desire of these oppositional fans (as such a correction might actually make their opponents seem less racist). Playing upon the natural proclivities of sports fans to take up positions against their opponents was one way of bolstering the number of sports fans across the country who would readily agree to the fact that the word "redskins" could even be considered a problem.

We can also see that the tactic of using radio advertisements as the primary vehicle for the name-change activists' political message takes the environment of fandom into consideration. Rather than attempting to convince sports fans of their cause in the space of their home stadium, activists conveyed their message to those who were listening to the radio while they were in their cars, at work, or in their homes. Moreover, through the earned coverage that their campaign was able to garner in a wide range of outlets—including local and national newspaper stories; sports magazines such as *Sports Illustrated*; sports websites such as Grantland.com, ESPN.com, and FoxSports.com; the radio programs *Mike and Mike* and the *Jim Rome Show*; and the television shows *First Take, His and Hers*, and the *Dan Patrick Show*—the distribution of their messaging continued well beyond these radio spots to reach a diverse and multifaceted audience of sports fans. Each of these forms of mediated messaging can then be consumed in an environment that potentially allows for more deliberative or thoughtful engagement than the rowdy, competitive arena of the stadium.

Furthermore, as we have seen above, sports fandom involves more than simply having an opponent or being set against outsiders—it also includes a positive identification as fans of the NFL, or of sports in general. This broader fannish identification offers important opportunities for activists, as NFL fans who do not root for the Redskins and sports fans who do not follow the NFL nevertheless both offer potential allies in the fight to change the Redskins name. They are removed enough not to take the activists as outsiders who are attacking their team, but connected enough to the league or to sports to identify with the embarrassment of the Redskins name. This larger utilization of an affective connection to sports fandom can be seen at work in the airing of the "Proud to Be" spot during the NBA Finals. This commercial was clearly meant to address sports fans, as it was aired during a major sports telecast whose audience ostensibly included fans of professional basketball and of the San Antonio and Miami teams who were competing. Although these specific sets of fans might not fall into a strongly oppositional position against football or the Redskins, we can still see this strategic positioning relying on some of the same principles—the targeting of those who are fans of sports, but who are not necessarily fans of football or the Redskins. It is their fandom and interest in sports that make the NBA Finals a more appropriate time to solicit support for the Redskins name change than other non-sports media events with high viewership, such as the Emmys or a presidential debate. Given the strategies of the name-change activists and the insights of oppositional fandom, even though FedExField might not be the most useful site for the activists to engage with Redskins fans, there exists a resource of NFL fans in thirty-one other stadiums, and of sports fans more generally around the country. Of course there may be other impediments within those environments, but the enthusiasm of oppositional fandom is nevertheless a valuable resource for fan activism.

Conclusion: The Results of Oppositional Fandom

Although Snyder has not yet budged on the name of the team, name-change activists have made important gains through their deployment of oppositional fandom. First, they have clearly renewed national interest in this issue of Native American mascots, with countless discussions taking place across news outlets, sports television programs, and social media, as well as within legislative sessions, boardrooms, schools, and homes. Second, they have managed to catch the attention of Snyder. In a rather misguided attempt to assuage activists, Snyder founded an organization called the Washington Redskins Original Americans Foundation. A letter to fans describing the work of this organization includes descriptions from his travels to reservations:

> The stories I heard and the experiences I witnessed were of children without winter coats or athletic shoes; students in makeshift classrooms without adequate school supplies; text books more than decades old; rampant and unnecessary suffering from preventable diseases like diabetes; economic hardship almost everywhere; and in too many places too few of the tools and technology that we all take for granted every day—computers, internet access, even cellphone coverage. (Snyder 2014)

He proposed to donate millions of dollars to reservations in order to combat these problems. As might be expected, this organization was roundly lambasted for simply attempting to pay off Native Americans to stop complaining about the name and almost immediately ceased functioning when tribes started refusing to take his money (Cox 2015).

Yet it seems that Snyder has finally been convinced to consider, to some degree, the lives and experiences of his team's supposed namesake.

Finally, through the rich and multifaceted coverage that this controversy has aroused, we can begin to see that Snyder's recognition is part of a broader trend. There is certainly a lot of work to be done in effectively mobilizing such discourse into meaningful action, but name-change activists have played an important role in pushing this dialogue forward and garnering national support in doing so. The groundswell created through name-change activism has provided the ideal context for actually discussing the needs of Native Americans across the country.

Using the appeal, accessibility, and widespread popularity of sport, these debates around the Washington Redskins provide a strong example of how activists can leverage a fannish engagement with sports franchises into discussions of political importance. As the scope of conversation about sports widens to include off-the-field issues such as domestic violence, drug and alcohol use, poverty, sexual orientation and gender identity, labor issues, and incarceration, activists working in these areas can use the particularities of sports fandom to aid their causes. In this way, sports remain an increasingly important arena in which to ask what it means to be a fan, what kinds of activities fans are participating in, and what the political implications are for these different forms of engagement.

NOTES

1   While some believe that the use of any Native American imagery or peoples as mascots is an offensive practice, others believe the use of words like "Chiefs" or "Warriors" is potentially respectful.

2   One website briefly promised free "love the team, hate the name" bumper stickers (www.lovetheteam.com), but these were supplied by a Native American organization, and it is unclear if the site originated from actual fans.

3   For evidence of the meaningful relationship between alcohol and sport, we can turn to the entire edited issue of *International Review for the Sociology of Sport* in 2014 that focused on research on alcohol within the field of sociology of sport.

WORKS CITED

Bennett, L 2014, "'If we stick together we can do anything': Lady Gaga fandom, philanthropy and activism through social media," *Celebrity Studies* 5(1–2): 138–52.

Bibel, S 2014, "NFL 2013 TV recap: 205 million fans tuned in; 34 of 35 most watched shows this fall," *TV By the Numbers*, January 8, tvbythenumbers.zap2it.com.

Boyle, R & Haynes, R 2000, *Power play: sport, the media, and popular culture*, Edinburgh University Press, Edinburgh.

Brady, E 2013, "Daniel Snyder says Redskins will never change name," *USA Today*, May 10, www.usatoday.com.

Bryant, J, Zillmann, D, & Raney, AA 1998, "Violence and enjoyment of media sport," in LA Wenner (ed.), *Media sport*, Routledge, New York.

Burwell, C & Boler, M 2008, "Calling on the Colbert Nation: fandom, politics and parody in an age of media convergence," *Electronic Journal of Communication* 18, www.cios.org.

ChangetheMascot.org n.d., "Supporters of change," www.changethemascot.org.

Cleland, J 2014, "Racism, football fans, and online message boards: how social media has added a new dimension to racist discourse in English football," *Journal of Sport and Social Issues* 38: 415–31.

Cochran, TR 2012, "'Past the brink of tacit support': fan activism and the Whedonverses," *Transformative Works and Cultures* 10, journal.transformativeworks.org.

Corte, U & Edwards, B 2008, "White power music and the mobilization of racist social movements," *Music and Arts in Action* 1(1): 4–20.

Cox, JW 2014, "In Minnesota, thousands of Native Americans protest Redskins' name," *Washington Post*, November 2, www.washingtonpost.com.

Cox, JW 2015, "Native American tribe votes to reject $25,000 offered by Washington Redskins foundation," *Washington Post*, August 5, www.washingtonpost.com.

Davis-Delano, L 2007, "Eliminating Native American mascots: ingredients for success," *Journal of Sport and Social Issues* 31(4): 340–73.

ESPN 2014, "Poll: 71 percent say keep Redskins," September 2, espn.go.com.

Foster, W, Hyatt, C, & Julien, M 2012, "'Pronger you ignorant ape . . . I hope you fall off space mountain!': a study of the institutional work of sports fans," in AC Earnheardt, P Haridakis, & B Hugenberg (eds.), *Sports fans, identity, and socialization: exploring the fandemonium*, Lexington, Lanham, MD.

Glassman, T, Werch, C, Jobli, E, & Bian, H 2007, "Alcohol-related fan behavior on college football game day," *Journal of American College Health* 56(3): 255–60.

Hofmann, S 2005, "The elimination of indigenous mascots, logos, and nicknames: organizing on college campuses," *American Indian Quarterly* 29(1/2): 156–77.

Irwin, B 2014, "The most important Super Bowl ad you didn't see," *Huffington Post*, February 3, www.huffingtonpost.com.

Jenkins, H 1992, *Textual poachers: television fans and participatory culture*, Routledge, New York.

Jenkins, H 2014, "Fan activism as participatory politics: the case of the Harry Potter Alliance," in M Ratto & M Boler (eds.), *DIY citizenship: critical making and social media*, MIT Press, Cambridge, MA.

Jenkins, H & Shresthova, S 2012, "Up, up, and away! The power and potential of fan activism," *Transformative Works and Cultures* 10, journal.transformativeworks.org.

Kian, EM, Clavio, G, Vincent, J, & Shaw, SD 2011, "Homophobic and sexist yet uncontested: examining football fan postings on Internet message boards," *Journal of Homosexuality* 58(5): 680–99.

King, RC, & Springwood, CF 2001, *Team spirits: the Native American mascots controversy*, University of Nebraska Press, Lincoln.

Kligler-Vilenchik, N, McVeigh-Schultz, J, Weitbrecht, C, & Tokuhama, C 2012, "Experiencing fan activism: understanding the power of fan activist organizations through members' narratives," *Transformative Works and Cultures* 10, journal. transformativeworks.org.

Lamerichs, N 2014, "Costuming as subculture: the multiple bodies of cosplay," *Scene* 2: 113–25.

Lanter, JR 2011, "Spectator identification with the team and participation in celebratory violence," *Journal of Sports Behavior* 34(3): 268–80.

Lopez, LK 2011, "Fan activists and the politics of race in *The Last Airbender*," *International Journal of Cultural Studies* 15(5): 431–45.

Love, A & Hughey, MW 2015, "Out of bounds? Racial discourse on college basketball message boards," *Ethnic and Racial Studies* 38(6): 877–93.

Palmer, C 2014, "Introduction to special issue on sport and alcohol: on the contemporary agenda of research on alcohol within the sociology of sport," *International Review for the Sociology of Sport* 49: 3–4.

Radway, J 1984, *Reading the romance: women, patriarchy, and popular literature*, University of North Carolina Press, Chapel Hill.

Rees, D & Schnepel, K 2009, "College football games and crime," *Journal of Sports Economics* 10(1): 68–87.

Roberts, J & Benjamin, C 2000, "Spectator violence in sports: a North American perspective," *European Journal on Criminal Policy and Research* 8(2): 163–81.

Sandvoss, C 2003, *A game of two halves: football, television, and globalization*, Routledge, New York.

Sloan L 1989, "The motives of sports fans," in JH Goldstein (ed.), *Sports, games, and play: social and psychological viewpoints*, Psychology Press, New York.

Smith, T 1987, "Civil rights on the gridiron: the Kennedy administration and the desegregation of the Washington Redskins," *Journal of Sport History* 14(2): 189–208.

Snyder, D 2014, "Letter from Dan Snyder," Washington Redskins Original Americans Foundation, March 24, www.washingtonredskinsoriginalamericansfoundation.org.

Steinberg, D 2013, "From Riley Cooper to 'Redskins,'" *Washington Post*, August 2, www. washingtonpost.com.

Taylor, M 2013, *Contesting constructed Indian-ness: the intersection of the frontier, masculinity and whiteness in Native American mascot representations*, Lexington, Lanham, MD.

Theodoropoulou, V 2007, "The anti-fan within the fan: awe and envy in sport fandom," In J Gray, C Sandvoss, & CL Harrington (eds.), *Fandom: identities and communities in a mediated world*, New York University Press, New York.

Wanzo, R 2015, "African American acafandom and other strangers: new genealogies of fan studies," *Transformative Works and Cultures* 20, journal.transformativeworks.org.

Williams, ME 2014, "What 'The Daily Show's' Redskins segment didn't show," *Salon*, September 29, www.salon.com.

PART V

Fan Labor and Fan-Producer Interactions

20

Ethics of Fansubbing in Anime's Hybrid Public Culture

MIZUKO ITO

Editors' Note: this chapter reprints a significant portion of "Contributors v. Leechers: Fansubbing Ethics and a Hybrid Public Culture" in **Fandom Unbound: Otaku Culture in a Connected World,** *edited by Mizuko Ito, Daisuke Okabe, and Izumi Tsuiji (New Haven, CT: Yale University Press, 2012).*

Today's massive international anime and manga audiences have been built through the energies of teams of highly dedicated fans who have localized and distributed Japanese content in diverse languages and regions.[1] Beginning with the activities of anime clubs in the 1980s, fansubbing (fan subtitling) has been a core practice of overseas fans, a necessary condition for access to the foreign cult media of anime. In the absence of commercial distribution overseas, the fan-to-fan traffic in fansubbed VHS tapes is credited for creating markets and audiences outside of Japan. With the growing availability of digital production tools and Internet distribution, fansubbing and its sister practice of scanlation (scanning and translating manga) have become a vehicle for large-scale distribution of anime and manga, dwarfing commercial efforts at localization and overseas distribution. The relationship between the anime industry and fansubbing is both symbiotic and antagonistic; each requires the other for its survival, and yet they compete to capture the attentions of a growing audience of anime viewers.

The case of fansubbing offers a window into the complex negotiations between media industries and fans as they negotiate their entry into a networked and digital age. Complicated by issues of transnational localization and flows, fansubbing provides a unique twist to the ongoing wrangling over intellectual property, peer-to-peer distribution, and non-commercial appropriation of digital content. A self-consciously non-commercial practice, fansubbing is driven by diverse motives, including the demand for high-quality localized content, a desire to contribute to the international fandom, and opportunities for learning, fame, and recognition. Although highly contested, fansubbing is framed by a set of ethical guidelines that dictate how fans should "give back to the industry" and what content is appropriate for subbing and distribution. These practices and norms surrounding fansubbing offer a model for a public culture that values both amateur noncommercial and professional commercial contributions.

This chapter draws from ethnographic research on fansubbing, part of a broader study of the English-language anime fandom. In the period from 2005 to 2008, my research team and I interviewed fifty-six North American fans, of whom fifteen had contributed to fansubbing in some capacity.[2] In addition to the interviews, we participated in major conventions, including Anime Expo, Fanime, Anime Weekend Atlanta, and Anime-LA, and conducted ongoing observations on online forums and Internet relay chat (IRC) channels related to fansubbing and fansubbed content.

Public Culture in a Networked Age

In the inaugural issue of *Public Culture*, Arjun Appadurai and Carol Breckenridge suggest that "the world of the late twentieth century is increasingly a cosmopolitan world. More people are widely travelled, are catholic in their tastes, are more inclusive in the range of cuisines they consume, are attentive to world wide news, are exposed to global media-covered events, and are influenced by universal trends in fashion" (1988: 5). They suggest the term "public culture" as a way of referencing an arena of cosmopolitan cultural forms and public life that lie at the intersection of the accelerating flows of people and media. From the vantage point of 2010, this view from 1988 appears prescient; as mobile phones and the Internet have become an everyday presence in the lives of many across the globe, the nature of publicity and sociability are deeply implicated in the flow of media and communications across various spatial boundaries. Today's networked publics are a site of ongoing struggle over the meanings of publicity, property, and common culture in a transnational arena (Russell et al. 2008; Varnelis 2008).

One of the defining struggles in our transition to a digitally networked public culture has centered on the tension between intellectual property regimes and the public domain. As amateurs and regular folks have gained status as producers and distributors of media online, media industries have fought to retain control of their intellectual property and distribution channels. What I would like to focus on is the broader so-ciocultural context of the sometimes synergistic and often hostile code-pendency between media fans and industries (see also Jenkins 2006).

Today's industry-fan relations surface foundational questions about the appropriate roles and norms for varied types of media makers and distributors in a reconfigured public culture. Although this debate has often been framed as a polarized fight between free-culture activists and greedy capitalists, the reality of everyday culture and practice is not so black-and-white. Most people inhabit a murky and ambivalent gray zone that values the output of professional cultural production while also ap-preciating the opportunities for peer-to-peer social sharing and amateur creativity that digital media offer us. Lawrence Lessig, a spokesperson for a cultural commons and a less oppressive copyright regime, focused in a recent book on hybrid models, such as Craigslist and Second Life, that integrate sharing and commercial economies (Lessig 2008).

We are still in the early stages of defining what these hybrid models might look like. Although we have a long history of studying the in-centives of commercial actors, we know much less about what drives what Lessig describes as the "sharing economy" (2008) or what Yochai Benkler (2006) has called "commons-based peer production." A small but growing body of research has been looking at the motivations and incentives that drive participation in voluntary, open, amateur, and non-commercial forms of work (Hippel 2005; Leadbeater 2004; Shirky 2010). Research on cases such as Wikipedia (Giles 2005; Swartz 2006), open-source software (Feller et al. 2005; Weber 2004), and game modding (Kow & Nardi 2010; Postigo 2010; Scacchi 2010; Sotamaa 2007) have indicated that these forms of production rely on motivations and norms that not only differ from financially driven ones but are often actually hostile to them. We are beginning to arrive at a more nuanced picture of the diversity of forms of participation in noncommercial production and collectives (see, for example, Lakhani & Wolf 2005). Sharing econo-mies and amateur production foreground incentives and motivations that center on learning, self-actualization, and reputation rather than financial rewards.

Within this broader body of examples of networked, digital, and non-commercial production, fan production raises unique issues. Unlike groups that center on fully open content, such as open-source software or Wikipedia, fan culture begins with the love of professional media content. While fans can irk the industry with practices such as unauthorized distribution and modification, they are fundamentally enthusiasts and evangelists for commercial media. Successful examples of industry-fan synergy have tapped into this fannish enthusiasm and the desire for legitimization by the industry. Fansubbing may look at first blush as if it is simply robbing commercial production and localization of their revenue streams, but the practice is framed by fans as an act of evangelism in the service of expansion of commercial markets for anime. Fans actively seek intimacy with and recognition by the industry while simultaneously being motivated by a fundamentally different set of incentives that they hold in common with other forms of noncommercial production.

Put differently, fan production is not technically what Benkler (2006) has described as commons-based peer production but instead relies on a hybridized vision of intellectual property that lies within the gray zone between proprietary and open regimes. What this suggests is not only a consideration of diverse motivations for production and participation but also a less singular vision of the commons or public domain. If we consider today's public culture as a space that includes the circulation of both commercial and noncommercial forms of culture, otaku culture inhabits the zone of translation and integration of the two. This zone has been fraught with tension, but it is also the site of generative new models that cannot be reduced to either a purely open commons-based model or a purely proprietary commercial one (Condry 2010).

Fansubbing arose to fill an unmet consumer demand not being served by commercial industries. Fans assumed the costs of localization, distribution, and marketing, converting commercial media into a non-commercial peer-to-peer regime out of necessity and passion. Gradually, fansubbing and distribution have taken on a life of their own, deeply integrated in the community and social practices of contemporary wired fans. In the remainder of this chapter, I describe the history and current practices of fansubbing in more depth, as well as the norms, ethics, and motivations on the fan side of the equation. I conclude by revisiting the issues of industry-fan relations encountered at this nexus between commercial and noncommercial culture, and I suggest that a hybrid version of public culture can provide a model for mediating the tensions between commons-based and proprietary markets.

Generations of Fansubbing

The practices of fansubbing originated in the mid-1980s with the advent of technology that enabled amateur subtitling.[3] Before this period, fans exchanged print versions of translated scripts and VHS tapes through a growing network of anime clubs in the United States. Initially, distribution was restricted to small networks of clubs and convention screenings, and there was a relatively close relationship between the leadership in the US fandom and the Japanese industry. Several fans I spoke to noted that many of those involved in the early fansub scene went on to work in the licensing and localization industries for anime.

Gilles Poitras, a prominent fan who was involved in these early years, describes how the VHS fansubbing days were characterized by a strong desire to support the anime industry and not compete with the commercial releases. "Back in the days of VHS, I met many people who had a little [anime] on VHS that they had fansubbed that they just adored. So what they would do is they would go and buy a copy of the Japanese release so they'd have the Japanese release and [. . .] then they would have their fansub. It was their way of supporting the industry." It was during this period that fansubbers established ethical guidelines that signaled their support of the industry and their noncompetitive intent. They defined their work as strictly noncommercial, and they would stop fansubbing and distribution as soon as a series was licensed for the US market. Fansubbers justified their work as an effort to build and test an audience for new series in the United States to encourage commercial release outside of Japan.

By the mid-1990s, VHS tapes of fansubbed anime had begun circulating more broadly through peer-based fan networks, and by the late 1990s, fans began turning to the Internet for anime distribution through sites such as eDonkey or IRC channels. This shift to online distribution happened in tandem with the growth of digisubbing through the use of accessible digital subtitling programs. The shift to digital production and distribution dramatically expanded the scope of fansubbing. With the advent of BitTorrent in the early 2000s, the distribution of fansubbed anime exploded, and we saw the birth of the contemporary digisubbing ecology. Fans involved in the early VHS years see the new generation of digisubbers as an entirely new breed. XStylus, who once timed scripts for VHS fansubbing, emphasizes that "there can be absolutely zero comparison between the VHS days of fansubbing and the digisubbing of today. [. . .] The anime club I went to was actually a subbing group, but they did not distribute what they subbed. [. . .] They would actually buy a show from overseas and translate it themselves."[4] In contrast to those early years, today's fansubbing teams are highly dispersed and organize online through IRC, and they see their mission as broad distribution. Anime industries began to take note, and occasional cease-and-desist letters were sent to groups, requesting that they stop subbing a series. For the most part, however, anime studios and localization companies have continued to turn a blind eye toward fansubbing practice.

While the scale and nature of the fansub scene have changed and expanded dramatically in the past decade, today's fansubbers still recognize many of the norms and ethical guidelines established in the early years of the practice. Almost everyone acknowledged the importance of "giving back to the industry" through the purchase of DVDs. Every fansubber I spoke to referenced the norm of dropping a series after licensing, though not all groups actually adhered to that norm. Many argued that they are continuing in the tradition of opening and testing markets for anime overseas. In turn, the generation of subbers who came of age in the first wave of digisubbing complains about the new generation of subbers who have lax ethical standards and fansub series that are already licensed and released on DVD.

As the technology and culture of fansubbing continue to evolve, we can expect to see ongoing generational differences between subbers who came of age during different moments in the scene. Despite the various discontinuities in fansubbing through the years, the practice has steadily developed an increasingly robust and efficient set of infrastructures for the peer-to-peer traffic of anime across national boundaries. The expansion of the fansub scene online was closely tied to the growing popularity of Japanese popular culture overseas. Gradually expanding into multiple regions and languages, fansubbing continues in its mission to make diverse and otherwise unavailable anime accessible to fans around the world. And despite each generation's complaints about the eroding ethics and discipline of the newer generation, the work ethic of fansubbing is remarkably robust. I turn now to the fansubbing work process and discipline in today's digisubbing scene.

The Fansubber's Work

Anyone who has had a glimpse of the work of fansubbing cannot help but be impressed by the discipline and dedication of teams who turn out subtitled episodes week after week as a purely volunteer endeavor. The way that teams and work processes are organized varies by group, but certain kinds of jobs and workflow have become fairly standardized in the scene. The process begins with the work of the raw capper, who captures the "raw" untranslated episode via television broadcast or through a Japanese file-sharing site. The process then moves to the translator, who listens to the episode and generates an English script. One or sometimes two editors or translation checkers will check the script and then turn it over to the timer, who segments it and times how long each segment should appear on-screen. The typesetter then chooses fonts and creates any signs or special effects, such as karaoke effects for songs. After the typesetting is complete, an encoder prepares an initial video for quality checking (QC). Most groups then put the episode through one or more rounds of QC and revision before turning it over to the encoder for a final encode and then to the distribution team, which releases the episode on IRC and through BitTorrent.

Because team members are dependent on one another to complete the finished project, groups generally have a high degree of camaraderie and coordination. As members finish their jobs on a particular episode, they coordinate handoffs. Often there is an expectation of turnaround within a certain amount of time. Team members are generally logged onto a closed "staff" IRC channel to coordinate these handoffs, as well as onto an open channel where the audience, known as "leechers," congregate and await announcements about new releases and staff openings. This collaborative and high-pressure work situation requires effective coordination and management and also leads to tensions and politics within and between groups. A few of the fansubbers I spoke to had founded their own groups or were part of the founding of groups. They described how groups were started with a spirit of fun and experimentation, gradually developing into more formally organized work teams. Even as he worked for other large groups in the scene, as a high schooler Kurechan started a group with his girlfriend, who was fluent in Japanese, as a fun project to do together. Akira also started a group when he was in high school, after he fansubbed an episode on his own and released it on an IRC channel he hung out in. People in the channel volunteered to help out with new releases, and a new fansub group coalesced. At the time I interviewed him, his group was a high-functioning work team that turned around quality episodes within days of release in Japan. He described his group as "family," with a strong sense of social cohesion and a disciplined work ethic, though other interviewees described the scene as at times "full of drama" and "highly political," as people move in and out of different roles and groups, and different fansub groups compete for recognition.

Different fansub groups have specialties and different emphases. Most groups have a reputation for subbing particular genres of anime. Some of the groups that fansub the most popular anime have set a standard that they will turn an episode around within twenty-four or even eighteen hours of broadcast in Japan. One group has described how it achieves this by having team members in different time zones to keep the workflow on a twenty-four-hour cycle. These groups are often described pejoratively as "speed sub" groups by fansubbers who subscribe to a more methodical pace and process. By contrast, "quality" groups will generally make an effort to keep up with the weekly broadcast schedule of a series, but they might take much longer, attributing delays to a more careful translation, typesetting, and QC process. The best of both types of groups work to exacting standards and are under constant scrutiny by peers, competitors, and audiences.

When different groups are subbing the same series, they compete to produce the quickest or the highest-quality releases to attract leechers. Groups make their decisions about which series to sub based on their personal tastes as well as whether they want to compete with the groups who have already signed on with a series. Playing out in both private and public forums online, groups can be highly critical of the quality of the releases of their competitors. Groups will keep track of the BitTorrent download numbers through trackers that they publicize on their sites.

The slower, quality-oriented groups will distinguish themselves by the high quality of their translations and the effort they put into typesetting. Typesetters from these groups will create custom titles and signs that closely mimic the on-screen text of the original episode, customizing text for storefronts, product labels, and other text that appears on screen. They also develop elaborate karaoke-style effects so that people can follow the timing of both the Japanese and the English translation of songs. Fansubbers I spoke to noted with pride that this kind of attention to detail far exceeds the industry standard of simply going with one default font regardless of its appropriateness for the series or scene.

Fansubbers frequently suffer from burnout, and most groups are relatively short-lived. Five years is considered a benchmark of a very well-established group, and only a handful of groups have survived for longer. Among the active fansubbers whom I interviewed, in the more than two-year span between then and this writing, most have dropped out of the scene though they continue to be part of anime fandom. Zalas describes how most groups "fizzle out" rather than going through a formal breakup process. The Internet is littered with fansub group sites that show no evidence of new activity in years, but new groups are constantly cropping up to take their place in the scene. The ecology of fansubbing is maintained through these processes in which new entrants can start or join new groups, develop new practices and standards, and then eventually retire from the scene. The scene also depends on a diverse set of motives for participation, for both contributing fansubbers and leechers. I turn now to a closer look at the specific motivations and ethics that fansubbers bring to their participation.

Contributors

In my interviews with fansubbers, one of the first social distinctions that I was introduced to was that between "contributors" and "leechers." Put simply, contributors are those who contribute labor and expertise to the process of fansubbing, and leechers are consumers who download and view fansubbed works. People involved in distribution lie in the middle of this spectrum. Although they contribute bandwidth and storage space to the infrastructure of fansubbing, because they do not contribute human labor and expertise, they are not generally included among the ranks of "full staff," and they are relegated to a separate "distro" channel. While the motivations that leechers bring to fansubbing are relatively uncomplicated—they want access to anime—the motivations of contributors are a bit more complex. The level of commitment that fansubbers devote to what is often grinding and boring work cannot be fully captured by either notions of altruistic volunteerism or the creative passions of the hobbyist.

Yochai Benkler in *Wealth of Networks* identifies new forms of noncommercial "peer production" as people have gained access to the processing power of computers and networks to connect, collaborate, and publicize. He notes that people have always had a diverse set of motives to produce culture and knowledge, only some that rely on market and financial incentives. On the nonmarket side, motivations and social practices are highly diverse and include governmental and educational institutions committed to public knowledge, as well as individual writers and creators "who play to 'immortality' rather than seek to maximize the revenue from their creation" (Benkler 2006: 47). More recently, Clay Shirky (2010) has suggested that we are living in a time when the world's "cognitive surplus" is being mobilized in new ways because of the networked and participatory nature of the online world. "Back when coordinating group action was hard, most amateur groups stayed small and informal. Now that we have the tools that let groups of people find one another and share their thought and actions, we are seeing a strange new hybrid: large, public, amateur groups."

Studies examining the motivations for participation in Wikipedia, open-source software development, and game modding have described different motives for participation, puzzling over why people would contribute effort and expertise with little or no financial rewards (Kow & Nardi 2010; Lakhani & Wolf 2005; Sotamaa 2007; Swartz 2006; Weber 2004). Though these groups differ on many details, research findings suggest a general pattern that participation in these groups is tied to a sense of autonomy and efficacy, which is in turn tied to the voluntary nature of the activity. Fansubbers, even while expressing a high degree of commitment and sense of obligation to their team and audiences, also underscored that it was "a hobby" that they did "for fun." Furthermore, this body of work also indicates that reasons for participation are diverse but cluster roughly around ideals about contributing to a shared collective vision or resource, learning and self-actualization, and status and social belonging. I have also seen these motivations at play in the case of the fansubbers I spoke to, and I touch on each set of motivations in turn.

Becoming a Contributor

When I queried fansubbers about what motivated them to start subbing, all of them cited some desire to "contribute" to the fandom. Most fansubbers started off as leechers and decided to become contributors after discovering some form of value they could provide to the scene. For example, zalas describes how he discovered the online fandom, started leeching, and eventually went on to start making anime music videos (AMVs). His AMV making led him to a pursuit of raw video files. "And eventually, I got a very good hang of it, and I was like, 'Maybe I should try to contribute back to these fansubbers. I can offer my services downloading raws for people.'" Similarly, Aren describes how he was part of the eDonkey file-sharing scene when he was thirteen years old, downloading anime through a modem connection. "I thought maybe I should contribute something to the communities [. . .] so I wasn't only downloading the stuff with my old modem but also contributing." Although his parents allowed him only two hours a day of modem time, he contributed this limited bandwidth by helping distribute anime. "It doesn't seem exciting watching something uploading, but it was kind of exciting to contribute something to the community because it was like oh, if they just keep leeching stuff it won't contribute to the community. Anime faces extinction." Moving on from these early experiences at contributing, zalas and Aren both went on to found their own fansub groups and become active participants in the fansub scene.

As is evident with Aren and zalas, fansubbers' sense of contribution was not generally framed in terms of the ethic of "giving back" to the anime industry per se, but more in terms of adding value to the anime fandom as a whole, a fandom that includes the interests of fansubbers, leechers, and the commercial industry. Razz says, "I enjoy bringing anime that's hot off the presses to people around the world." Similarly, Akira says that he subs "to be nice I suppose. [. . .] Just a community to contribute to because stuff we sub hundreds of thousands of people watch." As part of this broader sense of contribution, many fansubbers also noted the benefits to the industry: that they were opening new markets and recruiting new audiences for anime. Lantis ties his motivations to this ethic. "I just feel so good when I can release something that conforms to my standards and make it available to the world of anime the same way that fansubbers did back in the VHS days."

Lantis notes that his drive to contribute was also motivated by the desire to maintain the quality of fansubbing. He discovered fansubs when he was in high school and began following particular groups that he thought had high-quality editing. When one of his favorite groups advertised for a staff position, he immediately applied. Razz was motivated to take on the job of timer for a group because he noticed "bleeds," when a subtitle continues to be displayed on-screen after a scene change. "You won't see this kind of intricacy on any anime DVD, but [among fansubbers] it is generally considered an eyesore." Upon hearing his complaints, the leader of the group invited him to take on the job. After running his own group for many years, zalas has transitioned to a position of fansub critic for the scene and is involved in quality checking the translations of a game that he cares a lot about. "I want to give back to the community, kind of an ethical motivation I guess. [. . .] I tend to be a stickler over whether things are translated properly. [. . .] I feel like I'm this critic guy who looks over and makes sure things aren't screwed up."

These motivations that center on a sense of contributing to a broader good and community were also tied to the ethical positions that fansubbers took in their relationships with the anime industry. The long-standing ethic that groups should drop a series after licensing can run into conflict with the interests of leechers and the quality standards of fansub groups. For example, when a series is licensed midseason, fansubbers must make the call about whether they will drop the series or complete it for their viewers. They see their decision to start subbing a series as an ethical obligation to their viewers, and they are reluctant not to deliver on a completed season. Sai explains, "The argument of 'Well it's licensed but it won't get released for N many more months so it wouldn't be fair to the fans to make them wait.'" Groups that drop midseason get a negative reputation among leechers. Fansubbers also feel committed to upholding the quality standards that they have established. Leechers and fansubbers alike acknowledge that high-quality fansubs are more accurate, better executed, and truer to the original

Japanese source than their commercial versions. When a quality group drops a series, it means depriving audiences of a more high-quality viewing experience.

Some groups have modified the previous norm and have decided to stop subbing only after the DVD is actually released in their region. After licensing or after receiving a cease-and-desist letter, some groups have taken the remainder of the season underground, releasing under a different name so they can retain the ethical pedigree for their more public group identity. A few prominent groups that sub very popular and long-running series such as *One Piece*, *Naruto*, and *Inuyasha* have continued openly subbing and releasing even after licensing and broadcast in the United States, arguing that it is unreasonable to expect fans to wait for the industry to catch up on more than one hundred episodes that have already been fansubbed. Fans from the VHS days look askance at this shifting ethical landscape. Gilles Poitras argues, "I had to wait 10 years for *Nadia*. They can wait." XStylus also takes issue with fans who insist on access to fansubbed versions. "If a show does get licensed, the companies get bitched out because now the fansubs for that show cease. [. . .] The fans do not know how lucky they've got it. Unlike the big lawsuit happy assholes in Hollywood, the anime companies DO care, and do listen."

Although different fans and fansub groups take different positions on the ethics of when to stop subbing and distributing, all the fans I spoke to are united in their commitment to support the anime fandom. The debates boil down to differences in how they perceive the value of their contributions and the relative priority they give to different constituents in this hybrid public culture that includes both commercial and non-commercial interests. While fans from the VHS era see their interests in closer alignment with those of the anime industry and position themselves more as traditional media consumers, the newer generations of fans tend to align with a more fluid and hybrid networked public culture in which the industry does not have as privileged a position.

Learning and Self-Actualization

In addition to the values surrounding their sense of contributing to and improving the fandom, fansubbers also describe being motivated by a sense of learning, self-actualization, and pleasure in creative work. In this, they share participatory motivations similar to what we see with other amateur creative and fan groups. All the fansubbers I spoke to took pride in the quality of their work and valued fansubbing as an activity that helped them acquire skills and expertise. For example, Sai started fansubbing as a translator specifically to improve her Japanese. Having grown up in Japan, she was fully bilingual but was concerned about losing her Japanese after going to the United States for college.

Other subbers described how as they got involved in the scene they became attracted to certain specialties that they found intellectually or creatively stimulating. Aren moved from the German fansubbing scene to the US one, met other encoders who were much more accomplished than he was, and began to learn from them. "It just got interesting because other encoders were like 'Here are some tips and tricks' [. . .] so it got pretty interesting." Unlike the kind of learning that these young people were experiencing in school, learning within the fansub scene is embedded in an authentic set of work practices, in which they are able to connect with and learn from more experienced peers who share their passionate and specialized interests (Ito et al. 2009). This kind of learning and skills development is highly motivating and tied to a sense of autonomy and self-actualization. Kurechan got more involved in the scene as he was mentored by more experienced fansubbers in different specialties. "My tsing [typesetting] was *really* bad at first [. . .] but I worked hard and learned from the masters of the time. And I hung out @ doom9 forums (stuff for encoders) a lot. [. . .] Then I gradually branched out. Timing, then [typesetting], then edit and qc."

As they become more expert and established in the scene, fansubbers take on the role of experts and are motivated to help and teach others. The geek culture of expertise and learning norms that center on self-motivation and self-direction dictate, however, that fansubbers expect newcomers to do their initial homework on their own and not ask basic questions. Zalas participates actively on forums and will often help with technical questions people have, as long as they are intellectually challenging ones. "If it's something really trivial, I don't really feel bothered to actually go help them, but sometimes if it's something relatively advanced, it's kind of interesting to sort of walk people through it." Fansubbers enjoy knowledge exchange with respected peers, but they look down upon the mass of leechers and newbies who have yet to prove their self-worth. Akira sums up this attitude: "Fansubbing is half filled with people who don't know what they are talking about and the fans 99.9% of them don't know what they're talking about."

Status and Social Belonging

Fansubbers are also motivated by social belonging and reputation. When I ask razz what keeps him going in the two groups he is involved in, he says, "The people in the group are fun to work with. Both groups have really cool members." This team spirit and expectations drive a strong sense of commitment to the work. "Because [my group] was really struggling I felt personally obligated to do everything I could to help keep it alive," explains Sai. The tight-knit nature of the work team, and the immediate communication and feedback with both her team and her audience, drove her to become one of the most prolific translators in the scene. Of her peak years of fansubbing during college, she says, "The compulsion was unbelievable. [. . .] The feedback is immediate. It's IRC. [. . .] You'd have people jubilating because you're doing something at the time. I'm like, I'm translating [x series] and they're like, 'Oh, my God. That's awesome. Thank you.' You don't get that kind of feedback."

The large audiences for digisubbing mean that successful fansubbers can gain large followings. Akira sees one of the primary motivations of fansubbing as "instant reputation. Just saying you worked on a series gets you respect." The politics of how groups and individual subbers gain reputation in the scene often can be fraught. Kurechan describes "ego subbers" who gravitate toward the most popular shows as the quickest means to get a reputation and download numbers. His respect is reserved for fansubbers who achieve their status through high-quality and sustained work. For example, he argues that Sai had to translate nine hundred episodes before "she was recognized as a good tl [translator] by the masses" because she did not choose to translate popular shows. Fansubbers I spoke to all agreed that download numbers were not a proxy for quality and that motivations driven purely by leecher popu-larity were suspect. At the same time, all fansubbers also admitted that the numbers did matter to them. Lantis says, somewhat sheepishly, that "I'd be lying if I didn't check [the download counts] out of curiosity ^^;;

but it's not like I decide what to sub because I think I'll get more downloads that way." The quest for download counts also drives the quest for speed. "Usually the group that releases first, assuming equal quality, gets the most downloads," razz explains. "You can hear people talking about group reputations and what not, but the fact of the matter is that the average person will get [the episodes of] the group that releases first. [. . .] Deep down inside, every fansubber wants to have their work watched and a high amount of viewers causes them some kind of joy whether or not they express it."

In summary, all fansubbers bring to their work multiple motivations that are altruistic, personal, and social in nature. Zalas offers a concise summary. "Some people do it for fun because it's kind of neat to play around with this stuff. Some people do it because they want to be popular. [. . .] There's groups out there who just want to get as many downloads as possible because they'll be like, 'Oh. Wow. I'm so cool. I rule over a channel of 300 people.'" I ask about his own motivations. "Well, a lot of it is just socialization. I get to talk to people about things I like. Sometimes it's just I want to give back to the fansubbing community." Fansubbing has sustained itself as a noncommercial, voluntary, and participatory practice because it supports this entire constellation of motivations and ways of participating.

Toward a Hybrid Public Culture

By describing the practices, norms, and ethics involved in fansubbing, I have indicated the diversity of motivations that people bring to the scene. Although fansubbers subscribe to diverse norms and motivations, a commitment to building a sustainable, expanding, and high-quality public culture of anime content and communication is shared across all these groups. In this sense, the interests of fans are in close alignment with the interests of anime producers. The ethical norms to "give back to the industry" so it can continue to produce anime and the intense efforts to achieve high-fidelity translations and video are all propelled by fans' commitment to the medium that they love and the fandom surrounding it. Fansubbers are motivated to contribute enormous amounts of voluntary labor and expertise in the service of this broader sense of mission; they also contribute out of a sense of efficacy and for the recognition they achieve by successfully filling an unmet need for high-quality anime localized for different languages.

Contrary to some models of motivation, the presence of commercial actors does not necessarily crowd out the motivations of noncommercial participants. Many subbers I spoke to said they would be willing to sub for free for the industry and do not see fansubbing as part of their professional career trajectory. The key to effective enlistment of noncommercial players is the presence of compelling noncommercial motivations and incentives, including shared purpose and values as well as personal motivations for learning and recognition. Commercial motives and interests will not always corrupt the commons or the public domain; collective values and interests might at times best be served by an integration of commercial and noncommercial motives. The case of fansubbing also demonstrates how crucial it is to differentiate the motivations for participation between consumers and contributors to a shared public culture.

Despite alignment of many broad goals and interests, however, industry-fansubber relations are fraught with tension and controversy. In recent years, the DVD market has been collapsing, and prominent companies that had been distributing anime overseas, such as ADV and Central Park Media, have folded. These developments have contributed to the polarization of the debate about the legitimacy of fansubbing in supporting the anime industry and the fandom. Although earlier generations of fansubbers could justify their practices as opening new and untapped markets, today's English-language audiences for anime are now well established, and fansub distribution often goes head-to-head with its commercial counterpart. Fansubbers try to bring their practices into alignment with industry interests, but they often express frustration at the lack of what they see as viable alternatives that still meet the needs of fans for speedy and high-quality access to titles.

Some recent experiments in digital distribution are suggesting a model of a hybrid public culture in anime that resolves some of these tensions while meeting the broader goals that unite the fandom and the industry. In 2008, Crunchyroll, a site initially dedicated to streaming fansub content, received venture funding and began developing a model for legal, licensed online distribution of subtitled anime that is simultaneous with release in Japan. Crunchyroll has secured distribution deals for many popular series, and now it streams only content that is licensed and is subtitled by the commercial localization companies. Crunchyroll secured the licensing deal for *Naruto Shippuden*, one of the most popular of the current anime series. This prompted Dattebayo (the group that made its name subbing *Naruto*) to drop the series, although it had continued subbing the series for many years after it had started airing in the United States. Crunchyroll tried to license another major series that Dattebayo subs, *Bleach*. In an online press release, Dattebayo announced that it would drop *Bleach* because of Crunchyroll's plans, and it lobbied the site to allow the group to provide the subs for the series.[5] Within the press release was also an acknowledgment of the changing landscape of fansubbing. "DB came along at just the right moment in fansubbing. It has existed through the moments I feel were fansubbing's zenith. Now fansubbing is clearly in its decline, as it has been for two years now, replaced by legal alternatives."

Fansubbing arose to meet a compelling need of overseas fans that was not met by commercial alternatives. As the anime industry adapts to take advantage of the opportunities of online distribution, fansubbing's mission to distribute anime overseas will decline in importance. At the same time, as acknowledged in the Dattebayo press release, fansubbing still provides a unique value that is very difficult for commercial industries to compete with, which is high-quality "crowdsourced" (Howe 2009) subtitling. As other volunteer subtitling sites such as dotsub have demonstrated, translation is an activity that is uniquely well suited to peer production because tasks can be decomposed and people can contribute in a distributed fashion to translation, editing, and QC. Viikii.net is a commercial site that licenses and distributes Taiwanese and Korean dramas in multiple languages. It relies on crowdsourced fansubbing for its subtitles.

These experiments in online distribution suggest that there are viable hybrid models that integrate noncommercial peer production with professional media production, localization, and distribution. Just as the earlier generation of fansubbers opened a new market for anime industries overseas, today's digisubbers would see their interests served by new legal and revenue-generating forms of online distribution, if they would allow for fans to contribute to higher standards for localization and subtitling. Shifting the view from the question of who extracts value to a vision of who is allowed to add value changes the view of how a hybrid economy can work. Rather than assume that incorporation of volunteer labor for commercial gain is a form of digital sharecropping (Carr 2006; Terranova 2000), we should consider how the ability to contribute to a collectively meaningful endeavor can be itself a source of value and efficacy that often requires no other rewards. Individual motivations are tightly tied to collective public recognition and value creation. The fansubbing case demonstrates how economic models of individual value extraction and maximization provide an inadequate view into the motivations for contribution.

In this chapter, I have argued for attention to the underlying social patterns and meaningful values that motivate people's participation in and contributions to a shared and networked public culture. One of the key lessons of the networked age has been that the days of proprietary locked-down culture and winner-take-all scenarios are definitively over. Conversely, we cannot rely on a narrow vision of the commons or the public domain that is free of commercial interests and financial incentives. A notion of public culture has from the start been about collectives that include both commercial and noncommercial incentives for participation. Arguing for a hybrid public culture is not an act of capitulating to a capitalist imperative that reduces the pool of common culture, but rather it is a way of arguing for an enriching public life that values diverse forms of contribution.

NOTES

1 This research would not have been possible without the generosity of the fansubbers and fans who decoded the world of subbing and file sharing for me and my research team. I would particularly like to thank Zalas and Kinovas, who opened the doors to the fansub world for me. This work was supported by a grant from the John D. and Catherine T. MacArthur Foundation and by the Annenberg Center for Communication at the University of Southern California. My research assistants on this project included Rachel Cody, Renee Saito, Annie Manion, Brendan Callum, and Judy Suwatanapongched. Without them my knowledge of the anime fandom would have been much more impoverished, and cons would have been much less enjoyable. This work has also benefited from an ongoing collaboration and conversations with Jennifer Urban.

2 I was the lead researcher of a team that included the aforementioned research assistants. Jennifer Urban, a collaborator on this work, also participated in the fieldwork. When the observation or interview was conducted by somebody other

than me, this is noted in the text. I offered all fans the option of having their real names, fan names, or pseudonyms used in publications that resulted from the research. Most involved in fansubbing chose a pseudonym, and I have noted in a footnote only those instances when I have used a "real" fan name. In the case of leechers, to protect their identities, I have not mentioned their names or assigned pseudonyms, as their quotes were illustrative of generalized practices rather than individual life histories.

3 This history of fansubbing is derived from a more detailed history of fansubbing from 1979 to 1993 compiled by Sean Leonard (2005), my interviews with fans, and Lawrence Eng's (2012) history of the US fandom.

4 This is a real fan name.

5 See www.dattebayo.com.

WORKS CITED

Appadurai, A & Breckenridge, C 1988, "Why public culture," *Public Culture* 1(1): 5–9.

Benkler, Y 2006, *The wealth of networks: how social production transforms markets and freedom*, Yale University Press, New Haven, CT.

Carr, N 2006, "Sharecropping the long tail," *Rough Type*, www.roughtype.com.

Condry, I 2010, "Dark energy: what fansubs reveal about the copyright wars," in F Lunning (ed.), *Mechademia 5: fanthropologies*, University of Minnesota Press, Minneapolis.

Eng, L 2012, "Anime and Mange fandom as networked culture," in M Ito, D Okabe, & T Izumi (eds.), *Fandom unbound: Otaku culture in a networked world*, Yale University Press, New Haven, CT.

Feller, J, Fitzgerald, B, Hissam, SA, & Lakhani, KR (eds.) 2005, *Perspectives on free and open source software*, MIT Press, Cambridge, MA.

Giles, J 2005, "Special report: Internet encyclopedias go head to head," *Nature* 438: 900–901.

Hippel, EV 2005, *Democratizing innovation*, MIT Press, Cambridge, MA.

Howe, J 2009, *Crowdsourcing: why the power of the crowd is driving the future of business*, Three Rivers Press, New York.

Ito, M, Baumer, S, Bittanti, M, boyd, d, Cody, R, Herr-Stephenson, B, Horst, H, Martínez, KZ, Pascoe, CJ, Perkel, D, Robinson, L, Sims, C, & Tripp, L 2009, *Hanging out, messing around, and geeking out: kids living and learning with new media*, John D. and Catherine T. Macarthur Foundation Series on Digital Media and Learning, MIT Press, Cambridge, MA.

Jenkins, H 2006, *Convergence culture: where old and new media collide*, New York University Press, New York.

Kow, YM & Nardi, B 2010, "Who owns the mods?" *First Monday* 15(5), firstmonday.org.

Lakhani, KR & Wolf, RG 2005, "Why hackers do what they do: understanding motivation and effort in free/open source software project," in J Feller, B Fitzgerald, S

Hissam, & KR Lakhani (eds.), *Perspectives on free and open software*, MIT Press, Cambridge, MA.

Leadbeater, C 2004, *The pro-am revolution: how enthusiasts are changing our economy and society*, Demos, London.

Leonard, S 2005, "Celebrating two decades of unlawful progress: fan distribution, proselytization commons, and the explosive growth of Japanese animation," *UCLA Entertainment Law Review*, Spring, papers.ssrn.com.

Lessig, L 2008, *Remix: making art and commerce thrive in the hybrid economy*, Penguin, New York.

Postigo, H 2010, "Modding to the big leagues: exploring the space between modders and the game industry," *First Monday* 15(5), firstmonday.org.

Russell, A, Ito, M, Richmond, T, & Tuters, M 2008, "Culture: media convergence and networked participation," in K Varnelis (ed.), *Networked publics*, MIT Press, Cambridge, MA.

Scacchi, W 2010, "Computer game mods, modders, modding, and the mod scene," *First Monday* 15(5), firstmonday.org.

Shirky, C 2010, *Cognitive surplus: creativity and generosity in a connected age*, Penguin, New York.

Sotamaa, O 2007, "On modder labour, commodification of play, and mod competitions," *First Monday* 12(9): 131.193.153.231/www/issues/issue12_9/sotamaa.

Swartz, A 2006, "Who writes Wikipedia?," *Raw Thought*, www.aaronsw.com.

Terranova, T 2000, "Free labor: Producing culture for the digital economy," *Social Text* 18(2): 33–58.

Varnelis, K (ed.) 2008, *Networked publics*, MIT Press, Cambridge, MA.

Weber, S 2004, *The success of open source*, Harvard University Press, Cambridge, MA.

21

Live from Hall H

Fan/Producer Symbiosis at San Diego Comic-Con

ANNE GILBERT

Late on a Saturday afternoon in July, Hall H—the largest room at the San Diego Convention Center, a vast auditorium that seats upward of sixty-five hundred people—erupted in a spontaneous chant of "One more time! One more time!" Fans had just been treated to the premiere of a trailer for the upcoming superhero film *Deadpool* (2016), and were demanding a second showing of the exclusive footage. The panel moderator, nonplussed but game, declared, "We were only going to show it once, but I have the microphone. . . . Sure, let's run it again." The fans cheered, and were no less vocal during the trailer's second screening.

The event was 20th Century Fox's 2015 panel at San Diego Comic-Con. Though fans' specific demand for multiple screenings of footage was unusual, the moment itself is representative of the allocation of authority at the event. This exchange illustrates Comic-Con's identity as both a fan convention and major industry marketing event, an identity navigating the balance between interests of fans—savvy consumers who collectively voice demands for content, access, and media influence—and those of producers, who cede little control but who have a vested economic interest in the success of their promotions.

This chapter considers San Diego Comic-Con as a demonstration of complementary fan/producer interests, arguing that this site points to an entrenched interdependence of power, purpose, and reward between audiences and industry. To do this, I borrow Nick Couldry's (2000) concept of a "media world," combine it with emerging academic work on industry events and convention spaces, and argue that participants of the convention construct it as an environment distinct from the ordinary, a space in which promotions and marketing allow non-media people entry into an ephemeral world of media power. The relations are not antagonistic clashes between fans and industries, but asymmetrical power balances that structure participatory fandom as a way of promoting business and consumption. Media producers use the convention as a promotional opportunity, as it presents the chance to market directly to a desirable audience. Fans in attendance recognize their role as consumers, internalizing a relationship in which they are afforded less control because the perceived rewards are dependent on their position as idealized but circumscribed subjects. As one longtime Comic-Con attendee told me, "A lot is put into [Comic-Con] for the fans. Because 364 days out of the year, we're giving to [the industry], we're giving our time and our dedication, and our money [. . .] so this is the one time that we as a group get to reap the benefits." Put simply, San Diego Comic-Con reinforces hierarchies between media people and non-media people and rearticulates uneven power dynamics between fans and producers, but in doing so, reveals the investment of all sides in maintaining these systems in order to reap the benefits.

The Power of Media Worlds

San Diego Comic-Con (SDCC) occupies a space at the intersection of "media world" and "ordinary world." These terms, from Nick Couldry (2000), constitute a symbolic division, a separation between media spaces—populated by stars, creatives, producers, and distributors of popular media—and the everyday environment of non-media people, who are consumers and fans, subject to the social influence of the media world but not part of its creation. The difference between the media world and the ordinary world is one of kind, "not so much a distinction based on detailed comparison, but an absolute distinction that divides the world up in advance" (47). Though absolute, this distinction is naturalized so as to be largely invisible while at the same time, Couldry argues, structuring the social influence of media institutions (15). Designating the media world as exceptional reinforces and bestows a justification of media power: because the media world and its inhabitants are something beyond the ordinary, they deserve to be regarded with admiration. The legitimate boundary between the worlds of the media and the ordinary, then, becomes "automatically significant to cross or approach" (47).

Couldry's primary focus is on pilgrimages of ordinary consumers into or near media worlds, and he and others have researched the significance of media ritual constructed by fans or by after-market ventures that offer entrance into spaces of media power—media tours, for example, to shooting locations or sets, or visits to stars' former homes or grave sites. These events operate outside industrial systems of production and promotion, but others, such as film festivals, are integrated into media industries. Speaking about film festivals, Robert Moses Peaslee notes that these environments represent "a kind of rift through which a normally hidden or out-of-reach area of meaningful activity becomes visible to those not already connected to the event" (2013: 815). Attendees have the opportunity to briefly gain access or see beyond the boundary between the two worlds, access that can ultimately reinforce the distinction between media professionals and nonprofessionals. Though media tourists and festivalgoers can elide the separation between themselves and the media world, the reward of access reifies the value of those worlds (Peaslee 2013) by maintaining existing hierarchies. Couldry argues, "[A]lthough the hierarchy of value (between 'ordinary person' and 'media person,' 'ordinary world' and 'media world') is *constructed*, the difference of symbolic resources between those outside media institutions and those within them is *real*" (2000: 20) and, furthermore, that "[i]t is precisely the symbolic hierarchy of the media frame [. . .] that makes [media spaces] special and worth visiting" (32).

Other events, created for industry promotion and commerce (trade conventions, sales events), exist firmly within the media world. Few are open to the public, and fewer still have been subjects of extensive academic study. Timothy Havens argues that the analysis of industry spaces and events can generate a greater "understanding of the ways in which business practices concretize the general economic realities" of the entertainment industry (2003: 20), and existing work on trade conventions emphasizes how spatial, interpersonal, and economic issues at industry events shape content and consumption (Bielby & Harrington 2008). Research on SDCC operates to similar ends, and I would add it also illustrates the efforts to promote an image of media power for both professionals and audiences. Trade events foster a sense of media power as business strategy, an effort to promote upcoming media properties as a sound investment for backers, advertisers, and exhibitors. SDCC integrates these business goals with explicit outreach to fans, surrounding economic realities of industry practice with rhetoric of giving loyal consumers what they want.

SDCC is an immersive engagement with fandom, a pilgrimage into a media world that occupies a space of industry commerce and promotion. The convention is an ephemeral but vivid media space, one in which the interests of fans and those of industry participants are both best served by reinforcing the power dynamics of the media/ordinary distinction. By applying Couldry's concept of media worlds to a space that also houses industrial commerce, analysis of SDCC illustrates how media ritual is also a means of navigating the business of media: pilgrimages to industry spaces naturalize both the hierarchy of media people and non-media people, as theorized by Couldry, and fans' participation and consumption as central aspects of enacting media ritual. My findings are drawn from a larger project on SDCC, for which I attended SDCC from 2010 to 2015, conducted nearly one hundred interviews with fans, vendors, panelists, volunteers, organizers, and industry participants, and surveyed coverage produced by attendees, journalists, and industry marketers. From this, I argue that participants of SDCC are cognizant of the roles they play in rearticulating dynamics of fan/producer relationships, and the significance and continued success of the convention indicates the complex interdependence of industry benefit and fan reward.

San Diego's Pop Culture Mecca

San Diego Comic-Con is a fan convention on a massive scale. The activities are typical of those available to attendees of any media convention—a schedule of panels, an exhibition floor, autograph signings, screenings, gaming. At SDCC, these events are scaled to accommodate roughly 150,000 participants and are marked by considerable industrial investment, giving the convention the enviable patina of an entry point into the high-profile corporate media world.

On the trade floor, attendees buy and trade comic books, get autographs, and make friends with fellow fans. Here, small-press comic vendors set up shop next to sprawling booths from Marvel and DC, and independent artists and vendors sell collectibles, toys, apparel, books, games, posters, and custom art in pop-up shops interspersed among the lines for exclusives at the storefronts for Mattel, LEGO, and Hasbro. The floor is also a site of some of the most visible industry participation: major Hollywood studios erect elaborate displays to market upcoming films, cable networks sell exclusive merchandise and build sets for fans to experience upcoming programs, and video game makers offer the opportunity to play not-yet-released games.

Panel schedules, too, reflect a mix of fan camaraderie and industry marketing. At any given time, fourteen to eighteen rooms host panels, presentations, Q&A sessions, and workshops. In the smallest rooms are intimate discussions of costumes, the economics of comic book stores, and the role of women in fandom, attended by anywhere from a few dozen to a couple hundred people. The largest rooms house thousands of people who wait in line for hours to watch distributors parade out stars, directors, and producers to preview exclusive footage of upcoming releases and answer questions directly from the crowd.

The immense popularity of SDCC has seen the event expand well beyond the convention center where the trade floor and most panels are located. Nearby hotels house panel space, branded gaming lounges, and screening rooms for animation and festival films. Restaurants and storefronts in the adjacent Gaslamp neighborhood of downtown San Diego are decorated as advertisements for television networks and programs, and unofficial events trickle across the city. The local Major League Baseball stadium houses free events for badge holders, including concerts and interactive marketing displays, as well as paid events available to the public, such as a *Walking Dead* zombie run and ticketed Q&As with celebrities in town for the convention.

SDCC's sprawl and scale have made it impossible to experience in full. Participation at Comic-Con is necessarily about making choices: lining up for a chance at an autograph from stars of their favorite show might mean missing the panel for that same program, as demand makes attending both impossible. The choices made by fans at the convention, including the events for which they wait for hours and the ones they sacrifice in exchange, mark evidence of fans constructing both rituals and their significance by wielding a collective audience power; this meaning operates, however, within systems built for commerce and consumption.

Fan Interests, Fan Rewards

At SDCC, fan investment is celebratory. Over the past decade, SDCC has experienced a shift in size and prestige, and longtime attendees consistently observe that the "mainstreaming" of cult media has had a profound effect on the convention: longer lines, difficulties securing badges, bigger stars, more media properties that don't "belong." These changes fit a narrative of a fan convention that has been exploited by corporate industry interests, but that narrative does not reflect the evolution of SDCC; the benefits of this event have always been wrapped up with industry interests. Though attendees recognize the event has changed, they appreciate SDCC's newfound fame: "In some respects, the changes have got to be good. I mean, more mainstream means more stuff here, which means more coverage." Fans at Comic-Con are motivated by commerce and access, benefits that are more rewarding with increased industry involvement. Exclusive content, merchandise, and celebrity interaction are incentives that generate positive social capital among fans while reinforcing consumptive practices that have economic benefits for industry producers.

Fan interest in the commerce of the convention runs deep, and attendees' investment situates consumption as central to the meaning they construct of the event. Buying, acquiring, and collecting are ingrained practices in a fan identity (Hills 2002), and the trade floor and material giveaways at Comic-Con are dedicated to these practices. Lincoln Geraghty (2014) argues that the commodity consumption at an event like SDCC can generate closeness with a media text and a collective sense of memory that also extends to the convention itself. This is a performative mode of material acquisition: fans buy or receive sought-after items that become touchstones of cultural meaning, signaling fannish affiliation and participation in a significant event.

Conventions have long played a role in the fans' desire to build collections, but "the actual products being launched in San Diego [. . .] are no longer aimed at a niche audience—they are mass-market commodities with timeless comic book superheroes from DC and Marvel competing with new characters from the worlds of TV, film and anime" (Geraghty 2014: 97). SDCC "exclusive" comics, merchandise, and collectibles are big business, and lines for new product launches at LEGO, Mattel, and Hasbro are among the longest at the convention as fans vie for the chance to purchase new toys and tie-ins from their favorite media properties. The pilgrimage to SDCC is, for some, an annual shopping trip, with days at the convention organized into toy or comic "buying" days and "panel" days. The collectibles, comic books, art, apparel, and other merchandise available at SDCC visibly signify participation in geek culture, and fans' interest in buying makes commerce a significant influencer of the convention's economic structure.

SDCC is also a veritable mecca of free swag and promotional material; fans are aggressive and strategic in attempts to score the most desirable giveaways, positioning themselves near booths for television networks or film distributors to snag T-shirts, posters, buttons, reusable bags, and promotional tchotchkes branded with titles or corporate logos. Attendees organize swaps of free bags and shirts to get the best ones, and they proudly display goodie bags, inflatable chairs, even branded pajamas that they receive "just 'cause [they] sat there" in a panel presentation. Fans eagerly collect material goods that they can show off (or, for the more enterprising, resell), because they represent exclusive attachments: "It's not like anyone else has a *Covert Affairs* shirt. Especially in Michigan." Implicit in this desire for SDCC exclusive material goods is the cachet their relative rarity produces for attendees. Commerce at the convention allows attendees to create social capital within fan communities and among personal networks; it also provides tangible manifestations of the significance they attribute to the event itself, ones predicated on consumption that give substance to a user-generated aura of the importance of SDCC's media world.

SDCC's exclusivity affords attendees other benefits of "being there" not as visible as T-shirts or collectibles, but that are nevertheless marked by vivid, intangible rewards. The lure of the convention is the access it offers to industry professionals, from low-end laborers in the comic industry to the biggest Hollywood celebrities of film and television. SDCC invites fans into a world of celebrity and creativity, with panels offering behind-the-scenes looks at the making of upcoming television shows and films, access to exclusive footage, and the opportunity to speak directly to stars. These points of access, it should be noted, indicate SDCC's construction as a media ritual without specific textual affiliation; though much of the work on media pilgrimages analyzes fans seeking closeness with a particular beloved text, SDCC provides an opportunity to expand on this, illustrating practices of fans seeking a sense of intimacy with a broader media world.

Fans of small-scale enterprises, including lesser known comic series and television programs, note the intimacy afforded at the convention, despite the event's overwhelming size: "Because [SDCC is] not just about the comics any more, it's really easy to run into writers and artists that I admire and enjoy, and actually have like one-on-one conversations," noted a young woman who frequents small panels with fewer crowds. Desirable moments of contact and intimacy are characterized as fleeting, rare, and to be found only off the beaten track at an increasingly corporatized event, but are prized by fans who value the convention's opportunities for access to media figures.

The convention's high-profile industry identity also has benefits for those looking for a star moment. SDCC has built an image that anyone from a loyal fan to a movie star to Stan Lee himself might be wandering the floor; panels, scheduled autograph signings, and nights out in the Gaslamp create opportunities to stargaze. Fans who wait in line for more than twenty-four hours in order to be in the front of the room for the convention's biggest presentations in Hall H do so for the perceived intimacy with the major celebrities on stage: "It's so worth it [to watch panels from the front row]. [. . .] You spend so much of your time watching this show on TV, and then you get to see it in person and ask questions and hear what the actors have to say. [. . .] And they're not acting up there, they're like themselves. It's amazing." Comic-Con offers fans the chance to gain intangible but visceral joy through brushes with the highest echelon of media people.

SDCC's offer of access to the media world is desirable, in part, because of its liveness and ephemerality. The explicit purpose of industry presentations at Comic-Con is to make announcements about upcoming projects and to screen advance footage. The instantaneous nature of the Internet, however, has obviated the exclusivity of these rewards: any breaking news is simultaneously announced via the entertainment news media, and content is exclusive only until it plays at the convention, after which official streams or pirated copies immediately circulate online. Learning this information, however, cannot duplicate entirely the rewards offered by presence at the convention. Philip Auslander (1999) argues that live experiences bear greater symbolic capital than mediated ones because of the social construction of the performance as valuable. Auslander contends that live performances position spectators as members of a fleeting community; the moment of liveness cannot be fully captured, thus making "presence" at a particular time and place desirable but resolutely unattainable to those who are elsewhere. The fleeting affective incentive of sharing time and space with significant media people is sufficient for SDCC to constitute a point of desirable slippage between media worlds and ordinary ones.

Rewards for fans invested in commerce and access at SDCC are dependent on the connection these qualities have with the "extraordinariness" of the media world. Access operates as a benefit for fans precisely because of hierarchies that situate media people as something special and separate from non-media people: access to it is exciting only when the media world has power. SDCC constructs a space in which fans can get close to the media world but are reminded of their separation from it. Fans are discouraged from efforts to collapse the distinction—asking for favors during a Q&A, for instance, is explicitly prohibited in SDCC guidelines, and fans who ask questions while attempting to incorporate their own forays into the media world are met with vocal resistance from other attendees. If fans and celebrities do not occupy different worlds, there is little appeal to the portal offered by the convention to the spaces and individuals who wield great symbolic power; blurring the lines between fan and producer, in this space, reduces the pleasures on offer for the fans.

Media Industry Investment

Media industry presence at SDCC is designed to generate publicity and fan interest, capitalizing on consumer appetites for exclusive content to provide viable direct and indirect returns on financial investment. Industry participants range from small, independent comic book publishers and vendors to the world's largest multinational media conglomerates. It is these latter corporations that bring the greatest attention—and star power—to SDCC, as film distributors, broadcast and cable networks, video game producers, and book and comic publishers promote upcoming properties designed to appeal to an increasingly mainstream geek audience. The direct involvement of industry makes SDCC a fan event that also acts as a tool for corporate media interests. Combining analysis of SDCC as a media world and as an industry event makes it possible to understand that conventions in general, and SDCC in particular, are how users' media ritual practice can structure industrial business.

In his analysis of industry trade shows, Havens argues that these events offer a "variety of 'pre-sale' or 'non-selling' opportunities that are crucial to future sales," shoring up industrial dominance by circulating and reinforcing "common-sense assumptions about how the industry functions" (2003: 21). Because SDCC is an industry marketing event, but one that is attended by non-media people, these selling opportunities ask fans to engage in what Jonathan Gray calls "speculative consumption" (2010: 24). Producers use paratexts—previews, exclusive footage, merchandising, interviews, casting announcements—to build fan interest and, ideally, eventual consumption. Gray contends that paratexts serve to create an understanding of media texts, manage their meanings, and shape the experience of media consumption (6), and SDCC provides industrial participants the opportunity to introduce influential paratextual material to a particularly receptive fan audience. Taken as part of the convention programming, industrial paratexts are instructive about the media properties and fannish investment producers will promote in the coming months, and help instruct fan attendees about their role in media business practice.

At the convention, new television shows screen pilot episodes before bringing out the cast and producers for brief, moderated interview segments. Panels for returning shows rely more on fan interaction, in part because cast and crew have often not begun shooting new fall episodes; these panels show brief exclusive footage or behind-the-scenes extras and then open up to questions. Film promotion is often part of high-profile panels organized by distribution corporations that treat the presentation like an industry marketing showcase by featuring short clips of exclusive footage interspersed with short, fluffy interviews by friendly moderators that segue quickly from one to the next.

SDCC is a heavily covered event, and participation engages media industries in the production of hype. "The industry desperately needs its paratexts to work," Gray points out, "since both industry and audiences habitually count on paratexts' relative success or failure as an index to the success or failure of the text as a whole" (2010: 39). At SDCC, the work of paratexts is twofold: the promotional material tests audiences and reinforces fan engagement with long-term marketing strategies. For the first, exclusive footage is premiered and gauged at Comic-Con. SDCC audiences act as focus groups, their interest, reactions, and social media feedback to film teaser footage and pilot screenings providing a gauge for executives looking to tweak the content or marketing of an upcoming product. By using SDCC as a test market for their core audience, television and film studios can potentially use negative responses to adapt advertising campaigns, or even content, in the hopes of securing a more favorable result in release.

Positive response at SDCC does not guarantee market success. The purpose of promotional efforts in general, and industrial involvement at SDCC in particular, is to generate interest that translates into quantifiable monetary gains—television viewers, box office receipts, video game sales, and so forth. The fans in the SDCC test market can act as canaries in the entertainment economy coal mine: panels with empty seats, content with little word-of-mouth attention from fans, or properties with poorly selling exclusive merchandise can indicate future underperformance in ratings or at the box office. During the same 20th Century Fox presentation in which the fans so vocally demanded additional viewings of *Deadpool* content, for instance, the response to *Fantastic Four* promotional material was decidedly lackluster. The measured reaction might have presaged *Fantastic Four*'s disastrous US box office earnings, the worst for a superhero film in more than a decade (Hoad 2015). Industry participants at SDCC are implicitly instructing attendees on consumption practices, but are learning the ongoing significance that fans attribute to the event's features as well.

There are also instances in which SDCC heralds market success that never materializes, where the paratextual promotion does not yield returns. SDCC is a heavily hyped event that dominates the entertainment news cycle, so properties with a mediocre response at the convention can benefit from red carpet photos and complimentary news write-ups that mask a lack of genuine fan enthusiasm. Fans in attendance are aware of the instances in which their enthusiasm has not rewarded the industrial coffers: "A lot of studios [. . .] are also realizing that, from a marketing standpoint, if you do well at Comic-Con, it doesn't translate into actual box office numbers all the time. However, if you do badly here, it will actually really hurt you, and you'll have to work really hard to overcome it." Fans articulate their role as a test market easily, but do so in a way that acknowledges their role in the relationship with industry. In order for SDCC to offer benefits to fans who want access to stars and exclusive content, fans must reciprocate with genuine responses that can reliably translate into accurate economic projections.

Producers at Comic-Con also benefit from incentivizing fans' role in industry marketing, and from situating media consumption as a central component of the media ritual of the convention. Fans, like those at SDCC, are voracious and loyal consumers, and direct marketing to them thanks the fans for their dedication while at the same time asking them to do more. Producers encourage fans to post responses to the panels and reactions to exclusive content online, to advocate for beloved film and television shows to others, and to recruit friends, family, and strangers to buy tickets or tune in. The material promotional giveaways involve SDCC attendees in the business of advertising, such that even the act of reselling free merchandise after the convention can serve to market upcoming media properties. One of the benefits for producers of SDCC, then, is that inherent in the process of marketing to loyal fans are attempts to enlist those fans to become marketers themselves.

SDCC offers an opportunity for producers and industrial players to cut through the clutter of a marketing-saturated environment in order to reach a captive—and invested—audience of consumers. In a media environment rife with advertisement, media content and promotions become difficult to distinguish, as text, context, and paratext are disorganized and interwoven, making boundaries and entry points hard to discern (Gray 2010; Couldry 2000). To some extent, SDCC is emblematic of this saturation: the convention space has sponsorships and branded components from ceiling banners to restroom signs. Attending SDCC is an immersive experience, and San Diego itself becomes a consumer space, with pedicabs, hotel keys, public transit, city lampposts, and local businesses all advertising the convention or popular media, contributing to a nearly overwhelming marketing density. At industry trade events, the primary purpose is for commerce, and physical layouts are organized to facilitate dealmaking (Bielby & Harrington 2008), so that attendees navigate the space in such a way to make appropriate interpersonal and business connections along their paths. At SDCC, the space is similarly organized so that commerce and marketing are inescapable values that underscore how the convention is experienced by its participants and consumption is made integral to the understanding of SDCC as a media world.

At the same time, however, SDCC is an escape; consumption and promotions are part of fans' lives outside of the convention, but practices here are immersive, sensationalized, and extravagant, thus making marketing at SDCC the focus and not a banal distraction. Comic-Con attendees enjoy their time at the convention as an opportunity to be among their "tribe" and immerse themselves in geek culture; as one attendee notes, "We are all looking for something a little bit bigger; [Comic-Con] allows you to indulge in that." As part of attendees' inhabiting of a media world at SDCC, fannish pursuits like toy buying, cosplay, and comic collecting are privileged ahead of the obligations of everyday life. While the environment of the convention is arguably more saturated with promotions than the world beyond, attendees are focused on the practices of consumption, less distracted and more receptive to industrial marketing efforts. SDCC does not prime attendees to pay attention to a particular media property; however, the event's immersion in popular culture makes it a time in which fans' central focus is on consumption. At the convention, attention to promotion is not something producers must attempt to wrest away from competing interests.

Particularly striking is the manner in which these promotional strategies are framed. In industry rhetoric, marketing interests at SDCC are characterized as an incentive for fans, downplaying the economic benefits for producers in favor of emphasizing promotional content as a reward for fans' dedication. Fans are praised for waiting in long lines and attending panels in high numbers, and are thanked repeatedly for their loyalty. Celebrity panelists express awe at the level of enthusiasm and size of the crowd in the room. In short, producers explicitly recognize the affective labor that fans at SDCC do to popularize and proselytize beloved texts, and they capitalize on that loyalty by offering rewards in the form of exclusive content and celebrity sightings, thus using promotional material to market further. Promoting appropriate products to willing attendees is necessary for the speculative consumption at the convention to translate to actual consumption—and therefore economic returns—at a later date. The rhetoric employed at SDCC, that promotional efforts are an attempt to "give back" to fans, illustrates that the potential economic benefits for industry interests at the convention are deeply intertwined with fan participation.

Fan/Producer Power

SDCC and its participants shape the nature of the fan/producer relationships enacted there. Attendees and industry players invest their interests in the convention, but their roles are likewise structured by the limitations and affordances delineated by others. Fandom at SDCC, for example, is constructed as a consumptive practice rather than a productive one. Industry figures are overtly appreciative of fans' loyal and vociferous viewing, and the rewards offered to attendees are predicated on the depiction of fans as ideal consumers. The effect is that the division between media people and non-media people is reified while the potential for fans to act as petty producers, or for fannish creativity to blur the boundary between producer and consumer, is minimized. Industry's role at the convention as a marketing venture with economic motivations is likewise constructed and rewarded by fans. SDCC involves fans' apparent awareness of the mechanisms of media industry, including promotion, distribution, and marketing. Economic benefit for industry participants is shaped by fans' demands to be recognized as a viable, desirable segment of the market, sold to effectively.

These structuring principles indicate the interdependence of reward and power that takes place at SDCC. The relationship is far from symmetrical; industry remains the arbiter of creative control, and fans are consumers with little sway over production. Even as consumers, fans have means of exerting influence; at the convention and beyond, fans have avenues and activities beyond industry control (Geraghty 2014). At SDCC, the power of the attendees is omnipresent, collective, and frequently wielded: fans can choose to attend or reject industry offerings; they can, as I illustrated at the start of the chapter, make demands on the content shown; and their responses to (and potential rejection of) upcoming media properties are a powerful economic consequence of producers who fail to generate genuine fan interest. Piracy, too, remains a specter of fannish agency: in panels, audiences are strictly forbidden from photographing or filming exclusive content on the screen, yet leaked video of advance trailers inevitably finds its way online. In other words, there are behaviors available to the less powerful fans that thwart the notion of absolute media power, and these are a significant component of the convention's practices.

Couldry's division between media world and ordinary world, however, involves hierarchy as well as separation. At SDCC, the asymmetry of power dynamics in fan/producer relationships remains, despite the potential for subversive acts of defiance or the blurring of consumer/creator boundaries. Practices at the convention are invested in reinforcing and naturalizing the distinction of media power. Fan rewards and industry benefits are both dependent on the reproduction of existing dynamics, and thus the roles of each are highly interreliant. By including a consideration of the direct industry participation involved, San Diego Comic-Con augments research on media worlds to illustrate how the symbolic power of ritual serves the interests of both sides of the fan/producer relationship.

WORKS CITED

Auslander, P 1999, *Liveness: performance in a mediatised culture*, Routledge, New York.
Bielby, DD & Harrington, CL 2008, *Global TV: exporting television and culture in the world market*, New York University Press, New York.
Couldry, N 2000, *The place of media power: pilgrims and witnesses of the media age*, Routledge, New York.
Geraghty, L 2014, *Cult collectors: nostalgia, fandom and collecting popular culture*, Routledge, New York.
Gray, J 2010, *Show sold separately: promos, spoilers, and other media paratexts*, New York University Press, New York.
Havens, TJ 2003, "Exhibiting global television: on the business and cultural functions of global television fairs," *Journal of Broadcasting & Electronic Media* 47(1): 18–35.
Hills, M 2002, *Fan cultures*, Routledge, New York.
Hoad, P 2015, "Fantastic Four flop: the biggest superhero disaster since Catwoman," *Guardian*, August 11, www.theguardian.com.
Peaslee, RM 2013, "Media conduction: festivals, networks, and boundaried spaces," *International Journal of Communication* 7: 811–30.

22

Fantagonism

Factions, Institutions, and Constitutive Hegemonies of Fandom

DEREK JOHNSON

Disharmony has long held a contradictory place in studies of fandom and cult television.[1] While early works like Bacon-Smith's *Enterprising Women* (1992) stressed unity within fan communities, Jenkins's *Textual Poachers* acknowledged rifts among fans, producers, and even other fans, stressing the "passions that surround[ed] disputes" (1992: 130). However, Jenkins too deflected attention from conflict and dissent, emphasizing the consensual and positing that "disagreements occur within a shared frame of reference, a common sense of the series' generic placement and a tacit agreement about what questions are worth asking" (137). As Jenkins later explained, he "accented the positive" to distance fandom from perceptions of it as immature, deviant, and ultimately immaterial to academic study (Harrison 1996: 274). While tactically advantageous, this initial focus on consensus and unity underplayed the constitutive centrality of antagonism and power to television fandom.

Since then, Tulloch and Jenkins (1995) have shown that science fiction series attract heterogeneous fan groups with varying interests, diverse reading practices, and unequal positions of stature within the community. Baym (2000) and MacDonald (1998) have examined the internal hierarchical structures that frequently make fandom a site of exclusion. Externally, Gwenllian-Jones (2003) examines tensions between communities and institutions over unauthorized interactions with corporately owned intellectual properties. While these accounts begin to emphasize inequalities of power relative to fan culture, media studies would benefit from more expansive theorizations of constitutive, hegemonic antagonisms beyond the "moments of friction and dispute" that characterized *Textual Poachers* (Jenkins 1992: 132). Instead of conceiving of antagonism as momentary aberration within unified consensus, I propose that ongoing struggles for discursive dominance constitute fandom as a hegemonic struggle over interpretation and evaluation through which relationships among fan, text, and producer are continually articulated, disarticulated, and rearticulated.

Focusing on the cult television series *Buffy the Vampire Slayer* (1997–2003), this chapter argues that power-laden discursive struggles play a constitutive role in structuring the fan-text-producer relationship.[2] Through communicative contributions to websites, newsgroups, and bulletin boards, factions of *Buffy* fans construct competing "truths" about the series, its producers, and its relationship to fandom, endeavoring to fix fan identity in respectively advantageous ways. Discussions of the program erupt across a range of online venues, some dedicated exclusively to *Buffy*, others to the works of series creator Joss Whedon, and others to television at large. My sample, collected during the 2001–2 and 2002–3 seasons, neither is exhaustive nor confirms monolithic, representative attitudes within a singular, generalizable *Buffy* fan community. Rather, this study evidences antagonistic competition between discourses of interpretation and evaluation in the interaction of opposing factions operating *within* individual communities in defined virtual spaces.[3]

The significance of these struggles for discursive hegemony becomes apparent when considered in terms of the relationships between fans and textual structures discussed by Jenkins (1992) and Hills (2002). Hills coins the term "hyperdiegesis" to denote the consistent continuity that makes cult narratives like *Buffy* cohere overall as ontologically secure worlds (2002: 138). Hyperdiegesis provides audiences with constant, trustworthy, supportive environments for productive practices like discussion, speculation, and fan fiction. While hyperdiegesis is a quality of the primary text, Jenkins's "meta-text" is a tertiary, fan-made construction—a projection of the text's potential future, based on specific fan desires and interests (1992: 97). But diverse, divergent fan interests—generated from the same hyperdiegesis, but leading to different meta-textual conclusions—cannot, I argue, be met by any singular, canonical iteration of the series. Events in hyperdiegetic continuity that please one fan or interest group conflict with competing meta-textual interests of another. Co-present meta-texts, therefore, necessarily exist in opposition. Competing meta-textual evaluations of hyperdiegetic states will therefore play a crucial role in structuring the antagonistic ways fans relate to one another, producers, and the text.

Ultimately, this chapter proposes that practices of cult television fandom be considered in terms of "fantagonism"—ongoing, competitive struggles between both internal factions and external institutions to discursively codify the fan-text-producer relationship according to their respective interests. To illustrate, I will explore discursive conflicts, first within fan communities and, second, between fans and producers of *Buffy*.[4] At both levels, competing interests advocate rival "truths" that codify and recodify fandom within continually contested parameters. While factionalized internal interests vie for discursive hegemony, forces external to fan practice exercise their institutional power to define and delimit relationships among audience, production, and text. The struggles of fantagonism not only produce tertiary interpretations and evaluations but also (as I will show) encode contending constructions of the "normative" fantext-producer relationship into the primary television text. Antagonisms external and internal to fandom structure its practices, with fan and institutional interests competing to establish dominant meta-textual interpretative discourses while legitimizing specific audience relationships to the industrial production of the hyperdiegetic text.

Fan Factions and Aesthetic History

Though acknowledging diverse interests within fan groups, Tulloch and Jenkins stress the importance of shared, restricted meaning making, arguing that a "unified interpretative position is what makes fans a cultural unit, an interpretative community" (1995: 108). In the absence of institutional power, these interpretative communities wield discursive power "to write the aesthetic history of the show—dividing [it] into a series of 'golden ages' and 'all-time lows'" (1995: 145). But if, as Hills argues, communal schism occurs over "favourite characters, actors, periods in a series, films in a franchise, or according to differences in fans' interpretative strategies," the process by which competing interest blocs attempt to secure this aesthetic consensus comes into question (2002: 62). How do inequalities of status and textual interest give way to unified interpretation? Alternative positions and tastes must somehow be silenced so that divergent interests within a community can be unified as hegemonic interpretative consensus.

Within discussions of *Buffy*, interpretative schism frequently occurred in response to the visibility of "shippers" (short for "relationshippers"), fans whose meta-textual conception of the series advocated the romantic coupling of specific characters and whose ongoing pleasure depended in part upon sustained diegetic potential to spark or preserve those romances. While shippers are not limited to cult series, *Buffy* offered numerous dyads to create such interest: Buffy/Angel, Buffy/Spike, Buffy/Riley, Spike/Angel, and so on. Shippers often inhabit specialized online communities and discussion venues, but this multiplicity of romantic permutations regularly puts shipper interests in competition within larger *Buffy* fan communities.[5] Although some pairings proved more popular, the inability of the producers' official hyperdiegetic construction to satisfy all these shipper interests created grounds for struggle. While meta-texts coexisted paradigmatically, canonical hyperdiegesis could syntagmatically fulfill only one of them at a time. Thus, when the Buffy/Spike relationship began in season 6, the text foreclosed on meta-textual hopes for reunion with previous love interest Angel (or Riley). Thus, debates over hyperdiegetic developments erupted to negotiate the incompatible interests of concerned fans.

Some concerned fans, however, opposed any pairing. Endorsing alternative taste cultures that devalued romance as soap opera convention, these fans introduced further meta-textual incompatibility—intensifying existing antagonisms. As one particularly vitriolic fan wrote,

> There's nothing like wanting to rant and whine about the pathetic state *Buffy* [. . .] has sunk into only to open a message board [. . .] filled with a thousand "This is the best eva because Spike+Buffy 4eva!!!" dumb posts from 'Shippers to make me want to brain myself with a blunt, barbed metallic cleaver to end the pain.[6]

This fan demonstrates passionately, if impenetrably, that fans do not easily agree to disagree—differing opinions become co-present, competing interests struggling to define interpretative and evaluative consensus. While Buffy/Spike shippers welcomed developments furthering that relationship, others articulated such episodes, incompatible with their metatextual conception of the series, to a decline in quality. Continuing his diatribe, the same fan claimed,

> 'Shippers don't care that the plot is nonexistent, the pace plods, and everything sucks. [...] It doesn't matter that Spike tried to rape Buffy [...] [in] a shocking show of lack of continuity and lazy writing [...] because 'Shippers know that Spike and Buffy belong together. Just like how Angel and Buffy belong together. [...] [E]veryone ends up talking about baby names while genuine fans flee in terror.

Coyly demonstrating an inability to reconcile hyperdiegesis with metatext, this critique imposes a discursive framework not just on *Buffy*'s aesthetic history but also on *Buffy* fans at large. The equivalence posited here of nonshippers and "genuine fans" raises the stakes of the debate past textual evaluation to include the proper aesthetic orientation of fan to text.

Discursive attempts to retrospectively define golden ages and all-time lows aggravate this fragmentation of antagonistic fan communities. In constructing aesthetic histories, different factions foreground elements from the hyperdiegetic past that most strongly support their meta-textual interests, contrasting them with unsavory elements that do not—knowledge claims that, if reiterated, produce norms to either invalidate the series' status quo or legitimate it within a tradition of quality. During 2002–3, for example, many fans constructed the recent season 6 as *Buffy*'s aesthetic nadir—a truth claim contested by others in a debate tellingly titled "Season 6 was the biggest piece of shit ever."[7] This critical deliberation placed individual seasons—and fans who valued them—within hierarchies of taste. According to one fan, "to say that Season 6 was good is almost to dishonor those seasons that were actually good," elaborating that *Buffy*

> started out as a groundbreakingly great television series. [In season 6], for whatever reason, they decided to fall back on Soap opera clichés [...] [giving] the Up yours to the old school fans who would have loved a return to normalcy. [...] That isn't even going into the long term damage to the "heart" of the series that various arcs suggested.

Professing adoration for the series' past, the author nevertheless claimed that "old school fans" had been shortchanged by recent plot developments that veered from their shared meta-textual interests. Because supposedly shared desires for "normalcy" had been foreclosed upon by narrative developments, the author perceived a failure in ontological security, in the somehow truer hyperdiegetic "heart" of the series in which he or she had become invested—an investment devalued by recent episodes.

Proponents of season 6's meta-textual promise, however, launched their own attempts to reify it as a golden age within an alternative aesthetic history. One fan wrote, "Overall season 6 was the most experimental season of them all. A lot of the experiments failed, I'll admit, but a lot of them succeeded with flying colors." Another supporter, attacking a detractor, blasted, "I think you're an arrogant narcissist. [. . .] [F]orgive me for not taking seriously your hackneyed, uncreative argument, which by the way has been argued all over the Internet." The evaluative struggle again enlarged, forwarding truth claims not just about season 6 but also about competing factions of fans. For both sides, "true fan" status necessitated appreciation of one aesthetic, one prescribed evaluative relationship to the text.

Brooker describes similar struggles between "gushers" accused of uncritically accepting drivel and "bashers" charged with gratuitous harshness. Such hostile interpretative stalemates fragment online fan communities into splinter groups with "their own strongholds [. . .] where they consolidate and preach to the choir" (2002: 95–96). Only in rupture could the antagonisms of Brooker's *Star Wars* fans produce the unified consensus of interpretation observed by Tulloch and Jenkins. For the *Buffy* fans observed here, however, "commonsense" consensus of interpretation vis-à-vis season 6 formed hegemonically in debate, where a dominant discourse was legitimated before dissident secession became necessary. Detractors incorporated alternative interpretative values until most agreed that season 6 "had some of the best ideas of the entire series, but the way they were written was just awful." Even the staunchest season 6 supporter backpedaled: "this post has made me reconsider my opinion of season 6 as a whole. [. . .] I can say that I enjoyed this season more than any other, but I can no longer say it's the best." Those whose meta-textual interests meshed with season 6 (like Buffy/Spike shippers) could continue enjoying that season the most, but they lost the battle to legitimize truth claims about its excellence as dominant discourse. Their tastes were subordinated within a hierarchical, hegemonically consensual, group meta-text.

Not all *Buffy* fans, however, consensually accepted season 6 as a low point in the series; this discussion only evidences the process by which antagonism constituted a single unified reading formation. Although season 3 compared favorably in 2002–3 to season 6, elements of the former were framed when first aired as "a SLAP to the face," guilty of "turning our beloved show into crap."[8] Thus, fan interpretation is constantly shifting, never unified or maintaining the same valences over time. Despised eras may later become beloved if they retrospectively satisfy the meta-textual desires of dominant fan interests. This extended analysis of aesthetic debate is therefore representative not in the judgments it contains, but in the process by which those judgments were met. Consensus of interpretation legitimated some meta-textual constructions and evaluative discourse at the expense of marginalized others. By discursively framing textual history, competing power blocs attempt to fix the meta-textual projections that can be made from the hyperdiegetic text in the future. Reiterated over time, these antagonistic debates form a habitus, generating not explicitly declared rules and norms but reasonable, commonsense behaviors that reproduce the dispositions most favorable to it (Bourdieu 1999: 110). By reinforcing certain textual contingencies as desirable, fan consensus reproduces tastes predisposed to those particular interpretations. Although golden ages change, factionalized fan interests can provisionally install certain evaluations as hegemonic common sense through antagonistic, intracommunity discourse. By constructing consensual legitimizations of a particular season or story line, the habitus of fan discourse encourages future interpretations to evaluate narrative elements against a privileged meta-text. The interpretation of the cult text in the future is made to appear as the extension of a supposedly consensual and objective view of the past.

Fan Activism: Vilifying the Producer

While fantagonism structures hegemonies of textual interpretation, internal struggles to empower factional meta-texts often expand to challenge the discursive and productive monopolies of institutional forces outside fandom—often those in the industrial sphere of hyperdiegetic production. Corporate producers' creative choices often delimit the range of interpretation possible within fan meta-texts, authorizing some but denying others. While audiences can, via fan fiction, adapt the text to marginalized interests, they can also challenge corporate producers by constructing interpretative consensuses that delegitimize institutional authority over the hyperdiegetic text.

Early studies of television fandom engaged with external fan-producer antagonisms more openly than internal fan schisms. In Jenkins's view, fan fiction "involves not simply fascination or adoration, but also frustration and antagonism. [. . .] Because popular narratives often fail to satisfy, fans must struggle [. . .] to find ways to salvage them for their interests" (1992: 23). But salvage is not always possible. This antagonism moved into the institutional sphere when Jenkins's *Beauty and the Beast* fans, finding their meta-textual interests foreclosed upon, advocated the cancellation of the series—only a season after fighting to renew it. *Doctor Who* fans launched similar campaigns to "'save the programme' from its producer" (Tulloch & Jenkins 1995: 160). The producers of these series either eliminated narrative elements in which dominant fan factions had become invested, or else introduced new ones that prohibited significant meta-textual contingencies, therefore compelling some fans to defy their authority with what Pam Wilson calls "narrative activism" (2004: 337).

But like *Star Trek*'s Gene Roddenberry, *Buffy* creator Joss Whedon is often deified by the fan base. As an auteur, Whedon's authorial signature linked *Buffy*, spin-off *Angel*, and even the diegetically autonomous *Firefly* in an intertextual relationship (sometimes referred to as the "Whedonverse" or "Jossverse"), reinforcing the hyperdiegetic coherence of those worlds by promising consistency, continuity, and quality within and between texts. The ontological security he provided caused some fans to "agree with Joss that he knows what's best for our own good better than we do."[9] So if the author figure can so defuse fan discontent, where does fantagonism come into play?

Enter perceived pretender to the throne, executive producer Marti Noxon, whose collaboration with Whedon challenged the hyperdiegetic security of auteurism. While Whedon nurtured fledgling series *Firefly*, Noxon faced scrutiny and distrust while managing *Buffy*'s sixth season in his stead. The aforementioned hegemonic reading formation that de-valued season 6 worked simultaneously to delegitimize Noxon's produc-tive authority and privileged relationship to the text. Many fans vilified Noxon: one Frequently Asked Questions list insisted she was "widely considered the Devil,"[10] with some fans dubbing her "Marti Noxious." Mirroring evaluations of season 6 in general, criticisms of Noxon con-demned her production of "angsty and depressing episodes" akin to melodrama and soap opera.[11] While it is unclear whether such critics were unwilling to accept a woman as Whedon's show-running succes-sor, the female Noxon was nevertheless assigned the blame for the series' perceived dalliances in devalued, feminized storytelling forms (despite the series' prior melodramatic leanings). Even fans who admired Noxon held her, for better or worse, responsible for both the quality of that sea-son and any problems perceived during Whedon's absence. "I actually think that she 'gets' these characters better than Joss does," opined one fan, "which is why I was so surprised at how bad season six was with her at the helm."[12]

Not all disgruntled fans delegitimized Noxon in such a direct, con-structive manner. One fan authored a faux studio press release announc-ing Noxon as the next "Big Bad" (*Buffy*-speak for each season's recurring narrative antagonist):

> It was easy to make the audience hate [Noxon]. We purposely planted in-numerable inconsistencies into the weekly scripts, making the characters act very, well, out of character. According to Noxon, "They hate me. They really do. I've managed to tick off the Angel fans, Spike fans, the Willow fans [...] pretty much the whole lot of them. [...] Just check out some of the posting boards. [...] So, I guess I'm doing a good job. I mean, I'm the one Big Bad you just can't defeat."[13]

Highlighting a number of hegemonic (if often unduly severe) fan dis-courses surrounding Noxon, this critique charged her stewardship with breaking continuity and, thus, harming the narrative's hyperdiegetic coherence. Perceiving a diversity of fan factions each disgruntled and alienated by Noxon's productive control, this text evidences a potential point of commonality for a hegemonic consensus of interpretation between competing interests all feeling equally betrayed. These sentiments did not go unrecognized: "I get such hate mail, you wouldn't believe," echoed Noxon (Gottlieb 2002).

Fan attitudes toward Noxon, therefore, suggest a struggle for discursive and productive authority between fans and producer. By calcifying perceptions that Noxon had illegitimately taken over and sullied the series, these fans worked to negate her authority in support of their own metatextual interests. Because they so denied producerly and narrative competency, we might be tempted to call these viewers "anti-fans"—a term Gray proposes for audiences who approach texts in negatively charged, uninterested, or irritated ways (2003: 71). However, the militancy of these *Buffy* viewers remained symptomatic of fandom, not of anti-fandom in its own right. Though Gray importantly identifies alternative modes of audience engagement, anti-fans who hate a program (without necessarily viewing it) must be differentiated from disgruntled fan factions who hate episodes, eras, or producers because they perceive a violation of the larger text they still love. Fans may follow programs closely, even when meta-text and hyperdiegesis become so divergent that one would rather see the series end than continue on its displeasing current course. Fans may hate the current status quo, but their intense feelings and continued contribution to fan discourse stem from pleasurable engagement with the diegetic past. Negative discourse in these instances compartmentalizes dissatisfaction with part of the text so fans may continue enjoying other elements of it.[14]

Fan factions maneuver to secure extratextual, intracommunal interpretative dominance, but also to counter external threats to their interests posed by institutions, declaring their own authority in legitimizing cultural production and audience relationship to it. Each power bloc, formed around factional meta-textual interests, competes to wield enough discursive power within the community to mobilize appropriate challenges to the productive power of outside institutional/industrial forces. But given the unequal resources available to antagonistic fans, is the battle for authority over the fan-text-producer relationship one that any faction can hope to win? If producers like Noxon are the Big Bad, as some fans contend, what special powers work to prevent their defeat?

The Author Strikes Back: Disciplining the Fan

While besieged producers sometimes defend themselves in online fan forums, they also enjoy privileged means of answering challenges to their discursive, producerly authority. Corporate counterdiscourses discipline and reorient the relationship of fans to textual production, reinscribing unruly audiences who produce their own texts—both fan fiction and tertiary critiques—within consumptive roles that more efficiently translate fandom into corporate profits. Corporate producers intervene in the struggles of fantagonism by reasserting their productive dominance, reframing "normative" fandom within "proper" spheres of consumption.

This response often manifests as legal action. Issuing injunctions against online fan productions, *Star Wars* producer George Lucas is "in the ironic position of reclaiming control over an Empire, [. . .] stamping out 'rebel' interpretations such as slash fiction or films that infringe copyright" (Brooker 2002: 88). But his Lucasfilm, Ltd. is not the only corporation to serve cease-and-desist orders. "The Slayer's Fanfic Archive," a *Buffy*-oriented site, was similarly shut down by 20th Century Fox in 2003.[15] As Consalvo remarks, fans respond to these studio tactics by removing links to official corporate sites and organizing media blackout days that withhold the free advertising provided by fan sites (2003: 78–79). Arguably, such tactics only inconvenience media corporations; moreover, fans confronted by corporations are financially unable to mount a corresponding legal defense (Jenkins 2000: 104). Brooker (2002), Consalvo (2003), and Gwenllian-Jones (2003) have all also noted the assimilative tactics employed by studios; fans who migrate to official sites—submitting to institutional rules and surveillance—receive amnesty from corporate lawyers. Yet these legalistic measures target only those fan uses of copyrighted intellectual property that challenge corporate productive and distributional hegemony. Because copyright law cannot curb consumer dissent, alternative strategies must rejoin the challenges represented by fans' discursive power to construct aesthetic histories of corporate production.

To this end, the television text itself has been mobilized to narratively construct "acceptable" fan activity—bolstering extratextual legal measures by building critiques of unruly fans directly into the text that supports unauthorized discursive activity. Thus, while defiant fans made her a villain, Noxon concurrently oversaw the narrative construction of fans as the Big Bad in *Buffy*'s sixth season. Fancying themselves super villains ("like Dr. No"), unpopular geeks Warren, Jonathan, and Andrew become the "Evil Trio," the season's ongoing threat to Buffy. Instead of bringing the apocalypse, like most Buffy nemeses, these weak, ineffectual, pathetic villains complicate Buffy's attempts to manage greater (arguably soap-operatic) real-world problems. What distinguishes these flaccid antagonists, however, is their intertextual referentiality to cult texts. Trapping Buffy in a looped sequence of time in the episode "Life Serial," for example, they draw parallels between their actions and those featured on cult series from which they effectively poach:

> ANDREW: I just hope she solves it faster than Data did on the ep of
>   *TNG* where the *Enterprise* kept blowing up.
> WARREN: Or Mulder, in *The X-Files* where the bank kept blowing up.
> ANDREW: Scully wants me so bad.

Tailored to fan sensibilities, these characters make references that audiences with memories of these *Star Trek* and *X-Files* episodes alone would appreciate.

Simultaneously, however, such recognition implicates viewers in the deviance articulated to the Trio's social otherness and inappropriate relationship to media texts. The Trio's obsessive interest in *Star Wars* collectibles evidences their status as undisciplined consumers amassing trivial knowledge and possessions—an alterity that recalls their prior transgressions of social norms. In the fifth season, Warren had built a submissive robotic slave to replace his flesh-and-blood girlfriend Katrina. After attempting suicide in season 3, the eternally friendless Jonathan reconfigured the universe in season 4's "Superstar" to make himself the center of Buffy's world—demonstrating a fannish proclivity for unauthorized manipulation of the hyperdiegesis.[16] Though Andrew debuts in the sixth season, he is established as the brother of a previously encountered teen deviant. These outcasts' pathetic villainy therefore derives from substitution of constructs—robots, parallel universes, and media texts—for normative interpersonal relationships. The only chance these infantilized men have for a nonrobotic, heteronormative sexual encounter lies in placing a spell on Katrina in the episode "Dead Things." When this rape fails, and Warren kills Katrina, the articulation of fandom, social violation, and transgressive alterity calcifies, only reinforced by the devotion shown to Warren by an increasingly demasculinized and suggestively homosexual Andrew. Even as Buffy and Xander protect Andrew from unjust death at the hands of Willow in "Two to Go," they demasculinize him for demonstrating his fan knowledge (in this case, a triple *Star Wars* reference):

> ANDREW: You think your little witch buddy's gonna stop with us? You saw her! She's a truck driving magic mama! We've got maybe seconds before Darth Rosenberg grinds everybody into Jawa Burgers and not one of your bunch has the midichlorians to stop her!
>
> XANDER: You've never had any tiny bit of sex, have you?

Amid the "growing up" theme of season 6, the fan status ascribed to Xander in prior seasons is interestingly reduced and transferred to these new characters. In condemning fannish behavior, adult Xander understands the social unacceptability of filtering reality through fantasy texts. Xander no longer makes fan references without some kind of conscious self-deprecation to mark himself off from the Trio and thus from fan deviancy. Noxon characterizes the Trio as "trying to do anything to sort of shortcut having to do adult things, like getting a job or going to school" (*Sci-Fi Wire* 2002). Career and heterosexual relationships thus prevent Xander from being similarly constructed as deviant fan—unlike the Trio, whose inability to form relationships outside of cult media articulates fandom to immaturity, instability, and even the violations of rape.

While embodying cult fandom in general, the Trio also narrativizes *Buffy* fans specifically. Despite their relative insignificance, these powerless fans attempt to insinuate themselves into larger (narrative) goings-on. In posing challenges (like the time loop) that produce diagnostic knowledge of Buffy's abilities, the Trio plans to redirect her attention—and that of the series—away from soapy, real-world dilemmas and toward a more fantastical direction of their meta-textual choosing. While referencing other series at the diegetic level, their extradiegetic role is as stand-ins for outspoken *Buffy* fans. Tom Lenk, the actor who plays Andrew, explains, "We're playing what the truly obsessive *Buffy* fans would be [...] the writers have told us that we're basically them personified" (Topel 2002). As part of the industrial discourse working to constitute a disciplined fandom, the Trio reinforces the hegemonic "truth" that fans should be disregarded, mocked, and even feared as obsessive, socially deviant outcasts.

These representations further inhibit fandom's discursive productivity by disarticulating fans from storytelling practice and rearticulating them to compliant consumption. In season 7, Andrew (sole surviving member of the Trio) becomes Buffy's prisoner-yet-pseudo-ally. In "Storyteller," Andrew's fan practices expand from referentiality to unauthorized narrative production; he effectively authors a fan video about Buffy (and, extradiegetically, *Buffy* the series), filtering narrative events through his own interpretative perspective. Andrew also rewrites his own history, excusing his crimes while also embellishing his prior villainous prowess. His sexuality still uncertain, Andrew identifies with Anya, rather than Xander, as he films a romantic conversation between the two. This unruly storyteller is ultimately confronted by Buffy (at knifepoint over the Hellmouth!) and coerced into abandoning these textually productive practices: "Stop! Stop telling stories. Life isn't a story," Buffy commands, demanding that Andrew discontinue his interpretations of the hyperdiegetic past. To be redeemed and socially rehabilitated, deviant Andrew must cease and desist—give up storytelling and submit to the narrative as the authoritative Buffy experienced it.[17] His eventual redemption is punctuated by his transformation from sexually ambiguous nerd into confirmed heterosexual, suave sage, and trusted ally. Appearing on spin-off *Angel* the next season ("The Girl in Question"), a changed Andrew offers Angel and Spike advice about "moving on" before departing with a beautiful woman on each tuxedo-clad arm. Though he still references cult texts, Andrew, like Xander, has replaced fandom with a new social discipline—seemingly that of watcher in training.[18] Andrew's redemption thus promises a more proper, passive, socially acceptable fan consumption.

Deployed within larger institutional discourses, the Trio's reformation of fan-text-producer relationships should not be mistaken as the malicious response of a single producer like Noxon. Leyla Harrison, a recurring character on *The X-Files* (named in memory of a prominent fan fiction author), similarly enforces boundaries between the fan and textual productivity. Though a "fan" of Mulder and Scully, untrained Agent Harrison settles for reading reports of their exploits, rather than contributing to them. Even the *Star Trek* franchise, whose generic conventions prohibit overt acknowledgment of contemporary fandom, manages to pathologize unauthorized narrative production. Lieutenant Barclay, a recurring character on both *The Next Generation* and *Voyager*, is repeatedly disciplined for his addictive, unhealthy use of holodeck technology to appropriate the regular characters in virtual reality narratives. Although Hayward (1997) and Jenkins (2002) suggest that interactions between industry and audience enabled by television and new media convergence might blur the lines between production and consumption, characters like the Evil Trio allow television institutions to redraw that line and increase its resolution, rearticulating distinctions between normative audience and Othered fan, professional and amateur, producer and consumer.

Conclusion

This struggle to consensually legitimate competing knowledge claims about fans, cult texts, and their production—fantagonism—operates discursively to constitute hegemonies within factionalized fan communities. But internal constructions of communal interpretative consensus compose just one front on which the war for hegemony is waged; we must also look outward since it is in the productive authority of external corporate institutions that the greatest power is mobilized. Fans attack and criticize media producers whom they feel threaten their meta-textual interests, but producers also respond to these challenges, protecting their privilege by defusing and marginalizing fan activism. As fans negotiate positions of production and consumption, antagonistic corporate discourse toils to manage that discursive power, disciplining productive fandom so it can continue to be cultivated as a consumer base. Here I have added to our catalogue of the corporate arsenal a textual strategy through which producers work to subordinate fans to their discursive authority. However, while textual representations like the Evil Trio constitute an institutional bid to circumscribe fan activity, that textuality is negotiated in turn via interpretative and evaluative debates within fandom that, through their own redefinitions and reevaluations, keep antagonistic, discursive struggles for hegemony in play. As one writer observes of the Trio, "The controversial nerds were either loved or hated by the fan base. Some adored their comedic riffs on everything sci-fi and geek-based while others were irritated by the exact same thing" (DiLullo 2003). Thus, as the Trio and other textual manifestations of the external, institutional dimension of fantagonism enter into fan aesthetic historiography, they promise to inspire the same kind of internal, factional fan schism explored at the outset.

Whether through interpretative, legal, or narrative measures, fan activity is discursively dominated, disciplined, and defined to preserve hegemonies of cultural power at the local or institutional level. Ultimately, the multidimensional, antagonistic dynamics of cult fandom demand that we avoid utopian models of fan community and productive participation, and engage more directly with the constitutive negotiations of hegemony.

NOTES

1 Thanks to Julie D'Acci, Henry Jenkins, Jonathan Gray, Ron Becker, and Aswin Punathambekar for their helpful comments and insights on various drafts of this piece.

2 Theorizing fan-text-producer relationships complicates audience-text relationships as discussed by Nightingale (2003), accounting for both productive and consumptive fan practice and, following Gwenllian-Jones (2003: 174), industrial strategies designed to maximize audience involvement.

3 While relaxing limitations on group dynamic and generating alongside greater diversity of membership more disagreement and antagonism, online communication has not *introduced* conflictual relationships to fandom. Though insufficiently emphasized in previous scholarly work, real tensions, anxieties, and disputes were evidenced in offline fan relations (see Jenkins 1992: 187–91; Bacon-Smith 1992: 229). We might, however, still interrogate the amplifying or foregrounding effect of the Internet.

4 In addition to the dimensions of fans versus fans and fans versus producers, other dynamics of conflict could be similarly explored (fans versus academics, for example).

5 Although I distinguish between larger fan interests, communities, and competing factions within them, the boundaries of discrete interest groups do not prohibit individual fans from enjoying "dual citizenship" or visiting other communities; like-minded, consensual groups rarely operate in isolation without (antagonistic) interaction at a larger level. Thus, we might think of the larger fandom as a site of struggle just as we would the individual communities.

6   "Damn the 'Shippers,'" retrieved May 2, 2003, from mrsg.lunarpages.com.

7   "Season 6 was the biggest piece of shit ever," July 5–6, 2002, retrieved May 2, 2003, from fireflyfans.net.

8   "Why is Joss turning our beloved show into crap?," October 6, 1998, retrieved May 2, 2003, from alt.tv.buffy-v-slayer.

9   "The Remote Controllers," October 20, 2002, retrieved May 2, 2003, from www.whedonesque.com.

10 "Opinion FAQ," retrieved May 2, 2003, from www.slayage.com.

11 "Had an Idea," November 4, 2002, retrieved May 2, 2003, from firefly fans.net.

12 "Season 6 was the biggest piece of shit ever."

13 Headline: "Season Big Bad revealed (soilers) [sic]," retrieved May 2, 2003, from www.btvs-tabularasa.net.

14 Jenkins recognizes this compartmentalized disappointment in his often overlooked chapter on *Beauty and the Beast* fans (1992: 132).

15 See Chilling Effects (www.chillingeffects.com) for more accounts of media corporations taking legal action against fan producers.

16 Larbalestier (2002) discusses Jonathan as a textual embodiment of Buffy fans.

17 Andrew briefly relapses in the later episode "Dirty Girls," including a fight to the death with Mr. Spock in his history of rogue vampire slayer Faith. Andrew was, however, sternly reprimanded.

18 The need to cultivate enthusiastic media consumption makes it counterproductive for corporate discourse to entirely rehabilitate the fan. See Gwenllian-Jones (2003).

WORKS CITED

Bacon-Smith, C 1992, *Enterprising women: television fandom and the creation of popular myth*, University of Pennsylvania Press, Philadelphia.

Baym, NK 2000, *Tune in, log on: soaps, fandom, and online community*, Sage, Thousand Oaks, CA.

Bourdieu, P 1999, "Structures, habitus, practices," in A Elliot (ed.), *Contemporary social theory*, Blackwell, New York.

Brooker, W 2002, *Using the force: creativity, community, and Star Wars fans*, Continuum, New York.

Consalvo, M 2003, "Cyber-slaying media fans: code, digital poaching, and corporate control of the Internet," *Journal of Communication Inquiry* 27(1): 67–86.

DiLullo, T 2003, "Tom Lenk," *Altzone.com*, www.buffy.nu.

Gottlieb, A 2002, "Buffy's angels," *Oakland's Urbanview*, September 25, www.metroactive.com.

Gray, J 2003, "New audiences, new textualities: anti-fans and non-fans," *International Journal of Cultural Studies* 6(1): 64–81.

Gwenllian-Jones, S 2003, "Web wars: resistance, online fandom, and studio censorship," in M Jancovich & J Lyons (eds.), *Quality popular television: cult TV, the industry, and fans*, BFI, London.

Harrison, T 1996, "Interview with Henry Jenkins," in T Harrison et al. (eds.), *Enterprise zones: critical positions on Star Trek*, Westview, Boulder, CO.

Hayward, J 1997, *Consuming pleasures: active audiences and serial fictions from Dickens to soap opera*, University Press of Kentucky, Lexington.

Hills, M 2002, *Fan cultures*, Routledge, New York.

Jenkins, H 1992, *Textual poachers: television fans and participatory culture*, Routledge, New York.

Jenkins, H 2000, "Digital land grab," *Technology Review* 103(2): 103–5.

Jenkins, H 2002, "Interactive audiences?," in D Harries (ed.), *The new media book*, BFI, London.

Larbalestier, J 2002, "Buffy's Mary Sue is Jonathan: Buffy acknowledges the fans," in R Wilcox & D Lavery (eds.), *Fighting the forces: what's at stake in* Buffy the Vampire Slayer, Rowman & Littlefield, Lanham, MD.

MacDonald, A 1998, "Uncertain utopia: science fiction media fandom and computer mediated communication," in C Harris & A Alexander (eds.), *Theorizing fandom: fans, subculture, and identity*, Hampton, Cresskill, NJ.

Nightingale, V 2003, "Improvising Elvis, Marilyn, and Mickey Mouse," in V Nightingale & K Ross (eds.), *Critical readings: media and audiences*, Open University Press, Maidenhead, UK.

Sci-Fi Wire 2002, "Buffy getting darker," January 15, www.scifi.com.

Topel, F 2002, "Tom Lenk—Buffy baddie," *About.com*, actionadventure.about.com.

Tulloch, J & Jenkins, H 1995, *Science fiction audiences: watching Dr. Who and Star Trek*, Routledge, London.

Wilson, P 2004, "Jamming Big Brother: webcasting, audience intervention, and narrative activism," in S Murray & L Ouellette (eds.), *Reality TV: remaking television culture*, New York University Press, New York.

23

The Powers That Squee

Orlando Jones and Intersectional Fan Studies

SUZANNE SCOTT

For a field foundationally invested in identity politics and power dynamics, fan studies has historically privileged some identities and power structures, while remaining reluctant to critically engage others. As Rebecca Wanzo notes, race remains troublingly undertheorized within fan studies, "frequently treated as an add-on (or a should-be-addressed-somewhere-later)" (2015: n.p.). One rationale Wanzo offers for the citational erasure of work on African American fans and remix cultures within fan studies is the desire of scholars to continue to position fans as oppositional audiences, to frame "othering in a manner that valorizes people who have claimed otherness as opposed to having otherness thrust upon them" (2015: n.p.). In line with this often celebratory framing of fandom as an "oppositional" space, there have been myriad studies of industrial or authorial efforts to contain or circumvent fans' "resistant" interpretations and transformative textual production (see, for instance, Wexelblat 2002; Russo 2009; and Felschow 2010). Conversely, there has been minimal engagement with moments of "fantagonism" (to borrow a term from Derek Johnson's contribution to this collection) in which a fan community resists the fan credentials or fan identity of one of "the powers that be" (hereafter TPTB), an industrial category that has historically referred to studio/network executives, creators, and showrunners, but is increasingly being extended to include cast or crew who exert authority within fan spaces.

We can no longer neatly delineate between empowered producers and disempowered consumers within digital fan culture, but this doesn't mean we have moved beyond conversations of power and privilege. Many fan scholars remain attentive to industrial appropriations of fan labor in order to consider which modes of fan engagement are "empowered" or "marginalized." This essay addresses the other side of this trend, exploring the tensions surrounding instances in which TPTB claim (or are perceived to be co-opting) fan identities. Through this analysis, I wish to both stress the need for more intersectional conceptions of fan identity and highlight resistances to certain intersectional fan identities as we continue these vital conversations about the place of power and identity within fan studies.

There and Back Again: Toward a More Intersectional Fan Studies

Fandom was, and for many continues to be, conceptualized as a "vehicle for marginalized subcultural groups [. . .] to pry open space for their cultural concerns within dominant representations" (Jenkins 2007: 40). Rarely, though, have fan scholars interrogated our own tendencies toward dominant representations within our constructions of marginality. Because first-wave fan studies was informed by feminist theory, and transformative fan culture has been overwhelmingly populated by women, gender has been, and continues to be, the dominant axis of identity addressed by fan scholars. It is not my intent to critique fan studies' ongoing investment in the gendered politics of fan culture. On the contrary, I've repeatedly argued that these discussions are more vital now than ever before, particularly with regard to questions of fan labor and producer-fan interactions (see Scott 2013b, 2015). Rather, I want to suggest that in a moment of convergence for both fan culture and fan studies, it is increasingly vital to interrogate convergent fannish identities, precisely because it will allow us to reinvigorate and reimagine first-wave fan studies' focus on identity and power.

Revisiting these concerns of fan studies from the early 1990s also returns us to the cultural moment in which the term "intersectionality" was coined by Kimberlé Crenshaw to describe "the need to account for multiple grounds of identity when considering how the social world is constructed" (1993: 1245). This concept has since been taken up by scholars across disciplines to better theorize intersecting modes of oppression, or what Patricia Hill Collins in 1990 labeled the "matrix of domination" (2000: 203). Accordingly, when mapping fan culture's own matrices it is vital to reiterate Crenshaw's initial call to "summon the courage to challenge groups that are after all, in one sense, 'home' to us, in the name of the parts of us that are not made at home" (1993: 1299) in order to arrive at a more nuanced understanding of the power dynamics of producer-fan relationships in the digital age. Only then, Crenshaw suggests, can we "speak against internal exclusions and marginalizations, [and] call attention to how the identity of 'the group' has been centered on the intersectional identities of a few" (1993: 1299). My own call is to acknowledge our frequent failure, as fan scholars, to critically examine our focus on the identities of a few at the expense of developing a more intersectional conception of fans as a group. In doing so, though, I want to acknowledge that gender, despite its potentially problematic comforts as fan studies' conceptual "home," remains central to both our conception and our contestation of fan identity.

It is important to note from the outset that many fan scholars (most forcefully Hills 2002, Ford 2014, and Booth 2015) have previously and productively called for the need to nuance or move beyond some of fan studies' structuring binaries (e.g., consumerism/resistance, fanboy/fangirl, affirmational/transformative modes of engagement). On the surface, calling for a more intersectional conception of the fan within fan studies would appear to be a natural extension of these prior efforts to move away from false binaries. However, this chapter suggests that building a more intersectional fan studies is vital in large part precisely because it allows us to productively reinvigorate conversations around (or perhaps more thoroughly interrogate) the lingering power and place of these categories within fan culture and studies. Though a call for intersectionality in order to reassert the importance of the field's structuring binaries may seem conceptually counterintuitive, it would allow us to begin rectifying the historical erasure of fans of color, not to mention queer, transgender, or transcultural fans (see Morimoto & Chin, this volume), within conversations surrounding fan identity politics. Equally importantly, a reassertion/reassessment of these binaries and their lingering significance might expose the conceptual limits of intersectional fan identities within both fandom and fan studies.

The Powers That Squee: Orlando Jones as "Fangirl"

To ground this conversation, I put forward Orlando Jones as a rich test case to begin examining emergent intersectional fan identities, as both spaces of potential coalition and sites where long-standing boundaries to claiming fan identity are policed and power dynamics might be re-entrenched. Jones, an actor and comedian, first gained notoriety with fans and fan scholars alike in 2013 during his promotion of the Fox television series *Sleepy Hollow*, in which Ichabod Crane (Tom Mison) wakes up after 230 years in present-day Sleepy Hollow to assist a local cop, Abbie Mills (Nicole Beharie), in fending off the four horsemen of the apocalypse. Jones, in his supporting role as police Captain Frank Irving (for the show's first two seasons), initially played the straight man or foil for the show's supernatural shenanigans and man-out-of-time comedy. This characterization aligned nicely with Jones's early and oft-repeated claim that he was also an avid *Sleepy Hollow* fan: despite his intimate connection to the production, Jones watched weekly in a state of disbelief and delight alongside fans as the ecclesiastical drama unfolded, both in character and as himself on social media.

Even within a cultural moment in which social media interaction between content creators and fans is both an expected and an essential promotional strategy, Jones's immediate and apparently unconditional immersion into fan culture is an anomaly. Jones was credited by multiple outlets as one of the primary sources of *Sleepy Hollow*'s breakout success, and his "habitual fourth-wall breaking" and active engagement with fans of the show as a fellow fan on fannish platforms like Tumblr (in addition to more conventional promotional spaces like Twitter) was roundly celebrated as an unprecedented effort to break down "the traditional barriers between fans and the objects of their fandom" (Prudom 2013: n.p.). Jones's emphatic self-identification as a "fangirl" on social media and in interviews discursively disrupts his own identity markers, as an African American man in his late forties, and his active solicitation of fans' transformative works (including homoerotic fan texts featuring his character) complicates his producorial identity as one of TPTB.

In short, Jones forces us to interrogate many of the structuring binaries that have long occupied discussions of identity within fan studies (fanboy/fangirl, TPTB/fan) and the power dynamics associated with them, while simultaneously exemplifying how these binaries continue to be mobilized within fannish identity politics. Though gender and age are terminologically embedded in the terms "fanboy" and "fangirl," and race/whiteness and sexuality/heteronormativity perhaps problematically assumed, Jones requires us to consider not just the complexity of fannish subject positions, but how these might further intersect with his identity as one of TPTB. Thus, the conception of intersectional fan studies that I'm advocating for might also require more robust theorizations of liminal producorial identities as well as the emergent power dynamics produced by their convergence with fan identities (see Scott 2012 and 2013a). Moving toward an intersectional fan studies also produces a growing need to grapple with the ways in which unconventional "identity" categories like TPTB are also raced, gendered, aged, and so forth when considering the power they exert within fan culture.

From fan studies' inception, scholars have noted that the relationship between producers and fans is "often charged with mutual suspicion, if not open conflict" (Jenkins 1992: 32). The growing industrial incentive to cultivate and quantify fan/producer engagement across digital and social media platforms (for example, with the emergence of the Nielsen Twitter TV rating in 2013) has complicated, but in no way eradicated, these suspicions and conflicts. This culture of mutual suspicion, which is intrinsically tied to the relationship's inherent power differential, grows increasingly complex as the lines between affective, transformative, and promotional labor break down for producers and fans alike in digital culture. Since this is too limited a space in which to perform a comprehensive analysis of Jones's strategic (yet in no way synthetic) intersectional fan identity, I can only begin to unpack its complexity. Accordingly, I'm more interested in considering how Jones opens up a space for us to address the need for a more intersectional conception of fan identity, while simultaneously signaling the ongoing investment in gender as its primary axis, particularly when discussing the power dynamics between TPTB and fans.

"Fangirl Is the Correct Nomenclature"?

Jones is an emergent example of what Elizabeth Ellcessor calls a "star text of connection" (2012: 47). Ellcessor suggests that stars who use social media platforms to cultivate a sense of intimacy and immediacy in their interactions with fans become a "unifying force" or "an agent of further convergences" between media texts, platforms, and audiences (2012: 53). Jones is similarly situated as both a product and proponent of media convergence, though he differs in key ways from prior cult television personalities who have attempted to vacillate between promotional agent and fan participant, such as *Supernatural* cast member Misha Collins. Louisa Stein suggests that while Collins's popularity can be credited to his role on the show, his appeal to fans is "equally shaped by his perceived marginality and transgressiveness" (2013: 415). Though Collins has served as both a model for Jones's liminal identity performance and a frequent fannish sparring partner for Jones on social media, Jones's claims to marginality (as a person of color who self-identifies as a fangirl) and transgression (through his embrace of slash and other industrially contested forms of fan production and participation) are not only perceived, but actively presented as part of his claim to "authentic" fan identity and are central to his appeal to fans. Whereas Collins aligns himself with female fans through satirical performance, playing "the role of the masculine 'overlord'" to his "minions" (Stein 2013: 413), Jones mobilizes sincerity and camaraderie to breed intimacy. Rather than distancing himself, however playfully, from fans, Jones repeatedly and forcefully asserts his right to identify not only as a fan, despite his conflicted status as a content creator, but as a very specific type of fan: "I'm a true fangirl and nobody will ever be able to change that. And I've really always felt that I was part of this decent group that wasn't about being black, it was about our interests and things we got excited about" (Jones in Bandit 2015: n.p.).

Despite this fairly utopian, color-blind vision of fan culture, as a Black man in his late forties who self-identifies as a fangirl, Jones always already challenges culturally raced, aged, and sexed conceptions of fan identity. Interestingly, though, Jones often dismisses or elides the identity markers embedded in the term, framing "fangirl" as a mode of fan engagement rather than an identity or subject position, thus allowing him more easily to claim it. In a tweet from November 4, 2013, Jones wrote in response to a fan that when it comes to his own fan identity, "Fangirl is the correct nomenclature. Fanboys try to hide their feels to 'look cool.' I embrace them" (Jones 2013: n.p.). Jones can easily self-identity as a fangirl because, in his view, "Fangirling doesn't concern itself with color, creed, age or gender" (Jones 2014: n.p.), but is rather a state of doing and being.

Though fans' response to Jones's intersectional performance of fan identity has been overwhelmingly celebratory, some have actively challenged the implications of his claim to "fan" identity broadly, and "fangirl" identity specifically. In a March 2014 chat with Jones sponsored by the Organization for Transformative Works (Rebaza 2014: n.p.), one participant, Laura J., inquired: "Am I alone in (liking Orlando very much but) not liking his appropriation of 'fangirl'?" Jones's response was typical of previous challenges from fans on this point. After thanking Laura for sharing her perspective, Jones noted that he had "never thought of it as appropriation," but is "mindful that others do." Jones relayed that, in his mind, there is a clear distinction between fanboys and fangirls, but he "think[s] the terms are fair game for either gender," particularly as "we all possess masculine and feminine energy." He concluded with the mea culpa that "[e]ither way I realize some may find that response to be disingenuous but I use the term with respect, not derision." Some fans within the chat were quick to rally to Jones's defense, but others pressed the point. Laura J. replied that Jones's stance elided the lived realities of this identity, remarking he was "never going to be shamed for only be[ing] a girl." Others took issue with Jones's essentialist "equation of 'girl' with 'emotional,'" and Gabby took on the broader connotations of his statement: "I mean, Orlando, if you id as somewhat genderqueer, that's a thing and I would never begrudge anyone's right to self-identify. But if not, then it's side-eye material." Jones maintained his stance, but acknowledged, "I don't personally believe that self identifying as a fangirl implies that I have the ego or arrogance to suggest I am having the female experience. It's just a term that I believe applies to my own dynamic in fandom as the term itself is not gender specific in my own mind." As Kristina Busse has noted, "the widespread embrace of the white middle-class heterosexual male geek in popular culture redefines but does not erase boundaries of exclusion" (2015: 111). The lived realities of these exclusionary practices, as referenced by the fangirls in the chat above, make it clear that Jones, as a man, is in a privileged position to celebrate or revalue the perceived emotional excesses of the fangirl, and might also explain some of the disappointment surrounding his perceived lack of understanding (as he himself doesn't conform to the category of "white geek").

Mel Stanfill, one of the first fan scholars to tackle directly the common cultural construction of fans as white men, notes that though male geeks and fans might be culturally conceived as failing to behave "in a way consistent with constructed-as-white normative, middle-class, heterosexual masculinity," it is the fanboy's capacity to be recuperated into that category (and claim the privilege that accompanies it) that is central (2011: n.p.). Stanfill points out that nonwhite bodies are excluded from this recuperation narrative, and I would note that this cultural conception of the fan also excludes female and queer fans. Jones may neither racially conform to this cultural conception of the fan, nor biologically align with the "fan" that has historically been recuperated through fan studies, but a similar case might be made for Jones's capacity for recuperation (and the privilege that accompanies it), as both a male fan and one of TPTB.

This debate over Jones's claim to the identity of "fangirl," and whether we conceive of the term as a fannish disposition, a set of practices, or a gendered identity, is a prime example of what Crenshaw calls the "politics of naming" (1993: 1297). It is also exemplary of the ongoing tendency to privilege gender as the primary axis of both fannish identity and marginality. We see this clearly with these fan responses, but it is also present in Jones's somewhat paradoxical embrace of an explicitly gendered term that he insists isn't gender specific. Ironically, when Jones is celebrated for his immersion into fan culture, it is almost always for his willingness to break with his identity as a male fan (say, in his pointed adoption of "feminine" digital fan platforms, like Tumblr) or willingness to shed his paternalistic producorial identity (embracing female-driven fannish reading strategies that media industries do not traditionally comprehend or condone), without further consideration of the other identity markers in play. In the paragraphs to follow, I will consider how Jones's self-identification forces us to grapple with both what Matt Hills has called "gender plus" modes of fannish boundary policing, or "gender plus age or generation" (2012b: 123), as well as his racial identity.

After all, Jones self-identifies not merely as a fangirl, but as "a fourteen-year-old fangirl" (Jones in Bandit 2014). Jones's active presence on Tumblr is a vital component of his demographically dissonant claim to this identity, as Tumblr fan culture is not only predominantly female, but known for its youthful user base. Analyses of the platform as a distinctly aged fan space suggest that the Tumblr interface design "lends itself particularly well to the visual enactment of collective emotion," or what is colloquially referred to as "feels" within digital and fan culture (Stein 2015: 158). Stein contends that sites like Tumblr exemplify the ways in which "[m]illennial feels culture combines the aesthetics of intimate emotion—the sense that we are accessing an author's immediate and personal emotional response to media culture—with an aesthetics of high performativity, calling attention to mediation and the labor of the author" (2015: 158). Jones's Tumblr frequently traffics in these aesthetic paradoxes, often conveyed through the visual language of Tumblr feels culture, GIFs, and image macros. These fannish displays of platform-specific literacy (reinforced by his blog's pedagogic title "The Tumblr Experiment") are unquestionably a core component of Jones's "fangirl" performance, and central to his appeal. However, in calling attention to his own mediation of identity in these posts, Jones also inevitably exposes the fact that his labor is always already promotional, regardless of his intent. The intimacy produced between Jones and other fans in spaces like Tumblr may be real, but his status as one of TPTB will always provoke questions around the impetus behind this high performance of fan identity. This perception is further complicated by the fact that Tumblr is an increasingly intersectional platform, with industry-produced and fan-produced sites coexisting. Furthermore, the act of reblogging (a cornerstone of the fan's participation in and experience of community) creates a slippage between promotional content from industry and personalized messages from fans (see Kohnen 2012: n.p.).

Fannish Ecosystems and the Capacity for Coalition Building

Interestingly, though Jones is quick to invoke race when discussing media representations, and is a vocal critic of racism in its myriad forms, he (like many fans and fan scholars) has a tendency to leave race out of the conversation when discussing his own fan identity. We might simply read this as an extension of Jones's personal framing of fan identity as a mode of affective expression rather than a subject position. Or, one could cynically suggest that this is a strategic embrace of post-identity fan politics, framing fandom as the great equalizer in order to mitigate his own privileged positioning in a fandom in which he is also a creator of the fan object. Like any analysis of Jones, however, this reading would be too simplistic, particularly because, though he rarely engages his racial identity as a fan, he has used fannish tactics to vocally critique racialized violence.

For example, a little over one week after Michael Brown was killed by a police officer in Ferguson, Missouri, Jones textually poached (Jenkins 1992) the viral ALS ice bucket challenge to YouTube by dumping a bucket of bullets over his head, issuing a challenge to himself and viewers to move beyond the "us vs. them mentality" and "listen without prejudice, love without limits, and reverse the hate" (Roy 2014: n.p.). The video, which as of this writing has over 1,874,500 views, closes with the hashtags #justiceformichaelbrown, #weareallferguson, and #reversethehate. Even here, though, Jones's identity defies binary logics. In the span of one minute, Jones cites human rights activists of color such as Sister Chân Không, Martin Luther King Jr., and Mahatma Gandhi, critiques the "militarized police force threatening the rights of people to assemble," and presents himself as both a lifetime member of the National Rifle Association and a special member of the Louisiana Police Force. In a subsequent interview, Jones suggests he joined the NRA to "affect change in the organization," but more vitally and pointedly he rejects the cultural desire to reduce a reading of the video to his race alone: "Do I share all of [the NRA's] ideals? No. I'm not a monolith in culture. I don't agree with all black people on everything either. I'm a complex person and I wanted to make that point" (Roy 2014: n.p.).

Jones may be comparatively quiet on how race shapes his fan identity and experience in interviews, but he commonly frames fan culture broadly as both a space to speak back to the fact that African Americans and women are "grossly underrepresented" in the media, and a space for marginalized audiences to speak out against these biases (Jones in Granshaw 2014: n.p.). In this sense, Jones's views of fan culture often reproduce what the co-editors of this collection have identified as the "Fandom Is Beautiful" ethos of first-wave fan studies, in which fandom is conceptualized as a collective strategy to evade or challenge the hegemonic properties of media texts and industries (Gray, Sandvoss, & Harrington 2007: 2–3). In an interview with fan scholars Lucy Bennett and Bertha Chin, Jones stated that his interest in fans and fan studies is "born partially out of my own work as a creator, and the desire to better understand how fans relate to story worlds on a granular level," but also because fandom is

> a perfect little ecosystem, and in some ways it's a looking glass version of society at large, both positive and negative. This is the place where the disenfranchised and the marginalized have a voice, where they can express their dissatisfaction with the status quo and demand a more concerted effort by the media establishment to improve diversity, to expand beyond tropes, idioms, and stereotypes. (2014: n.p.)

Crenshaw argues that any movement toward intersectionality first demands recognition that "the organized identity groups in which we find ourselves in are in fact coalitions, or at least potential coalitions waiting to be formed" (1993: 1299). Here, in these comments, we see Jones's myriad identities articulated and fused together, and perhaps his own coalition mentality can model how we might better recognize coalitions waiting to be formed within the field and within fan culture.

That said, there are massive cultural and ideological barriers to the development of such coalitions, within both fan ecosystems and society at large. Authorial engagements with fans in the digital age have historically attempted to codify, rather than collapse, analog power dynamics between producers and consumers. Because of this, fans are justifiably wary of industrial "fanagement," or "the attempted management of fan readings, responses and activities" (Hills 2012a: 425). Jones, who was quick to claim during his time on *Sleepy Hollow* that 20th Century Fox wasn't dictating how he interacted with fans, has admitted that "[w]hat I'm not as surprised about, but what occasionally makes me sad, is the level of distrust my presence in fandom seems to engender at times. [. . .] Trust is obviously something that needs to be earned, but at a certain point, it starts to become uninteresting to constantly have to prove myself and demonstrate my authenticity" (Bennett & Chin 2014: n.p.). Much like Wanzo, who is justifiably critical of fan scholars who disproportionately valorize "people who have claimed otherness as opposed to having otherness thrust upon them" (2015: n.p.), fans who have expressed discomfort or open hostility toward Jones's claim of fannish "Otherness" overwhelmingly do so because of the identity markers he cannot control (TPTB), rather than those he's actively adopted (fangirl).

One recent incident exposing these tensions was Orlando Jones's controversial appearance at a 2015 *Supernatural* fan convention, which spawned an anti–Orlando Jones tag on Tumblr. Though Jones repeated insists that he was, and is, a "fan first" (Jones in Kyle 2014: n.p.), and routinely engages in fan practices surrounding *Supernatural*, including live-tweeting episodes, discussing the show with other fans, and shipping a popular slash pairing (Destiel), the fan backlash to Jones's presence suggests his inability to ever fully divorce himself from his identity as a "media industry insider" (Chin 2015: n.p.). Because of his affiliation with TPTB, Jones's own fan predilections are tainted, or are perceived to be unfairly privileged, as "fans continue to assume that his words equals [industrial] endorsement" of particular readings and character pairings (Chin 2015: n.p.). Even when Jones's "insider status" and position of relative power is positively framed as a part of his fan identity, it invariably separates him from other fans. For example, Jones has embraced the fannish performance of "shipping," short for "relationshipping," or supporting or desiring a particular romantic pairing between characters. Jones's repeated fannish references to "Ichabbie" (a portmanteau for those invested in the relationship of *Sleepy Hollow*'s protagonists Ichabod Crane and Abbie Mills) led to some *Sleepy Hollow* fans dubbing Jones the "Captain" of the S.S. Ichabbie, a designation that concurrently reveals his acceptance into the fan community and his inevitable position of privilege within it.

Conclusion: Check Your Fannish Privilege

Foregrounding intersectional conceptions of fan identity, much less those that move beyond conventional identity markers to also consider producorial identities, requires that fans, producers, and scholars alike check their privilege, particularly when conceptualizing the shifting power dynamics between media producers and fans. The notion of a privilege check is concerned with whose stories are told or obscured within cultural narratives of progress, who is telling them, and how they're told. In order to develop a "more fluid, interactive, and contextual mechanism by which to identify the complex processes at the heart of fan/industry interaction" (Booth 2015: 5), further examination of privileged fan identities, the industrial privileging of particular types of fans within convergence culture, and what we as fan scholars privilege in our work is necessary. The challenge, as Kristen Warner's exemplary intersectional work on black female *Scandal* fans makes clear, is that neither fandom nor fan studies is

> necessarily made up of scholars with an investment in diversity or checking their privilege or even seeing their own selves as racialized bodies in a system designed to benefit some and disadvantage Others. Thus, the gap between beginning a conversation on intersectionality and concluding with real, viable solutions is a long and weary journey many fans are not interested in taking. (2015: 36–37)

Even this chapter, which does not begin bridging this gap, and merely suggests the need to expand conceptions of "intersectional fan identity" to include instances in which TPTB claim fan identities, makes clear how even invested scholars can become mired in privileging some identity markers (here, gender) over others. If "the original sin of fandom studies was its silence about race" (Jenkins 2015: n.p.), then perhaps the sin of contemporary fan studies is our silence about the rewards and roadblocks we encounter along the journey toward more intersectional analyses of fan identity. Even a cursory analysis of a liminal figure like Jones suggests that while many of the structuring binaries of fan studies may be problematic, they also remain powerfully entrenched and potentially valuable modes of articulating fan identity politics and expressing concerns about a media system designed to benefit some (TPTB) more than others (fans). The above analysis, which only begins to gesture to the challenges inherent in intersectional work, as well as the growing inability to "bracket" authorial or industrial identities from the field's focus on fan identity, suggests that these intersections are only growing more complex. Figures like Orlando Jones open up a space to examine the Infinite Diversity in Infinite Combinations of contemporary fan identities, but more significantly he articulates the need to begin actively grappling with that diversity (and its discontents).

WORKS CITED

Bandit 2014, "Orlando Jones: the man, the myth, the fourteen year old fangirl," *The Geekiary*, October 14, thegeekiary.com.

Bandit 2015, "We are fandom: an interview with Orlando Jones at SDCC," *The Geekiary*, July 23, thegeekiary.com.

Bennett, L & Chin, B 2014, "Exploring fandom, social media, and producer/fan interactions: an interview with Sleepy Hollow's Orlando Jones," *Transformative Works and Cultures* 17, dx.doi.org/10.3983/twc.2014.0601.

Booth, P 2015, *Playing fans: negotiating fandom and media in the digital age*, University of Iowa Press, Iowa City.

Busse, K 2015, "Fan labor and feminism: capitalizing on the fannish labor of love," *Cinema Journal* 54(3): 110–15.

Chin, B 2015, "'Orlando Jones needs to GTFO of our fandom': *Supernatural* conventions and gate-keeping," *On/Off Screen*, July 6, onoffscreen.wordpress.com.

Collins, P 2000, *Black feminist thought: knowledge, consciousness, and the politics of empowerment*, 2nd ed., Routledge, New York.

Crenshaw, K 1993, "Mapping the margins: intersectionality, identity politics, and violence against women of color," *Stanford Law Review* 43(1241): 1241–99.

Ellcessor, E 2012, "Tweeting @feliciaday: online social media, convergence, and subcultural stardom," *Cinema Journal* 51(2): 46–66.

Felschow, L 2010, "'Hey, check it out, there's actually fans': (dis)empowerment and (mis)representation of cult fandom in *Supernatural*," *Transformative Works and Cultures* 4, dx.doi.org/10.3983/twc.2010.0134.

Ford, S 2014, "Fan studies: grappling with an 'undisciplined' discipline," *Journal of Fandom Studies* 2(1): 53–71.

Granshaw, L 2014, "Orlando Jones: 'Sleepy Hollow' fans should 'expect the unexpected' next season," *Daily Dot*, August 8, www.dailydot.com.

Gray J, Sandvoss C, & Harrington CL 2007, "Introduction: why study fans," in J Gray, C Sandvoss, & CL Harrington (eds.), *Fandom: identities and communities in a mediated world*, New York University Press, New York.

Hills, M 2002, *Fan cultures*, Routledge, New York.

Hills, M 2012a, "*Torchwood*'s trans-transmedia: media tie-ins and brand 'fanagement,'" *Participations* 9(2), 409–28.

Hills, M 2012b, "Twilight fans represented in commercial paratexts and inter-fandoms: resisting and repurposing negative fan stereotypes," in A Morey (ed.), *Genre, reception, and adaptation in the Twilight series*, Ashgate, Surrey.

Jenkins, H 1992, *Textual poachers: television fans and participatory culture*, Routledge, New York.

Jenkins, H 2007, *Fans, bloggers, and gamers: exploring participatory culture*, New York University Press, New York.

Jenkins, H 2015, "'Somewhat diverse?' Remarks to the Science Fiction Research Association Conference," *Confessions of an Aca-Fan*, August 19, henryjenkins.org.

Jones, O 2013, twitter.com/theorlandojones.

Jones, O 2014, twitter.com/theorlandojones.

Kohnen, M 2012, "Creating a spark: official and fan-produced transmedia for *The Hunger Games*," *Antenna*, May 11, blog.commarts.wisc.edu.

Kyle, T 2014, "Orlando Jones talks fandom, celebrity involvement, and diversity," *Hypable*, July 26, www.hypable.com.

Prudom, L 2013, "What every TV show can learn from *Sleepy Hollow*," *The Week*, December 3, theweek.com.

Rebaza, C 2014, "Transcript for the Future of Fanworks entertainment industry chat," Organization for Transformative Works, March 29, transformativeworks.org.

Roy, J 2014, "Inspired by Ferguson, *Sleepy Hollow* star Orlando Jones launches 'Bullet Bucket' Challenge," *Fusion*, August 19, fusion.net.

Russo, J 2009, "User-penetrated content: fan video in the age of convergence," *Cinema Journal* 56(5): 125–30.

Scott, S 2012, "Who's steering the mothership? The role of the fanboy auteur in transmedia storytelling," in A Delwiche & J Henderson (eds.), *The Participatory Cultures Handbook*, Routledge, New York.

Scott, S 2013a, "Dawn of the undead auteur: fanboy auteurism and Zack Snyder's 'Vision,'" in J Gray & D Johnson (eds.), *A Companion to Media Authorship*, Wiley-Blackwell, Hoboken, NJ.

Scott, S 2013b, "Fangirls in refrigerators: the politics of (in)visibility in comic book culture," *Transformative Works and Cultures* 12, doi:10.3983/twc.2013.0460.

Scott, S 2015, "'Cosplay is serious business': gendering material fan labor on *Heroes of Cosplay*," *Cinema Journal* 54(3): 146–54.

Stanfill, M 2011, "Doing fandom, (mis)doing whiteness: heteronormativity, racialization, and the discursive construction of fandom," *Transformative Works and Cultures* 8, doi:10.3983/twc.2011.0256.

Stein, L 2013, "#Bowdown to your new god: Misha Collins and decentered authorship in the digital age," in J Gray & D Johnson (eds.), *A Companion to Media Authorship*, Wiley-Blackwell, Hoboken, NJ.

Stein, L 2015, *Millennial fandom: television audiences in the transmedia age*, University of Iowa Press, Iowa City.

Wanzo, R 2015, "African American acafandom and other strangers: new genealogies of fan studies," *Transformative Works and Cultures* 20, dx.doi.org/10.3983/twc.2015.0699.

Warner, K 2015, "ABC's *Scandal* and Black women's fandom," in E Levine (ed.), *Cupcakes, Pinterest, and ladyporn: feminized popular culture in the early twenty-first century*, University of Illinois Press, Urbana.

Wexelblat, A 2002, "An auteur in the age of the Internet: JMS, *Babylon 5*, and the Net," in H Jenkins, T McPherson, & J Shattuc (eds.), *Hop on pop: the politics and pleasures of popular culture*, Duke University Press, Durham, NC.

24

Measuring Fandom

Social TV Analytics and the Integration of Fandom into Television Audience Measurement

PHILIP M. NAPOLI AND ALLIE KOSTERICH

Fan activities can take a variety of forms, some of which are readily observable by media industry stakeholders such as content producers, distributors, and advertisers, while others are less so. Media industries have a variety of incentives for comprehensively observing these fan activities, ranging from policing copyright violations to gaining feedback that could be employed to alter/improve the content and potentially even monetizing these activities in a variety of ways. This intersection of fan activity and industry interests in observing, analyzing, and monetizing these activities takes us into the realm of the *measurement of fandom*. The notion of *measurement* suggests something more comprehensive and systematic than mere casual, impressionistic, or ad hoc observation. Measurement implies a more rigorous effort at observing and aggregating fan activity in a way that is conducive to subsequent analysis. And, as with many dimensions of contemporary human activity, technological changes are making fan activities more measurable than they have been in years past, with social media being a key driver of this process.

The question of how fandom is measured—and the potential implications of such measurement—appears to have received relatively little attention thus far in the fan studies literature, no doubt due to the relatively recent emergence of measurement systems that seek to capture select aspects of fandom. In this chapter, we seek to address this gap through an exploration of the differences between two contemporary systems for measuring television audience behaviors, one of which (traditional Nielsen ratings) relies upon sample-based measurement of audiences' exposure to television programs, the other of which (Nielsen Twitter

Television Ratings) relies upon social media activity related to individual programs, which has emerged as a significant new mechanism via which television fandom is expressed (Bore & Hickman 2013; Highfield, Harrington, & Bruns 2013). An examination of the different representations of the hit programs produced by these different measurement systems can provide insights into the extent to which measuring and valuing television audiences as fans means something very different from measuring and valuing television audiences as consumers.

Distinguishing among Audiences, Consumers, and Fans in Television Viewing

Given that the goal here is to consider the measurement of fandom in comparison to what is traditionally referred to as *audience measurement*, it is useful to start with a consideration of the relationship—and points of distinction—between measuring audiences and fans. On an intuitive level, the distinction between audiences and fans from a measurement standpoint may seem fairly clear, with the notion of fandom connoting higher levels of engagement, appreciation, and activity than those that are traditionally associated with the notion of audience. However, exploring how these distinctions are articulated as related to measurement in the audience and fan studies literatures is nonetheless a useful starting point for this analysis.

Perhaps the most important takeaway from these discussions is that fans are best thought of as a subset of the broader concept of audiences. According to Lewis, "Fans are, in fact, the most visible and identifiable of audiences" (1992: 1). This statement also forges an immediate connection with the issue of measurement, through its implicit contention that fans are essentially the easiest category of audience to observe and measure, since they are the most "visible" and "identifiable" type of audience.

This embeddedness of fans within the larger audience construct is also reflected in Abercrombie and Longhurst's description of fans as "a form of skilled audience" (1998: 121). Abercrombie and Longhurst place fans in the second position on an "audience continuum" that begins with another category—*consumers*—and continues on with other categories, such as *cultists* and *enthusiasts*. The logic of this continuum is premised upon differences among audiences in the intensity of their media usage, media-related activities, and social organization. The focus here is limited to the distinctions between fans and consumers, given that the traditional measurement apparatus within the television industry has focused primarily on audiences as consumers. From this standpoint, the skills referenced by Abercrombie and Longhurst represent some of the key means by which fans are distinguished from consumers and establish their distinct identity within the larger construct of audiences. These skills include technical, analytical, and interpretive abilities related to the consumption, processing, sharing, and creation of media content.

Another point of distinction identified by Abercrombie and Longhurst (1998) that separates fans from consumers is greater engagement in communal activities. Along related lines, Bielby, Harrington, and Bielby emphasize, "To 'view' television is to engage in a relatively private behavior. To be a 'fan,' however, is to participate in a range of activities that extend beyond the private act of viewing and reflect an enhanced emotional involvement with a television narrative" (1999: 35). Of course, as media-usage-related behaviors move from private to public contexts, the opportunities for measurement are enhanced.

In industry discourse, we are beginning to see clear articulations of how industry stakeholders distinguish fans from the larger population of audiences of which they are a part. Internet investment analyst Mary Meeker, in a discussion of the emerging value of fans ("fans trump audiences," she declares), distinguishes television fans from the larger concept of television audiences as follows: "An audience changes the channel when the show is over. A fan base shares, comments, creates content when the show is done, magnifying the show's reach and engagement with existing and potential new audiences" (as quoted in Bloom 2014: 1). Here again, the key distinguishing characteristics are oriented around the volume and intensity of activities and expression related to the programming.

Measuring Television Audiences and Fans

The different dimensions of audiencehood discussed above force us to confront the extent to which what has traditionally been dubbed "audience measurement" in the television industry really only has been scratching the tip of the iceberg (or, to adopt Abercrombie & Longhurst's

[1998] perspective, the beginning of the continuum) in its approach to measuring audiences. As Napoli (2011) discusses, traditional approaches to audience measurement have historically focused on fairly superficial indicators of audience exposure to media content. In this regard, the consumption dimension of the audience continuum is all that has mattered to these measurement systems (and, thus, to some extent, to the industry stakeholders who rely on these measurement systems). When rival measurement systems have emerged and attempted to distinguish themselves through the measurement of audience appreciation, the marketplace has not embraced them (Napoli 2011). Ultimately, these characteristics of traditional audience measurement are both a reflection and a driver of the fact that, historically, "[i]n the business of television viewers matter more than fans" (Bielby, Harrington, & Bielby 1999: 35).

With any meaningful dimensions of fandom residing outside the dimensions of institutionalized systems of audience measurement, industry mechanisms for understanding fandom have tended to be less systematic and more ad hoc. Perhaps the earliest mechanisms via which television fandom has been measured have been fan letters expressing enthusiasm for specific programs. These activities date back at least as far as the original *Star Trek* television series, which achieved renewal despite lackluster ratings, due in part to the volume of fan letters that NBC received in support of the program (see, e.g., Cochran 2012; Collins 1997). Throughout television history, there have been a number of instances of such fan activities (sometimes organized independently by fan communities; sometimes organized and supported by program producers) at least temporarily sustaining programs whose ratings performance would otherwise have merited cancellation (Brower 1992). Television executives have used the volume of fan letters as an indicator that it may make sense to give an underperforming program a little more time before pulling the plug (Sabal 1992).

In some instances, this fan activism has taken other forms, including organized campaigns to support individual program sponsors, or engaging in other organized, public displays of support and enthusiasm (Savage 2014). With the diffusion of the Internet, expressions of fan support found a new outlet. Fan web pages and online communities and discussion boards became important mechanisms via which fans expressed their opinions about television programs, as well as a mechanism via which program producers and networks could monitor and analyze—and even respond to—this fan activity (Scardaville 2005).

In all of these cases, the key, from a fan activism standpoint, was to produce some measurable indicator of the size and intensity of fan support, whether in the form of the volume of letters received or the aggregate dollar value of their support for program sponsors. As Savage emphasizes, an important dimension of fan activism on behalf of their preferred programs is for the fans to effectively demonstrate their value to the programmer: "The evolution of fan campaigns taught fans that audience attention would often not be enough" (2014: n.p.).

As Gray has noted, "Intentionally or not, audience research often equals fan research" (2003: 64). However, audience *measurement* represents something different from audience research; and, as this section has illustrated, audience measurement has never equaled fan measurement. Rather, fandom measurement has remained a more impressionistic, ad hoc endeavor, largely disconnected from the institutionalized system of television audience measurement that long has provided the economic foundation of the industry.

Social Media and Television Fandom

This state of affairs has begun to be disrupted by the emergence of social media and the role that it plays in fan-related activities and expression (see, e.g., Bore & Hickman 2013; D'heer & Verdegem 2015; Harrington & Bruns 2013). Social media platforms make certain aspects of television fandom more visible and, thus, more measurable. According to Nielsen (2014), over one million people per day discuss television programming on Twitter, with those television-related tweets garnering over eleven million readers.

One could certainly critique social media activity as a robust indicator of fandom. One might argue, for instance, that social media activity represents too low of an activity/engagement threshold to meaningfully distinguish fans from audiences in general. Nonetheless, the visibility of "fans" on social media is increasingly utilized by network executives in programming decisions, specifically as an indicator of fandom. For example, CW President Mark Pedowitz justified the renewal of one show over a canceled higher-rated show because it was a "fan favorite" with higher social engagement (Hibberd 2014). Fandom may also have contributed to the renewal of NBC's relatively low-rated *Hannibal*, spearheaded by the "rapid appearance and organization of the show's fans, who dubbed themselves 'Fannibals,'" on Tumblr (Hall 2013: 4). Ultimately, social media platforms have facilitated "newly visible" forms of fan activity (Hills 2013: 144), and with this visibility also comes greater incentive and opportunities for implementing rigorous systems of measurement.

Social TV Analytics

This section discusses the specific systems that have been put in place to measure, aggregate, report, and analyze this social media activity in ways that serve the interests of television programmers. Essentially, then, the focus here is on how fan activity is being transformed into an "institutionally effective" (Ettema & Whitney 1994) form of audience information for the industry.

Most social TV analytic services utilize some form of "web scraping," in which the conversations posted on a wide range of social media platforms (which can include Twitter, public Facebook pages, blogs, and online discussion boards, depending upon the individual service) are aggregated and classified via language processing and classification algorithms and/or (in the case of Twitter) the use of program-specific hashtags. Some services also categorize social media activity in terms of the sentiment (positive/negative) expressed. Over the past few years, Nielsen Twitter Television Ratings (NTTR) has emerged as the industry standard (Kosterich & Napoli forthcoming). NTTR distributes a weekly ranking of the top ten most social episodes of prime-time television according to four different metrics, which include unique audience, impressions, unique authors, and tweets. As a syndicated metric, NTTR operates in a similar capacity to traditional audience ratings. However, it is important to emphasize that there are other systems that individual media companies can utilize to conduct their own analyses, as a large number of firms of different types compete in the social TV analytics industry.

Whereas traditional TV ratings require individuals to agree to be part of the measurement sample, social TV analytics draw from the entirety of the online population's expressions, with the key limitation being the range of online platforms that are incorporated into the data-gathering process. NTTR focuses exclusively on Twitter activity (though other social media analytics services cast a wider net), which of course raises the question of whether Twitter-based discussion of television programming is reflective of the broader social media space. And, of course, there is the related question of whether the demographics of Twitter's user base (or the online population as a whole, for that matter) are reflective of the television viewing population as a whole; they most likely are not (Duggan et al. 2015; Napoli 2014). As these issues make clear, this emergent system of fandom measurement does not operate under the same guiding principle as traditional television audience measurement, in terms of the measurement system seeking to accurately represent the activities of the population as a whole. Rather, in terms of social TV analytics, the population under analysis is defined by their expressive activities and the platforms they utilize to engage in these activities.

There are other measurement issues that should be noted as well. For instance, one commonly identified phenomenon involves fan communities hijacking hashtags, manipulating Twitter's Trending Topics list, or engaging in other coordinated efforts to "game" the systems via which program-related expression is disseminated, consumed, and evaluated (Highfield, Harrington, & Bruns 2013). This is important from a measurement standpoint in that it raises the question as to whether such activities are motivated primarily by expressions of fandom or primarily by efforts to manipulate or disrupt social media conversation, with the object of communication being secondary. If the answer is the latter, then of course the nature of the social media activity taking place is somewhat questionable as a meaningful expression of fandom.

In sum, social TV analytics represent a flawed, incomplete measure of television fandom in many of the same ways that traditional television ratings have long been a flawed, incomplete measure of television audience exposure (Napoli 2003). However, they appear to have reached a point of "institutional effectiveness" in that they seem to have been embraced by the industry as sufficiently robust to serve as a meaningful complement to the traditional Nielsen ratings (Kosterich & Napoli forthcoming). They now serve as the primary means by which notions of fandom are interpreted and acted upon by television industry decision makers.

Consumption- versus Fandom-Oriented Approaches to Audience Measurement: A Comparative Analysis

Given the dramatic methodological differences, it is not surprising that a more fandom-centric measurement approach such as social TV analytics may produce a very different portrait of hit programs than is produced by more traditional methods. Programs that produce high volumes of social media conversation do not necessarily reach relatively large audiences (Napoli 2014; Deller 2011). Academic researchers have yet to engage in substantive analyses of how the representation of successful programs differs across the two measurement systems. Delving into this subject can give us a sense of how the stronger integration of television fandom into programmers' understanding of the audience might produce alternative perceptions of what constitutes a hit program—and thus might influence industry dynamics and decision making.

In order to provide a more concrete sense of how measuring fandom can reconfigure perceptions of program success, this section presents the results of a comparative analysis of twenty-five weeks of audience ratings data across Nielsen's traditional ratings and Twitter ratings systems. Specifically, this analysis focuses on the top ten prime-time program lists generated by each measurement system for twenty-five weeks, ranging from September 22, 2014, through March 15, 2015. This hits dataset was constructed from weekly ratings information on the top ten ranked shows made publicly available by Nielsen.

In order to analyze comparable data, information from Nielsen's traditional ratings reports was compiled via multiple outlets to best match the parameters provided by Nielsen's social ratings. NTTR provides a weekly report of the top ten episodes based on a measure of social activity from three hours before, during, and three hours after broadcast of new or live prime-time episodes on broadcast or cable television networks.[1] Thus, traditional ratings data were collected based on the live plus same-day metric of both broadcast and cable prime-time television episodes. It is also worth noting that the demographic skew of typical Twitter users is users under fifty years old (Duggan et al. 2015); as such, the constructed dataset utilizes the traditional ratings information from the demographic of adults ages eighteen to forty-nine. Repeat episodes and sports programming were discarded from traditional Nielsen reports as NTTR ranks only new episodes of prime-time programming; the remaining top ten episodes were then retained for the dataset. In essence, the unit of analysis is the ranking slot and $N = 500$ slotted shows, 250 slots from each measurement system.[2]

The programs in the dataset were categorized across two primary variables in order to facilitate comparisons across the two systems. First, each program was categorized according to its genre. Genre classifications were obtained from an institutionalized genre classification system.[3] There were sixteen distinct genre categories among the total programs ranked by both measurement systems.[4] Analysis included both the total number of genre categories and the total number of programs within each genre to account for differences in composition.

Genre composition was measured with the Hirschman-Herfindahl Index (HHI) to account for the degree of concentration of programming into few genre categories (Li & Chiang 2001). A highly diverse composition of genres would produce programming evenly distributed across genre categories and an HHI that approaches zero. Television hits from only one genre would have an HHI of 10,000. In addition, t-tests were conducted to determine if the average weekly number of different genres represented by each system's hits were statistically significant from one another. With this analytical approach, it is possible to determine whether a measurement approach that incorporates fandom results in a greater or lesser diversity of program types emerging as hits than is the case under the traditional ratings system.

We also identified the source of each program that appears in the top ten lists. In this case, source was identified in terms of the network on which the program aired. There were a total of thirty-two distinct sources responsible for the five hundred ranked programs. Both the total number of distinct sources and the total number of ranked shows appearing from each source were accounted for in order to test for diversity differences between the two approaches to measuring television audiences. HHI and t-tests were once again computed. With this information, it is possible to determine whether a fandom-oriented approach to audience measurement corresponds with an increase or decrease in the diversity of sources of hit programs.

Results

Under the traditional ratings system, 53 different programs appeared in the top ten lists during this time period, while under the social TV analytics measurement system, 84 different programs appeared. Table 24.1 shows the distribution of hit programming from each measurement system across sixteen genres. The hit programs (i.e., the 250 top show slots, as totaled by the top ten lists over twenty-five weeks) as reflected by traditional Nielsen ratings fall across eleven genre categories and have 2201.92 HHI. According to social TV analytics, the hit programs (again, 250 show slots) of the television marketplace fall across fourteen genre categories and have a 1923.2 HHI.

TABLE 24.1. Composition by program genre

Genre	Traditional Nielsen ratings		Social TV analytics		Percentage difference
	Raw number	Percentage	Raw number	Percentage	
Reality	54	21.6	70	28	−6.4
Drama	66	26.4	68	27.2	−0.8
Horror	1	0.4	13	5.2	−4.8
Crime drama	21	8.4	5	2	6.4
Suspense	0	0	1	0.4	−0.4
Historical drama	0	0	1	0.4	−0.4
Sitcom	76	30.4	6	2.4	28
Special event	12	4.8	39	15.6	−10.8
Documentary	0	0	6	2.4	−2.4
Talk	9	3.6	7	2.8	0.8
TV movie	3	1.2	4	1.6	−0.4
Musical comedy	1	0.4	1	0.4	0
Pro wrestling	0	0	25	10	−10
Comedy	0	0	4	1.6	−1.6
Newsmagazine	6	2.4	0	0	2.4
News	1	0.4	0	0	0.4
HHI	2201.92		1923.2		

Note: N = 250. This table depicts the raw number, percentage, and percentage difference of all genres represented by the top-rated programs according to each measurement system over the twenty-five-week period of data collection. HHI scores are noted for each.

In addition, the average number of different genres represented by television's hits each week according to traditional Nielsen ratings was 4.08. The average number of different genres represented by television's hits each week according to social TV analytics was 4.58. As Table 24.2 shows, this difference in aggregate means was statistically significant ($t25 = 1.73$, $p < .10$). As such, the television hits produced by the measurement system that better integrates fandom are more evenly distributed across the sixteen genre categories.

TABLE 24.2. Charting placement for different genres

	Traditional Nielsen ratings	Social TV analytics	Difference
Different genres	4.08 genres/week (s.d. = 0.95)	4.58 genres/week (s.d. = 1.00)	−0.50* ($t25 = 1.73$, $p < .10$)

Note: All figures are means, standard deviation indicated as s.d.
*Significant at $p < .10$.

Next, we looked at the representation of source diversity across the two measurement systems. Table 24.3 shows the distribution of networks responsible for the top programming according to each week's ratings reports. Traditional Nielsen ratings portray a TV marketplace with only eight different networks responsible for top-ten programming (and a corresponding 2261.44 HHI). According to social TV analytics, top-ten programming is produced by thirty-two different networks (with a corresponding HHI of 1168.70).

TABLE 24.3. Diversity according to program source (percentage)

Channel	Traditional Nielsen ratings	Social TV analytics
ABC	28.8	22.13
ABC Family	0	3.69
AMC	9.6	6.56
BBC	0	0.41
BET	0	1.23
Bravo	0.4	0.82
CBS	30	3.69
CMT	0	0.41
CNBC	0	0.41
CNN	0.4	0.41
Comedy Central	0	1.64

TABLE 24.3. (cont.)

Channel	Traditional Nielsen ratings	Social TV analytics
CW	0	1.23
Discovery	0	0.41
E!	0	2.05
ESPN	0	1.64
FNC	0	0.41
FOX	14.8	6.56
FX	1.2	6.97
HLN	0	0.41
Lifetime	0	1.23
MTV	0	0.82
NBC	14.8	20.08
NFL Network	0	0.82
OWN	0	0.82
Oxygen	0	0.41
PBS	0	0.41
Syfy	0	0.41
Telemundo	0	0.41
TV One	0	0.41
Univision	0	0.41
USA	0	9.02
VH1	0	3.69
HHI	2261.44	1168.70

Note: This table depicts the percentage of various sources responsible for the top-rated programs according to each measurement system. HHI scores are noted for each.

In addition, the hits portrayed by traditional Nielsen ratings present an average of 4.24 different network sources each week. The hits portrayed by social TV analytics present an average of 7.28 different channel sources each week. As depicted in Table 24.4, here too the difference was statistically different ($t25 = 9.99$, $p < .01$).

TABLE 24.4. Charting placement for different network sources

	Traditional Nielsen ratings	Social TV analytics	Difference
Different sources	4.24 sources/week (s.d. = 0.88)	7.28 sources/week (s.d. = 1.24)	−3.02* ($t25 = 9.99$, $p < .01$)

Note: All figures are means, standard deviation indicated as s.d.
*Significant at $p < .01$.

Conclusion

To the extent that the television industry embraces an approach to measuring and valuing audiences that better integrates dimensions of fandom through increased emphasis on social TV analytics, the industry is going to be confronted with a significantly different understanding of the types of programming that constitute hits and the sources from which these hit programs arise.

This pattern suggests that the traditional system of television audience measurement, with its focus on audience exposure to programming, has provided a relatively constrained portrait of the nature of audiences' preferences. An exposure-focused approach to television audiences produces a narrower set of hits, allowing fewer types of programs, from a more limited range of sources, to emerge as successful. When, however, a hit is redefined in terms of the amount of social media conversation and activity that it inspires, the diversity of the types and sources of hit programs expands significantly.

These patterns may be a function of the disparity between the type of programming that generates viewership and the type of programming that generates *engagement* (see Napoli, 2011). To some extent, these findings may serve as a contemporary reminder of the "least objectionable programming" philosophy that long characterized the television industry (Reeves, Rodgers, & Epstein 1996). Under this approach, programmers seeking large audiences produced programs that the largest number of viewers would find acceptable, rather than programs that would incite more intense feelings of appreciation or dislike. Then, as now, the dynamics of consumption are likely very different from the dynamics of engagement. The results here suggest that a much narrower range of types of programs are capable of producing large audiences than are capable of producing highly engaged audiences—and that a much narrower range of programmers are capable of producing the type of programs that attract these large audiences.

These findings also may reflect the concerted efforts by programmers who are unable to fare well under the traditional measurement system to take full advantage of this new measurement system. That is, the barriers (i.e., production and marketing budgets, wide distribution) to achieving large audiences are likely higher than the barriers to achieving high levels of social media activity. Programmers who are inherently less able to achieve success under the primary measurement system/currency may instead be focusing their efforts on the social media realm, where the competitive playing field may be a bit more level.

Or, it may be that the type of audiences that engage in social media activity about television programs are fundamentally different from the type of audiences that take part in Nielsen's traditional audience measurement system. Social media analytics may be tapping into categories of audience tastes and preferences that have simply gone unobserved via traditional Nielsen ratings panels.

In any case, the primary implication is that if social TV analytics establish themselves as an influential source of information in decision making related to programming and (perhaps most important) the allocation of advertising dollars, then this alternative, more fan-centric approach to audience measurement could have a diversifying effect on the industry as a whole, encouraging the production of a greater array of content types and facilitating a more competitive television landscape in which a greater diversity of program sources share in the highest levels of programming success. As decision makers observe, internalize, and respond to the alternative portrait of the television audience presented by social TV analytics, the programming, and the marketplace as a whole, will evolve accordingly.

In the end, the institutionalization of social TV analytics as a way of measuring and valuing television audiences represents a more direct and potentially powerful mechanism via which fandom can influence television production (assuming, of course, we accept social media activity as a valid indicator of fandom). We have described here a transition in which there is increasing value placed on the notion of fans and their role in the media system. And, as the data analysis presented in this chapter illustrates, a media system that increasingly relies upon indicators of fandom to guide its decision making is likely to be one that will serve a more diverse range of tastes and preferences and that will support programming from a greater diversity of program sources. In these ways, institutionalized representations of fandom can affect cultural production in ways that, from a normative standpoint, are desirable and beneficial, in that they connect to long-standing media system structure and performance values such as diversity and competition (Napoli 2001).

It is important to recognize that this evolutionary potential is limited by the extent to which social TV analytics seem to have settled into a secondary, supplementary role in the television audience marketplace, with traditional ratings still serving as the primary audience information source that guides decision making (Kosterich & Napoli 2016). However, the extent to which the virtually exclusive emphasis on traditional exposure-based ratings finally appears to have been disrupted could still have significant ramifications for the television industry and the type of programming it produces.

NOTES

1 Nielsen Twitter Television Ratings (NTTR) provide information on four metrics including unique audience, impressions, unique authors, and tweets. Program ranking of the top ten weekly ratings report was ordered according to the total tweets metric. For more details regarding specific NTTR methods and metrics, please see Nielsen (2014).

2 This accounted for the discarding of sixty slots from the traditional Nielsen ratings.

3 Genre categories were collected from zap2it.com, a television guide website owned by Tribune Company. These program genre classifications frequently have been employed in academic research (Kordus 2014; Napoli & Yan 2007).

4 The sixteen genre categories represented include comedy, crime drama, documentary, drama, historical drama, horror, musical comedy, news, newsmagazine, pro wrestling, reality, sitcom, special event, suspense, talk, TV movie.

WORKS CITED

Abercrombie, N & Longhurst, B 1998, *Audiences: a sociological theory of performance and imagination*, Sage, Thousand Oaks, CA.

Bielby, DD, Harrington, CL, & Bielby, WT 1999, "'Whose stories are they?' Fans' engagement with soap opera narratives in three sites of fan activity," *Journal of Broadcasting & Electronic Media* 43(1): 35–52.

Bloom, D 2014, "'Fans trump audiences,' Mary Meeker tells Code Conference," *Deadline*, May 28, deadline.com.

Bore, I-LK & Hickman, J 2013, "Studying fan activities on Twitter: reflections on methodological issues emerging from a case study on *The West Wing* fandom," *First Monday* 18(9).

Brower, S 1992, "Fans as tastemakers: viewers for quality television," in LA Lewis (ed.), *The adoring audience: fan culture and popular media*, Routledge, New York.

Cochran, TR 2012, "'Past the brink of tacit support': fan activism and the Whedonverses," *Transformative Works and Cultures* 10, journal.transformativeworks.org.

Collins, C 1997, "Viewer letters as audience research: the case of *Murphy Brown*," *Journal of Broadcasting & Electronic Media* 41(1): 109–31.

Deller, R 2011, "Twittering on: audience research and participation using Twitter," *Participations* 8(1): 216–45.

D'heer, E & Verdegem, P 2015, "What social media data mean for audience studies: a multidimensional investigation of Twitter use during a current affairs TV programme," *Information, Communication & Society* 18(2): 221–34.

Duggan, M, Ellison, NB, Lampe, C, et al. 2015, "Social media update 2014: while Facebook remains the most popular site, other platforms see higher rates of growth," Pew Research Center, www.pewinternet.org.

Ettema, JS & Whitney, DC 1994, *Audiencemaking: how the media create the audience*, Sage, Thousand Oaks, CA.

Gray, J 2003, "New audiences, new textualities: anti-fans and non-fans," *International Journal of Cultural Studies* 6(1): 64–81.

Hall, E 2013, "Meet the 'Hannibal' Fannibals, TV's newest and most intense Fandom," *BuzzFeed*, May 31, www.buzzfeed.com.

Harrington, S & Bruns, A 2013, "More than a backchannel: Twitter and television," *Participations* 10(1): 13–17.

Hibberd, J 2014, "CW explains renewing 'Beauty' while axing 'Tomorrow People,'" *Entertainment Weekly*, May 15, www.ew.com.

Highfield, T, Harrington, S, & Bruns, A 2013, "Twitter as a technology for audiencing and fandom," *Information, Communication & Society* 16(3): 315–39.

Hills, M 2013, "Fiske's 'textual productivity' and digital fandom: Web 2.0 democratization versus fan distinction?," *Participations* 10(1): 130–53.

Kordus, D 2014, "What's on (digital) TV? Assessing the digital television broadcast system, its potential and its performance in increasing media content diversity," *Communication Law & Policy* 19(1): 55–86.

Kosterich, A & Napoli, PM 2016, "Reconfiguring the audience commodity: the institutionalization of social TV analytics as market information regime," *Television & New Media* 17(2): 254–71.

Lewis, LA 1992, "Introduction," in LA Lewis (ed.), *The adoring audience: fan culture and popular media*, Routledge, London.

Li, SS & Chiang, C 2001, "Market competition and programming diversity: a study on the TV market in Taiwan," *Journal of Media Innovations* 14(2): 105–19.

Napoli, PM 2001, *Foundations of communications policy: Principles and process in the regulation of electronic media*, Hampton Press, Cresskill, NJ.

Napoli, PM 2003, *Audience economics: media institutions and the audience marketplace*, Columbia University Press, New York.

Napoli, PM 2011, *Audience evolution: new technologies and the transformation of media audiences*, Columbia University Press, New York.

Napoli, PM 2014, "The institutionally effective audience in flux: Social media and the reassessment of the audience commodity," in LJ McGuigan & V Manzerolle (eds.),

The audience commodity in a digital age: revisiting a critical theory of commercial media, Peter Lang, New York.

Napoli, PM & Yan, MZ 2007, "Media ownership regulations and local news programming on broadcast television: an empirical analysis," *Journal of Broadcasting & Electronic Media* 51(1): 39–57.

Nielsen 2014, "Nielsen Twitter TV ratings: Frequently asked questions," April 15, en-us. nielsen.com.

Reeves, JL, Rodgers, MC, & Epstein, M 1996, "Rewriting popularity: the cult files," in D Lavery, A Hague, & M Cartwright (eds.), *Deny all knowledge: reading the X-Files*, Syracuse University Press, Syracuse, NY.

Sabal, R 1992, "Television executives speak about fan letters to networks," in LA Lewis (ed.), *The adoring audience: fan culture and popular media*, Routledge, London.

Savage, C 2014, "Chuck versus the ratings: savvy fans and 'save our show' campaigns," *Transformative Works and Cultures* 15, journal.transformativeworks.org.

Scardaville, MC 2005, "Accidental activists: fan activism in the soap opera community," *American Behavioral Scientist* 48(7): 881–901.

LUCY BENNETT completed her PhD in online fandom at JOMEC, Cardiff University. She is the co-chair of the Fan Studies Network and co-editor of *Crowdfunding the Future* and *Seeing Fans: Representations of Fandom in Media and Popular Culture*.

DENISE D. BIELBY is Distinguished Professor of Sociology at the University of California, Santa Barbara, and affiliate of Film & Media Studies. Her research on media culture focuses on the industries and audiences of television and film. Her ongoing project is on cultural voice and authority: who speaks, how, and the ways in which appraisal matters to cultural legitimation.

WILL BROOKER is Professor of Film and Cultural Studies at Kingston University, London, and editor of *Cinema Journal*. He is the author of many books and articles on popular culture, including *Batman Unmasked, Using the Force, Alice's Adventures, The Blade Runner Experience*, and *Hunting the Dark Knight*. His most recent book is *Forever Stardust: David Bowie Across the Universe*.

KRISTINA BUSSE is an independent scholar and media fan. She writes on fan fiction and fan communities and is the co-editor of several fan studies collections and founding co-editor of the open access fan studies journal *Transformative Works and Cultures*.

DANIEL CAVICCHI is Dean of Liberal Arts and Professor of American Studies at Rhode Island School of Design. His latest book is *Listening and Longing: Music Lovers in the Age of Barnum*.

DAYNA CHATMAN is George Gerbner Postdoctoral Fellow at the University of Pennsylvania's Annenberg School for Communication. Her research focuses on race and the business of television production and promotion in the post-network era and Black American fans' online engagement around television programs with Black women in lead roles.

BERTHA CHIN lectures at Swinburne University of Technology (Sarawak). She has published extensively, is a board member of the Fan Studies Network, and is co-editor of *Crowdfunding the Future: Media Industries, Ethics, and Digital Society*.

MELISSA A. CLICK is Lecturer of Communication Studies at Gonzaga University. Her work on popular culture, audiences, and fans has been published in the *International Journal of Cultural Studies*, *Men and Masculinities*, and *Television & New Media*.

ABIGAIL DE KOSNIK is Associate Professor at the University of California, Berkeley in the Berkeley Center for New Media and the Department of Theater, Dance & Performance Studies. She is the author of *Rogue Archives: Digital Cultural Memory and Media Fandom*.

MARK DUFFETT is Reader in Media and Cultural Studies at the University of Chester. He's author of *Understanding Fandom*, plus editor of *Popular Music Fandom* and *Fan Practices and Identities in Context*.

ANNE GILBERT is Assistant Professor of Entertainment and Media Studies at the University of Georgia. She researches media industries, fans, and audience cultures, and is writing a book on San Diego Comic-Con and its position in contemporary participatory culture.

JONATHAN GRAY is Professor of Media and Cultural Studies at the University of Wisconsin–Madison. His books include *Show Sold Separately: Promos, Spoilers, and Other Media Paratexts*, *Television Studies* (with Amanda Lotz), and *Television Entertainment*.

C. LEE HARRINGTON is Professor of Sociology and Social Justice Studies at Miami University. Her research focuses on media industries, audiences, and fan communities. Her current focus of research is on questions related to aging, death, and media.

KATRIINA HELJAKKA, toy researcher and toying artist, is Postdoctoral Researcher at the University of Turku (digital culture studies) and continues her research on toys, toy fandom, and the visual, material, digital, and social cultures of play.

MATT HILLS is Professor of Media and Journalism at the University of Huddersfield, and co-director of the Centre for Participatory Culture based there. He is the author of six books, beginning with *Fan Cultures*, and has published widely on media fandom.

MIZUKO ITO is a cultural anthropologist of technology use who studies youths' changing relationships to media and communications. She is Professor in Residence and MacArthur Foundation Chair in Digital Media and Learning at the University of California, Irvine.

HENRY JENKINS, Provost Professor of Communication, Journalism, Cinematic Art, and Education at the University of Southern California, is the author of *Textual Poachers: Television Fans and Participatory Culture*, *Convergence Culture: Where Old and New Media Collide*, *Spreadable Media: Creating Meaning and Value in a Networked Society*, and *By Any Media Necessary: The New Youth Activism*, among others.

DEREK JOHNSON is Associate Professor of Media and Cultural Studies in the Department of Communication Arts at the University of Wisconsin–Madison. He is the author of *Media Franchising: Creative License and Collaboration in the Culture Industries*.

ALLIE KOSTERICH is a doctoral candidate in the School of Communication & Information at Rutgers University. Her research on media industry transformation has been published in venues such as *Television & New Media* and *International Journal on Media Management*.

JASON KIDO LOPEZ is Lecturer of Media and Cultural Studies in the Communication Arts Department and the Integrated Liberal Studies Program at the University of Wisconsin–Madison. He is the author of *Self-Deception's Puzzles and Processes: A Return to a Sartrean View*.

LORI KIDO LOPEZ is Assistant Professor of Media and Cultural Studies in the Communication Arts Department at the University of Wisconsin–Madison. She is the author of *Asian American Media Activism: Fighting for Cultural Citizenship* and co-editor (with Vincent Pham) of *The Routledge Companion to Asian American Media*.

ALEXIS LOTHIAN is Assistant Professor of Women's Studies at the University of Maryland, College Park. Her research on queer theory, digital media, and social justice movements has been published in *International Journal of Cultural Studies, Cinema Journal,* and many other venues.

LORI HITCHCOCK MORIMOTO is an independent scholar of transcultural fandom. She has published in *Scope, Transformative Works and Cultures,* and *Participations,* and is currently writing a monograph on the Japanese female fandom of Hong Kong stars in the 1980s–90s.

PHILIP M. NAPOLI is James R. Shepley Professor of Public Policy in the Sanford School of Public Policy at Duke University. His research focuses on media institutions, audiences, and policy.

ASWIN PUNATHAMBEKAR is Associate Professor of Communication Studies and Founding Director of the Global Media Studies Initiative at the University of Michigan–Ann Arbor. He is the author of *From Bombay to Bollywood: The Making of a Global Media Industry.*

CORNEL SANDVOSS is Professor of Media and Journalism and co-founder of Centre for Participatory Culture at the University of Huddersfield. His work focuses on forms of fandom across the spectrum of popular culture from sports to music, art, and politics. His books include *Fans: The Mirror of Consumption.*

SUZANNE SCOTT is Assistant Professor of Media Studies at the University of Texas at Austin. Her current book project explores the gendered tensions underpinning the media industry's embrace of fans as a tastemaker demographic within convergence culture.

REBECCA TUSHNET is Professor of Law at Georgetown, focusing on intellectual property law and the First Amendment. She is a founder of the Organization for Transformative Works, a nonprofit dedicated to supporting and promoting fanworks.

INDEX

Abercrombie, Nicholas, 6, 403
academia, 8; aesthetic evaluation and,
61–66; judgment in, 69–70. *See also*
scholar-anti-fans
Action Comics #900 (DC Comics), 273
activism: racial activism of Jones, O., 396.
See also fan activism
Adams, Lillian, 145–46
Aden, Roger, 157–59, 166
Adorno, Theodor, 35, 145
adulthood, 91
adult toy collectors: adults as, 94–96;
aesthetic experience of, 95, 101; on
children, 100; commercially manufactured toys for, 96; culture of, 93–94; joy
of, 96; motivations for, 94–95; nostalgia
of, 94–95; preferences of, 98; on social
media, 95; on toy condition, 89–90
adult toy fandom, 92–93; future of, 102–3;
play aspects in, 102–3
adult toy play, 91, 92; fantasy in, 100; social
object players in, 94; toy collecting in,
94
aesthetic evaluation: academics and,
61–66; as defamiliarization, 40; in film
studies, 66–67; in forms of textuality,
41–42; in media/cultural studies, 60,
64–66, 71–72; political evaluations and,
66–67; reading and, 41; value of, 63–64
aesthetic experience, 95, 101
Alito, Samuel, 261
Althorp, William, 121
American Revolution, 110
Anderson, Benedict, 174

Ang, Ien, 177, 180
anime, 333–34, 337, 338, 350
anime music videos (AMVs), 343
Annett, Sandra, 176–77
anti-fans, 67–68, 378; of *Scandal*, 301–11; of
Stewart, M., 203
Appadurai, Arjun, 334
The Apprentice, 21
The Apprentice: Martha Stewart, 198
"Arcana" (Brunson), 48; contexts of, 51–52;
ephemeral traces in, 54; as fan fiction
representation, 56; id celebration in, 55;
mpreg in, 56; as WIP, 50
Art Stern (fictional character), 231–32
Asquith, Daisy, 4
Atlantic Monthly, 121
attribution, 79; in fan fiction, 84; moral
rights and, 88; in trademark law, 82–83
audience: defining of, 40–41; of fan fiction,
52–53; fans as subset of, 403; and fans
of television, 404–6; measurement of,
404–6, 409–16; as normal, 9–10; role
of, 74; text with, 38. *See also* "Before the
Dawn," Bush, K., technology request
Auslander, Philip, 362
authenticity: in "Before the Dawn," Bush,
K., technology request, 136, 137–38;
technology and, 129–30, 135
authorization, 84

BabyDee, 274
Bachchan, Amitabh, 285–86
Bacon-Smith, Camille, 369
Bal, Mieke, 225